Social Science Research

A Cross Section of Journal Articles For Discussion and Evaluation

Edited by

Robert F. Szafran

Stephen F. Austin State University

Pyrczak Publishing
P.O. Box 39731
Los Angeles, CA 90039
(213) 660–7600

Editorial assistance provided by Holbrook Mahn, Randall Koss, and Robert Morris.

ISBN 0–9623744–8–2

Contents

Continued ⇒

INTRODUCTION

Students who are learning how to read research can practice their skills on these 34 articles. The articles were selected because they are generally short, clearly written, employ straightforward research designs, deal with interesting topics, and, as a group, illustrate a variety of methodological techniques.

The articles represent a cross section of social science research. Although sociology, social work, and criminal justice are most heavily represented, works from other disciplines are also included. The 34 articles come from 20 different journals.

Learning How to Read Research

Social science students, instructors, researchers, and practitioners all read far more research than they conduct. The ability to read research well is clearly a useful skill, but it is not a skill most people acquire naturally. It needs to be learned.

Like most learned skills, one gets better through instruction and practice. A classroom teacher can provide instruction, but learning to read research well also requires practice. Structured practice which begins with easy research articles and advances to more difficult ones is best. That is exactly what this collection of articles provides.

Unlike most published research, these articles can be understood and evaluated by students who are just beginning to learn research methods. Students who practice their research reading skills on this collection of articles are likely to gain confidence in their ability, a desire to learn more, and an appreciation of the utility of their newly acquired methodological knowledge. Compare that to the frustration felt by the student who randomly selects research articles from social science journals only to find that these articles remain incomprehensible despite the hours spent studying methods.

Stimulating Student Research

In addition to providing appropriate practice in reading research, the articles can serve another purpose as well. Many research methods courses require students to complete research proposals or research projects. Students are often unable to think of a research problem they could address and a simple research design they could execute. Because these articles provide numerous examples of such simple but often elegant problems and designs, they can help students generate ideas of their own. To put it simply, many of these articles show how simple good research can be.

Spotting Errors and Reading Statistics

Although most of the articles in this collection represent quality research, that is, research that is theoretically and methodologically sound, the articles were not necessarily selected because they were of high quality. Indeed, a few of the articles contain relatively serious flaws. But the same can be said about all published research: most is good but some is flawed. Thus, this collection provides the opportunity for students to recognize both strengths and weaknesses in published research.

Most of the articles in this book employ relatively simple statistical procedures. There are exceptions, however. It is almost certain than every reader will encounter some statistical techniques with which he or she is not familiar. This happens not just to students but to professionals as well. Unless directed differently by an instructor, in these situations focus on the author's *interpretation* of the statistics, which will usually be comprehensible, and consider whether the conclusions drawn by the author are reasonable in light of the research methodology.

Organization of this Book

The articles in this book are arranged into eight groups. The first four groups of articles represent basic methods of gathering data: "Content Analysis," "Analysis of Existing Records," "Observational Research," and "Survey Research." The next three sections group articles that share a common type of analysis ("Qualitative Research"), a common research design ("Experimental Research"), or a common research purpose ("Evaluation Research"). The eighth section ("The Next Level") contains three articles that are more complex in nature and, therefore, more appropriate for use near the end of an introductory research course or in a more advanced research course.

Appendices, Factual Questions, and Discussion Questions

For most students, primary instruction in reading research articles comes from a classroom instructor. Parts of this book may help in that instruction. Appendix A contains an excellent article by Schroeder, Johnson, and Jensen that explains the purpose of each of the parts of a standard research article: heading, abstract, introduction, method, results, and discussion. Appendix B contains a short list of questions developed by Royse to be used in evaluating the quality (theoretical and methodological soundness) and usefulness of research articles. A wise reader might begin this book by reading these two appendices.

The factual and discussion questions, which appear at the end of each article, should also help with instruction in how to read research. The factual questions usually address major points, particularly the methodological issues, of the article. These factual questions can be answered directly from the article itself. The fact that the paragraphs in each article are numbered should help in documenting answers. These questions should sensitize students to the types of information in research articles that are substantively important and should be noticed.

The discussion questions require students to evaluate the quality and usefulness of the article. These questions are generally based on Royse's questions which appear in Appendix B. Student answers to these discussion questions may differ. Answering these discussion questions should provide students with an internalized set of critical questions to ask when reading any research article or report.

Acknowledgments

No work is done without assistance. My thanks go to John Harlan for an overview of criminal justice research journals, Michael Daley for a comparable overview of social work journals, and Fred Kitterle for technical assistance.

Robert F. Szafran
Professor of Sociology
Stephen F. Austin State University
Nacogdoches, Texas

Notes:

Article 1

Ronald Reagan and the Social Issues: Rhetorical Support for the Christian Right

Matthew C. Moen
The University of Maine

While scholars have studied the manner in which the Christian Right supported President Reagan, they have neglected to examine Reagan's support for the Christian Right. The purpose of this research is to analyze the public support Reagan accorded the legislative objectives of the Christian Right, through an examination of his State of the Union addresses. Among the findings are that Reagan devoted limited (but significant) attention to the social issues, focused primarily on the need for traditional values, anti-abortion, and school prayer legislation, and employed rather restrained language in support of the social issues.

(1)   Since its rapid rise in the late-1970s, the Christian Right has been a focal point for research on religion and politics. Much of that research has focused specifically upon the support that the Christian Right accorded Ronald Reagan in the 1980 and 1984 elections.[1] Virtually no research, however, has focused on the support that Reagan, in turn, provided the Christian Right.[2] That void in the literature is unfortunate, because the true nature of the relationship between Reagan and the Christian Right is skewed by such a one-sided focus.

(2)   The purpose of this research is to examine systematically a key facet of Reagan's support for the Christian Right: his public support for its legislative objectives, as it was expressed in his State of the Union addresses. Such an inquiry will partially redress the existing gap in the literature, as well as enhance scholarly understanding of the Reagan presidency. The inquiry begins with a brief discussion of the State of the Union and the Christian Right's political agenda, then moves to the analysis.

The State of the Union

(3)   The Constitution requires the president to give information about the State of the Union to the Congress. For years, scholars have argued that the most thorough and candid expression of an administration's legislative priorities may be found in that address.[3] In fact, Light asserts it is "*the* statement of legislative priorities;" Kingdon concurs, noting that ". . . agencies all over the government, staffers in the White House, interest groups, and others all vie for a place in the message."[4]

(4)   The State of the Union address is such a frank expression of a president's legislative agenda for three

Reprinted with permission from *The Social Science Journal,* 27(2): 199-207. Copyright © 1990 by JAI Press Inc. All rights of reproduction in any form reserved. ISSN: 0035-7634.

Direct all correspondence to: Matthew C. Moen, Department of Political Science, 27 North Stevens Hall, The University of Maine, Orono, Maine 04469. Telephone (207) 581-1871.

The author gratefully acknowledges the helpful comments of three anonymous reviewers.

reasons. First, it is delivered in the House chamber, an opportunity which presidents seize to personally convey their wishes to members of Congress. Second, it is delivered at the beginning of the legislative year, when Congress begins its work. Third, it is prepared far in advance of its delivery, after much deliberation. According to Light, who examined State of the Union addresses across five administrations, "There is conflict over the positioning of requests within the address, over the length of sentences, over punctuation."[5] What emerges from that process is a carefully crafted synthesis of presidential priorities.

The Christian Right Agenda

(5)　　What are the legislative priorities of the Christian Right that we should look for in the State of Union addresses in order to ascertain Reagan's rhetorical support for the movement? Crawford suggested the priority issues were opposition to abortion, busing, gay rights, and the Equal Rights Amendment, as well as concern over the content of school textbooks.[6] Jorstad added to that list both opposition to pornography and support for school prayer; Guth argued that gay rights, pornography, abortion, and school prayer were the main issues.[7] Moen interviewed the legislative directors of the Moral Majority, Christian Voice, and the National Christian Action Coalition in the first Reagan term, and discovered that they considered school prayer, abortion, and tuition tax credits their major legislative objectives.[8]

(6)　　Taken together, a reasonably consistent and coherent list of salient issues emerges: abortion, school prayer, pornography, gay rights, the Equal Rights Amendment, busing, school textbooks, and tuition tax credits. Added to that list, in a more generic vein, is erosion of "traditional values."[9] While those were not the only issues that motivated the Christian Right in the Reagan era,[10] they were the priority items. It was with them that the Christian Right enjoyed its niche in the conservative movement. Our task is simply to examine the support Reagan gave those social issues in his State of the Union addresses. In doing so, a picture of his public support for the Christian Right's agenda will emerge.

Method

(7)　　A content analysis was performed for each of the seven State of the Union messages delivered by Reagan from 1982-1988. Content analysis entails the creation of mutually exclusive and exhaustive categories within which some analytic unit (such as words) is actually tallied and placed.

(8)　　Although content analysis yields simplistic empirical results (percentages), it possesses numerous virtues: it allows scholars to study inaccessible subjects (like presidents); it avoids all problems of subject reactivity; it permits longitudinal analysis; it possesses face validity, since the words tallied are a first-person account.[11] Then too, a number of problems usually associated with content analysis are avoided in this particular study: there is no selective survival, incompleteness, or lack of access with respect to documents; there is no sampling error since the entirety of the documents is examined; there is no comparability problem since all of Reagan's addresses are similar in format and purpose.

Analysis

(9)　　The first step in the analysis is to tally the total number of words spoken on behalf of all social issues (abortion, school prayer, school textbook content, pornography, gay rights, the Equal Rights Amendment, school busing, tuition tax credits, and traditional values) for each State of the Union address.[12] The numbers are presented in Table 1.

Table 1. Number of Words on the Social Issues in Ronald Reagan's State of the Union Speeches

Year	Total Words
1982	53 (.01%)[1]
1983	134 (.02%)
1984	508 (.10%)
1985	292 (.07%)
1986	284 (.08%)
1987	64 (.02%)
1988	464 (.10%)

[1]Figure in parentheses is the percentage of the entire State of the Union address devoted to the social issues.

(10)　　For each year, there was some attention accorded the social issues. The fewest number of words Reagan spoke on those issues was 53 in 1982, followed by 64 in 1987. In the former case, the Administration was still focused on its initial budget and rearmament goals; in the latter case, it bowed to the reality that the Republicans lost control of the Senate in 1986, and that little action on the social issues was likely to occur in 1987. The most words Reagan delivered on the social issues were 508 in 1984 and 464 in 1988. Thus, the social issues received the most attention in presidential election years, suggesting that Reagan, at least in part, may have promoted the social issues to agitate an evangelical electoral constituency.

(11)   It is interesting to note that the number of words Reagan delivered each year on behalf of all the social issues was a mere fraction of his total speech. He devoted no more than one-tenth of 1% of his address to the social issues in any given year. Such inattention may have served his interest by limiting rhetoric on divisive social issues, and tempts one to conclude that he tried to "buy off" the Christian Right with token references. However, while the number of words Reagan spoke on the social issues was very modest in proportion to his total speeches, the State of the Union is by nature a far-reaching address outlining broad visions and particular proposals. It is consistent with the character of the speech that limited consideration is given to specific issues. The paucity of attention to the social issues cannot 'ipso facto' be interpreted as an effort to "buy off" the Christian Right via token references. After all, the State of the Union is a key presidential speech, whose provisions are advanced substantively and symbolically.[13] That Reagan chose it each and every year to convey his support for the social issues suggests a genuine commitment and constituted tangible assistance.

(12)   The next step in the analysis is to break down the total number of words Reagan spoke on behalf of the social issues into subcategories. A separate category was created for each of the social issues and the total number of words in it were tallied for each year. The results of the breakdown appear in Table 2.

(13)   The first finding that may be culled from this table is that Reagan paid no attention to three key issues on the Christian Right's agenda: the content of school textbooks, gay rights, and school busing. None of those issues received a single word in the course of seven State of the Union addresses, an inattention generally mirrored in other public addresses of the President.[14]

(14)   On the other side of the equation, the President spoke the most words on behalf of such "traditional values" as the importance of family, community, work, and neighborhood, with a total of 597 words delivered in four separate speeches. Of those speeches, the 1984 one is particularly interesting: Reagan devoted an entire section in it to "traditional values," which in part, may have been a subtle signal to the "American Coalition for Traditional Values," a Christian-Right organization set up to register evangelical Christians for Reagan.[15] The emphasis on traditional values was followed in order by abortion (451 words), school prayer (358 words), the ERA (181 words), tuition tax credits (118 words), and pornography (94 words). Of those issues, school prayer received the most consistent treatment, with mention in six of the seven State of the Union addresses. It was followed by traditional values and abortion, both of which received attention in four speeches.

(15)   Contrary to what one might expect, there were no major first and second term differences with respect to the social issues. In his first term, Reagan delivered an average of 231 words and mentioned six of the social issues; in his second term, he delivered an average of 276 words and mentioned five of those issues. Thus, he had somewhat more breadth in the first term and somewhat more depth in the second. Moreover, the abortion, school prayer, pornography, tuition tax credits, and traditional values issues were all mentioned at least once in both terms. Thus, the "lame duck" status of the

Table 2. Number of Words on Each Social Issue in Reagan's State of the Union Addresses[1]

Year	Abortion	Prayer	Pornography	ERA	Tuition Tax	Trad. Values
1982	—	—	—	53	—	—
1983	—	21	—	94	19	—
1984	101	113	34	34	81	145
1985	95	66	—	—	—	131
1986	58	18	60	—	18	130
1987	—	64	—	—	—	—
1988	197	76	—	—	—	191
Total	451	358	94	181	118	597

[1] There was no mention of the following issues in any of the State of the Union addresses: content of school textbooks, gay rights, school busing.

President after his 1984 reelection did not affect his support for the Christian Right's agenda in any demonstrable way. That finding again undercuts the view that Reagan rhetorically "whipped up" the Christian Right for his own benefit. He publicly advocated their issues for four years after his last election to public office.

(16)   The lone exception to the aforementioned pattern was the Equal Rights Amendment. Reagan delivered 181 words from 1982-1984 on that issue, implying that the ERA was unnecessary to eradicate discrimination. The complete absence of such rhetoric in his second term is probably explained by the defeat of the ERA in the Democratic House of Representatives in November 1983.[16] After that defeat, the ERA was a moot issue on the congressional agenda. Reagan spoke only 34 words on women's rights two months later in his 1984 speech, thereafter simply dropping the matter.

(17)   The final step in the content analysis is to examine the nature of the language employed by the President on behalf of the social issues. Bailey has noted that in addition to the frequency with which items appear, the nature of the language used in documents often reveals their contents.[17] The table below summarizes the gist of Reagan's language.

(18)   Looking first at the abortion issue, it is clear that Reagan supported anti-abortion efforts. His language in support of those efforts, however, was quite restrained. The dominant theme in his speeches was that Americans should assume a fetus is alive until it is proven otherwise—a passive endorsement which left open the possibility that it could be so proven. That rhetoric hardly reflected the views of ardent anti-abortion advocates, who claimed abortion is murder.

(19)   Complementing that rhetoric, the President also called for legislation to end abortion and advocated adoption as an alternative to it. The former rhetoric was substantive, but somewhat late, coming two years after the Senate defeated an anti-abortion constitutional amendment;[18] the latter rhetoric was passive, since few people oppose adoption. Only in 1986 did Reagan employ strong rhetoric, calling abortion "a wound on the national conscience" and advocating a "right-to-life."

(20)   With the school prayer issue, Reagan sounded several themes repeatedly: that Congress was permitted to begin its day with a public prayer, that "God had been expelled from the schools," and that remedial legislation was needed. He sounded at least one of those themes in the six years he mentioned school prayer. In contrast to his abortion language, Reagan's prayer rhetoric was strong. He directly challenged the Congress to halt the "double-standard" of prayer on Capitol Hill, but not in schools, as well as asserted the inherent virtue of prayer, the importance of God to the American founding, the "expulsion of God" from the public schools, and the need for remedial legislation. His school prayer rhetoric was as powerful as the Christian Right's own language, perhaps reflecting the broader base of support for that issue.[19]

(21)   Reagan's rhetoric vis-a-vis pornography was consensual in nature. He addressed pornography only in terms of the danger it presented to children, leaving aside First Amendment questions. He tackled only that aspect of the pornography issue which was non-controversial.

(22)   The equal rights rhetoric focused on ways that women could be assisted, apart from passage of the ERA. Reagan constructed a task force to uncover discriminatory state laws and called for amelioration of wage discrimination, stronger child support laws, better child care, and fairer pension equity. Apart from general references to the need for gender equality, he otherwise ignored the ERA. He chose to focus on alternatives, rather than directly challenge the need for the ERA.

(23)   Finally, the rhetoric on traditional values was straightforward, with little intensity behind it. In four speeches, the President spoke of the need to strengthen the values of family, neighborhood, faith, and work. Furthermore, he spoke of witnessing a reaffirmation of religious faith. Except in 1988, when Reagan suggested that America was something of a "special trust" of God, the rhetoric in support of traditional values was an obligatory exegesis of the need for such values.

(24)   Taken together, the rhetoric delivered by the President can only be described as quite restrained. With pornography, the ERA, and traditional values, Reagan offered language of the lowest common denominator. On abortion, with one salient exception (his 1986 speech calling abortion a "wound on the national conscience"), his words were similarly restrained, focused on the desirability of adoption and the belief that a fetus should be presumed alive. With the exception of the school prayer issue, which Reagan strongly favored either on its merits or for its political popularity, he opted for the most passive language possible which still conveyed his position on the social issues.

(25)   The reason Reagan opted for restrained endorsement of the social issues may go back to the nature

Table 3. Nature of Reagan's Language on the Social Issues

Issue	Themes
Abortion	assume fetus alive until disproven (1984–1986)[1]
	need legislation to stop abortion (1985, 1988)
	abortion a wound on national conscience (1986)
	adoption as alternative to abortion (1985, 1988)
	right-to-life is needed for fetuses (1986)
School Prayer	God has been expelled from schools (1983, 1987)
	need legislation to permit prayer (1983, 1985, 1986, 1988)
	Congress has prayer, why not schools (1984, 1988)
	religion was part of founding period (1984, 1987)
	importance of equal access to legislation (1985)
	importance of religion to society (1988)
Pornography	danger of pornography to children (1984, 1986)
Equal Rights	equal rights for women are needed (1982–1984)
	task force on discriminatory state laws (1982)
	wage discrimination is wrong (1983)
	strengthen child support laws (1983, 1984)
	importance of child care (1984)
	pension inequities must be remedied (1983, 1984)
	need for Individual Retirement Accounts (1984)
Tuition Tax	need to enact such legislation (1983, 1984)
	credits would soften parental burden (1984)
	tax credits targeted to less advantaged (1984)
	credits would increase school competition (1984)
	vouchers for parents to pick schools (1986)
Trad. Values	strengthen values of family, neighborhood, work, faith (1984, 1985, 1988)
	witnessing renewal of trad. values (1985, 1988)
	witnessing reaffirmation of religion (1986)
	seeing technological affirmation of faith (1986)
	America is special trust of God (1988)

[1] Numbers in parentheses are years in which Reagan mentioned this theme.

5

of the State of the Union address. It is designed as a "consensus" speech, intended to provide a president momentum as the Congress tackles his legislative agenda. Reagan's advocacy of the social issues, using moderate language, is consistent with the purpose of the speech: provoke the Congress to act, without provoking opposition.

Conclusion

(26)   Reagan's support for the legislative agenda of the Christian Right is open to interpretation. It is evident that he devoted only a fraction of his State of the Union messages to the social issues and that he offered mild endorsement of them. However, both the paucity of attention and the mild language used vis-a-vis the social issues, is consistent with the nature of the State of the Union address. Moreover, it must be recalled that Reagan mentioned six of the Christian Right's top agenda items in those important speeches, a major coup for any pressure group.

(27)   Despite the fact that Reagan's treatment of the social issues was terse and often passive, his efforts were exceedingly useful to the Christian Right. Its issues retained a prominent place on the congressional agenda—evidenced by tussles on Capitol Hill over abortion, tuition tax credits, school prayer, pornography and the ERA.[20] Its leaders profited by pointing out to their constituencies that their issues were receiving attention in the highest echelons of government. In a different vein, Reagan's attention to the social issues bequeathed secular legitimacy to the claims of religious conservatives, thereby "mainstreaming" them and their concerns into politics.

(28)   Clearly, the relationship which existed between President Reagan and the Christian Right is exceedingly complex. For his part, the President needed the votes that Christian Right leaders could muster for him personally in 1980 and 1984, as well as for his Republican Party in 1982 and 1986; the grassroots and elite lobbying resources those leaders could marshal for a gamut of conservative causes, including aid to the Contras and support for the Strategic Defense Initiative; and, the religious credentials those leaders could provide a president who not only lacked roots in any particular religious tradition, but also had often shunted "mainline" Protestant leaders during his tenure in office and had been attacked by the Catholic hierarchy on a variety of peace and social justice issues. The Christian Right, in turn, craved the supportive rhetoric, access, and political credentials the President could provide, as well as needed his personal support and his institutional

base as it pressed its agenda on Capitol Hill. To assert that either party somehow "used" the other is entirely too simplistic. It ignores the intricate and symbiotic nature of the relationship between Ronald Reagan and the Christian Right.

Notes

1. See Steven D. Johnson and Joseph B. Tamney, "The Christian Right and the 1980 Presidential Election," *Journal for the Scientific Study of Religion* 21 (1982): 123-131; Arthur H. Miller and Martin P. Wattenberg, "Politics From the Pulpit," *Public Opinion Quarterly* 48 (1984): 301-317; Jeffrey L. Brudney and Gary W. Copeland, "Evangelicals as a Political Force," *Social Science Quarterly* 65 (1984): 1072-1079; Jerome H. Himmelstein and James A. McRae, Jr., "Social Conservatism, New Republicanism and the 1980 Election," *Public Opinion Quarterly* 48 (1984): 592-605; Emmett H. Buell, Jr. and Lee Sigelman, "Popular Support for the Moral Majority in 1980," *Social Science Quarterly* 66 (1985): 426-434; Lee Sigelman, Clyde Wilcox, and Emmett H. Buell, Jr., "An Unchanging Minority," *Social Science Quarterly* 68 (1987): 876-884; Corwin Smidt, "Born-Again Politics," in Tod A. Baker, Robert P. Steed, and Laurence W. Moreland (eds.) *Religion and Politics in the South*, 27-56. (New York: Praeger, 1983); Clyde Wilcox, "Popular Support for the Moral Majority in 1980: A Second Look," *Social Science Quarterly* 68 (1987): 157-166; Emmett Buell and Lee Sigelman, "A Second Look at 'Popular Support for the Moral Majority in 1980: A Second Look,' " *Social Science Quarterly* 68 (1987): 167-169; Jeffrey L. Brudney and Gary W. Copeland, "Ronald Reagan and the Religious Vote." Paper delivered at the Annual Meeting of the American Political Science Association, Washington, D.C., 1988; Corwin Smidt, "Evangelicals and the 1984 Election," *American Politics Quarterly* 15 (1987): 419-444.
2. One popularly written book tackles the subject in part. See Richard G. Hutcheson, Jr., *God in the White House* (New York: Macmillan, 1988).
3. John Kessel, "The Parameters of Presidential Politics." Paper delivered at the Annual Meeting of the American Political Science Association, New York, 1972, p. 3; Erwin C. Hargrove and Michael Nelson, *Presidents, Politics, and Policy* (New York: Alfred A. Knopf), 1984, p. 50.
4. Paul Light, *The President's Agenda* (Baltimore: Johns Hopkins University Press, 1983), p. 160; John Kingdon, *Agendas, Alternatives, and Public Policies* (Boston: Little, Brown & Co., 1984), p. 197.

5. Light, *The President's Agenda*, p. 160.
6. Alan Crawford, *Thunder on the Right* (New York: Pantheon, 1980), p. 144.
7. Erling Jorstad, *The Politics of Moralism* (Minneapolis: Augsburg, 1981), p. 76; James L. Guth, "Southern Baptist Clergy: Vanguard of the Christian Right?" in Robert C. Liebman and Robert Wuthnow (eds.) *The New Christian Right*, 117-130. (New York: Aldine, 1983).
8. Matthew C. Moen, *The Christian Right and Congress* (Tuscaloosa: University of Alabama Press, 1989), p. 86.
9. Hutcheson, *God in the White House*, pp. 189-191.
10. For other issues, see Jorstad, *The Politics of Moralism*, pp. 76-77; Allen D. Hertzke, *Representing God in Washington* (Knoxville: University of Tennessee Press, 1988), pp. 133-134; Matthew C. Moen, "Status Politics and the Political Agenda of the Christian Right," *Sociological Quarterly* 29 (1988): 429-437.
11. Kenneth Bailey, *Methods of Social Research* (New York: Free Press, 1978), pp. 267-290.
12. For all of the issues (except "traditional values" and the ERA), the total number of words in an entire sentence in which a direct issue reference was made was tallied. It was a straightforward process because of Reagan's proclivity to address each social issue separately and sequentially. For "traditional values" and the ERA, the total number of words in an entire sentence were tallied for direct and thematic references. Thus, the phrases "traditional values" and "shared values" and "family values" were included, along with the phrases "ERA" and "women's rights."
13. Light, *The President's Agenda*, p. 160; Kingdon, *Agendas, Alternatives, and Public Policies*, p. 197.
14. A look at his papers reveals that Reagan never mentioned gay rights or school textbook content, and mentioned busing only sporadically. See *Public Papers of the President: Ronald Reagan* (Washington, D.C.: Government Printing Office, 1981-1986).
15. The American Coalition for Traditional Values was composed of prominent television ministers and local ministers from populous cities in twenty-two states, which made it an organization worth sending a subtle message of support. It should be added, however, that the phase "traditional values" was used regularly by other Christian Right groups, which also explains Reagan's usage of it. For a discussion of the American Coalition for Traditional Values, see Kenneth L. Woodward and Eleanor Clift, "Playing Politics at Church," *Newsweek*, July 9, 1984, p. 52.
16. "House Key Votes," *Congressional Quarterly Almanac 1983* XXXIX (1984): 8c.
17. Bailey, *Methods of Social Research*, p. 287.
18. Nadine Cohodas, "Senate Rejects Amendment Designed to Ban Abortion," *Congressional Quarterly Weekly Report*, July 2, 1983, p. 1362.
19. Hertzke, *Representing God in Washington*, pp. 120-122.
20. Moen, *The Christian Right and Congress*, pp. 93-140.

Factual Questions

1. What single book does the author note as an example of previous research on President Reagan's support of the Christian Right?

2. What is the purpose of this research?

3. What are the principal social agenda items of the Christian Right?

4. What does content analysis entail?

5. What are the virtues of content analysis?

11. Does the introduction provide a clear notion of the research problem, the purpose of the research, and its significance?

6. Why is it wrong to assume that a small number of words devoted to an issue in a State of the Union address reflects weak support from the President?

12. Does the literature review seem relevant to the research problem?

7. How many words did President Reagan devote to the abortion issue in his 1988 State of the Union address?

13. Why were State of the Union addresses selected for this analysis? Should other speeches have been included?

8. What Christian Right agenda item got the greatest total number of words across all seven State of the Union addresses?

14. To what population would you generalize the results of this study?

9. What is the basis for the statement that "the 'lame duck' status of the President after his 1984 reelection did not affect his support for the Christian Right agenda."?

15. Is there enough information on the research instruments and procedures to allow you to replicate this study?

10. What is the basis for the conclusion that President Reagan's support for school prayer was stronger than his support for anti-abortion efforts?

16. Should there be more information about the reliability and validity of the research instruments and procedures?

17. Does the analysis include sufficient statistical information? Are the statistics that are used appropriate?

18. Are the conclusions supported by and do they logically follow from the data that have been presented?

19. Are the findings discussed in terms of their implications and/or practical significance?

Notes:

Article 2 _____

Do Contemporary Women's Magazines Practice What They Preach?

Jeanne A. Ortiz
Larry P. Ortiz
Houghton College

Using the Consciousness Scale for Media Sexism developed by Butler-Paisley and Paisley-Butler (1974), this paper examines 288 advertisements in the April, August and December issues of four contemporary women's magazines, *Ms., Self, Working Mother*, and *Working Woman* between 1981 and 1984. It was found that despite attempts by publishers to create segmented publications geared towards the needs of contemporary women, a majority of women in advertisements are portrayed in stereotypical, sexist roles.

Introduction

(1)   The status of women in American society has received considerable scrutiny since the advent of the women's movement in the 1960s. The issue of the status of women is closely linked to traditional roles for women; roles which have been limited and stereotypical. Studies have looked at sex-stereotyping in many forms of common culture such as the electronic and print mediums (Beuf 1974; Courtney, Whipple 1983; Skelly, Lundstrom 1981; Glazer 1980). Concern regarding sex stereotyping in media stems from the assumption that media is an important educational force in society that reinforces the perception of traditional, limiting, and demeaning role expectations for women and men.

(2)   As a vehicle of informal education, traditional women's magazines such as *Good Housekeeping* and *Ladies Home Journal* have provided information which helped to shape and reinforce the lives and roles of American women (Friedan 1963). Analyses of the advertising content of these magazines reveals that

> . . . advertising still presents the typical woman at home; her labor force role is underrepresented, she is known as a housewife and mother dependent upon male authority for decisions, she needs product benefits to satisfy and serve her husband and family, and it is from this service that she draws her self-esteem. (Courtney, Whipple 1983, p. 24)

(3)   Since the early 1970s, new publications geared for women have appeared on the newsstand. These publications are designed for contemporary women and contribute to their education on issues relevant to their lifestyles. These magazines also represent attempts by publishers to use technology to demassify the media by matching various segmented communication opportunities with various markets. How are women portrayed in the advertisements of these contemporary women's magazines?

Reprinted with permission from *Free Inquiry in Creative Sociology, 17*(1): 51-55. Copyright © 1989 by University of Central Oklahoma.

(4)   The study reported here is an attempt to go beyond previous research on media sexism by trying to measure the portrayed images of women in the advertisements of contemporary women's magazines. Using qualitative indicators of sexism developed by Matilda Butler-Paisley and William Paisley-Butler (1974), magazine advertisements were assessed on a continuum of sexist to nonsexist portrayals of women in magazine advertising. While stereotyping of men in magazine advertising is also a valid concern, it is not examined in this research.

(5)   Although previous studies have concluded that women in advertising are portrayed with a narrow range of social, family or occupational settings, these images, in and of themselves, do not constitute sexism. However, when the majority of images presented show women in one role, homemaker, this constitutes sexism (Pingree et al. 1976). It matters that sexist images are presented because these images do not accurately represent the many and varied roles of women today. This study cannot document the effects of advertising stereotyping. However, it has been speculated that "concentrating imagery into one particular group over an extended time period must have some effect on self-perception and self-value" (Scott 1976, p. 223). Speculations regarding the social consequences of portraying women in particular social or occupational roles are discussed.

(6)   Since Betty Friedan's impressionistic work on the portrayal of women in magazines, many questions have been raised. The major focus of these questions is the way in which the sexes have been portrayed in all forms of media and advertising. Much research has been conducted in the area of sex stereotyping and its potential consequences (Belkaoui, Belkaoui 1976; Courtney, Lockeretz 1971; Goffman 1979; Millum 1975; Sexton, Haberman 1974; Venkatesan, Losco 1975; Wagner, Banos 1973). These studies point to two significant conclusions. First, the portrayals of both men and women do not reflect the wide range of lifestyles they experience. Advertising is criticized as contributing to the perpetuation of this situation by its neglect in showing both sexes utilizing their diverse capabilities and individualities. Secondly, the area of visual imagery in advertising as documented through content analysis requires additional study, particularly in magazines which claim to show women in a wider range of activities.

Methodology

(7)   This study examines the advertising of four different types of women's magazines which have emerged since the 1970s. They are *Ms., Working Woman, Working Mother,* and *Self.* Each of these magazines is designed to address different issues related to feminism. *Ms.* began publication in 1971 by the Ms. Foundation for Education and Communication, Inc. Its purpose is to serve as a lifeline for women isolated by geographical, familial, or other circumstances. Widely available, *Ms.* magazine is able to carry women's movement news and awareness to many women who might not otherwise know about feminist issues (Katz, Katz 1982 910). *Self* began publication by Conde' Nast Publishing, Inc. in 1979. This magazine is designed for the self-development of women, with a psychological perspective. The articles are on par with *Cosmopolitan,* stressing superficial beauty and fashion. Although it is considered a contemporary magazine, it does not deal with topics related to women's issues and concerns (Katz, Katz 1982 905). *Working Mother* began publication in 1978 by the McCall Publishing Company and is designed to be a service magazine for young women (20s and 30s) who combine marriage, children, home and career. Editorial content focuses on the problems and challenges of coping with diverse lifestyles, emotional stressors, health concerns, and child rearing (Katz, Katz 1982 906). *Working Woman* began publication in 1976 by Hal Publishing Inc. and focuses on professional women who not only work at careers for 40-plus hours a week, but also put in an additional 40 hours caring for their homes and families. The emphasis, however, is on career related topics (Katz, Katz 1982 715). All these magazines have large circulations and national audiences.

(8)   Six advertisements containing a picture of a woman and covering at least 1/6 of a magazine page were randomly selected from the April, August and December issues of four magazines between 1981 and 1984. A total of 288 advertisements were analyzed.

(9)   Content analysis was the method used to analyze the advertisements in the four contemporary women's magazines. Content analysis is a

> multipurpose research method developed specifically for investigating any problem in which communication serves as the basis of inference. (Holisti 1969, p. 104)

There are several problems associated with content analysis research. As an attribute, content analysis shows what is there, but does not explain the variables. In the case of women in advertisements, a count of women in advertisements can be easily made, but it is difficult to determine how sexist an advertisement is. In order to compensate for this shortcoming, what is needed is an ordinal scale which includes qualitative categories of sexism and can identify images on a continuum of sexist to non-sexist portrayals of women (Pingree et al. 1976).

(10)   Butler-Paisley and Paisley-Butler (1974) devised an ordinal consciousness scale that looks at how women, as presented in magazine advertisements, are portrayed in special roles and relationships. This scale, which measures both qualitative and quantitative measures of sexism, served as the basis of this research. *Level I* shows women being put down, the idea of "the dumb blond, the sex object, the whimpering victim who is less than a person, a two-dimensional image" such as a woman standing beside a car with no purpose, "or a woman's body as a decorative object, or in situations where the woman relies on others to do her thinking for her." In *Level II,* women are portrayed engaged in traditional womanly functions such as wives, mothers, secretaries, clerks, teachers and nurses. Advertisements for cosmetics, perfume, and clothing would fall into this category. Negative Level II advertisements might show women struggling with jobs that are beyond them such as executives, professionals, or doctors in which they develop unwomanly traits. In *Level III* women are portrayed more progressively by giving them two places. The notion is that women can work as professionals as long as they have the home taken care of, dinner on the table, the children clean, and the wash done. Their career is viewed as something extra, housework and mothering come first. These types of women sometimes work outside the home professionally, but always work inside the home. *Level IV* acknowledges that women are fully equal to men by showing women as professionals. These advertisements do not remind the reader that housework and mothering are women's major responsibilities. *Level V* is non-stereotypic. Individual men and women are viewed as superior in some respects and inferior in others. In this type of advertisement it is not necessary to perceive women as being equal to men. This type of advertisement is not very easily found in the media (Pingree et al. 1976 194-5).

(11)   This sexism scale was tested by Pingree et al. (1976) and looked at the level of sexism in four major national magazines: *Ms., Time, Newsweek,* and *Playboy* between June 1973 and June 1974. Findings suggested that each magazine, regardless of focus, included sexist advertisements, with *Playboy* having the highest

number of Level I advertisements, *Time* and *Newsweek* having a similar number of Level I advertisements, and *Ms.* having the fewest number.

(12)   In this study, a panel of three judges were employed. All three were graduate students. One was a master's student in home economics education. The others were two doctoral candidates, one in educational administration and the other in sociology. In order to determine the reliability of the five levels in the consciousness scale, the interraters coded each of 288 advertisements. As with the Pingree et al. study, disagreements in ratings were noted and referred back to a committee for the final decision. The interrater reliability score is shown in Table 1. The overall interrater reliability score was 92 percent. Reliability or the ability to reproduce the findings is of critical importance in content analysis. Categories must be reliable so that there is consensus regarding which category the population belongs to. Eighty-five percent interjudger reliability

Table 1. Interrater Reliability

Magazine	Percentage
Self	94
Ms.	93
Working Mother	89
Working Woman	93

scores are acceptable, while scores of less than 80 percent are suspicious (Holisti 1969). For all 288 advertisements there were only 22 disagreements. As with the Pingree et al. research, these findings suggest that the scale is relatively reliable in identifying media sexism.

Findings

(13)   Consistent with the Pingree et al. study which found 56 percent of the sampled advertisements for *Ms.* magazine falling either in Level I or Level II between June 1973 to June 1974, we found that 58 percent of the sample fell in these two levels almost ten years later. Many of the Level I or Level II advertisements attempted to sell cosmetics and personal items. An interesting difference, however, is in the findings for Levels III, IV, and V. The Pingree et al. study (1976) found only three percent of the advertisements in *Ms.* magazines portrayed women as individuals (Level V). In contrast, we found 22 percent of all advertisements in *Ms.* to be in this category. There was also an increase in the number of women portrayed as wife, mother and

Table 2. Levels of Consciousness of Advertisements in Four Contemporary Women's Magazines (Percents)

Level of Consciousness	*Ms.* N = 72	*Working Mother* N = 72	*Working Woman* N = 72	*Self* N = 72	Total N = 288
Level I	11	31	8	14	16
Level II	47	51	50	71	55
Level III	7	6	6	3	5
Level IV	13	8	8	8	9
Level V	22	4	28	4	15

worker (from 3% to 7%). There was a decrease in the number of advertisements portraying women as equal to men (37% to 13%).

(14)   In our study, on the average, 16 percent of all advertisements portrayed women at Level I (8% to 31%). These advertisements portrayed pensive, glassy-eyed women staring off into the distance at cars, a man, or even at a piece of candy! On the average, Level I advertisements were identified second most frequently (Table 2).

(15)   A surprising finding was that most of the advertisements portrayed women at Level II (55%). The majority of these advertisements did not portray women in domestic responsibilities, but rather were advertisements for cosmetics, perfume, clothing or hosiery. Some advertisements portrayed women in romantic situations, usually with the male perceived as the aggressor. The large percentage of advertisements in *Self* magazine (71%) which fell into Level II substantiate the editorial and advertising focus of the magazine. *Self* is thought to be in competition with *Cosmopolitan* (Katz, Katz 1982).

(16)   Few of the magazine advertisements show women fulfilling both domestic and work outside the home roles (Level III). This is surprising particularly for *Working Mother* magazine whose editorial focus is geared toward dual responsibilities. Most advertisements in the sample from that magazine were geared toward cosmetics, perfume, and clothing. As an interesting note, several Level II advertisements were for children's toys. Portrayed was a female adult, presumably a mother, playing with her child.

(17)   Both *Ms.* and *Working Woman* magazines had the highest percentage of advertisements geared for women as individuals. This seems to be consistent with the editorial focus of these magazines which is geared towards individual self-fulfillment through career achievement. The type of advertisements which would portray women as individuals included a Samsonite ad showing a woman traveler, a woman in an executive business role, a woman engaged in individual-oriented sports, painting, or fishing.

(18)   Although it is not necessarily the presence of Level I or Level II advertisements that constitute sexism, when these are the majority of images presented, this constitutes or reinforces sexism. Certainly it is not sexist to show a woman as a wife or mother or to show her trying to look attractive, but it is sexist to show women this way the majority of the time.

Discussion

(19)   The results of this survey show many things, but one thing in particular. Even though media technology has demassified itself by creating contemporary women's magazines which appeal to the changing roles of women, the advertising still reflects the two lowest positions of the sexism consciousness scale. This finding seems somewhat ironic considering the genesis of these contemporary women's publications. What might be possible interpretations for this finding? First, there are differences in objectives between advertisers and the publishers. On one hand the publisher wants to advance a theme, feminist issues, while on the other hand the advertiser wants to sell a product. Both parties need the other so they coexist without sharing the same objective. These magazines are published for women with the intention of raising their consciousness. Editors, nevertheless, must depend upon selling advertising space, even if the advertisements run in the spaces are inconsistent with the overarching editorial focus. Making ends meet is the bottom line for these magazines if women are to have a forum to express their issues.

Editors may not always be in a fiscal position to control the advertisements submitted to their publications. This explanation can be interpreted as women "selling out" for the purpose of keeping their ideas alive, or it may be interpreted simply in pragmatic terms. The result, as indicated in this study, is a contradictory message. Indeed this is a most perplexing situation, it leaves women in the position of allowing for exploitation while attempting to raise their collective consciousness. However it is interpreted, the one thing that seems very clear is that economically, women are still in a dependent position and their real status has changed little. Men are still the owners of the means of production and the products, and thus the controllers of social images.

(20)   This study clearly demonstrates that sexism abounds in contemporary advertising, to the extent that our sample is representative. Contemporary women's magazines are found to contain significant levels of sexism in their advertising content. One cannot help but wonder about the mixed messages given the readership as they scan and read these periodicals. What kind of images do women gain of themselves when they read articles designed to raise their consciousness as independent thinking and feeling beings and then turn the page only to see graphically, images of themselves portrayed as objects? Do these periodicals really practice what they preach?

References

Belkaoui A, J Belkaoui 1976 A comparative analysis of the roles portrayed by women in print advertisements 1958, 1970, 1972 *J Marketing Res* 13 168-172

Beuf A 1974 Doctor, lawyer and household drudge *J Communications* 24 142-145

Butler-Paisley M, WJ Paisley-Butler 1974 Sexism in the media: frameworks for research. Paper presented at the annual meeting of the Association for Education in Journalism, San Diego.

Courtney AE, SW Lockeretz 1971 Women's place: an analysis of the roles portrayed by women in magazine advertisements *J Marketing Res* 8 92-95

Courtney AE, TW Whipple 1983 *Sex Stereotyping in Advertising* Lexington, MA: Lexington Books

Friedan B 1963 *The Feminine Mystique* NY: Basic Books

Glazer N 1980 Overworking the working woman: the double day in a mass magazine *Women's Stud Internat Qrtly* 3 79-93

Goffman E 1979 *Gender Advertisements* Cambridge, MA: Harvard U Press

Holisti OR 1969 *Content Analysis for the Social Sciences and the Humanities* Reading, MA: Addison-Wesley

Katz B, LS Katz 1982 *Magazines for Libraries* NY: RR Bowker Company

Millum T 1975 *Images of Women* Totowa, NJ: Bowman and Littlefield

Pingree S, RP Hawkins, M Butler, W Paisley 1976 A scale for sexism *J Communication* 26 193-200

Scott R 1976 *The Female Consumer* NY: John Wiley & Sons Inc

Sexton D, P Haberman 1974 Women in magazine advertisements *J Advertising Res* 14 41-46

Skelly G, WJ Lundstrom 1981 Male sex roles in magazine advertising *J Communication* 31 52-57

Venkatesan M, J Losco 1975 Women in magazine ads: 1959-1971 *J Advertising Res* 15 49-54

Wagner LC, J Banos 1973 A woman's place: a follow-up analysis of the roles portrayed by women in magazine advertisements *J Marketing Res* 10 213-214

Factual Questions

1. What is the name of the article written by Beuf in 1974?

2. How does this research attempt to go beyond previous research on the topic?

3. Which of the four contemporary women's magazines examined in this study deals least with women's issues and concerns?

4. How many advertisements were examined and how were they selected?

5. What is content analysis?

6. What problem with content analysis is mentioned by the authors?

7. Describe the five levels of the Butler-Paisley and Paisley-Butler sexism scale.

8. What was the interrater reliability for advertisements appearing in *Working Mother*?

9. What percentage of the advertisements appearing in the four magazines were classified as Level I? Level III?

10. According to the authors, when do Level I and Level II advertisements constitute sexism?

11. What mixed messages are the authors referring to in the final paragraph?

Questions for Discussion

12. Does the introduction provide a clear notion of the research problem, the purpose of the research, and its significance?

13. Does the literature review seem relevant to the research problem?

14. Is the number of advertisements examined sufficient? To what population would you generalize the results of this study?

15. Is there enough information on the research instruments and procedures to allow you to replicate this study?

16. Do the research instruments and procedures have adequate reliability and validity?

17. Does the analysis include sufficient statistical information? Are the statistics that are used appropriate?

18. Why might this study have found different percentages of *Ms.* advertisements in levels III, IV, and V than in the Pingree et al. (1976) study?

19. Are the conclusions supported by and do they logically follow from the data that have been presented?

20. Are the findings discussed in terms of their implications and/or practical significance?

Notes:

Sex-Role Stereotyping of Children on Television: A Content Analysis of the Roles and Attributes of Child Characters

Kate Peirce

Southwest Texas State University

A content analysis of child characters on prime-time television revealed that while boys and girls are significantly different on only four out of 13 character traits (boys are considered more active, aggressive, rational and unhappy than are girls) they do differ significantly in the types of activities in which they participate. Girls talk on the telephone, read and help with housework, and boys play sports, go places and make mischief.

(1)   Roles, according to sociological definition, are the expectations attached to social positions, and sex-role expectations are the behaviors, attitudes, emotions and personality traits appropriate for each sex (Boudreau et al. 1986, p. 8). These expectations depend on what Berger and Luckman (1966) term socially constructed reality, a definition of reality that members of a society learn.

(2)   The processes that contribute to this definition of reality are institutionalization, patterns of interactions based on rules, laws, customs and rituals that become habits; legitimation, which justifies and explains why things are done the way they are; and internalization, which occurs when individuals accept the group's norm as their own (Boudreau et al. 1986, p. 9-10).

(3)   According to this perspective, a social definition of what is male and what is female is transmitted to the young. Society defines what is male and what is female. In social learning theory, the dominant explanation of sex-role socialization, children are thought to learn sex roles through observation as well as through rewards and punishments. They have the opportunity to watch members of their own sex in order to discover how they are supposed to behave and feel. Models of the opposite sex can provide direction for what is to be avoided (Maccoby and Jacklin 1974, p. 363).

(4)   The media—especially television—can contribute to children's sex-role socialization by providing models for observation. Many researchers have looked at television's part in sex-role socialization, asking such questions as: What are the role models to which children are being exposed on television, and what behaviors are being reinforced as culturally acceptable?

(5)   This study examines the images of children projected through the media by investigating the attributes of younger characters on prime-time television.

Reprinted with permission from *Sociological Spectrum, 9*: 321-328. Copyright © 1989 by Taylor & Francis, Inc. Request reprints from Kate Peirce, Department of Journalism, Southwest Texas State University, San Marcos, TX 78666.

Based on previous content analyses of adult characters on television, it can be hypothesized that characters and roles of children will be as stereotyped as those of adults.

(6)   Researchers using content analysis have focused on adult behaviors, attributes and activities, and have concluded that the media do little to dispel the stereotypes of sex roles and, in fact, present the sex-stereotyped views of males and females that prevail. Both men and women, they found, are portrayed stereotypically in television programs. On the one hand, women have been judged to be younger, more attractive and less aggressive than men (Miller and Reeves 1976), as well as sociable, peaceful, warm and happy (Tedesco 1974), affectionate, forgiving, submissive and fragile (Busby 1974). Men, on the other hand, were judged to be powerful, rational, smart, stable, active, independent, mature and serious (Tedesco 1974).

(7)   Other researchers have found that the most popular role for women characters is housewife (Smythe 1954; Downing 1974; Miller and Reeves 1976; Long and Simon 1974) while men are often portrayed as doctors, lawyers and policemen (Miller and Reeves 1976). Seggar (1975) found that women were portrayed as less competent than men in any of the occupations they held, which included housewife, secretary, receptionist, police-related jobs, student and nurse. Women are more frequently cast as victims and men as heroes (Gerbner 1972; Head 1954; Tedesco 1974). The marital status of women is more crucial than that of men (Downing 1974) and more women than men are married (Gerbner 1972; McNeil 1975; and Tedesco 1974).

(8)   Busby (1986) summarized the research of the last 15 years by saying that females are underrepresented, appear in limited roles and are most often associated with domesticity, while males are associated with paid employment, entertainment and leisure. Women are often victims, are often identified by their relationships with men, and tend to be younger but age more quickly than males.

(9)   Perhaps more important than the portrayals themselves is that children learn from these portrayals. They learn from television and consequently learn a stereotypical view of the world (Himmelweit et al. 1958; Bailyn 1959; DeFleur and DeFleur 1967; Beuf 1974). The more they watch, the more likely they are to have stereotypic beliefs (Beuf 1974; Freuh and McGhee 1975).

(10)   Busby (1986) also reports that children model the behavior they see in the media: boys use physical strength and dynamic action as criteria for selecting models, while girls use physical attractiveness. She says that children learn typical roles so thoroughly that they depend on them to remember media content, while non-stereotypic models lessen children's stereotypical attitudes.

(11)   Based on the findings of adult depictions, it is predicted that girl characters will be described by the use of adjectives that have been associated with women: inactive, passive, weak, irrational, unstable, happy, naive, nonviolent, dumb, attractive, warm, friendly and troubleshooter. Boys will be described with the opposites: strong, rational, stable, worldly, violent, active, cold, unfriendly, unhappy, unattractive, smart, aggressive and troublemaker. Additionally, it is predicted that boys will be observed participating in more typically male activities (outdoor and athletic) than will girls, and girls will participate in more typically female activities (household and sedentary) than will boys.

Methods

(12)   In order to test the assumptions about the stereotyped images of young characters, it was decided that all characters up to the age of 20 appearing on prime-time television would be rated by at least two independent coders. The values accorded by the observers were averaged to provide summary scores on each dimension.

(13)   It was assumed that characters would be at their most developed stage during February or "sweeps" month, the time period in which networks attempt to attract the largest audience. One week in this month was chosen at random. Thus the three major networks were to be watched for the three hours between 7 p.m. and 10 p.m. for seven consecutive days. During this period, coders would rate the attributes of all relevant characters and monitor their activities.

(14)   The programs that had youthful characters were "Who's the Boss?" "Family Ties," "The Cosby Show," "The Cavanaughs," "Kate and Allie," "Facts of Life," "Growing Pains," "My Sister Sam," "Gimme a Break," "You Again," "Valerie," "Head of the Class," and "Scarecrow and Mrs. King." A total of 20 male and 13 female characters appeared on these shows during the assigned time period.

(15)   Each of 15 coders (eight females and seven males) was assigned a total of six hours of viewing. They were assigned evenings and networks in a manner that assured at least two coders were viewing all prime-time shows for one full week. The intercoder reliability measures, ranging from .73 to .93, are high, given that all of the raters were naive, i.e. they were directed to use the adjective check list without any definition of the terms. Keeping them naive was calculated because it is assumed that typical viewers would interpret the characters in a similarly naive manner.

(16)   Coders rated each character on a five-point semantic differential-type scale, using 13 bipolar adjectives, such as active-inactive, aggressive-passive and smart-dumb. These scales have been used in previous content analyses of adult characters (Tedesco 1974; Miller and Reeves 1976) and were derived from sex-role inventories designed to measure masculinity and femininity (Broverman et al. 1972). Sex-role researchers have found that people tend to categorize both traits and activities as masculine, feminine and androgynous (Kaplan and Sedney 1980, p. 3; Basow 1986, p. 3). Discriminant analysis, developed to measure group differences for which multiple predictor variables have been obtained, was used to determine whether it is possible to distinguish between male and female characters using the 13 scales.

(17)   In addition, coders described the activities the characters engaged in to see if actions as well as attributes were sex-typed. The activities were then judged by independent coders to be masculine, feminine or sex-neutral. Coder reliabilities were above 90 percent. Activities were then analyzed by chi square tests to see if there were significant differences in the types of activities in which the characters engaged.

Findings and Discussion

(18)   A stepwise discriminant analysis, which eliminates weak or redundant variables, was conducted to determine which of the 13 variables best separate males from females.[1] Four of the 13 variables were retained in the analysis: active-inactive, aggressive-passive, rational-irrational and unhappy-happy. The standardized discriminant function coefficients are presented in Table 1. The larger the coefficient, the more important the variable is to the discriminant function.

(19)   The coefficients indicate that boys are associated with the traits active, aggressive, rational and

Table 1: Standardized Canonical Discriminant Function Coefficients for Male and Female Traits

active-inactive	1.05256
aggressive-passive	0.48280
rational-irrational	0.89560
unhappy-happy	0.68196
eigenvalue	2.4549
canonical correlation	0.8429
chi square	35.3340
df	5
probability less than	0.001
group centroids	
group 1 (female)	-1.88358
group 2 (male)	1.22433

unhappy. The analysis produced a function that classified correctly 94 percent of the characters. The exceptions were two females.

(20)   The prediction that girl characters will be described with adjectives different from those used to describe boy characters is, therefore, only partially supported. Boy and girl characters are not significantly different on all 13 attribute scales, but there are four attributes that separate the boys from the girls.

(21)   Table 2 suggests support for the second prediction: boys participated in male activities and girls participated in female activities. Activities designated by the coders as typically female include playing dress up, playing with dolls, helping in the kitchen and talking on the phone. Watching television, reading and studying are also considered female activities because they are sedentary activities and were done inside the home. Activities considered to be typically male include participating in sports and other outdoor activities, being a radio disc jockey and running through the house. Mischievous activities, such as removing labels from all the canned goods and conning parents or friends, are considered male activities because "troublemaker" is an adjective most often associated with males. Other activities—talking with friends and family, going to parties and dating—are considered sex-neutral.

---

[1] An examination of the means for boys and girls on each dimension and t-tests performed on the variables retained in the discriminant analysis corroborated the results of the analysis.

Table 2. Crosstabulation of Portrayed Activities of Child TV Characters by Sex of Character Participating

Activities	Stereotyped female activities	Stereotyped male activities	Sex neutral
Females	17 (89%)	0	9 (53%)
Males	2 (11%)	17 (100%)	8 (47%)
Total	19 (100%)	17 (100%)	17 (100%)

chi square = 28.9 with 2 df, p < .001

(22)   Other than sex-neutral activities, there was little crossover between the sexes. In fact, television watching is the only activity in which there was crossover, and it could be argued that watching television is sex-neutral. Reading and studying, which should be sex-neutral, are apparently the province of females, who were the only ones ever seen reading or studying. The girls spent the rest of their time helping around the house, talking on the phone, playing with dolls and just sitting around, while the boys spent their time in a variety of pursuits, active and inactive, indoor and outdoor. Both sexes participated in the normal teenage activities of trying to get dates, dating and falling in love.

(23)   For example, "Growing Pains," a half-hour situation comedy, illustrates well the non-stereotyped attributes of the children and the stereotypical activities in which they engage. The daughter, Carol, was judged more intelligent, rational and stable than her older brother, Mike, who was judged more aggressive, attractive, worldly and troublesome than Carol. In one episode, Carol spends her time helping her mother wash and iron curtains even though it is clear from conversation that she is the computer expert in the family. Mike, who is supposed to be painting his room, is instead conning a friend into doing it for him. The youngest child, Ben, while talking with the furnace repairman, manages to do something that results in a sooty mess all over the house. Clearly, the girl is the obedient, helpful child and the boys are the mischief-makers. The network obviously realizes the changing roles of women and is attempting to portray them; the mother is a newspaper reporter and the daughter is an intellectual who is good with numbers. But neither was seen in any capacity other than housewife/housedaughter.

(24)   The socially constructed reality that children learn from television, then, is one in which a girl can be smart and a boy can be attractive, but it is also one in which the girl's place is in the home and the boy's place is wherever he wants it to be. Though the argument can be made that network television has in some ways improved its portrayals of females, there is still work to be done to create role models for children that do not teach segregation of the sexes.

References

Bailyn, L. 1959. "Mass Media and Children: A Study of Exposure Habits and Cognitive Effects." *Psychological Monographs* 73:1-48.

Basow, S. 1986. *Gender Stereotypes.* California: Brooks/Cole.

Berger, P. and T. Luckman. 1966. *The Social Construction of Reality.* Garden City, New York: Doubleday/Anchor.

Beuf, A. 1974. "Doctor, Lawyer, Household Drudge." *Journal of Communication* 24:142-145.

Boudreau, F., R. Sennott and M. Wilson. 1986. *Sex Roles and Social Patterns.* New York: Praeger Publishers.

Broverman, I., S. Vogel, D. Broverman, F. Clarkson and P. Rosenkrantz. 1972. "Sex Role Stereotypes: A Current Appraisal." *Journal of Social Issues* 28:59-78.

Busby, L. 1974. "Defining the Sex Role Standard in Network Children's Programming." *Journalism Quarterly* 51:690-696.

_____. 1986. "The Mass Media and Sex-Role Socialization." Pp. 267-295 in *Broadcasting Research Methods,* edited by J. Dominick and J. Fletcher. Boston: Allyn and Bacon.

DeFleur, M. and L. DeFleur. 1967. "The Relative Contribution of Television as a Learning Source for Children's Occupational Knowledge." *American Sociological Review* 32:777-789.

Downing, M. 1974. "Heroine of the Daytime Serial." *Journal of Communication* 24:130-137.

Freuh, T. and P. McGhee. 1975. "Traditional Sex Role Development and Amount of Time Spent Watching TV." *Developmental Psychology* 11:109.

Gerbner, G. 1972. "Violence in Television Drama: Trends and Symbolic Functions." Pp. 28-187 in *Television and Social Behavior, Vol. 1: Media Content and Control,* edited by G.S. Comstock and E.A. Rubenstein. Washington, D.C.: U.S. Government Printing Office.

Head, S. 1954. "Content Analysis of Television Dramatic Programs." *Quarterly of Film, Radio and Television* 9:175-194.

Himmelweit, H., A. Oppenheim and P. Vince. 1958. *Television and the Child.* New York and London: Oxford University Press.

Kaplan, A. and M.A. Sedney. 1980. *Psychology and Sex Roles: An Androgynous Perspective.* Boston: Little, Brown.

Long, M. and R. Simon. 1974. "The Roles and Statuses of Women on Children and Family TV Programs." *Journalism Quarterly* 51:107-110.

Maccoby, E.E. and C.N. Jacklin. 1974. *The Psychology of Sex Differences.* Stanford, CA: Stanford University Press.

McNeil, J. 1975. "Femininity and the TV Series: A Content Analysis." *Journal of Broadcasting* 19:259-271 and 283-288.

Miller, M. and B. Reeves. 1976. "Dramatic TV and Sex Role Stereotypes." *Journal of Broadcasting* 20:35-49.

Seggar, J. 1975. "Women's Imagery on TV: Feminist, Fair Maiden or Maid?" *Journal of Broadcasting* 19:289-294.

Smythe, D. 1954. "Reality as Presented by Television." *Public Opinion Quarterly* 18:143-156.

Tedesco, N. 1974. "Patterns in Prime Time." *Journal of Communication* 24:119-124.

Factual Questions

1. What are sex roles?

2. What adjectives are predicted to describe girl characters?

3. What activities are boys predicted to be typically doing and what activities are girls predicted to be typically doing?

4. How many youthful characters were observed in prime time during one week?

5. Why were the coders not given definitions for the adjectives on the checklist?

6. In addition to using the adjective checklist, what else were the coders instructed to do for each character?

7. Who decided whether a particular activity should be classified as typically male, typically female, or sex-neutral?

8. What four traits were more often associated with boys than with girls?

9. The article mentions seven activities that were designated by the coders as typically female. What were they?

10. How many times were male characters observed engaging in stereotyped female activities? How many times were female characters observed engaging in stereotyped male activities?

Questions for Discussion

11. Does the introduction provide a clear notion of the research problem, the purpose of the research, and its significance?

12. Does the literature review seem relevant to the research problem?

13. Are the stated hypotheses reasonable? Do they appear to reasonably follow from the review of the literature?

14. Is the number of television shows studied sufficient? To what population would you generalize the results of this study?

15. Is there enough information on the research instruments and procedures to allow you to replicate this study?

16. Do the research instruments and procedures have adequate reliability and validity?

17. Does the analysis include sufficient statistical information? Are the statistics that are used appropriate?

18. Are the conclusions supported by and do they logically follow from the data that have been presented?

19. Are the findings discussed in terms of their implica-
    tions and/or practical significance?

96-945

Notes:

Article 4

Crime and the Magic Kingdom

David Fabianic
University of Central Florida

(1)   Rapid population growth is a salient fact of social and economic life in many parts of the country. The State of Florida is among those areas which have experienced substantial population growth since the 1960s. The migratory trend to Florida has been inspired by several factors, including the climate, tax advantages and relative economic prosperity. Among the items accounting for the latter has been the developing tourism industry which includes the construction of tourist attractions and the other facilities and services necessary to support them.

(2)   The Central Florida area, the area surrounding the city of Orlando, has been in the forefront of this development. In particular, the advent of Disney World has been a major force in subsequent development of other tourist attractions such as Sea World and Epcot Center and the construction of hotels, restaurants, stores, shopping centers and other commercial establishments. Today the Orlando area is recognized as one of the premier places for economic development and population growth.

(3)   Accompanying the growth and development are an assortment of problems and difficulties which are normally associated with rapid population growth and social change. The literature in sociology details the effects of rapid population growth on community resources. Primarily this literature concerns "boom town" effects in communities experiencing rapid growth because of energy development (Freudenburg 1981, 1984; Jobes & Parsons 1975). These communities undergo significant in-migrations of individuals from outside the community. People enter a social community and contribute to ongoing normative change. Consequently, there are at least two factors influencing community change. First, the normative structure of the community is diluted and weakened, and there is less community cohesiveness with which to identify and develop normative ties. And second, people coming into the community from other areas bring with them different patterns of behavior and expectations, some of which may be in conflict with those of their new community.

(4)   These thoughts are often expressed by the citizenry of Orlando and the surrounding area (*Orlando Sentinel* 1989 a-g; 1990). Frequently comparisons are made to an alleged period of relative calm which preceded the settlement of the Disney Corporation in Orange County in the late 1960s. Newcomers are often held in mild contempt by some of the more vocal natives and media personalities. While there is an appreciation for the good things which have emerged as a result of the development, there is also concern and alarm often expressed about some unfavorable things also regarded as a consequence of the change.

(5)   Next to horrendous traffic congestion, a principal factor of concern which arises in public forums is that of crime. In particular, a part of conventional wisdom among people currently residing in the area is the belief that crime is much worse today than it was before Disney's construction of the Magic Kingdom and the subsequent growth, that the rapid development of the area is a key factor in the emergence of crime, and that crime has become worse in the Orlando area and a

special and extraordinary problem. It is this contention which is examined here as an instance of a very special case of social growth and development. That is, the question of crime in Orlando, its growth and its relationship to crime in the state in general is an appropriate question to examine not only to respond to the popular proposition that the Magic Kingdom of Disney has produced crime in the process of producing prosperity. It is also relevant because Orlando is unique in that no other place has experienced as much growth centered around a single tourist attraction. Information pertaining to this question is appropriate to our understanding of social change and the manner in which communities grow. The facts pertaining to the changes in the Orlando area represent those which are relevant to scholars interested in the processes and effects of rapid population growth and social change.

Background Literature

(6)   The literature regarding the effects of rapid population growth has its roots at least as far back as Durkheim (1964) He speculated that social change could lead to the weakening or disappearance of social norms in a community. Individuals might suffer as well by being unable to accurately anticipate the actions of others and becoming detached from unifying values and beliefs. Crime was regarded as one manifestation of this occurrence.

(7)   More recent research and literature has focused on more specific aspects of the impact of rapid population growth. This literature reflects the complexity of the proposition that rapid growth necessarily results in increased patterns of deviance (Covey, Menard 1984; Diamond 1971; Finsterbusch 1982; Freudenburg 1981,1984; Wilkerson et al 1982). While yielding results generally compatible with Durkheim's central proposition, recent studies have done much to identify exceptions and qualifications as well.

Research Questions

(8)   The general proposition to be examined concerns a comparison of crime rates in Orlando (Orange and Seminole counties), with: 1) several points in the past; and 2) crime rates for other areas. That is, concerns expressed in the media by citizens, politicians and journalists indicate these as legitimate points of reference for current perceptions of crime. These perceptions are critical for many reasons, one of which is that state policy regarding prison construction and correctional practices are heavily influenced by them. However, it is also significant to note that these perceptions of crime

may not be accurate or consistent with the facts. Also what is precisely meant by "crime" in the general sense may vary from one source to another.

(9)   As a result of a tourist based economy in Orlando, the area is affected by a unique feature. In addition to the in-migration population growth, the tourists add people to the day-to-day population, presenting an undetermined but substantial number of uncounted people in the area. The Orlando area as defined in this study includes approximately one million people, but another 15 million people visit the area each year as tourists. These people are consumers and users, and by their presence present opportunities as both victims and perpetrators of crime.

Data

(10)   In order to examine these questions, standard data and definitions were employed. The measure of crime employed was the number of offenses known to the police. In addition to providing the greatest comparability across the time period under consideration, this index of criminality more properly reflected community concern about crime than did that of arrests. Data were gathered from the *Crime in the United States, Uniform Crime Reports* (1966-1988); *Florida Statistical Abstract* (1967–1988); the *Crime In Florida Annual Report* (1971–1987); and the *County and City Data Book* (1967, 1972, 1977, 1988). Crime was defined as those acts reflected in the serious crime index. The focus of this study was the Orlando area which for purposes here consisted of Orange and Seminole counties. Disney World and other major tourist attractions in the general area are located in Orange County, and the impact of related growth has been registered throughout Orange and Seminole Counties. The regions of interest were the data for the United States (USA); the South Atlantic region of the United States (SATL) which included the states of Delaware, Florida, Maryland, Georgia, North Carolina, South Carolina, Virginia, West Virginia and Washington, D.C.; the State of Florida (FL); the Florida Standard Metropolitan Statistical Areas (FSMSA); and the Orlando Standard Metropolitan Statistical Area (ORLANDO). The latter consisted of Orange and Seminole counties in 1966, the first year of the comparison. In 1987 the Orlando SMSA included Osecola County as well and therefore the figures for that county were subtracted out of the total in order to provide comparability with 1966. The figures for Orange and Seminole Counties were subtracted from the total figures for the Florida SMSAs and from the totals for the State of Florida as well. This permitted a comparison of the Orlando

SMSA with larger units of which it was a part without including its direct effects on the totals of these units.

(11)   The years selected for comparison were 1966, 1972 and 1987. The year 1966 was selected because it was that which preceded the announcement by Disney that the corporation was contemplating development in Central Florida. The year 1972 marks the year Disney World opened and Central Florida began to become a major tourist attraction. The year 1987 was the latest year for which crime statistics permitting this examination were available.

Results

(12)   One of the principal elements in the proposition of the relationship between rapid growth and escalating crime is the addition of people to the population ranks. Table 1 contains the figures for population growth in the five areas examined. The Florida component grew much more than that for the United States (USA) or the South Atlantic Region (SATL). Within Florida, it can be seen that the FSMSAs grew more than Orlando or the remainder of the state. Orlando (Orange and Seminole Counties) grew more than the rest of the State of Florida, but not as much as the FSMSAs. It is clear that rather phenomenal growth did

occur in Florida, Orlando and the FSMSAs over the time periods under review.

(13)   The basic exercise for this study was the examination of the crime rate for Orlando (Orange and Seminole Counties) over a 21 year period, and a comparison of its crime rates with other geographical units. This was accomplished in two ways. First, the crime rate for Orlando was compared with those of the United States (USA), the South Atlantic Region of the country (SATL), the State of Florida (FL), and the other Standard Metropolitan Statistical Areas in the State of Florida (FSMSA). Second, the rates of change across the designated years were compared within and among the regions to examine relative changes in the rate of crime growth.

(14)   The first comparison is a simple one examining the crime rates for the five areas at three time periods. From Table 2 it can be seen that Orlando ranked third in crime rates in 1966, 1972 and 1987. The crime rates increased for all the areas under consideration, but Orlando's rank did not change. The only change in rank occurring during this period was between the USA and the SATL areas which reversed their rank order between 1972 and 1987. Therefore, the Orlando area has had a general crime rate below that of the State of

Table 1. Percentage Change in Population and Crime Rate

Region	Year	Population	Violent Crimes	Non-Violent Crimes	All Crimes
USA	1966–72	6	85	69	71
	1972–87	17	53	103	96
	1966–87	24	183	243	235
SATL	1966–72	9	72	75	75
	1972–87	31	30	132	115
	1966–87	43	125	307	276
FL	1966–72	22	65	73	72
	1972–87	65	83	123	117
	1966–87	101	203	286	274
FSMSA	1966–72	50	55	58	58
	1972–87	86	74	114	108
	1966–87	180	169	238	228
ORLANDO	1966–72	26	46	73	70
	1972–87	72	118	113	114
	1966–87	117	219	269	262

Florida, and below that of other SMSAs in Florida throughout the period under examination. At the same time, Orlando's crime rate has been above that for the SATL Region and the USA as a whole throughout this period.

(15)   Having established how the Orlando crime rate compares to other areas, the second task was to examine the relative rates of change from 1966 to 1987. The rate of change in the crime rate for each area was examined

Table 2. Crime Rates, By Region and Year

Region	Year	Crime Categories		
		Violent	Non-Violent	Total
USA	1966	215	1441	1656
	1972	398	2432	2830
	1987	610	4940	5550
SATL	1966	270	1298	1568
	1972	466	2277	2742
	1987	607	5286	5893
FL	1966	341	1950	2291
	1972	564	3379	3943
	1987	1032	7532	8564
FSMSA	1966	404	2338	2741
	1972	624	3699	4323
	1987	1086	7909	8994
ORLAN	1966	289	1835	2125
	1972	423	3179	3602
	1987	922	6769	7691

Crimes per 100,000 people.

for the time periods of 1966 to 1972; 1972 to 1987; and 1966 to 1987. The results are also in Table 1.

(16)   In the period 1966 to 1972, the rate of change for Orlando crime was greater than that for FSMSAs, but less than that for the USA, FL or SATL. From 1972 to 1987, the post-Magic Kingdom era, the rates of change in general crime rates were similar for Orlando, FSMSAs, SATL and FL, although the rate of change for the USA lagged behind.

(17)   Overall from 1966 to 1987, the rate of change was greatest for the SATL, followed closely by FL.

Third in descending order was Orlando, followed by some distance by USA and FSMSAs.

(18)   Examining the information for the entire period more closely, it can be seen that Orlando had the third highest crime rate in 1966 and 1987, and the third highest rate of change in the general crime rate over this period of time as well. The crime rates for FL and the FSMSAs were higher than that of Orlando in both 1966 and 1987, and the rates for the USA and SATL were lower for both years. The rate of increase between 1966 and 1987 was higher for SATL and FL than for Orlando, and lower for USA and FSMSAs than that for Orlando. This latter figure is likely affected by the point at which the initial figure for calculating change is marked. An area with an initial low rate of crime has more potential for increase than that which is high. To some extent, this is reflected in the data in that the area with the lowest initial rate of crime (SATL) was that with the greatest rate of change. Conversely, the area with the highest initial rate of crime (FSMSAs) was that which had the lowest rate of change.

(19)   Another factor involved in the interpretation involves what aspect of crime one is considering and how this is generalized to the perception of crime. The most salient aspect of the total crime picture is that of violent crime. That is, many people think of violent crime first when they think of crime. These types of offenses are those which seem most threatening personally, are easily sensationalized and commonly reported by the media. The question then becomes one of whether or not the impression of Orlando as having become an area with a disproportionate amount of crime is one that is predicated on impressions of particular crime categories. Put another way, is there an instance within the general crime profile which conforms more closely to the popularly held belief that Orlando has had a disproportionate growth in crime since the advent of the Magic Kingdom?

(20)   The two broad categories of crime included within the general crime index are violent and nonviolent crime. Considering violent crimes, in 1966 the lowest rate among the five areas under review was for the USA, and the highest rate was for the FSMSAs. Orlando had the third highest violent crime rate in 1966. In 1987, USA and SATL region had the lowest violent crime rates, the FSMSAs had the highest, and Orlando remained third highest. Therefore, Orlando's relative position with regard to the violent crime rate did not change from 1966 to 1987.

(21) With respect to the amount of change in the violent crime rate between 1966 and 1987, the percent change was calculated for each area and are presented in Table 1. Between 1966 and 1972, Orlando experienced the lowest percentage change in violent crime rate, and the USA had the highest. However, between 1972 and 1987, Orlando had the highest rate of increase, and for the overall period of 1966 to 1987, Orlando had the highest rate of increase for violent crimes. Therefore, Orlando remained third in rank among the areas from 1966 to 1987 as far as violent crime rate was concerned; however, its violent crime rate grew at a faster rate than in other areas during that time period.

(22) With respect to the other major category of crime within the general crime profile, that of nonviolent crime, Table 1 indicates that the nonviolent crime for Orlando ranked third among the areas in 1966, 1972 and in 1987. Over the same time period the rate of nonviolent crime in Orlando grew at a rate greater than that for FSMSAs and the USA, but less than that for FL and SATL. Therefore, when compared to other areas, the more substantial change in the general crime profile in Orlando has been in violent crime and not in the nonviolent crime category.

Discussion

(23) Whether or not one regards the rate of crime in Orlando increasing disproportionately depends on several factors, among them the point of reference in time and the area to which the comparison is being made, and what aspect of crime is being singled out. The basic question being addressed here is whether or not Orlando has experienced more crime since the advent of the Magic Kingdom than what otherwise would have been expected as a consequence of being part of Florida, the South Atlantic region, or another SMSA in Florida. No attempt is made here to separate out the effects of growth from the singular effect of the development of Disney. The meaning of Disney to the inhabitants of the Orlando area is inextricably bound to the growth and social change it inspired.

(24) Between 1972 and 1987, the post-Magic Kingdom years, the crime rate grew in Orlando at about the same rate as the other areas, except that of the USA which grew more slowly. It is possible to conclude that the Magic Kingdom has meant little in the way of increased general crime rate during this period over what one might expect of other areas in the SATL region or in the State of Florida in general. Thus, from this perspective the increase in crime rate in Orlando after the Magic Kingdom is not extraordinary.

(25) Between 1966–87, Orlando's crime rate increased although its rate of growth is comparable to that of SATL and FL. Therefore, in terms of general crime, there is not unqualified support for the claim of extraordinary crime growth in Orlando during the period 1966–87. At the same time, however, the crime rate in Orlando rose more than that for the USA or other FSMSAs. Thus, if the point of reference is the latter areas, the extraordinary growth contention is unsupported. If the point of reference is the former, the contention is supported.

(26) It is possible, however, that the belief of an extraordinary increase in crime is created by the sharp increase in violent crime. It is reasonable to conclude that to the extent to which the belief of increased crime is valid in Orlando, it applies to violent crime from 1966 to 1987. To the degree to which violent crimes contribute to the popular image of crime in general, concentration on these types of offenses correctly reinforces the notion that there is substantially more crime in Orlando today than in the time period preceding the Magic Kingdom. In addition, the rate of increase for violent crimes is greater in Orlando than for other areas. The increase in violent crimes is consistent with "boom town" growth. The literature on many of these communities also alludes to an abnormal increase in rates of violent offenses. Thus, to at least some degree, the "boom town" communities whose growth was based on energy development are similar to Orlando whose growth is due to tourist attraction development.

(27) It would appear then that the image that the Magic Kingdom and its associated growth have produced an extraordinary increase in crime is reinforced by the violent crime rate in particular. These crimes are the more salient ones, the ones that concern the public more strongly. Violent crimes receive more coverage from the media and are easier to sensationalize. Thus, the increasing rate of violent crimes, and perhaps their media coverage, produce an overall impression of the Magic Kingdom having a negative effect on the Orlando community with respect to crime.

References

County and City Data Book 1967, 1972, 1977, 1988 United States Department of Commerce, Bureau of Census, Superintendent of Documents. Washington, DC: USGPO

Covey HC, S Menard 1984 Response to rapid social change *J Police Sci Admin* 12 161-169

Crime in Florida Annual Report 1971-1987 Tallahassee, FL: Florida Department of Law Enforcement

Crime in the United States, Uniform Crime Reports 1966-1988 Washington, DC: Federal Bureau of Investigation, United States Department of Justice

Diamond S 1971 The rule of law versus the order of custom *Soc Res* 38 42-72

Durkheim E 1964 *The Division of Labor in Society* NY: Free Press

Finsterbusch K 1982 Boomtown disruption thesis *Pacific Sociolog Rev* 25 307-22

Florida Statistical Abstract 1967-1988 Bureau of Economic and Business Research, College of Business Administration, University of Florida, Gainesville, FL: U Presses of Florida

Freudenburg WR 1981 Women and men in an energy boomtown *Rural Sociol* 46 220-44

_____ 1984 Boomtown's youth *Amer Sociol Rev* 49 697-705

Jobes P, M Parsons 1975 *Satisfaction, Coal Development and Land Use Planning: A Report of Attitudes Held by Residents of the Decker-Birney-Ashland Study Area* Helena, MT: Montana Energy Advisory Council

Orlando Sentinel 1989a Lamar left his critics frustrated. January 1, a-1

_____ 1989b The Floridian of the year, Jack Eckerd's project. January 1, h-1

_____ 1989c Crime figures rated a master of disguise. April 25, a-1

_____ 1989d Compiling crime figures–a mind-boggling job for law agencies. May 9, a-9

_____ 1989e Florida's crime report–who, when and how. May 9, a-1

_____ 1989f State faces 'nightmare' in prisons. August 8, a-1

_____ 1989g When the bad guys go free in Florida, special report. August 13, 14, 15, 16, a-1

_____ 1990 Crime image haunts Atlanta. April 22, g-4

Wilkerson KP, JG Thompson, RR Reynolds Jr, LM Ostresh 1982 Local social disruption and western energy development *Pacific Sociolog Rev* 25 275-96

Factual Questions

1. What tourist attraction played a particularly important role in the initial growth of the Orlando area?

2. Why were the crime totals for the Orlando area subtracted from the crime totals for the Florida SMSAs and Florida state before making comparisons?

3. Why were the years 1966, 1972, and 1987 chosen for the study?

4. Which comparison area had even more population growth than Orlando?

5. How did Orlando's overall crime rate compare with the overall crime rates for the U.S., the South Atlantic area, the Florida SMSAs, and the State of Florida in 1966 and 1987?

6. How did the rate of change in Orlando's overall crime rate from 1966 to 1987 compare with the rate of change in overall crime rates for the U.S., the South Atlantic area, the Florida SMSAs and the State of Florida during the same time period?

11. Does the introduction provide a clear notion of the research problem, the purpose of the research, and its significance?

7. All other things being equal, why are areas with initially low crime rates more likely to show a higher rate of increase in crime than are areas with initially high crime rates?

12. Does the literature review seem relevant to the research problem?

8. How did Orlando's violent crime rate compare with the violent crime rates for the U.S., the South Atlantic area, the Florida SMSAs and the State of Florida in 1966 and 1987?

13. Should the author have compared crime rates for more than three time points?

9. How did the rate of change in Orlando's violent crime rate from 1966 to 1987 compare with the rate of change in violent crime rates for the U.S., the South Atlantic area, the Florida SMSAs and the State of Florida during the same time period?

14. To what population would you generalize the results of this study?

15. Is there enough information on the research instruments and procedures to allow you to replicate this study?

10. What similarity does the author find between boomtowns based on energy development and Orlando—a boomtown based on tourism?

16. Should there be information about the reliability and validity of the research instruments and procedures?

17. Does the analysis include sufficient statistical information? Are the statistics that are used appropriate?

18. Are the conclusions supported by and do they logically follow from the data that have been presented?

19. Are the findings discussed in terms of their implications and/or practical significance?

Article 5

The Human Costs of "Giving the Kid Another Chance"

Waln K. Brown, Timothy P. Miller
Richard L. Jenkins, Warren A. Rhodes

This study is based on a 10- to 25-year follow-up of 500 randomly selected cases of juveniles adjudicated delinquent in the juvenile court of Dauphin County, Pennsylvania. Of 243 juveniles adjudicated delinquent in juvenile court on their first referral to juvenile justice, 20% went on to adult prison after the age of 18. Of 233 juveniles not taken to juvenile court on their first referral to juvenile justice, 43% were imprisoned in adult life after the age of 18. Early referral to the juvenile court of juveniles who commit delinquent acts appears to greatly reduce the likelihood that these individuals will go on to prison in adult life.

Introduction

(1)   When a child commits a delinquent act, unless it is a very serious act, there is usually hesitation about referring the matter to the juvenile justice system. Such hesitation is particularly strong if the child is not yet a teenager. Even if the referral is made, there is further reluctance about actually taking the child into the juvenile court for adjudication. This is all understandable in accordance with our protective feelings toward children.

(2)   We all desire to see offending children give up their antisocial behavior. Labeling theory postulates that labeling a child delinquent initiates a self-fulfilling prophecy, in which the child becomes what we label him or her. This makes us very hesitant to take a child into juvenile court, where the label "delinquent" is likely to be made official.

Present Study

(3)   The present study was undertaken in part as an effort to shed light on the foregoing question. Five hundred juvenile delinquents were randomly selected from the files of the juvenile probation office of Dauphin County, Pennsylvania, for the years 1960–1975 (Brown, Miller, & Jenkins, 1987). We found that the percentage of those referred to juvenile justice who were actually taken into court and adjudicated delinquent on their first referral varied with their age.

(4)   Of 105 juveniles ages 7–12 years on first referral, only 29 (28%) were taken into juvenile court and adjudicated delinquent on the first referral.

Reprinted with permission from *International Journal of Offender Therapy and Comparative Criminology, 35*(4): 296-302. Copyright 1991 held by Guilford Press.

This project was made possible through a grant from the Pennsylvania Commission on Crime and Delinquency.

Waln K. Brown, Ph.D., Executive Director, William Gladden Foundation, P.O. Box 7222, York, Pennsylvania 17404, USA. Timothy P. Miller, M.S., William Gladden Foundation, P.O. Box 7222, York, Pennsylvania 17404, USA. Richard L. Jenkins, M.D., Professor of Child Psychiatry, Emeritus, College of Medicine, The University of Iowa, Iowa City, Iowa 52242, USA. Warren A. Rhodes, Ph.D., Professor of Psychology, Delaware State College, Dover, Delaware 19901-2275, USA.

(5)   Of 273 juveniles age 13–15 years on first referral 134 (49%) were taken into juvenile court and adjudicated delinquent on first referral.

(6)   Of 98 juveniles ages 16–17 on first referral, 80 (82%) were taken into juvenile court and adjudicated delinquent on first referral.

(7)   The tendency to delay the referral to juvenile justice of very young children (and to delay their adjudication further) is in accord with our protective feelings for the very young. It is also in accord with labeling theory, which, as we have indicated, holds that labeling a juvenile a delinquent becomes a self-fulfilling prophecy. Adjudicating a juvenile to be a delinquent is clearly and officially labeling the juvenile.

(8)   Our 10- to 25-year follow-up of a randomized sample of 500 youths adjudicated delinquent in the juvenile court of Dauphin County, Pennsylvania, in the years 1960–1975 suggests that, by our reluctance to take juvenile offenders into juvenile court, we are doubling the proportion of juvenile delinquents who go to prison as adults. Are, then, the widespread efforts to "give the kid another chance" by postponing juvenile court adjudication until the *next* referral misguided?

(9)   It has long been known that the younger the age of a child when he or she first begins to commit delinquent acts, the worse the prognosis for his/her future involvement in the criminal justice system. A study of 300 boys paroled from the New York State Training School for Boys at Warwick revealed this (Jenkins, Hart, Sperling, & Axelrad, 1942). The boys were admitted to the training school during the years 1933 and 1934. An important finding was that the younger the boy at his first juvenile court appearance for delinquency, the less favorable the prospect that he would be discharged from parole for good adjustment, and the more likely that his parole from the training school would be terminated by his commitment to a correctional institution.

(10)   The same relation—that the younger the age at first delinquency the worse the prognosis—is true concerning the delinquent's self-report of the age at which he/she committed the first delinquent act (Jenkins, 1991).

(11)   It is our finding, based on evidence we will present here, that the unfavorable outcome attending early-age collision of juveniles with the juvenile justice system can be accounted for by a practice widely regarded as "giving the kid another chance", by not taking him/her into juvenile court on their first juvenile justice referral.

(12)   In 1987 we published on the favorable effect of adjudication in the juvenile court on first referral to juvenile justice (Brown, Miller, & Jenkins, 1987). Our report was based on the same randomized sample of 500 of the youths adjudicated delinquent in the juvenile court of Dauphin County, Pennsylvania, during the years 1960–1975 (Brown, Miller, & Jenkins, 1987).

(13)   To insure that our sample had no selective bias, the entire population of 2500 cases in the juvenile probation department files of Dauphin County for the years 1960-1975 was put in numerical order, and every fifth case was selected. When this sample was examined, it was found that about 200 cases were not cases of delinquency, but were cases referred for dependency, neglect, or other nondelinquent reasons. These cases were rejected, and every fourth case was selected, until 500 cases of adjudicated delinquents had been assembled. The method of follow-up has been described elsewhere (Brown & Miller, 1988). The data on imprisonment included checking the files of the Pennsylvania State Police and the district attorney's office. Some subjects were located by contacting correctional institutions or adult parole officers. A total of 476 of the 500 subjects were located, and of these 204 or 40.8% of the original 500 agreed to complete and return a survey form.

(14)   Comparisons were made, contrasting individuals who have a known record of having gone to prison as an adult, with individuals with no known record of imprisonment as an adult.

Results

(15)   Tables 1 to 4 are from the 10- to 25-year follow-up of 500 youths randomly selected from those adjudicated delinquent in the juvenile court of Dauphin County. These figures are taken from Table 1 of our report, "The favorable effect of juvenile court adjudication of delinquent youth on first contact with the juvenile justice system" (Brown, Miller, & Jenkins, 1987).

(16)   Table 1 reveals that subjects first referred to juvenile justice at ages 7 to 12 years have a rate of criminal imprisonment in adult life of 41%, while the group, 13 and older, have a rate of imprisonment in adult life of only 28.8%. χ^2 is 5.56, $p = .0184$, indicating there is less than one chance in 500 that such a difference would occur on a chance basis.

Table 1. Age at First Referral to Juvenile Justice Related to Adult Prison on Follow-up: All Cases

Age	No Prison	Prison	Total	Percent Imprisoned
7–12	62	43	105	41.0
13 & Over	264	107	371	28.8
Total	326	150	476	31.5

$\chi^2 = 5.56; p = .0184$

Table 2. All Cases

At First Referral	No Prison	Prison	Total	Percent Imprisoned
Case Adjudicated	192	51	243	20.1
Case *Not* Adjudicated	134	99	233	42.5
Total	326	150	476	31.5

$\chi^2 = 25.5; p < .0001$

Table 3. Ages 7–12 at First Referral

At First Referral	No Prison	Prison	Total	Percent Imprisoned
Case Adjudicated	22	7	29	24.1
Case *Not* Adjudicated	40	36	76	47.4
Total	62	43	105	41.0

$\chi^2 = 4.68; p = .0304$

Table 4. Ages 13 and Over at First Referral

At First Referral	No Prison	Prison	Total	Percent Imprisoned
Case Adjudicated	170	44	214	20.6
Case *Not* Adjudicated	94	63	157	40.1
Total	264	107	371	28.8

$\chi^2 = 16.89; p < .0001$

(17)   Clearly the juveniles in our sample who are first referred to juvenile court before the age of thirteen have a substantially greater likelihood of going to prison in adult life than do those who are first referred to juvenile court at age 13 or older.

(18)   Table 2 divides the total group of cases between 243 who were adjudicated at first referral, and 233 who were adjudicated at a later referral. Those adjudicated on first referral had 20.1% who went to adult prison. Of the 233 who did not go to juvenile court until a later referral, 42.5% of the individuals went to adult prison. This is a very substantial difference in favor of those taken to court on their first referral.

(19)   Contrasting rates of those adjudicated on first contact going to prison with the rates of those not

adjudicated on first contact going to prison, we found the difference statistically significant $\chi^2 = 25.5$, $p < .0001$.

(20)   The same relationship is evident in Table 3 which includes only those ages 7-13 on first referral. Those adjudicated among those taken to court on first referral have a ratio of improvement of 24.1% as compared with an imprisonment of 47.0% for those not adjudicated for their first referral $\chi^2 = 4.68$, $p = .0304$.

(21)   Table 4 includes only those individuals who were 13 years of age or older on first referral to the juvenile justice system. Of 170 cases taken to court and adjudicated on this first referral, 44 (20.6%) went to prison as adults. Of 94 cases not adjudicated on the first referral, 63 (40.1%) went to prison in adult life.

Discussion

(22)   One point deserves emphasis. In our material those juveniles *not* adjudicated on their first juvenile justice referral have a rate of going to prison in adult life which is double that of those adjudicated on their first referral. This applies to preteenagers as well as teenagers.

(23)   Among those adjudicated at first referral, there is no difference in rate of imprisonment as adults between those with first referral at ages 7-12 and those whose first referral was at age 13 or over ($\chi^2 = .20$, $p = .66$). Likewise, among those *not* adjudicated on first referral, there is no difference in rate of imprisonment in adult life between those whose first referral was at ages 7-12 and those whose age at first contact was 13 or over ($\chi^2 = 1.10$, $p = .29$). This makes it clear that the high rate of imprisonment in adult life of those only 7-12 at first referral can be explained by the fact that fewer of them are taken into juvenile court on first referral.

(24)   In each age group, those adjudicated on first referral have approximately half the rate of imprisonment as adults shown by those *not* adjudicated at first contact. Assuming that these relationships would hold, and had the 76 juveniles who were ages 7-12 and who were not taken to court on first referral been adjudicated on first referral, presumably only 18 of those youths, rather than 36 would have been imprisoned as adults.

(25)   In all likelihood, the results would have been even more favorable than this, for the cases that appeared at less risk would be *less* likely to be taken to

court on first referral and the cases judged to be at more risk would be *more* likely to be taken to court at first referral. Such an effect should increase the contrast we find.

(26)   On this basis, it would appear that for the juveniles who are caught in a delinquent action, any systematic tendency *not* to take some category of such juveniles into juvenile court promptly is in effect discriminatory. We believe this to be the case.

(27)   The group most discriminated against were the youngest group — those age 7–12 on first referral to juvenile justice. Only 28% of this group were adjudicated on first referral, while 51% of the total group were so adjudicated on first referral. Another group so discriminated against were the nonwhites. While 60% of whites were adjudicated on first referral, only 40% of nonwhites were so referred. The nonwhites (who are overwhelmingly black in our sample) were treated as younger children in this regard (Brown, Miller, Jenkins, & Rhodes, 1990). Deferral of adjudication was to their disadvantage, and apparently increased the number who went to prison.

Conclusion

(28)   By the same mathematical projection which has been presented, it would be expected that if the 157 juveniles age 13 or older who were *not* adjudicated at first contact, had been so adjudicated, the number committed to prison in adult life would be only 31, not 63. Thus, the human cost of "giving the kid another chance" by not taking him/her to juvenile court on the first referral for a delinquent act and not having him/her adjudicated delinquent and put on probation or in placement, appears to be doubling the likelihood of his/her going to prison in adult life.

References

Brown, W. K., & Miller, T. P. (1986). Post-intervention outcomes of previously adjudicated delinquents: An overview. Report submitted to the Pennsylvania Commission on Crime and Delinquency, June 13, 1986.

Brown, W. K., & Miller, T. P. (1988). Following up previously adjudicated delinquents: A method. *In R. L. Jenkins & W. K. Brown (Eds.), The abandonment of delinquent behavior: Promoting the turnaround* (1988). New York: Praeger Publishers.

Brown, W. K., Miller, T. P., & Jenkins, R. L. (1987). The favorable effect of juvenile court adjudication of delinquent youth on the first contact with the juvenile justice system. *Juvenile and Family Court Journal, 38,* 21-26.

Brown, W. K., Miller, T. P., & Jenkins, R. L. (1988). The fallacy of radical nonintervention. *Annals of Clinical Psychiatry, 1,* 55-57.

Brown, W. K., Miller, T. P., & Jenkins, R. L. (1990). Juvenile probation department experiences compared by adult outcome. *Journal of Offender Counseling Services and Rehabilitation, 15,* 109-116.

Brown, W. K., Miller, T. P., & Jenkins, R. L. (1990). The negative effect of discrimination on minority youth in the juvenile justice system. *International Journal of Offender Therapy and Comparative Criminology, 34,* 89-91.

Jenkins, R. L., Hart, H. H., Sperling, P. J., & Axelrad, S. (1942). Prediction of parole success. *Journal of Criminal Law and Criminology, 33,* 38-45.

Jenkins, R. L. (1991). Lights warning of delinquent rocks and shoals. In W. A. Rhodes and W. K Brown (Eds.), *Why some children succeed despite the odds.* New York: Praeger.

Factual Questions

1. What does labeling theory postulate?

2. How were the subjects for this study selected?

3. All of the juveniles studied in this article eventually did go to juvenile court and were adjudicated delinquent. For some this happened on their first referral to the juvenile justice system, for others it happened on a later referral. How does the probability of a juvenile being taken to juvenile court and adjudicated delinquent on first referral differ by age of the juvenile?

4. If you wanted a more detailed description of how the researchers followed-up each juvenile case to see if the juvenile later spent time in an adult prison, where would you look?

5. Although surveys were completed by just 204 subjects, information on whether the subject ever spent time in an adult prison was obtained for how many subjects?

6. In 1985 when the research was actually done, how many years had passed since the subjects had been referred to juvenile court and adjudicated delinquent?

7. What percentage of the 243 juveniles adjudicated delinquent on first referral eventually went to adult prison? What percentage of the 233 juveniles adjudicated delinquent on a later referral eventually went to adult prison?

Questions for Discussion

8. Does the introduction provide a clear notion of the research problem, the purpose of the research, and its significance?

9. Does the literature review seem relevant to the research problem?

10. Is the number of research subjects sufficient? To what population would you generalize the results of this study?

11. Does the article report what percentage of juveniles not adjudicated delinquent on their first referral never got into trouble again? Would that information be relevant?

12. Is there enough information on the research instruments and procedures to allow you to replicate this study?

13. Should there be information about the reliability and validity of the research instruments and procedures?

14. Does the analysis include sufficient statistical information? Are the statistics that are used appropriate?

15. Are the conclusions supported by and do they logically follow from the data that have been presented?

16. Are the findings discussed in terms of their implications and/or practical significance?

Article 6

Family Size and Occupational Mobility, Indianapolis: 1860–1880

Douglas B. Downey
Indiana University

This paper uses U.S. Census data from Indianapolis to compare occupational attainments of fathers in 1860 with sons in 1880, classified by family size. A son from a small family was more likely than a son from a large family to rise above his father's occupational category.

(1)   Researchers consistently find a strong inverse relationship between number of siblings and status attainment variables such as educational attainment and occupational attainment, even after controlling for parents' socioeconomic status (Blau and Duncan, 1967; Featherman and Hauser, 1978; Sewell and Hauser, 1977; Blake, 1981; Steelman and Mercy, 1980; Blake, 1985; Steelman and Powell, 1989; Blake, 1989a). The importance of number of siblings for understanding status attainment in contemporary America is evidenced by its strength (often as great or greater than father's occupational position) in predicting educational attainment (Blake, 1989b). Additional siblings, at least in twentieth century America, have been a major obstacle toward status attainment. Since status attainment researchers attach such importance to father's occupational status as a predictor of men's educational attainment (see, for example, Blau and Duncan 1967, chs. 1, 5, 9 and 12; Duncan, Featherman, and Duncan 1972, chap. 3), the equal or greater effect of number of siblings also merits attention.

(2)   Although contemporary evidence for an inverse relationship between number of siblings and attainment is convincing, this study considers the question: Did an increased number of siblings have adverse effects on an individual's status attainment

opportunities in the nineteenth century? Curiously, while several social scientists have studied attainment processes in the nineteenth century (Rogoff, 1953; Hardy, 1978; Tully et al., 1970) none have highlighted the role of number of siblings. This study fills a major gap in our understanding of the historical aspect of status attainment and the role of familial structure in that process.

(3)   Theoretical explanations for the inverse relationship between number of siblings and status attainment found in contemporary society remain speculative and mostly untested. The "resource dilution" model is posited by some as the best explanation (Spaeth, 1976; Blake, 1981; 1985; 1989a). The "resource dilution" model states that since parents' resources (e.g., time, emotional and physical energy, money, attention) are finite, increasing the number of children results in the dilution of these important resources, which in turn has negative consequences for the children. In addition, since the mother is pregnant or recovering from pregnancy more often in large families, the strains of producing a large family also affect parental childrearing capabilities (Blake, 1989a). In one of the few studies testing this model, Powell and Steelman (1989) found, in support of the model, that students from large families receive less financial aid for college from their

parents than students from small families. In addition, the resource dilution model implies that the inverse relationship between number of siblings and attainment variables should remain even when cultural norms support large families.

(4)   An alternative to the resource dilution explanation is that existing cultural norms concerning family size influence how sibling size affects status attainment. For example, if in a given society a family with five children is considered optimal, children growing up with four siblings would be advantaged (or at least not disadvantaged) compared to children growing up with only one sibling. Indeed, although Blake (1989) supports the resource dilution perspective, she finds that the effect of number of siblings on educational attainment is less pronounced among Catholics, who support large families, than it is among Protestants. This suggests that a pure "resource dilution" explanation may not always be appropriate. The relationship between number of siblings and attainment may depend on cultural context.

(5)   Although it is difficult to choose definitively between these two perspectives, an examination of another time period may provide additional support for one or the other. Thus, a test of whether family size influenced intergenerational occupational mobility in late nineteenth century Indianapolis is appropriate.

Data and Method

(6)   This study focuses on how additional siblings affected occupational mobility, for those living in Indianapolis between 1860-1880. Several studies of nineteenth century status attainment have chosen Indianapolis as a city representative of the country's general industrial trends of the time (Rogoff, 1953; Tully et al., 1970; Hardy, 1978).

(7)   The universe for this study is all individuals (between ages 18-40) listed in the 1860 Federal Census of Indianapolis. In the first stage of data collection, a random sample of 517 individuals was drawn from this source. This group from the 1860 census serves as the "fathers" for the analysis.[1] The 1860 census provided information on a variety of characteristics such as age, gender, address, occupation, place of birth, year born, names of others in the household, year married, and children's names, ages, and genders. This information allowed the fathers and their families to be carefully tracked through yearly city directories and the 1870 and 1880 census manuscripts. Of the original 517 cases, 145 (28%) were located in 1880. This seemingly low

percentage of the original sample over a twenty-year period is roughly similar to the nineteenth century decadal persistence rates of one-third to one-fifth found by other researchers (Knights, 1969; Thernstrom, 1969; Thernstrom and Knights, 1971; Hardy, 1978). Since it was only possible to study those respondents whose children remained in Indianapolis, the sample is biased toward those individuals who were more likely to remain in Indianapolis (stayers) and biased against those who were more likely to move elsewhere (movers). Comparing stayers with movers, movers tended to be unmarried, younger, and in lower occupational categories, which is consistent with what Hardy (1978) found in her study of Indianapolis in the 1850s.

(8)   Of the 145 cases found in 1880, 116 (the working sample) fit the criteria for this study: the father had (1) an occupation listed for 1860 (father's occupation), (2) at least one son[2] with an occupation listed in the 1880 census (son's occupational score). Each case, therefore, represents one father and at least one son. .

Measures

(9)   Family size was measured by using the "father's" response to the 1880 census question, "How many children have you had that lived?"

(10)   Both father's and son's occupations were coded using a collapsed version of the 9-category vertical Philadelphia Social History Project (PSHP) code developed by Hershberg and Dockhorn (1976). Three broad hierarchical categories were developed: (1) high white-collar professional, low white-collar and proprietary occupations, (2) skilled craftsman e.g, shoemaker, blacksmith, cabinet maker, and (3) unskilled workers e.g., "laborer, factory worker, ditch digger."[3] Since specific occupations may have changed in skills, qualifications and wages over time, the occupational categories are defined broadly, so that any change in category represents genuine changes in occupational positions.[4]

(11)   One problem with comparing the father's occupation level in 1860 and the son's occupational level in 1880 is that some of the fathers in 1860 were as young as 18 years old and may not have reached their highest occupational level yet. Similarly, some of the sons in 1880 may not have reached their highest occupational level. This could affect the amount and direction of mobility in unknown ways. Mobility studies commonly resolve this issue by making observations of occupational levels at about the same point in the careers of both the fathers and the sons. Although these data only provide occupational measures at a given

point in time rather than a point in individual's careers, a comparison of the ages of both sons and fathers from small and large families provides insight into the direction of bias. Fathers from large families were, on average, two years older than fathers from small families while there was no statistical difference between the ages of sons from small and large families. If bias exists due to when the individuals were observed in their careers, fathers from large families are probably advantaged since they are slightly older than fathers from small families.

(12)   In addition, since information for more than just the eldest son is available, an additional variable, sons' average occupational score, was generated by averaging all of the sons' occupational levels for each family. The average scores were then converted back into the original three categories by collapsing sons' average occupational scores in the following manner: (1 to 1.49 = 1, 1.50 to 2.49 = 2, 2.50 to 3 = 3). There were only minor differences when the data were analyzed with respect to the occupation of the eldest son (for which data were available) rather than the sons' average occupational category. Since including all of the sons uses more information and represents a larger picture of occupational mobility, the results using the sons' average occupational score are presented.

Results

Overall Patterns of Mobility

(13)   There was considerable intergenerational occupational mobility, most of it upward, between fathers and their sons in late nineteenth century Indianapolis (Table 1). Table 1 shows the cases in the sample in which the sons (on average) inherited their father's position (those cells along the diagonal, 43%) or in which

upward mobility occurred (those cells below the diagonal, 40%) or downward mobility occurred (those cases above the diagonal, 17%). While 43 percent of the sons inherited their father's occupational category the remaining 57 percent were occupationally mobile (those off the diagonal). Of those cases in which intergenerational mobility occurred, roughly 2/3 of it was upward and 1/3 downward, similar to what Hardy (1978) found in Indianapolis a decade earlier.[5] The greater upward rather than downward mobility can be accounted for by the increased number of white-collar positions available in 1880 for the sons (49) compared to the number available to the fathers in 1860 (25).

Mobility and Family Size

(14)   Given that intergenerational mobility was frequent, were sons from small families more likely to be upwardly mobile than sons from large families? To explore this question the mobility table was partitioned by family size. Table 2 shows that sons from small families were more likely to be upwardly mobile than sons from large families (small families = 50%, large families = 26%) and less likely to inherit their father's position (small families = 33%, large families = 56%). However, sons from small families were just as likely as sons from large families to experience downward mobility (small families = 17%, large families = 18%).

(15)   To determine whether these initial observations from Table 2 are merely chance fluctuations, regression analysis using the uncollapsed family size measure was performed. The results from Table 3 indicate that increases in family size resulted in lower occupational positions for sons, holding father's occupational level constant.[6]

Table 1. Intergenerational Mobility Table for Fathers' 1860 Occupational Category and Sons' Average Occupational Category in 1880, Indianapolis

		Sons' Average 1880 Occupational Category			
		A	B	C	Totals
Fathers'	A	<u>17</u>	4	4	25
1860	B	26	<u>26</u>	12	64
Occupation	C	6	14	<u>7</u>	27
Totals		49	44	23	116

A = High white-collar professional, low white-collar, and proprietary occupations.
B = Skilled craftsman.
C = Unskilled laborers.

Table 2. Fathers' Occupational Category in 1860 by Sons' Average Occupational Category in 1880 by Family Size, Indianapolis

	Sons' Average 1880 Occupation							
	Small Family (1–4 children)				Large Family (5 or more children)			
Fathers' Occupation in 1860	A	B	C	Totals	A	B	C	Totals
A	<u>10</u>	2	3	15	<u>7</u>	2	1	10
B	21	<u>8</u>	6	35	5	<u>18</u>	6	29
C	4	8	<u>4</u>	16	2	6	<u>3</u>	11
Totals	35	18	13	66	14	26	10	50

A = High white-collar professional, low white-collar, and proprietary occupations.
B = Skilled craftsman.
C = Unskilled laborers.

Table 3. Unstandardized Regression Coefficients of Sons' Average Occupational Category in 1880, Regressed on Father's Occupational Category in 1860, Indianapolis

Variable	Parameter Estimate	Standard Error
Father's Occupation	0.28**	0.10
Family Size	0.07*	0.03
Intercept	0.90	0.25
$R^2 = .11$		

*p < .01   **p < .001

Discussion and Conclusion

(16)   The negative relationship between family size and status attainment is not merely a recent phenomenon. While this inverse relationship has been well documented for contemporary society, these results indicate that family size also played an important role in status attainment opportunities over 100 years ago as family size had a major impact on sons' chances for moving into white-collar positions in nineteenth century Indianapolis.

(17)   These findings are consistent with the resource dilution model which claims that children from small families should enjoy a larger percentage of parental resources than children from large families and should therefore experience advantages (Blake, 1989a). The finding that sons from small families were advantaged provides necessary but not sufficient support for the dilution hypothesis. In addition, since an inverse relationship between family size and occupational opportunities was found in a society valuing large families (average number of children = 4.4), family size may have a negative effect on status attainment even when social norms support large families.

(18)   In conclusion, one case has been provided in which historical data are consistent with the contemporary relationship between number of siblings and status attainment. Future analyses of historical and/or cross-cultural data are needed for a more complete understanding of the pattern. Based on this one study, however, it appears that the American occupational structure has historically been more open for men from small rather than large families.

Notes

1. If we sampled a female, we used her spouse's occupational category (rather than her own) as a measure for the father's occupational category.
2. We chose not to study daughters since they were more difficult to follow and fewer entered the workforce.
3. Since our sample was urban, only 5 individuals (2 fathers and 3 sons) were listed as farmers. Since Hershberg and Dockhorn (1976) found farmers to be closer to unskilled laborers with respect to income and wealth, we followed their classification and grouped farmers with unskilled laborers.
4. Hershberg and Dockhorn (1976) warn against using the PSHP code for social mobility studies due to the difficulty in discerning between actual occupational

change and changes in census coding. Instructions in the census manuscript for describing occupational titles changed in 1870, requiring census marshals to designate jobs with greater detail than they had in previous enumerations. Although this is a problem for studies using the nine-category vertical code, since our occupational categories are broad, we can be confident that any changes between the 1860 occupation measure and the 1880 occupation measure can be attributed to real changes in occupational level rather than simply the new rules applied to recording data.

5. The only difference when only the eldest son is analyzed is that of those cases in which mobility occurred, 65% of it was upward compared to 67% when all sons are included.

6. Multinomial logistic regression analysis indicates that family size is particularly strong for predicting moves into white-collar positions, but weak for predicting moves into skilled craftsman positions. The odds of sons obtaining a white-collar position versus a skilled craftsman job decreased by a factor of .78 for each additional sibling, holding father's occupation constant. Similarly, a unit increase in father's occupational category resulted in an increase by a factor of 3.49 in the odds of sons' being in white-collar professional rather than skilled craftsman positions, holding family size constant. Family size had no effect, however, on the odds of sons being in skilled craftsman versus unskilled laborer positions.

Sons' chances of obtaining a white-collar job were reduced by roughly the same magnitude by either 1) lowering father's occupation one category, or 2) adding three siblings to the family. In other words, an individual's chances of obtaining a white-collar position were influenced as much by large family size changes as by the father's occupation.

Interestingly, a large family size was a barrier for moving into white-collar positions but not for moving into skilled craftsman positions. Perhaps the greater education needed to move into white-collar professional jobs separated children from small families who could afford the education from those from large families whose parents were less capable of providing education for all of their sons. Indeed, contemporary studies have found the inverse relationship between family size and attainment to be most pronounced with respect to education (Blau and Duncan, 1967; Blake, 1981; Blake, 1989b).

References

Barr, Alwyn. 1970. "Occupational and geographic mobility in San Antonio, 1870-1900." *Social Science Quarterly* 51:397-403.

Blake, Judith. 1981. "Family size and the quality of children." *Demography* 18:421-442.

_____1985. "Number of siblings and educational mobility." *American Sociological Review* 50:84-94.

_____1989a. *Family Size and Achievement.* Los Angeles: University of California Press.

_____1989b. "Number of siblings and educational attainment." *Science* 245:32-36.

Blau, Peter and Otis Dudley Duncan. 1967. *The American Occupational Structure.* New York: Wiley.

Duncan, Otis Dudley, David Featherman, and Beverly Duncan. 1972. *Socioeconoic Background and Achievement.* New York: Seminar Press.

Featherman, David and Robert Hauser. 1978. *Opportunity and Change.* New York: Academic Press.

Feinberg, Stephen E. 1985. *The Analysis of Cross-Classified Data, 2nd Edition.* Cambridge: The MIT Press.

Goldin, Claudia. 1981. "Family Strategies and the family economy in the late nineteenth century: The role of secondary workers." In Theodore Hershberg (ed.) Philadelphia: *Work, Space, Family, and Group Experience in the 19th Century.* New York: Oxford University Press.

Griffin, Clyde. 1972. "Occupational mobility in nineteenth century America: problems and possibilities." *Journal of Social History* 5:310-330.

Hardy, M. 1978. "Occupational mobility and nativity-ethnicity in Indianapolis, 1850-1860." *Social Force* 57:205-221.

Hershberg T. and R. Dockhorn. 1976. "Occupational Classification" in *Historical Methods Newsletter,* vol. 9 nos. 2-3 (March/June).

Knights, P.R. 1969. "Population turnover, persistence, and residential mobility in Boston, 1830-1860." In S. Thernstrom and R. Sennett (eds.) *Nineteenth-Century Cities.* New Haven: Yale University Press.

Rogoff, N. 1953. *Recent trends in occupational mobility.* New York: Free Press.

Sewell, W.H., and Hauser, R.M. 1977. "On the effects of families and family structure on achievement. " In P. Taubman (ed.) *Kinometrics: The determinants of economic success within and between families,* 35-96. Amsterdam: North Holland.

Spaeth, Joe L. 1976. "Cognitive Complexity: A Dimension Underlying the socioeconomic achievement process." In William Sewell, Robert M. Hauser, and David L. Featherman (eds.), *Schooling and*

Achievement in American Society. New York: Academic Press.

Steelman, Lala Carr and James A. Mercy. 1980. "Unconfounding the confluence model: A test of sibship size and birth order effects on intelligence." *American Sociological Review* 45:571-582.

Steelman, Lala Carr and Brian Powell. 1989. "Acquiring capital for college: The constraints of family configuration." *American Sociological Review* 54:744-755.

Thernstrom, S. 1969. "Immigrants and WASPs: Ethnic differences in occupational mobility in Boston, 1890-1940." In S. Thernstrom and R. Sennett (eds.), *Nineteenth–Century Cities.* New Haven: Yale Univ. Press.

Thernstrom, S. and P.R. Knights. 1971. "Men in motion: some data and speculation about urban population mobility in nineteenth-century America." in T.K. Kareven (ed.), *Anonymous Americans.* Englewood Cliffs: Prentice Hall.

Tully, J., Elton Jackson and R. Curtis. 1970. "Trends in occupational mobility in Indianapolis." *Social Forces* 49:186-199.

Manuscript was received January 17, 1990 and reviewed January 25, 1990.

Factual Questions

1. What is the author's research question?

2. What percentage of the individuals sampled from the 1860 census was located in the 1880 census?

3. Each of the cases in the working sample represents what?

4. How was family size measured?

5. Why did the author collapse the nine-category occupational code developed by Hershberg and Dockhorn (1976) into just three categories when measuring fathers' and sons' occupations?

6. What did the researcher do when he had information on more than one son's occupation?

7. What percentage of the sons in 1880 was in the same occupational category as their father was in 1860? What percentage was not?

8. Of those sons not in the same occupational category as their father, what fraction were in "better" occupations and what fraction were in "worse" occupations?

9. How were small families and large families operationally defined?

10. How did the occupational mobility of sons from large families compare to the occupational mobility of sons from small families?

Questions for Discussion

11. Does the introduction provide a clear notion of the research problem, the purpose of the research, and its significance?

12. Does the literature review seem relevant to the research problem?

13. What would the "resource depletion" model predict about the relationship between number of siblings and status attainment in the 19th century? What would the "cultural norms" model (described in paragraph 4) predict?

14. Is the number of research subjects sufficient? To what population would you generalize the results of this study?

15. Is there enough information on the research instruments and procedures to allow you to replicate this study?

16. Should there be information about the reliability and validity of the research instruments and procedures?

17. Is the fact that fathers of large families were on average two years older than fathers of small families a problem for the research and its conclusions?

18. Does the analysis include sufficient statistical information? Are the statistics that are used appropriate?

19. Are the conclusions supported by and do they logically follow from the data that have been presented?

20. Are the findings discussed in terms of their implications and/or practical significance?

Notes:

Ethnic Consistency in Remarriage

Davor Jedlicka

Ethnicity of consecutive spouses was selected to study how the characteristics of the first spouse may relate to the selection of the second spouse after divorce. The sample consisted of 4,525 women and 4,066 men who married, divorced, and remarried in Hawaii between 1943 and 1967. For each person in this sample ethnicity of the first spouse was compared to the ethnicity of the second spouse. The results showed a strong tendency for men and for women to remarry consistently in or consistently out of their own ethnic group. Some implications of consistency in remarriage are discussed within the framework of the related literature.

(1) It was Farber (1964) who first recognized serial monogamy as a trend in mate selection and marriage. That emerging trend of yesteryear has become so prevalent that today in 46 percent of the marriages at least one spouse had been previously married (National Center for Health Statistics, 1989). Judging by this high proportion of serial marriages, it is not surprising that increasing attention in family research is focused on remarriage. Specifically, the question of how the first marriage may influence the choice of second spouse remains a vexing issue for marriage counselors and therapists.

(2) Among a multitude of sociopsychological characteristics of spouses that could be used to research this question, ethnicity of spouses was selected in this study for two reasons. One, ethnicity is a robust variable; it does not vary due to changes in subjects' recall. And two, the related literature portrays ethnic background as an important determinant of interpersonal attraction, marital happiness, and divorce (Stephens, 1968; Lewis and Spanier, 1979; Becker, 1973; Bumpass and Sweet, 1972; Cherlin, 1977; Norton and Glick, 1976; Teachman, 1983). These authors share the view that "people from different backgrounds will have different values

habits, and perhaps even personalities, and that these differences will make it difficult to get along in a marriage" (Whyte, 1990:181). Based on these conclusions, it seems logical to expect that a person would not likely follow one intermarriage with another.

(3) The findings which suggest that marital satisfaction increases in second marriages are consistent with this expectation (Cherlin, 1981:91). Some researchers even describe remarriage as a mechanism for replacing poor marriages with better ones (Glenn, 1981; Spanier and Furstenberg, 1982; Weingarten, 1985). These researchers reason that after divorce a person is better able to avoid attachment to incompatible persons. According to Benson-von der Ohe (1981:29), "second-marriage people do choose mates who are in some respect different from those chosen by first marriage respondents." Again, the literature leads to the hypothesis that ethnicity of the second partner would tend to be different from the ethnicity of the first, especially if the first marriage was exogamous.

(4) What appears rational to some researchers, however, seems improbable to others. Demographers, for example, have shown that divorce rates tend to be

Reprinted with permission from *Family Perspective*, *25*(3): 237-245. Copyright 1991 held by Brigham Young University. Davor Jedlicka, Ph.D., is a professor in the Department of Sociology, The University of Texas at Tyler, Tyler, TX.

higher when at least one spouse was previously married than when both were married for the first time (Monahan, 1958; Glick, 1980). The obvious question these findings raise is, if the remarriage were indeed an improvement on the first marriage, why would divorce rates increase?

(5)   Among several possible answers, some literature suggests that some proportion of remarrying people may be repeating one poor marriage after another at frequencies higher than could be expected by chance alone. Dean and Gurak (1978) supported this contention when they concluded that heterogamy in remarriage occurred even when heterogamy was a likely contributor to the break up of the first marriage. Similarly, Kalmuss and Seltzer (1986) showed that the people who at first marry an abusive spouse tend to do the same in the second marriage. Freeman (1955) also found that ethnic consistency may begin before marriage. In his study of interethnic dating, partner after dating partner was sought from the same ethnic group even after disillusionments.

(6)   The findings presented below provide additional support for the consistency hypothesis of remarriage. The data set in this study, however, does not elucidate why consistency seems to be the rule with respect to ethnic background of partners. Without such deeper insight into remarriage patterns much of the psychodynamics of serial marriage will remain a mystery.

Methods

Population Studied

(7)   This study used about 130,000 marriage records accumulated by the Department of Health, State of Hawaii, in the period from 1943 to 1967. These records are a part of a larger collection which dates back to the beginning of this century and continues through the present. The middle period was selected because during that time first and second marriage records were linked for each person marrying twice in Hawaii between 1943 and 1967 (Jedlicka, 1975).

(8)   A record in this collection pertains to prospective brides and grooms who answered a series of questions on their marriage license applications. These questions included ethnicity of brides' and of grooms' parents. Using these responses, I classified subjects whose parents shared the same ethnicity into one of eight most frequently occurring ethnic groups. If they represented some small group they were classified as "other." Subjects whose parents differed in their ethnic backgrounds were classified as "multiethnic."

(9)   Subjects with single ethnic background included: Black, Caucasian, Chinese, Filipino, Hawaiian, Japanese, Korean, and Portuguese. People in Hawaii perceive and identify themselves by these categories; historically, non-Caucasian ethnic groups remained distinct, whereas distinctions among various Caucasian ethnicities became obscured and unimportant in everyday life.

(10)   Subjects whose parents represented different ethnic groups were categorized into "multiethnic" category. The most common combinations in this category included Eurasian, part Hawaiian, and various combinations of Chinese, Japanese, Korean, and Filipino parentage. Distribution of ethnic parentage of remarrying divorced persons is shown in Table 1.

Table 1. Distribution of Ethnic Categories by Sex of Remarrying Divorced Persons, State of Hawaii, 1943–1967

Ethnic Category	Male	Female
Part Hawaiian	870	1252
Japanese	836	1078
Caucasian	680	314
Filipino	468	384
Portuguese	332	367
Other Multi-ethnic	259	380
Hawaiian	193	274
Chinese	153	200
Black	142	131
Korean	75	89
Other "Pure"	27	14
Eurasian	22	31
Biethnic Asian	9	11
Total	4066	4525

(11)   In general, part Hawaiians tend to identify themselves with Hawaiian population rather than with any Asian or Caucasian group. Therefore, for the analysis of consistency patterns "part Hawaiian" and "Hawaiian" were combined into one category. All remaining biethnic and multiethnic combinations were combined into "multiethnic" category.

Representativeness of Sample

(12)   A relevant question about these 25-year-old data is do they reflect mate selection patterns today? Over the last 25 years, judging by the recent marriage statistics from Hawaii, ethnicity has become less of a barrier to marriage than at any time in the past (Department of Health, State of Hawaii, 1989). Also, new ethnic groups have increased in number and in importance in the marriage market. If this study were done using marriage records since 1967, Vietnamese and Samoans would be added to the list of ethnic groups while the number of Portuguese origin brides and grooms would be excluded because they have become too small to classify.

(13)   Considering these changes in ethnic composition and the lapse of time, the data may be relevant today to the extent that the forces that attract people to each other are not based on chance alone. If the forces of attraction tend to remain unchanged, the assumption is that mate selection patterns will also remain constant.

(14)   The validity of this assumption may be inferred from cross-cultural comparisons. Each ethnic group immigrated at different times in Hawaii's history. Hawaiians, for example, have lived there for hundreds of years, while at the time of this study Koreans and

Filipinos were primarily first generation. If the results show variations in consistency among these ethnic groups, then indeed the validity of the data would be questionable. On the other hand, if similar remarriage patterns characterize each ethnic group, then one may generalize cautiously beyond this one data set. After all, with regard to mate selection, the people of Hawaii have much in common with the people in the rest of the United States. As is the case on the mainland United States, romantic love and free choice of marriage partners characterized Hawaii 25 years ago as it does today.

Analysis

(15)   For each sex/ethnicity category, the marriage to remarriage data were arranged in a matrix with rows representing ethnicity of the first and columns of the second spouse. Entries along the diagonals of each matrix represented all possible consistent ethnic combinations. Off-diagonal entries represented various inconsistent combinations.

(16)   For index persons of each gender, consistent and inconsistent sequences were expressed as percentages of total marriages for that gender within each ethnic group. Consistently endogamous sequences were combined to represent consecutive marriages within one's own ethnic group. Consistently exogamous

Table 2. Ethnic and Racial Consistency in Remarriage for Women, State of Hawaii, 1943–1967

Ethnicity or Race	Consistent						Inconsistent		Both
	Total		Endogamy		Exogamy				
	%	N	%	N	%	N	%	N	N
Korean	83.2	74	7.9	7	75.3	67	16.8	15	89
Multi-ethnic	80.1	338	2.8	12	77.3	326	19.9	84	422
Chinese	75.5	151	16.0	32	59.5	119	24.5	49	200
Japanese	72.9	786	46.7	503	26.2	283	27.1	292	1078
Caucasian	72.9	229	57.3	180	15.6	49	27.1	85	314
Portuguese	69.8	256	10.4	38	59.4	218	30.2	111	367
Filipino	66.9	257	37.7	145	29.2	112	33.1	127	384
Black	66.4	87	24.4	32	41.0	55	33.6	44	131
Hawaiian	62.8	958	22.5	344	40.2	614	37.2	568	1526
Other	64.3	9	7.1	1	57.1	8	35.7	5	14
Total	69.5	3145	28.6	1294	40.9	1851	30.5	1380	4525

Note: chi-square = 75.73, d.f. = 9, p < .001

Table 3. Ethnic and Racial Consistency in Remarriage for Men, State of Hawaii, 1943–1967

Ethnicity or Race	Consistent Total %	N	Endogamy %	N	Exogamy %	N	Inconsistent %	N	Both N
Japanese	82.9	693	74.3	621	8.6	72	17.1	143	836
Multi-ethnic	79.0	229	4.8	14	74.1	215	21.0	61	290
Caucasian	75.3	527	22.1	155	53.1	372	24.7	173	700
Chinese	71.9	110	26.8	41	45.1	69	28.1	43	153
Portu-uese	70.2	233	12.4	41	57.8	192	29.8	99	332
Black	68.3	97	28.9	41	39.4	56	31.7	45	142
Korean	66.7	50	12.0	9	54.7	41	33.3	25	75
Hawaiian	64.9	690	43.5	462	21.4	228	35.1	373	1063
Filipino	61.5	288	26.7	125	34.8	163	38.5	180	468
Other	88.0	24	3.7	1	85.2	23	11.1	3	27
Total	72.0	2941	37.0	1510	35.0	1431	28.0	1145	4086

Note: chi-square = 90.67, d.f. = 9, p < .001

sequences, on the other hand, refer to the consecutive marriages out of one's own ethnic group. All inconsistent sequences represent persons who married once exogamously and once endogamously, regardless of which type of marriage came first.

(17)   The two types of consistent sequences were combined to represent the overall tendency toward consistency for each gender. This combined frequency distribution was compared to the corresponding consistent sequences using the Chi-square measure of statistical significance.

Results

(18)   Tables 2 and 3 show that differences between consistent and inconsistent frequencies are large and highly significant (p<.001 with nine degrees of freedom) for men and for women. Korean women and Japanese men exhibited the highest tendency toward consistency: over 83 percent of Korean women and about the same percentage of Japanese men. In no ethnic group did inconsistent ethnic sequences emerge as a dominant pattern for either gender. The lowest level of consistent ethnic sequences characterized Filipino men, 61.5 percent, and Hawaiian women, about 63 percent.

(19)   It is interesting to note that 79 percent of men and over 80 percent of women from multiethnic backgrounds had extremely low rates of "endogamy" even though marriage between any two multiethnic spouses was classified as endogamous. The fact that a small percentage of multiethnic brides and grooms either marry or remarry others of mixed ethnic parentage may reflect a tendency to choose a spouse from one of the parents' ethnic groups (Jedlicka, 1980, 1984).

(20)   Overall, 69.5 percent of women and 72 percent of men remarried consistently. Consistent endogamy was more common among men, 37 percent of whom stayed within their own ethnic group compared to 28.6 percent for the women. Frequency of inconsistent sequences, on the other hand, were remarkably similar for each sex: 30.5 percent for women and 28 percent for men.

Conclusion and Discussion

(21)   The data used in this study lacked a dimension needed to explain why some people marry consistently with respect to ethnicity while others do not. The data do show, however, that with respect to ethnicity men and women in each ethnic group studied were more likely to marry consistently than to marry inconsistently. That is, those who at first married into their own

ethnic group were more likely to remarry into their ethnic group after divorce than those who at first married out of their own group. Similarly, those who initially married out of their own group were more likely than expected by chance alone to repeat their experience after divorce. Unless the measure of consistency used in this study entirely fails to reflect personal choice in selection of consecutive marriage partners, it can be concluded that consistency rather than change is a characteristic of remarriage.

(22)   Consistent exogamy in remarriage poses a dilemma for researchers who support the contention that "people from different backgrounds will have different values, habits, and perhaps even personalities, and that these differences will make it difficult to get along in a marriage" (Whyte, 1990: 191). If Whyte's assessment of intermarriage is correct, it is intriguing that consistent exogamy nevertheless seems to be the prevalent pattern.

(23)   At this point we are left with an unanswered question: Does consistent exogamy indicate failure to learn from the experience during the first marriage, or have the researchers assumed incorrectly that interethnic marriages as a rule are fraught with problems?

(24)   Regardless of how these questions may be answered, the findings of this study do not stand alone. Others have shown that certain types of divorce-prone heterogamy occur consistently from marriage to marriage (Dean and Gurak, 1978) It has even been shown that a spouse abused in the first marriage is likely to be abused in remarriage (Kalmuss and Seltzer, 1986). Demographic data available for this study add some support to the hypothesis that consistency may be a rule of remarriage. If future research confirms this contention, then the idea that "remarriage is a mechanism for improving marriage" may lose its intuitive appeal among counselors and other family specialists.

References

Becker, G.
1973   "A theory of marriage." Journal of Political Economy 81:813-845.

Benson-von der Ohe, E.
1981   First and Second Marriages. New York: Praeger.

Bumpass, L. and Sweet, J.
1972   "Differentials in marital instability: 1970." American Sociological Review 37:754-766.

Cherlin, A. J.
1977   "The effect of children on marital instability." Demography 14:165-172.
1981   Marriage, Divorce, Remarriage. Cambridge, MA: Harvard Univ. Press.

Dean, G., and Gurak, D. T.
1978   "Marital homogamy the second time around." Journal of Marriage and the Family 40:559-570.

Department of Health, State of Hawaii
1989   Statistical Report 1988. Research and Statistics Office, pp. 58-66.

Farber, B.
1964   Family: Organization and Interaction. San Francisco: Chandler Publishing.

Freeman, L. C.
1955   "Homogamy in interethnic mate selection." Sociology and Social Research 39:369-377.

Furstenberg, F. F., Jr., and Spanier, G. B.
1984   Recycling the Family: Remarriage after Divorce. Beverly Hills, CA: Sage.

Glenn, N. D.
1981   "The well-being of persons remarried after divorce." Journal of Family Issues 2:61-75.

Glick, P. C.
1980   "Remarriage: Some recent changes and variations." Journal of Family Issues 1(4):726-724.

Jedlicka, D.
1975   Ethnic Serial Marriages in Hawaii: Application of a Sequential Preference Model. Unpublished Doctoral Dissertation, University of Hawaii.
1980   "A test of the psychoanalytic theory of mate selection." Journal of Social Psychology 112:259-299.
1980   "Indirect parental influence on mate choice: A test of the psychoanalytic theory." Journal of Marriage and the Family 46:65-70.

Kalmuss, D., and Seltzer, J. A.
1986   "Continuity of marital behavior in remarriage: The case of spouse abuse." Journal of Marriage and the Family 48: 113-120.

Lewis, R. A., and Spanier, G. B.
1979   "Theorizing about the quality and stability of marriage." Pp. 268-294 in W. Burr, R. Hill, F. Nye, and I. Reiss (eds.), Contemporary Theories about the Family. (Vol. 1). New York: Free Press.

Monahan, T. P.
1958   "The changing nature and instability of remarriage." Eugenics Quarterly 5:73-85.

National Center for Health Statistics

1989 "Advance report of final marriage statistics, 1986." Monthly Vital Statistics Reports 33 (3):12

Norton, A., and Glick, P.

1976 "Marital instability: Past, present, and future." Journal of Social Issues 34:5-20.

Spanier, G. B., and Furstenberg, F. F.

1982 "Remarriage after divorce: A longitudinal analysis of well-being." Journal of Marriage and the Family 43:709-720.

Stephens, W. N.

1968 "Predictions of marital adjustment." Pp. 119-133 in W. Stephens (ed.), Reflections on Marriage. New York: Thomas Crowell.

Teachman, J.

1983 "Early marriage, premarital fertility, and marital dissolution: Results for blacks and whites." Journal of Family Issues 4:105-126.

Weingarten, H. R.

1985 "Marital status and well-being: A national study comparing first-married, divorced, and remarried adults." Journal of Marriage and the Family 47:653-662.

Whyte, M. K.

1990 Dating, Mating, and Marriage. New York: Aldine de Gruyter.

Factual Questions

1. What does the author mean when he refers to ethnicity as a robust variable?

2. How does Freeman's (1955) study differ from the study described in this article?

3. Why were marriage records from 1943 through 1967 used?

4. How many remarried men and remarried women were included in the sample for this study?

5. The author acknowledges that the data are not recent and raises the question of whether these data reflect current mate selection patterns. What does the author suggest be examined to determine the validity of the assumption that mate selection patterns have remained constant?

6. According to Table 2, what percent of women of Japanese ethnicity in the sample consistently married husbands of Japanese ethnicity?

7. In how many ethnic groups were inconsistent remarriage patterns (one marriage endogamous and one marriage exogamous) more common than consistent remarriage patterns (both marriages endogamous or both marriages exogamous)?

8. What percentage of the women in the sample married within their own ethnic group both times? outside their ethnic group both times? once inside their ethnic group and once outside their ethnic group?

9. What percentage of the men in the sample married within their own ethnic group both times? outside their ethnic group both times? once inside their ethnic group and once outside their ethnic group?

10. What unanswered question does the author pose based on his findings?

Questions for Discussion

11. Does the introduction provide a clear notion of the research problem, the purpose of the research, and its significance?

12. Does the literature review seem relevant to the research problem?

13. Is the number of research subjects sufficient?

14. Is there enough information on the research instruments and procedures to allow you to replicate this study?

15. Should there be information about the reliability and validity of the research instruments and procedures?

16. Does the analysis include sufficient statistical information? Are the statistics that are used appropriate?

17. Are the conclusions supported by and do they logically follow from the data that have been presented?

18. Do you agree with the author that cross-cultural comparisons within the data set can determine the validity of the assumption that mate selection patterns have remained constant over the 25 years since the data was collected?

19. Are the findings discussed in terms of their implications and/or practical significance?

Article 8

Factors Influencing Pedestrian Cautiousness in Crossing Streets

W. Andrew Harrell
Centre for Experimental Sociology
University of Alberta

In an observational study of the perception of risks and cautionary behaviors displayed by 571 pedestrians waiting to cross signal-controlled intersections in Edmonton, Alberta, Canada, cautiousness was measured by distance stood from the curb and whether a pedestrian checked for traffic before crossing. Female and older pedestrians were more perceptive of risks and were more cautious. Greater caution was demonstrated when outside temperatures were warm rather than cold, when traffic volumes were low, when crosswalks were icy rather than dry, and when pedestrian volumes were low. The impact of pedestrian volumes was interpreted in terms of a diffusion of responsibility and the concept of safety in numbers. Width of crosswalk and time of day did not significantly affect cautiousness.

(1)   The perception of traffic hazards by pedestrians and the measures they take to reduce their exposure to risk is the subject of a growing body of literature. Among the factors shown to influence awareness of those hazards and to elicit behaviors avoiding or minimizing risk include the age of the pedestrian (Harrell, 1990; Jonah & Engel, 1983; Jorgensen, 1988; Kastenbaum & Brisco, 1976; Mathey, 1983; Vestrup & Reid, 1989; Winter, 1984), pedestrian's gender (Henderson & Lyons, 1972; Hill & Roemer, 1977; Mackie & Older, 1965), the volume of traffic passing through the pedestrian crosswalk (Harrell, 1989), slipperiness of streets (Harrell, 1989), and cues from other pedestrians regarding whether it is safe to cross an intersection (Wagner, 1981).

(2)   Practices that may reduce the likelihood of pedestrian accidents include looking both ways and checking for traffic (Grayson, 1980; Mathey, 1983; Wilson & Grayson, 1980; Wilson & Rennie, 1980); standing back from the curb, away from passing traffic (Harrell, 1990); crossing roads quickly to reduce the time of exposure to oncoming traffic (Harrell, 1989); using marked crosswalks instead of jaywalking (Jonah & Engel, 1983); avoiding busy intersections (Mathey, 1983; Wagner, 1981); and obeying signals (Retzko & Androsch, 1974; Wilson & Rennie, 1980). In general, these studies tend to show that older pedestrians and women are more perceptive of hazards and exercise more caution when crossing streets. In addition, a study by Harrell (1989) found that crossing times were faster when streets were icy or slippery and when traffic volumes were moderate (i.e., when more vehicles were on

The Journal of Social Psychology, 131(3): 367-372. Reprinted with permission of the Helen Dwight Reid Educational Foundation. Published by Heldref Publications, 1319 Eighteenth St., N.W., Washington, D.C. 20036-1802. Copyright © 1991.

Requests for reprints should be sent to W. Andrew Harrell, Centre for Experimental Sociology, Tory Building 5-21, University of Alberta, Edmonton, Alberta, Canada T6G 2H4.

the road and able to travel at a reasonably high rate of speed, thereby increasing the likelihood of potentially more injurious vehicle-pedestrian encounters).

(3)   The present investigation expanded on the Harrell (1989) research by examining the effects of traffic volume and road conditions on a composite measure of pedestrian safety: whether a pedestrian checked for oncoming traffic and the distance he or she stood away from the curb. It was predicted, as was the case with crossing times, that pedestrians would be more likely both to check for traffic and to stand back from the curb when confronting higher volumes of rapidly moving traffic and when roads were icy rather than dry. Icy roads were assumed to increase the danger of vehicles being unable to stop, thus endangering pedestrians by careening through crosswalks .

(4)   Research by Wagner (1981) found that pedestrians use the cues of other pedestrians as indicators of the relative safety of crossing an intersection. "Backfielders" (i.e., pedestrians in the back of a group waiting to cross) tended to look only at the backs of "frontliners" in front of them. When the frontliners crossed, the backfielders followed them without checking for traffic themselves, assuming it was safe to do so. Frontliners varied in their behavior, sometimes looking up the street for traffic and sometimes looking only at the signal light. Wagner reported that pedestrians were more likely to check for traffic when there were no other pedestrians present; their absence prevented the delegation of responsibility for traffic-checking. Lone pedestrians and some frontliners may also look to pedestrians across the street for cues as to when it is safe to cross. Thus, in the present study, it was hypothesized that subjects would show lower levels of caution when other pedestrians were present to provide cues of safety.

(5)   Outside temperature has been shown to affect pedestrian walking speed when crossing intersections (Harrell, 1989), with colder temperatures increasing the pace. It was hypothesized that low temperatures would also increase pedestrian vigilance and caution.

(6)   Finally, the impact of the width of the street being crossed was examined. It was expected that pedestrians would be more cautious when crossing wide as opposed to narrow streets because of longer exposure to vehicular traffic when crossing and the potential for coming into contact with greater volumes of rapidly moving traffic on wide streets.

Method

Subjects

(7)   Participants were 571 pedestrians using one of four crosswalks in Edmonton, Alberta, Canada, in October of 1986 and 1987. Only unaccompanied pedestrians presumably over the age of 17 were observed. Data were collected by four two-person observation teams extensively trained in observational techniques at four crosswalks on busy downtown streets with traffic passing through the intersections in four directions. Crosswalks were signal controlled. Two of the crosswalks were 78 feet in width; two were 42 feet in width. All observations were made on Monday through Friday, from 10:00 a.m. until 8:00 p.m.

Procedure

(8)   Pieces of tape were placed unobtrusively on the sidewalk leading into the intersections at intervals of 1 foot or less from the curb, 2 feet from the curb, and 3 feet or beyond. Pairs of observers noted the distance from the roadway at which pedestrians stood while waiting to cross; they also noted whether pedestrians checked for oncoming traffic by recording when the pedestrians explicitly moved their heads to the left or right to look for traffic. Those who first stepped into the intersection and then moved their heads were not counted as checking, nor were those who may have used peripheral vision rather than moving their heads. Pedestrians were retained for observation only if they were fully stopped at a crosswalk before the light changed and if they were in the front row (i.e., the group closest to the curb). The measure of caution was constructed by adding together a subject's score on curb position and traffic checking. A person standing 1 foot or less from the curb was assigned a value of 1; a person 2 feet away, a value of 2; and a person 3 feet or more away, a value of 3. A person who did not check for traffic was assigned a value of 0, a person who looked in only one direction was given a value of 1, and a person looking both ways received a value of 2.

(9)   Observation periods were divided into three 10-min segments for each 30 min of observation. During the first and third 10-min segments, observer pairs counted the number of vehicles crossing through the intersection. The counts were averaged to arrive at an estimate of traffic volume experienced by pedestrians during the 30-min period. The middle 10-min segment was devoted to recording pedestrian behavior.

(10)   In addition to recording a pedestrian's age and gender, observers also recorded the number of pedestrians on the other side of the intersection, crossing against the subject, to obtain the measure of pedestrian volume.

(11)   Outside temperature, time of observation, and whether roadways and crosswalks were clear and dry or icy and covered with compacted snow were also recorded (See Harrell, 1989 for a fuller treatment).

(12)   A multiple analysis of variance was made of the data. Two factor variables, road condition (icy vs. dry) and pedestrian's gender, and six covariates, traffic volume, pedestrian volume, time of observation, outside temperature, pedestrian's age, and width of roadway, were investigated.

Results

Descriptive Statistics

(13)   Cautiousness in crossing ranged from a low value of 1 to a maximum of 5. The mean level of cautiousness was 2.94 (SD = 0.92). Traffic volume ranged from 9 to 531 vehicles, with a mean of 88.36 (SD = 64.30). Time of observation ranged from 1000 hours (10:00 a.m.) to 2000 hours (8:00 p.m.) with a mean of 1595.79 (SD = 331.44). Temperatures ranged from -30C to +20C, with a mean of 2.61C (SD = 11.77). Pedestrian volume ranged from 0 to 58 pedestrians, with a mean of 16.63 (SD = 16.25). The modal age group was in the 21 to 30 year bracket. Forty-nine percent of the crossings took place at the narrow crosswalks and 51.2% at the wide crossings. Fifty-nine percent of the subjects were men; 41.16% were women. Twelve percent of the crossing occurred under icy road conditions and 88.44% under dry conditions.

Analysis of Variance

(14)   Four of the six covariates were statistically significant. Only time of day when observations were made and width of intersection were not significant. Age had the strongest impact, $F(1, 561)$ = 17.37, p < 0.001, with older subjects showing greater caution when crossing than younger pedestrians. Traffic volume had an inverse relationship to cautiousness, $F(1, 561)$ = 6.88, p < 0.01, with lower traffic volumes yielding greater cautiousness. Pedestrians showed greater cautiousness when outside temperatures were relatively warmer, $F(1, 561)$ = 6.24, p < 0.05. Finally, the greater number of pedestrians crossing the intersection with the subject, the less caution shown by the subject, $F(1, 561)$ = 3.80, p < 0.05.

(15)   Both factor variables, gender of subject, $F(1, 561)$ = 15.56, p < 0.001, and road conditions, $F(1, 561)$ = 3.16, p < 0.05, were statistically significant. Female pedestrians showed higher mean levels of cautiousness (M = 3.18) than male (M = 2.77). Icy roads evoked greater caution (M = 3.01) than dry roads (M = 2.92). The interaction of these two variables was not statistically significant.

Discussion

(16)   This study reaffirmed the finding that older adults and women were both more cognizant of traffic hazards and more likely to exercise caution as pedestrians. The elderly may realize that they are at greater risk of being involved in a fatal accident than younger pedestrians (Brainard, Slauterbeck, Benjamin, Hagaman, & Higie, 1989; Vestrup & Reid, 1989; Winter, 1984). Women's cautiousness may derive from a lesser propensity than that of men to take risks in a variety of endeavors and settings.

(17)   Surprisingly, this study found that cautiousness was greater for low than high traffic volumes, perhaps because vehicles traveled at faster speeds when volumes were low. High traffic volumes were observed to compact vehicular traffic, slowing the speed of vehicles considerably. It may be that speed of vehicle rather than absolute number of vehicles on the road is the salient warning factor for pedestrians.

(18)   This study found that the presence of large numbers of pedestrians on the opposite side of the street served to reduce cautiousness; a "diffusion of responsibility" effect may have occurred in which the subject delegated the task of checking to other pedestrians. When fewer pedestrians were available to act as lookouts, the subjects assumed the responsibility for themselves. Another explanation may be a "safety in numbers" effect that may occur when many other pedestrians are also crossing; one might assume that oncoming traffic is better able to see pedestrians and come to a stop when there are many of them huddled at the crosswalks. Consequently, there may be greater trust placed in drivers of motor vehicles to stop under these conditions, eliminating the need for caution by the pedestrian.

(19)   As predicted, icy roads evoked greater caution than dry roads. However, lower outside temperatures tended to reduce cautiousness. Perhaps under very cold

conditions, pedestrians are largely intent on escaping the cold and may focus their attention on their internal state of discomfort rather than on the external hazards around them. Fast walking when outside temperatures are low may reflect a desire to escape the cold rather than the risk of a traffic accident per se.

References

Brainard, B. J., Slauterbeck, J., Benjamin, S. B., Hagaman, R. M., & Higie, S. (1989). Injury profiles in pedestrian motor vehicle trauma. *Annals of Emergency Medicine, 18,* 881-883.

Grayson, G. B. (1980). The elderly pedestrian. In Oborne, D. J., & Levis, J. A. (Eds.), *Human factors in transport research* (Vol. 2). London: Academic Press.

Harrell, W. A. (1989). Pedestrian avoidance of risk: Traffic density and the speed of crossing icy streets. *Man-Environment Systems.*

Harrell, W. A. (1990). Perception of risk and curb standing at street corners by older pedestrians. *Perceptual and Motor Skills, 70,* 1363-1366.

Henderson, L. F., & Lyons, D. J. (1972). Sexual differences in human crowd motion. *Nature, 240,* 246-255.

Hill, M. R., & Roemer, T. T. (1977). Toward an explanation of jaywalking behavior: A linear regression approach. *Man-Environment Systems, 7,* 342-349.

Jonah, B. A., & Engel, G. R. (1983). Measuring the relative risk of pedestrian accidents. *Accident Analysis and Prevention, 15,* 193-206.

Jorgensen, N. O. (1988). Risky behavior at traffic signals: A traffic engineer's view. *Ergonomics, 31,* 657-661.

Kastenbaum, R., & Brisco, L. (1976). Street crossing patterns. *Human Behavior, 5,* 33.

Mackie, A. M., & Older, S. J. (1965). Study of the pedestrian risk in crossing busy roads in London inner suburbs. *Traffic Engineering Control, 7,* 736-750.

Mathey, F. J. (1983). Attitudes and behavior of elderly pedestrians. *International Journal of Aging and Human Development, 17,* 25-28.

Retzko, H. G., & Androsch, W. (1974). Pedestrian behavior at signalised intersections. *Traffic Engineering and Control, 15,* 735-738.

Vestrup, J. A., & Reid, J. D. (1989). A profile of urban pedestrian trauma. *Journal of Trauma, 29,* 741-745.

Wagner, J. (1981). Crossing streets: Reflections on urban pedestrian behavior. *Man-Environment Systems, 11,* 57-61.

Wilson, D. G., & Grayson, G. B. (1980). Age-related differences in the road crossing behavior of adult pedestrians. *Transport and Road Research Digest,* LR 933.

Wilson, J. R., & Rennie, A. M. (1980). *Elderly pedestrians and road safety: A summary report.* Loughborough, United Kingdom: Loughborough University of Technology, Institute for Consumer Ergonomics.

Winter, D. J. (1984). Needs and problems of older drivers and pedestrians: An exploratory study with teaching/learning implications. *Education Gerontology, 10,* 135-146.

Factual Questions

1. What pedestrian characteristics have previous researchers found to influence awareness of traffic hazards?

2. What hypothesis does the author state regarding the effect of outside temperature on pedestrian vigilance and caution?

3. How many subjects were observed and how many observation sites were there?

4. During what time of day were observations of pedestrian behavior made?

5. Were any of the subjects crossing the intersection in violation of the signal?

6. How did observers determine if a pedestrian checked for traffic?

7. How was the measure of caution calculated?

8. What was the modal age bracket of the pedestrian subjects?

9. Were pedestrians more cautious when traffic volume was high or low? Were pedestrians more cautious in warmer weather or cooler weather?

10. Which of the author's hypotheses were not supported?

11. How does the author explain the unexpected finding that more caution is exercised when traffic volume is low than when it is high?

Questions for Discussion

12. Does the introduction provide a clear notion of the research problem, the purpose of the research, and its significance?

13. Does the literature review seem relevant to the research problem?

14. Are the stated hypotheses reasonable? Do they appear to reasonably follow from the review of the literature?

15. Is the number of research subjects sufficient? To what population would you generalize the results of this study?

16. Is there enough information on the research instruments and procedures to allow you to replicate this study?

17. Should there be information about the reliability and validity of the research instruments and procedures?

18. Does the analysis include sufficient statistical information? Are the statistics that are used appropriate?

19. Are the conclusions supported by and do they logically follow from the data that have been presented?

20. Are the findings discussed in terms of their implications and/or practical significance

Sensitivity and Reciprocity in the Play of Adolescent Mothers and Young Fathers with Their Infants

Mary Ann McGovern

Fifteen 4-month-old infants were videotaped for 15 minutes of free play with their adolescent mothers and another 15 minutes with their fathers. Comparisons using paired t tests were made between mothers and fathers on type of play, and parental sensitivity and reciprocity. Findings indicate that fathers' type of play is very similar to mothers' with the exception that fathers engage in more social play. However, fathers are found to be less sensitive than mothers to their infants' communications for they often missed cues, or responded slowly or inappropriately to the infant's signals. Fathers also tended to demonstrate less reciprocity in the interactions. These findings emphasize a need for parent educators to teach young fathers how to understand and respond to their children.

(1) There is general consensus among child developmentalists and practitioners who teach parenting programs that a central component of effective parenting is parental sensitivity. Although some studies have examined parental sensitivity in adult parents, very few studies have looked at this phenomenon in adolescent mothers and the fathers of their young infants. Parental sensitivity involves the parent's ability to provide contingent, consistent, and appropriate responses to his/her infant's cues (Ainsworth, Blehar, Waters, & Wall, 1978).

Literature Review

(2) Parental sensitivity and responsiveness can be observed during parent-child interactions, particularly those involving play. When parents behave in an attentive, responsive manner, their infants are more likely to develop trustful or secure attachment relationships and to experience accelerated cognitive development (Ainsworth et al., 1978; Lamb, Thompson, Gardner, Charnov, & Estes, 1984). Furthermore, older children with sensitive parents appear to be more self-confident, assertive, and socially competent (Baumrind, 1975). Conversely, when parents are insensitive, unstim-

Reprinted with permission from *Family Relations, 39*: 427-431. Copyright 1990 by the National Council on Family Relations, 3989 Central Ave. NE, Suite 550, Minneapolis, MN 55421.

Based on a paper presented at the April 1987 meeting of the Society for Research in Child Development, Baltimore. This research was supported by The Department of Health and Human Services, Division of Nursing, National Research Service Award Grant No. NU05885-02. The author would like to thank Rita Peterson and Ruth Harding-Weaver for their assistance with coding and Ric Luecht for his help with analysis.

Mary Ann McGovern is on leave from the University of Wisconsin-Milwaukee where she is an assistant professor in the School of Nursing. She is currently living in Europe, 31 Bis Boulevard Suchet, 75016 Paris, France.

ulating, rejecting, or overstimulating, their infants are more likely to develop distrustful, insecure attachments and their older children are apt to be more dependent and socially incompetent.

(3)   The investigators who have studied the responsiveness of adolescent parents to their infants have looked predominately at mothers (Jones, Green, & Krauss, 1980) and have found them to be less responsive to their infants' cues than are adult mothers. Another group (Lawrence et al., 1981) found some adolescent mothers to engage in aggressive, inappropriate behaviors, such as picking, poking, and pinching their infants. With regard to young fathers, data on the interaction of these men with their infants are rare. One study examined adolescent mothers and their partners interacting with their 6-month-old infants and found that in the triadic context, adolescent mothers were more responsive to their infants than were fathers (Lamb & Elster, 1985).

(4)   Among adult parents, the findings in regard to parents' sensitivity and responsiveness have been mixed. Some studies with adult parents have found mothers to be more engaging and responsive to their infants than fathers (Belsky, Gilstrap, & Rovine, 1984) while other studies have found mothers and fathers to be equally responsive to their infants (Parke & Sawin, 1980).

(5)   Previous data gathered during the interactions of adult, middle-class parents and their children have shown that when fathers interact with their infant they tend to be more involved in playful, physical, social interaction while the mothers are more apt to be nurturant and verbal with their infant (Lamb, 1976, 1977b; Kalasch, 1981). Fathers, more than mothers, have been found to spend a larger proportion of their time playing with their child and fostering social development (Field, 1978; Lamb, 1977a; Yogman, Dixon, Tronick, Als, & Brazelton, 1976). Fathers may also enhance sex role development in their sons by showing preferential treatment towards boys in their second year of life (Fagot, 1984).

Purpose of the Study

(6)   This study examines the play of adolescent mothers and the fathers of their 4-month-old infants in a dyadic context. Parent and infant behaviors were observed and videotaped during a 15-minute play session between each of the parents and his/her infant. One aim of the study is to determine whether there are differences between the mothers' and fathers' style of play

with their infants and the type and number of objects used in play. Another aim is to observe parental sensitivity and responsivity to the infants' cues.

(7)   This research is based on Sameroff's Transactional Model (1975, 1986) which indicates that each of the three interacting members of the family brings a set of components to the family system that will influence the relationships the members have with each other. These components include constitutional make-up, role attitudes, values, and past experiences and learning. The young parents' ability to sensitively and responsively play with their infant is dependent not only on their own personality, but on their previous experiences and learning, as well as certain qualities in their infant.

Methods

Subjects

(8)   Parents and infants were recruited from a midwest Teen Pregnancy Clinic which provides interdisciplinary outpatient care to pregnant adolescents (13 to 18 years of age), adolescent mothers, and their infants from delivery until the infants' second birthday. All parents had to be the biological parents of the infant and the infant had to be their first child. Infants had to be 36-44 weeks gestational age, of a single birth and free from major abnormalities or disease at birth and at the time of the play session. The sample was composed of 15 adolescent mothers, the fathers of their babies, and their infants. The mothers' ages ranged from 14-19 years ($M = 17$ yrs.) while the fathers' ages ranged from 15-26 years ($M = 19$ yrs.). Thirteen of the mothers were under 18 years of age, but only 7 of the fathers were under 18 years. Only 2 of the couples were married. Five couples lived together with their infant but 3 of these couples lived with the fathers' family. Seven mothers and infants lived with the mothers' family, 1 mother and infant lived alone, and 2 mothers and infants lived with others. The racial composition included 5 black couples, 7 white couples, 2 Hispanic couples, and 1 Hispanic mother and Indian father. The mean grade completed by both mothers and fathers was 11th grade. Six mothers were still in school, 4 attending full-time and 2 attending part-time. Five fathers were attending school, 3 full-time and 2 part-time. Three mothers worked, 1 full-time and 2 part-time. Eight fathers were working, 4 full-time and 4 part-time.

(9)   All of the infants were 4 months old at time of testing. This age was chosen because by 4 months, parents and infant have had time to get acquainted; the infants' vocal repertoire is expanding and their

pseudo-imitation skills make reciprocal vocal exchange possible; the infants' physical development is progressing so that they will be able to reach out to the environment and hold some small toys; and visual recognition is increasing. Five of the infants were males and 10 were females. None of the infants had any health problems at the time of testing.

(10)   The adolescent mothers were asked to identify their major source of support. Seven stated their own mother, while 6 stated the father of their baby. One mother said no one and another said a family member. Twelve of the mothers stated that they were satisfied with the support they received which included both emotional and physical support (i.e., assistance with the infant). Although they were satisfied with the support received, less than half relied on the infant's father.

(11)   The Coopersmith Self-Esteem Inventory (1984) was given to both mothers and fathers. This was used as a measure of the parents' self-evaluation in social, academic, family, and personal areas of experience. Mean scores were slightly below the standardized norm of 70 for mothers ($M = 64$) and at norm for fathers ($M = 72$) since the score tends to rise with age. No significant differences existed between the two groups.

(12)   Prior to data collection, an assessment was made of the fathers' involvement in his infant's care. Parents were asked how many times per week the father had seen the infant in the month prior to the onset of the study. For inclusion in the study, the father had to be with the infant at least three times per week. After signing consents, parents were asked to keep a diary for 3 days. In this diary they had to note who performed certain child care tasks and how often they were performed. Results indicated that mothers performed significantly more tasks than did fathers (Table 1). Thus

fathers stated that they were involved with their infants, but they did little child care.

Procedure

(13)   At 2 months of age, infants were seen at the clinic for a routine evaluation of their health and development. During their appointment the investigator visited with the adolescent mother and her partner if he was present. The study was explained to them, and they were invited to participate. A few parents who originally had agreed to participate were lost by 4 months because they failed to come to clinic for their infant's appointments and could not be contacted since they did not have telephones. A few other parents had to be dropped when it was learned that the male partner had previous children, was not the biological father, or was no longer involved with his infant. Some other subjects initially refused because of the difficulty of getting to clinic, but this was resolved when the researcher agreed to pick up the parents and infant at their home, drive them to the session at the clinic, and then return them home. Although each parent was given a $10.00 stipend for participating, this did not appear to be a great incentive for recruiting these parents.

(14)   Parents were contacted a second time when the infant had his/her 4 month-old visit. If parents were still willing to participate, consent forms were signed and parents were assured that all information obtained from the study would be kept strictly confidential. An appointment was then made for them to return for the play session.

The Play Session

(15)   The play sessions were videotaped in a naturalistic laboratory setting in a room a few floors below the

Table 1. Percentage of Mothers' and Fathers' Performance of Child Care Tasks

	Mothers		Fathers		
	M	*SD*	*M*	*SD*	*t*
Feed liquids	.60	.21	.25	.18	3.73*
Feed solids	.60	.35	.15	.21	3.71*
Diaper	.60	.24	.25	.26	3.02*
Bathe	.50	.35	.35	.36	.87
Morning care	.68	.29	.19	.22	4.10**
Sleep	.65	.24	.22	.22	3.73*

*$p < .01$. **$p < .001$.

clinic. The room contained a couch, some lounge chairs, and a rocking chair along with a number of age appropriate toys. Mothers and fathers were observed separately with their infants so that a more precise assessment could be made of each parent's interaction with his/her infant. Each interaction session lasted for 15 minutes. The order of the sessions was counterbalanced so that an equal number of each sex parent was filmed first. Two people did the videotaping — a white female filmed the mothers playing with their infant and a black male filmed the fathers playing with their infant. It was felt that having members of both sexes collect data would make the parents, particularly the fathers, feel at ease.

(16)   The investigator and the videotaping equipment were hidden behind a curtain with only the lens of the camera visible. Videotaping was carried out while the infant was awake, alert, and in a playful mood. The parents were instructed that the researcher was interested in learning how babies play with their parents and that they should just play with their infants as they would do at home. Parents were told that they could use any of the toys that were present but that they did not have to use the toys. Toys included three which the infant could hold and which would make a noise when shaken; a small teddy bear and a small doll; stacking rings that provided color and with the parent's help, could be stacked; a teething ring; a book with big colorful pictures that the parents could show the child; and a colorful wooden train. If the infant became fussy and needed to be fed or changed, videotaping was stopped so that the parent could attend to the infant. Videotaping was resumed again when the parent and infant were ready to play.

Coding of Data

(17)   The coding system developed for this study was based on previous observational studies of parents and infants in interaction (Belsky, 1980; Clarke-Stewart, 1973; Lamb & Elster, 1985; Stevenson & Roach, 1984a) as well as refinement of a coding system that the investigator used in a pilot study. It was designed to record differences in the types of play parents engaged in with their infants and the objects used in play. Additionally, an assessment was made of parental sensitivity and reciprocity during the interaction.

(18)   *Types of play.* Types of play and their definitions for this study are: (a) physical play — parent is involved in active, bodily play with the infant, often tossing the infant; (b) social play — occurs when the parent plays repetitive, turn-taking games with the

infant, such as imitating facial expressions or sounds; (c) object play — parent gives, shows, or offers the infant a toy, such as the squeaky dwarf, teething ring, doll, or teddy; (d) active object play — when parent is offering a toy, parent shakes or rattles a toy, or points out pictures in a book.

(19)   *Objects used.* The objects used in play included those previously mentioned plus another category for those personal toys the parent insisted on using.

(20)   *Reciprocity.* Reciprocity was characterized by contingent responsivity and engagement on the part of both parent and infant. The scale used in this study was based on one developed by Clark (1985) and consisted of 5 points with 1 being *no reciprocity* and 5 being *reciprocity* in almost all instances.

(21)   *Sensitivity.* Sensitivity reflects the parents' ability to perceive and to accurately interpret the signals and communication implicit in their infant's behavior, and given this understanding, to respond to them appropriately and promptly. This scale was based on one developed by Ainsworth, Bell, and Stayton (1974). It too had 5 points with 1 being *highly insensitive* to infant's cues and 5 being *highly sensitive.*

(22)   Videotaping permitted use of a multiple pass coding system. One pass was done to score play and play objects, and another pass for coding sensitivity and reciprocity. Types of play and objects of play were observed and scored in 10-second intervals. Each type and object was mutually exclusive and scored only once during the particular time sampling interval regardless of the number of actual onsets. Qualitative assessments of reciprocity and sensitivity in the interactions were scored once every minute in a global rating since they could not adequately be assessed in shorter intervals.

(23)   An independent coder who was totally "blind" to the aims of the study was trained by the investigator to code the videotaped observations. Practice videotapes were used to define and discuss the passes. A 78% or greater agreement (Kaye & Fogel, 1980) was reached on two consecutive observations for each pass. Additional assessments were made during the coding period to assure continued reliability. These assessments reached a 77% or greater reliability.

(24)   Comparisons between mothers and fathers were performed with paired *t* tests since the data from the mothers and fathers were not independent of each other (Loftus & Loftus, 1982).

Results

(25)   Review of the mothers' and fathers' play behaviors shows that fathers' style of play was comparable to mothers' in each category (Table 2) except that fathers were slightly more apt to engage in social play. Both mothers and fathers used a similar number of toys during the play session (Table 3). However paired *t* tests between the mothers and fathers demonstrated that mothers used the squeaky dwarf more than fathers but the fathers used the teething ring more than did mothers (Table 3). Regarding sensitivity and reciprocity during the interaction, mothers were found to be consistently more sensitive to their infants than were fathers and slightly more responsive (Table 4).

Table 2. Frequency of Play Behaviors Per 15-Minute Play Session

	Fathers		Mothers		
	M	*SD*	*M*	*SD*	*t*
Physical play	23.07	16.05	18.20	17.02	.81
Social play	1.33	2.19	.13	.35	2.02*
Object play	28.00	15.45	23.60	17.04	.68
Active object play	29.60	17.77	37.73	20.09	1.55

*$p < .10$.

Table 3. Objects of Play and Number of Times They Were Used

Objects	Mothers		Fathers		
	M	*SD*	*M*	*SD*	*t*
Doll	4.33	6.03	3.07	3.96	.58
Teddy bear	8.93	10.29	9.07	9.11	.05
Book	9.07	11.09	6.73	13.69	.52
Rattle	8.53	7.41	8.20	8.12	.09
Rings	6.00	4.86	4.07	5.22	.88
Train	3.27	3.24	3.20	5.38	.05
Squeaky dwarf	13.40	10.90	6.27	5.16	2.41*
Teething ring	2.00	2.48	9.07	9.11	3.18*
Total number of objects used	5.93	2.05	6.40	2.03	.57

*$p < .05$.

Table 4. Rating of Sensitivity and Reciprocity in the Interactions

	Fathers		Mothers		
	M	*SD*	*M*	*SD*	*t*
Sensitivity	3.28	.42	3.63	.65	2.15**
Reciprocity	3.09	.27	3.38	.51	2.03*

*$p < .10$. **$p < .05$.

Discussion

(26)   This research involved a special group of fathers who wished and were able to continue their relationship with their infants for at least 4 months following the birth. This may have occurred because the clinic encouraged father involvement and made this fact known to the mothers and maternal grandmothers who sometimes preferred not to have the fathers involved with the infants. It may also have been related to the fathers' age, since half of them were 19 years and older. A younger group might not have responded similarly.

(27)   The study sought to extend the early studies on fathers' interactions with their infants where adult fathers were found to be more involved in physical play and less involved in social play than were the mothers (Lamb, 1977a, 1977b). However these findings did not carry over to younger fathers. Perhaps this occurred because the infants were only 4 months old, whereas infants in earlier research ranged in age from 8 to 24 months (Lamb, 1977b; Power & Parke, 1979) when infants are more mobile and expressive.

(28)   These findings regarding types of play coincide with Stevenson, Leavitt, Thompson, and Roach (1983), Pederson, Anderson, and Cain (1980), and Belsky (1980) all of whom found minimal differences in the type of play of mothers versus fathers. Pederson and colleagues (1980) attribute their findings to their parents being committed consciously, or implicitly, to "androgynous" parenting. It is doubtful that the parents in this study were committed to androgynous parenting. A more likely explanation is that both these mothers and these fathers enjoyed a certain amount of physical play and object play with their infants.

(29)   The mean number of objects used during play was similar for both mothers and fathers. Out of a possible nine objects, approximately six were used by parents in each group. This was sufficient to provide a variety of stimulating objects for the infant. Bornstein (1985) found that infants whose mothers frequently encouraged them to attend to properties, objects, and events in the home environment in the first 6 months of life excelled in verbal development during their second year and scored higher on a psychometric assessment of intelligence at 4 years. Perhaps if these parents could be encouraged to continue to stimulate their infants with a variety of objects and events, these infants would perform well in preschool. It is not known why the mothers used the squeaky dwarf more than the fathers. Perhaps mothers liked to hear noise. Fathers may have used teething rings more often because they perceived the infant to have great oral needs.

(30)   With regard to social play, neither mothers nor fathers engaged in this type of play very often. When social play did occur, fathers did more of it than mothers. Social play occurs when parents play repetitive, turn-taking games with their infants. It is possible that the parents could not perceive of their infants as being capable of these types of games. It is also known that adolescent mothers speak to their infants less frequently than do adult mothers. Another possible explanation is that the parents have not had good role modeling in regard to social play. Conversely, parents may not have had many toys at home for their infants and thus when given a variety of toys, they preferred to use these rather than ignore them. Future studies could inquire about toys that parent and infant play with at home.

(31)   The fact that mothers were consistently more sensitive to their infants than were fathers may be related to the mothers' having received more information on parenting and child care from the nurse parent-educator at the clinic. Fathers were invited to these sessions that were held throughout the mothers' pregnancy and early postpartum period but the parent educator said the fathers usually did not attend. Perhaps if the classes were co-taught by a male, there would be greater male attendance. A different interpretation is that mothers may have been exposed to more role modeling than were fathers since father involvement in infant care is a recent phenomenon. The Transactional Model (Sameroff, 1975) states that role attitudes and previous learning are two of the components influencing the interaction. Future research should assess these factors.

Implications for Practitioners

(32)   This research has demonstrated that a number of young fathers wished to be involved with their infants but provided very little child care and did not know how to consistently respond to their infants' cues in a sensitive manner. These involved fathers may have been an unusually motivated group, but there may be others like them who are unknown to social service providers. Hence practitioners who are planning parenting programs for adolescent mothers should make a point to include the fathers of these infants, or possibly hold a separate session or provide a support group for fathers. These programs or support groups could assist the father in his own development and furnish information on child development, child care skills, and the parent-child relationship. Perhaps some of these programs could be given by male parent educators so the fathers

could witness a little role modeling. Barret and Robinson (1982) blame poor father involvement on the neglect of fathers by service providers, yet it is difficult to motivate the fathers to attend programs (Berland, 1987). One motivating incentive for fathers to attend parenting classes might be to provide the fathers with some snacks or a meal during the program. Additionally, if male educators were available, they could recruit fathers by making a personal contact with them. Westney, Cole, and Munford (1988) state that when adolescent prospective fathers were provided with the knowledge of infant development and child care, these fathers tended to report more supportive behaviors toward the mother and infant. Hence if involvement was fostered and fathers became more supportive of their partners and their infants, it might result in some real benefits to society. Parents might share child care tasks, thus allowing one another the opportunity to attend school or hold a job, as was the case with a few of the couples in this study.

(33)   Although most funding in recent years has been geared towards reducing the number of adolescent pregnancies, it is unrealistic to think that these pregnancies will not occur. Given the fact that a certain percentage will continue, practitioners should be more attuned to providing both parents with the skills needed to become good parents. These young men were involved with the adolescent mother before she became pregnant, and this study and others (Berland, 1987; Klinman & Sander, 1985; Westney et al., 1988) give reason to believe that some fathers want to continue the relationship beyond pregnancy and extend the relationship to their children. Would it not be better to teach fathers some responsible skills of child care and encourage their support of children, than to add to the already staggering number of female-headed families?

References

Ainsworth, M. D., Bell, S. M., & Stayton, D. J. (1974). Infant-mother attachment and social development: 'Socialization' as a product of reciprocal responsiveness to signals. In M. P. Richards (Ed.), *The integration of a child into a social world* (pp. 99-135). New York: Cambridge University Press.

Ainsworth, M. D., Blehar, E., Waters, E., & Wall, S. (1978). *Patterns of attachment: A psychological study of the strange situation.* Hillsdale, NJ: Erlbaum.

Baumrind, D. (1975). *Early socialization and the discipline controversy.* Morristown, NJ: General Learning Press.

Barret, R. L., & Robinson, B. (1982). A descriptive study of teenage expectant fathers. *Family Relations,* **31**, 349-352.

Belsky, J. (1980). A family analysis of parental influence on infant exploratory competence. In F. A. Pederson (Ed.), *The father-infant relationship: Observational studies in a family setting* (pp. 87-110). New York: Praeger.

Belsky, J., Gilstrap, B., & Rovine, M. (1984). The Pennsylvania Infant and Family Development Project, I: Stability and change in mother-infant and father-infant interaction in a family setting at one, three, and nine months. *Child Development,* **55**, 692-705.

Berland, A. (1987). Young fathers support group. *Pediatric Nursing,* **13**(4), 255-256 & 276.

Bornstein, M. (1985). How infant and mother jointly contribute to developing cognitive competence in the child. *Proceedings of the National Academy of Science, USA,* **82**, 7470-7473.

Clark, R. (1985). *The parent-infant early relational assessment.* Unpublished manuscript.

Clarke-Stewart, A. K. (1973). Interactions between parents and their young children: Characteristics and consequences. *Monographs of the Society for Research in Child Development,* **38**, (6-7, Serial No. 153).

Coopersmith, S. (1984). *Self-esteem inventories.* Palo Alto, CA: Consulting Psychologists.

Fagot, B. I. (1984). Sex differences in toddlers' behavior and parental reaction. *Developmental Psychology,* **10**, 554-558.

Field, T. (1978). Interaction behaviors of primary vs. secondary caretaker fathers. *Developmental Psychology,* **4**, 183-184.

Jones, F. A., Green V., & Krauss, D. R. (1980). Maternal responsiveness of primiparous mothers during the postpartum period: Age differences. *Pediatrics,* **65**, 575-584.

Kalasch, B. S. (1981). Fathers and infants: Reported caregiving and interaction. *Journal of Family Issues,* **2**, 275-296.

Kaye, K., & Fogel, A. (1980). The temporal structure of face-to-face communication between mothers and infants. *Child Development,* **16**, 454-464.

Klinman, D. G., & Sander, J. H. (1985). *The Teen Parent Collaboration: Reaching and serving the teenage father.* New York: Bank Street College of Education.

Lamb, M. E. (1976). The role of the father: An overview. In M. E. Lamb (Ed.), *The role of the father in child development* (pp. 1-63). New York: John Wiley & Sons.

Lamb, M. E. (1977a). Development of mother-infant and father-infant interaction in the second year of life. *Developmental Psychology, 13*, 637-649.

Lamb, M. E. (1977b). Father-infant and mother-infant interaction in the first year of life. *Child Development, 48*, 167-181.

Lamb, M. E., & Elster, A. B. (1985). Adolescent mother-father-infant relationships. *Developmental Psychology, 21*, 768-773.

Lamb, M. E., Thompson, R. A., Gardner, W. P., Charnov, E. L., & Estes, D. (1984). Security of infantile attachment as assessed in the "strange situation": Its study and biological interpretation. *Behavioral and Brain Sciences, 7*, 127-147.

Lawrence, R. A., McAnarney, E. R., Aten, M. J., Iker, H. P., Baldwin, C. P., & Baldwin, A. L. (1981). Aggressive behaviors in young mothers: Markers of future morbidity? *Pediatric Research, 15*, 443.

Loftus, G., & Loftus, E. (1982). *Essence of statistics*. Monterey, CA: Brooks/Cole.

Parke, R. D., & Sawin, D. B. (1980). The family in early infancy: Social interaction and attitudinal analyses. In F. A. Pedersen (Ed.), *The father-infant relationship: Observational studies in a family setting* (pp. 40-70). New York: Praeger.

Pedersen, F. A., Anderson, B. J., & Cain, R. L. (1980). Parent-infant and husband-wife interactions observed at age five months. In F. A. Pedersen (Ed.), *The father-infant relationship: Observational studies in the family setting* (pp. 70-86). New York: Praeger.

Power, T. G., & Parke, R. D. (1979, March). *Towards a taxonomy of father-infant and mother-infant play patterns*. Paper presented at the biennial meeting of the Society for Research in Child Development, San Francisco, CA.

Sameroff, A. (1975). Transactional models in early social relations. *Human Development, 18*, 65-79.

Sameroff, A. (1986, April). *Description of transactional model*. Paper presented at Comparisons of Theoretical Models Symposium conducted at the meeting of the International Conference on Infant Studies, Beverly Hills, CA.

Stevenson, M. B., Leavitt, L., Thompson, R., & Roach, M. (1983, April). *Play in the family: Fathers and mothers with their infants and preschoolers*. Paper presented at the biennial meeting of the Society for Research in Child Development, Detroit, MI.

Stevenson, M. B., & Roach, M. (1984a). *Behavior codes for recoding interaction between 4-month-old infants and their mothers*. Unpublished manuscript.

Stevenson, M. B., & Roach, M. (1984b, April). *Fathers' and mothers' interactions with their one-year-olds: Analyses of behavioral frequencies and contingencies*. Paper presented at the International Conference on Infant Studies, New York, NY.

Westney, O., Cole, J., & Munford, T. (1988). The effects of prenatal education on unwed prospective adolescent fathers. *Journal of Adolescent Health Care, 9*, 214-218.

Yogman, M. J., Dixon, S., Tronick, E., Als, H., & Brazelton, T. B. (1976, April). *Development of infant social interaction with fathers*. Paper presented to the Eastern Psychological Association, New York, NY.

Factual Questions

1. What are the positive consequences for children of parental sensitivity and responsiveness?

2. On what theoretical model is the research based?

3. How many couples with infants were studied?

4. How many of the couples lived together with their infant?

5. What was the mean grade completed by mothers? By fathers?

6. Were mothers and fathers found to significantly differ in average self-esteem?

7. Why were some parents who initially agreed to participate in the study eventually not included in this study?

8. How long were the videotaped play sessions?

9. Why were two different people used to videotape the play sessions?

10. What instructions were given to the parents about the videotaping session?

11. What differences between mothers and fathers were found in sensitivity and reciprocity?

Questions for Discussion

12. Does the introduction provide a clear notion of the research problem, the purpose of the research, and its significance?

13. Does the literature review seem relevant to the research problem?

14. Is the number of couples studied sufficient? To what population would you generalize the results of this study?

15. Is there enough information on the research instruments and procedures to allow you to replicate this study?

16. The father-infant session was videotaped before the mother-infant session for approximately half of the families. The order was reversed for the remainder of the families. Why was this done?

17. What is a "multiple pass coding system"?

18. Do the research instruments and procedures have adequate reliability and validity?

19. Does the analysis include sufficient statistical information? Are the statistics that are used appropriate?

20. Are the conclusions supported by and do they logically follow from the data that have been presented?

21. Are the findings discussed in terms of their implications and/or practical significance?

Overt and Covert Parental Conflict and Adolescent Problems: Observed Marital Interaction in Clinic and Nonclinic Families

Shaun Whittaker
Brenna H. Bry

When adolescents behave in socially unacceptable ways, overt interparental conflict is widely held to be the cause. Empirical studies, however, have been inconsistent in supporting this assumption. Some researchers therefore have speculated that covert conflict also plays a role. In the current observational study, evidence was found that both overt parental conflict and some forms of covert conflict play roles. During problem-solving family discussions, parents of adolescents whom they had brought into an outpatient clinic for treatment overtly disagreed with each other significantly more often than did parents with adolescents who did not require treatment. Families of clinic adolescents also exhibited significantly more silence during their discussions, and mothers spent significantly less time talking than did their nonclinic counterparts. The implications that both the overt and covert conflict may have for adolescent behavior are discussed.

(1)   When adolescents behave in socially unacceptable ways, interparental conflict or discord is held to be a major cause (Minuchin, 1974). The theory states that parental discord prevents them from providing the developing adolescent with a unified message and model of appropriate behavior. When researchers investigated this assumption empirically, however, their findings were inconsistent. Some studies strongly supported a relationship between interparental conflict and adolescent problems, whereas others did not.

(2)   Early studies using parent questionnaires found clear correlations between self-reported marital acrimony and younger children's behavior problems, even when other possible explanatory variables such as poverty were controlled (e.g., Shaw & Emery, 1987). Literature reviews warned, however, that conclusions about the relationships should not be based upon (a) a single age group, (b) a single source of self-report, (c) self-report alone, or (d) a single definition of marital discord (Emery, 1982). There are multiple types of marital discord, such as overt conflict and covert

Reprinted with permission from *Adolescence, 26*(104): 865-876. Copyright © 1991 by Libra Publishers, Inc.

This study is based on a master's thesis submitted to Rutgers University by the first author under the direction of the second author. This research was partially supported by NIDA grant DA05112 to Dr. Brenna H. Bry. The authors are grateful to Cornelius Schutte for assistance with the data analysis.

Shaun Whittaker, M.S., Department of Psychology, Rutgers University.

Reprint requests to Brenna H. Bry, Ph.D., Associate Professor of Clinical Psychology, Graduate School of Applied and Professional Psychology, Rutgers University, P.O. Box 819, Piscataway, New Jersey 08855.

hostility, which may be related to adolescent behavior problems.

(3)   Addressing two of the above issues, Long, Forehand, Fauber, and Brody (1987) found a relationship between parent conflict and child problems when they extended the research to adolescent-aged subjects and compared parent-reported levels of marital conflict with independently observed levels (teacher ratings) of adolescent social and cognitive competence. Forehand and McCombs (1989) then found that not only parent-perceived (particularly mother) but also adolescent-perceived parent conflict was related to levels of adolescent functioning. However, the cross-sectional, self-report nature of the findings leaves questions about the form that this parental conflict takes. As Wierson, Forehand, and McCombs (1988) stated, "Our understanding of the nature of this conflict is currently limited" (p. 708).

(4)   When Forehand and McCombs (1989) administered questionnaires that assessed dimensions of parent conflict, they discovered, somewhat surprisingly, that open, heated arguments, even between highly dissatisfied parents, were rarely reported. The authors speculated that an active component of parent relations was "lingering hostile feelings, which interfere with child/adolescent functioning through inconsistent parenting" (p. 247). Forehand and McCombs went on to suggest:

> It is possible that the conflict that occurs is more subtle than overt, heated arguments. For example, a parent may not have an explosive argument with the other parent but, rather, may criticize and berate him/her in front of the adolescent. Thus . . . there may be an ongoing "negative attitude" about the other parent, occasionally punctuated by arguments, whereas for [other] parents the arguments may occur in the context of a more amiable atmosphere. (p. 248)

(5)   After finding only a low association between observed marital conflict and behavior problems in 4- to 13-year-olds, Reid and Crisafulli (1990) also wondered if some subtler form of marital conflict might account for child behavior problems. To add to the confusion, in another observational study, Henggeler, Edwards, and Borduin (1987) found overt conflict to be *lower* between parents of male adolescent juvenile delinquents than between parents of well-adjusted adolescent males during family negotiations. Another interesting finding, however, was that fathers of delinquents showed significantly more domination over their wives than did fathers of well-adjusted adolescents.

(6)   This domination of one parent over another is reminiscent of Alexander and Parson's (1973) finding that families of delinquents showed less egalitarianism, or greater differences in talktime, than did families of nondelinquents. Alexander and Parsons also found that there was more silence when families of delinquent adolescents engaged in discussions. Perhaps amount of talktime and silence are observable manifestations of the covert marital conflict that Forehand and McCombs (1989) and Reid and Crisafulli (1990) believe is associated with offspring behavior problems.

(7)   Another measure of covert parent conflict that may be associated with adolescent problems is what Gottman and Krokoff (1989) call "withdrawal from interaction." They found that this subtle communication pattern, characterized by the listener's ignoring the speaker, changing the topic, or making an incoherent response, is associated with long-term marital dissatisfaction.

(8)   To examine the hypothesis that adolescent problems are positively associated with both overt and covert forms of parent conflict, the current study compared observed marital interactions in families of adolescents with problems to those in families of adolescents without problems. During a 10-minute problem-solving discussion, the two groups of parents were compared on frequency of overt conflict and four forms of covert conflict — amount of silence, amount of mother talktime, amount of father talktime, and frequency of withdrawal from interaction.

Method

Subjects

(9)   Subjects were sixteen married parents, who, along with sixteen of their adolescent and preadolescent offspring, had been recruited for a previous study. Warren (1986) recruited four of the married couples and their conduct-disordered adolescents and other offspring through the Psychological Clinic of the Graduate School of Applied and Professional Psychology at Rutgers University. The adolescent problem behaviors generally included substance abuse, problems with the law, and difficulties with school and family functioning. The research protocol formed part of the pretreatment evaluation of the families who utilized the professional services provided by the clinic. These families received

a clinical evaluation free of charge for participating in the study.

(10)   Warren (1986) also recruited four comparable married couples with nonproblematic adolescents and preadolescents through Rutgers University support staff personnel. They were invited to the clinic for an assessment session, and were paid $40.00 for their involvement in the study. The nonclinical couples were informed that the purpose of the research was to ascertain how families with adolescents function.

(11)   Clinic and nonclinic families were compared on demographic variables, including family size; age of the oldest child; number, age, and sex of children present for the assessment; and parents' years of education. All families had two parents who were in first marriages, although one clinic couple was in the process of separating. The Mann-Whitney U statistic (two-tailed) showed a significant difference on one demographic variable, age of oldest offspring. The oldest offspring in the clinic group were, on average, older ($U = 0$, $p < .028$). However, since these older offspring (adult children) were less likely to come to the assessment session, the mean ages of offspring at the session did not differ between groups. Clinic fathers included two blue-collar workers, one professional, and one lower level manager; fathers in the nonclinic group were two blue-collar workers, one self-employed retailer, and one industrial salesman. All subjects were white except for one black family. There was no significant difference between the groups regarding family size; number, age, and sex of children present for the assessment; and parents' years of education.

(12)   Family size ranged from 4 to 7 members, with an average of 5. Age of oldest child ranged from 15 to 27 years, with a mean of 16 years in the nonclinic families and 23 years in the clinic families. Average number of children in the study was 2, ranging from 1 to 3. Their ages ranged from 11 to 19 years, with an average age of 15 years. Fifty-six percent of the children were female. Parents' education ranged from 12 to 19 years, with an average of 14.5 years.

Procedure

(13)   Warren (1986) had each couple and their adolescents participate in two structured interaction tasks, videotaping them during the 10 minutes of interaction. The videotapes were reanalyzed for this study. The two tasks were chosen for the high level of interaction they generate, and both have been widely used in research with families. The first task required discussion of a specific current problem which was chosen for each family based on their responses on an issues checklist — a modification of Prinz, Foster, Kent, and O'Leary's (1979) Issues Checklist. It included common areas of parent-adolescent conflict such as "smoking" and "coming home on time." One of the less intense issues that the majority of family members endorsed was selected in order to compare the interactions of clinic and nonclinic families. The problems discussed by families included: adolescents' talking back to parents, homework, use of the telephone, and taking the dog out.

(14)   The second task required the family to plan something they could all do together. The interaction among family members was also videotaped. The interviewer was absent from the room during both interaction tasks.

Observational Measures

(15)   For a previous study, the videotapes of the family interactions were transcribed without identifying information, and divided into discrete utterances or complete grammatical units (Greene, 1989). For the present study, the transcripts were coded by the first author in randomized fashion. Each utterance was examined and coded if it included a form of marital conflict. Only one code was given for each utterance. Each videotape was also viewed with a stopwatch so that silences and parent talktime could be calculated. An advanced clinical psychology student coded 25% of the transcripts, chosen at random, to check for reliability. The measures of marital conflict were: overt conflict, withdrawal from interaction, silence, mother's talktime, and father's talktime.

(16)   *Overt conflict* was coded when a person's utterance was in direct disagreement with the partner's opinion. Overt conflict was defined as conflict between the spouses that was verbally expressed in the form of a contradiction, a misgiving, a criticism, or a sarcastic utterance. Utterances were coded as overt conflict: (a) when spouse A used words like "No," "I disagree," "We cannot do that" in interacting with spouse B, or stated directly that the previous utterance of spouse B was wrong or impossible; (b) when spouse A expressed a misgiving in interacting with spouse B, for example, "We'll see"; (c) when spouse A expressed sarcasm in interacting with spouse B, for example, "Oh, is that what it is?"; (d) when spouse A expressed criticism in interacting with spouse B, for example, "You are off the topic."

(17) *Withdrawal from interaction* was coded when an opposing view was not directly or candidly expressed, the other person's verbal behavior was incompatible with the partner's, or the partner's utterance was disregarded by not responding to a direct request for a response and/or by changing the direction of the interaction. Withdrawal from interaction was thus manifested as an interruption, an implicit contradiction, an inappropriate change of the direction or content of interaction, or when spouses ignored each other. Utterances were coded as withdrawal from interaction: (a) when spouse A interrupted spouse B, the utterance of spouse A was coded; (b) when spouse A ignored the utterance of spouse B by remaining quiet, the next subsequent utterance of spouse A was coded; (c) when spouse A changed the direction or content of interaction following an utterance of spouse B, the utterance of spouse A was coded; (d) when spouse A implicitly contradicted spouse B and an unspoken "no" or "but" could be added to the utterance of spouse A without changing the meaning.

(18) *Silence* refers to the number of seconds during the 10-minute videotape when no one was talking.

(19) *Mother's talktime* refers to the number of seconds during the 10-minute videotape when the wife was talking.

(20) *Father's talktime* refers to the number of seconds during the 10-minute videotape when the father was talking.

(21) The general rules of coding were: (a) when an independent thought (usually in a full sentence) was expressed in two or more utterances, all the utterances were coded separately; (b) when an utterance made sense independently, only that utterance was coded; (c) when the same utterance was repeated, both utterances were coded; (d) when words or sentences were unclear, these were not coded; (e) only verbal behavior was coded; (f) when the same utterance had components of both overt conflict and withdrawal from interaction, the utterance was coded as overt conflict.

Reliability

(22) Interrater reliability on coding was calculated using the following formula: percentage agreement equals total utterances where coders agreed divided by total number of coded utterances. The percentage agreement between coders was calculated for overt conflict (.87), withdrawal from interaction (.81), talktime (.98) and silence (.97).

Results

Overt Conflict

(23) A t test revealed that parents of adolescents with problems exhibited significantly more frequent overt conflict than did parents of adolescents without problems, $t(7) = 2.17$, $p < .05$ (one-tailed). Parents of the clinic adolescents exhibited a mean of 11.25 instances (range of 7-16) of overt conflict during the 10-minute interaction, whereas the parents of the nonclinic adolescents exhibited a mean of only 4 such instances (range of 2-5).

Withdrawal from Interaction

(24) No significant difference was found between clinic and nonclinic parents in withdrawal from interaction. A mean of 13 instances (range of 5-20) was coded for clinic couples, and a mean of 14 instances (range of 9-25) was coded for nonclinic couples.

Silence

(25) A t test revealed that significantly more silence was observed during the clinic family discussions than during the nonclinic family discussions, $t(7) = 1.9$, $p < .05$ (one-tailed). A mean of 46.3 seconds of silence (range of 23-84) occurred during the 10-minute discussion for clinic families, whereas a mean of only 8.5 seconds (range of 0-26) occurred for the nonclinic families.

Mother Talktime

(26) Mothers of clinic adolescents talked during the family discussions for significantly less time than did nonclinic mothers, $t(7) = 1.89$, $p < .05$ (one-tailed). Clinic mothers talked for a mean of 110.3 seconds (range of 68-173), whereas nonclinic mothers talked for a mean of 213 seconds (range of 144-299).

Father Talktime

(27) There was no significant difference between the talktimes of clinic and nonclinic fathers. Clinic fathers talked for a mean of 163 seconds (range of 44–275), and nonclinic fathers for a mean of 163 seconds (range of 91–280).

Discussion

(28) The study supports the widely held notion that adolescent functioning is positively related to parental marital interaction. Parents whose adolescents had

problems exhibited significantly higher rates of marital conflict during family problem-solving discussions than did parents with problem-free adolescents. These findings, which are based upon observed marital interactions in the laboratory in the presence of their adolescents, are consistent with previous findings based on self-report. Further, the current study employed multiple measures of conflict, and found that both overt and covert forms of conflict differentiated parents with and without adolescents experiencing problems.

(29)　A confirming observational study was recently reported by Mann, Borduin, Henggeler. and Blaske (1990). Using a factor analytically derived composite of frequency counts and global ratings, they also found greater overall marital conflict during problem-resolution discussions at home for parents of adolescent delinquents than for other parents of adolescents. Henggeler et al.'s (1987) findings that parents of male delinquents showed less conflict than did parents of well-adjusted adolescents are difficult to reconcile with the present study's findings as well as those by Mann et al. Henggeler et al.'s measure of conflict/hostility appears to be slightly different from Mann et al.'s, but this difference does not seem substantive enough to account for Henggeler et al.'s differing results.

(30)　The microanalytic observation technique employed in the current study has the advantage of providing a precise picture of the nature of the differentiating parental conflict. While heated arguments are rare (Forehand, Wierson, McCombs, Brody, & Fauber, 1989), explicit disagreement between spouses with a troubled adolescent are extremely frequent. The coders recorded a mean of 11.25 instances in 10 minutes. It is not very difficult to imagine that such an atmosphere could have a negative effect on a developing adolescent. Few unified parental messages regarding appropriate behavior could result. As Bry and Krinsley (1990) have shown in a case study, behavioral standards set by one parent are canceled by the other during parental conflict, leaving the adolescent with little parental guidance.

(31)　Adolescent behavioral problems can be seen as the result of ineffective parental influence. Of course, there are many reasons why parents are unsuccessful, but the current study suggests that a high degree of conflict can prevent parents from providing clear, consistent messages that would optimize appropriate behavior. Relatedly, a high degree of conflict can also prevent parents from providing consistent discipline for inappropriate behavior.

(32)　Besides resulting in inconsistent parenting, frequent parent conflict also reduces adolescents' opportunities to observe and practice appropriate interpersonal problem-solving and negotiation skills. Patterson, Dishion, and Bank (1984) found that overly aggressive older boys were rejected by their socially acceptable peers early in their school careers for this behavior. The researchers assume that these boys had difficulty getting along with their peers because they had not learned interpersonal problem-solving and negotiation skills from their parents.

(33)　In the current study, in addition to frequent explicit disagreements, there were also more subtle forms of conflict that differentiated couples who had adolescents with problems from those who did not. One was amount of silence during family discussions. This silence could be due to what Forehand and McCombs (1989) labeled "lingering hostile feelings." Regardless of what caused it, silence during family discussions certainly limits opportunities for family members to reconcile different points of view and to practice problem solving. Silence allows disparate parental guidelines regarding appropriate behavior to remain disparate.

(34)　According to the present results, whereas the talktime of the mothers with troubled adolescents was significantly less than that of mothers with adjusted adolescents, the fathers' mean talktimes were identical. It is not known whether the talktime of the mothers with troubled adolescents was less because of depression, which Forehand, Long, Brody, and Fauber (1986) have shown is related to adolescent problems, or because of withdrawal from interaction, which Gottman and Krokoff (1989) have shown is related to eventual marital dissatisfaction. In this study, the reduced mother talktime did not seem to be due to submission to father domination. Despite the fact that, as a group, the mothers of troubled adolescents talked significantly less than did the other mothers, half of the mothers with troubled adolescents talked more than did their husbands.

(35)　The overall mean father talktime fell between that of the mothers with adolescents having problems and that of the other mothers. The finding that the fathers showed no group difference is consistent with those of studies by Patterson (1980) and Krinsley and Bry (in press). In neither study did fathers whose offspring had problems show substantial differences in communication from fathers whose offspring were adjusted. Patterson (1980) labeled fathers as "guests" in the home. The current findings are also consistent with Gottman and Krokoff's (1989) conclusion that wives serve as managers of conflict in families. If wives and husbands disagree and then the wife falls silent, as our results suggest, then husbands may not respond too much differently than they would if their wives had not fallen silent. Sequential analyses of marital interaction during discussions with their adolescents may shed more light on these results.

(36)   This study's last measure of covert conflict, withdrawal from interaction, did not differentiate couples with and without adolescents experiencing problems. It may be that this subtle form of marital conflict has no implications for adolescent problems, but it may also be that withdrawal from interaction was measured differently in this study than it was in Gottman and Krokoff's (1989) study. Because Gottman and Krokoff found that withdrawal from interaction related to longterm marital dissatisfaction, and because withdrawal from interaction theoretically could undermine positive parental influence on an adolescent's behavior (just as more overt conflict could do), the possible role of parental withdrawal from marital interaction in the etiology of adolescent problems seems worth investigating further.

(37)   Other possible reasons for negative results may be the limitations in the research design. The sample size was small enough to render all results preliminary. The artificiality of laboratory settings is also known to reduce couple conflict below what is seen in homes (Gottman, 1979). In addition, the motivations to participate in the study were inherently not equivalent across the two groups of couples. The couples who brought their adolescent into the clinic may have been more motivated to portray themselves as good parents and their offspring as problematic than were the other parents. Larger samples of marital couples observed in their homes could address the former limitations, whereas only a prospective study might eliminate the latter.

(38)   A prospective study could also tackle another limitation of the current study, namely, the indeterminant directionality of causality. In this study, parent conflict could be the result of adolescent problems instead of the cause, as was hypothesized. Patterson et al. (1984) investigated this question and found that adolescent problems can indeed be predicted prospectively from negative parental communication patterns, among other variables. Patterson (1982) has even shown a dose-response relationship: the greater the amount of parental "nattering" (aversive exchanges), the greater the probability of delinquency. Thus a reasonable interpretation of the present data is that parental conflict plays a causative role in adolescent problems; however, the relationship is probably reciprocal, with adolescent conflict in turn exacerbating already strained marital relations.

(39)   A final possible limitation of this study is the simultaneous use of five t tests. Multiple tests can cause an elevation in Type I error rate. On the other hand, the small sample size substantially reduced the power of the t tests and increased the chance of Type II error. Consequently, all of the results must be seen as preliminary.

(40)   In summary, as has been assumed over the years by family therapists, this study offers evidence that overt and covert conflict is greater in couples whose children develop problems than in couples whose children do not. Although its cross-sectional design allows for the interpretation that the adolescent's problems caused the marital conflict, other research points to the interpretation that marital conflict plays a causal role in adolescent problems. It is plausible that marital conflict prevents parents from providing unified standards of conduct for their teenagers. Marital conflict also could interfere with consistent discipline practices. Finally, a significantly greater amount of silence in family discussions could leave problems unresolved and deprive young people of opportunities to observe successful interpersonal problem solving and negotiation.

References

Alexander, F. J., & Parsons, B. V. (1973). Short-term behavioral intervention with delinquent families: Impact on family process and recidivism. *Journal of Abnormal Psychology, 81,* 219-225.

Bry, B. H., & Krinsley, K. E. (1990). Adolescent substance abuse: A case study. In E. L. Feindler & G. R. Kalfus (Eds.), *Casebook In adolescent behavior therapy* (pp. 275-302). New York: Springer.

Emery, R. E. (1982). Interparental conflict and the children of discord and divorce. *Psychological Bulletin, 92,* 310-330.

Forehand, R., Long, N., Brody, C. H., & Fauber R. (1986). Home predictors of young adolescents' school behavior and academic performance. *Child Development, 57,* 1528-1533.

Forehand, R., & McCombs, A. (1989). The nature of interparental conflict of married and divorced parents: Implications for young adolescents. *Journal of Abnormal Child Psychology, 17,* 235-249.

Forehand, R., Wierson, M., McCombs, A., Brody, G., & Fauber, R. (1989). Interparental conflict and adolescent problem behavior: An examination of mechanisms. *Behaviour Research and Therapy, 27,* 365-371.

Gottman, J. M. (1979). *Marital interaction: Experimental investigations.* New York: Academic Press.

Gottman, J. M., & Krokoff, L. J. (1989). Marital interaction and satisfaction: A longitudinal view. *Journal of Consulting and Clinical Psychology, 57,* 47-52.

Greene, D. M. (1989). *Problem solving in families: A descriptive analysis of solution statements in relation to other verbal behaviors.* Master's thesis. Rutgers University, New Brunswick, NJ.

Henggeler, S. W., Edwards, J., & Borduin, C. M. (1987). The family relations of female juvenile delinquents. *Journal of Abnormal Child Psychology, 15,* 199-209.

Krinsley, K. E., & Bry, B. H. (in press). Sequential analyses of adolescent, mother and father behaviors in distressed and nondistressed families. *Child & Family Behavior Therapy.*

Long, N., Forehand, R., Fauber, R., & Brody, G. H. (1987). Self-perceived and independently observed competence of young adolescents as a function of parental marital conflict and recent divorce. *Journal of Abnormal Child Psychology, 15,* 15-27.

Mann, B. J., Borduin, C. M., Henggeler, S. W., & Blaske, D. M. (1990). An investigation of systemic conceptualizations of parent-child coalitions and symptom change. *Journal of Consulting and Clinical Psychology, 58,* 336-344.

Minuchin, S. N. (1974). *Families and family therapy.* Cambridge, MA: Harvard University Press.

Patterson, G. R. (1980). Mothers: The unacknowledged victims. *Monographs of the Society for Research in Child Development, 45* (5, Serial No. 186).

Patterson, G. R. (1982). *Coercive family process.* Eugene, OR: Castalia Publishing.

Patterson, G. R., Dishion, T. J., & Bank, L. (1984). Family interaction: A process model of deviancy training. *Aggressive Behavior, 10,* 253-267.

Prinz, R. J., Foster, S., Kent, R. N., & O'Leary, K. (1979). Multivariate assessment of conflict in distressed and nondistressed mother-adolescent dyads. *Journal of Applied Behavior Analysis, 12,* 691-700.

Reid, W. J., & Crisafulli, A. (1990). Marital discord and child behavior problems: A meta-analysis. *Journal of Abnormal Child Psychology, 18,* 105-117.

Shaw, D. S., & Emery, R. E. (1987). Parental conflict and other correlates of adjustment of school-age children whose parents have separated. *Journal of Abnormal Child Psychology, 15,* 269-281.

Warren, C. S. (1986). *Comparing cohesion and adaptability in clinic and nonclinic families with adolescents using observational and self-report methods.*

Master's thesis, Rutgers University, New Brunswick, NJ.

Wierson, M., Forehand, R., & McCombs, A. (1988). The relationship of early adolescent functioning to parent-reported and adolescent-perceived interparental conflict. *Journal of Abnormal Child Psychology, 16,* 707-718.

Factual Questions

1. What warnings do literature reviews make regarding conclusions about the relationship between marital discord and adolescent behavior problems?

2. How many parents participated in this study? how many children? how many families?

3. On what one characteristic did clinic and nonclinic families significantly differ? Did clinic and nonclinic families significantly differ on average age of children present for the assessment?

4. What two tasks were parents and their children asked to do?

5. Was the researcher in the room when the family discussions occurred?

6. How was overt conflict coded?

7. What was the agreement percentage between coders for overt conflict and withdrawal from interaction?

8. On which variables were there significant differences between clinic and nonclinic families?

Questions for Discussion

9. Does the introduction provide a clear notion of the research problem, the purpose of the research, and its significance?

10. Does the literature review seem relevant to the research problem?

11. Is the number of research subjects sufficient? To what population would you generalize the results of this study?

12. Is it legitimate to "reuse" the videotapes of a prior study's subjects for the purpose of another study?

13. Is there enough information on the research instruments and procedures to allow you to replicate this study?

14. Paragraph 15 states that the first author coded the transcripts in a randomized fashion. Why was it done in a randomized fashion?

15. Do the research instruments and procedures have adequate reliability and validity?

16. Does the analysis include sufficient statistical information? Are the statistics that are used appropriate?

17. Are the conclusions supported by and do they logically follow from the data that have been presented?

18. Are the findings discussed in terms of their implications and/or practical significance?

19. Why can't we conclude from this study that parental conflict "causes" adolescent behavior problems?

Notes:

Differences in Male and Female Patterns of Communication in Groups: A Methodological Artifact?

Susan A. Wheelan
Anthony F. Verdi
Temple University

This study investigated communication patterns in an all-male, all-female, and mixed-sex group. All participants were white and middle class. These groups met for longer periods of time than those in most previous studies that reported differences between men and women in task and maintenance communication patterns. Most previous research investigations were based on groups that met for an hour or less and used unacquainted undergraduates. In this study, no significant differences were found in seven categories of verbal input. While there were no significant differences, the typical pattern reported in the literature was present in the first 30-60 minutes of the groups. After that time period, no consistent patterns were noted, and stereotypic sex differences vanished. This has led the authors to tentatively conclude that the findings of previous research may be due to the limited time period used in most investigations. Men and women did not differ on task and maintenance input, or other categories of verbal input, in groups meeting for 4 ½ hours or 6 hours.

(1)   The purpose of this research was to investigate the effects of gender composition on communication patterns in groups. In 1956, Strodtbeck and Mann studied 12 mixed-sex groups to determine whether there were significant differences in the quantity and content of the verbal contributions of men and women. The 12 subjects in each group were obtained from lists of potential jurists. Each group's task was to listen to a recorded trial, deliberate the guilt or innocence of the defendant, and return a verdict. The deliberations were tape-recorded and later coded using Bales' (1950) system of Interaction Process Analysis. Findings of that study included the fact that the total activity rate of men was significantly higher than women. Also, men were significantly overrepresented in Bales' task categories. Women, on the other hand, contributed significantly more social-emotional, or maintenance, statements than men.

(2)   Task statements are those that contribute to group goal achievement such as giving suggestions, opinions, or information, or requesting these types of information from others. Social-emotional or maintenance statements are those that contribute to the affective life of the group such as agreeing, helping, supporting, and the like (Bales, 1950, 1970). According to Bales' theoretical model, both task and maintenance statements are necessary to adequate group functioning.

Task input is essential to goal achievement and maintenance input facilitates a supportive climate in which group members can work.

(3)   Since the publication of Strodtbeck and Mann's (1956) study, a large number of similar studies have been conducted to explore this area further. Twenty-eight studies were located that investigated whether women or men contributed more task statements in groups. Of these, 19 concluded that men contributed significantly more task statements than women in mixed or homogeneous groups (Bartol & Butterfield, 1976; Crocker & McGraw, 1984; Denmark, 1977; Ellis & McCallister, 1980; Eskilson & Wiley, 1976; Forsyth, Schlenker, Leary, & McCowen, 1985; Geis, Brown, Jennings & Corrado-Taylor, 1984; Geis, Boston, & Hoffman, 1985; Greene, Morrison, & Tischler, 1981; Hare, 1976; Lockheed, 1975; Lockheed & Hall, 1976; Mabry, 1985; Nemeth, Endicott, & Wachtler, 1976; Piliavin & Rosemann Martin, 1978; Stein & Heller, 1983; Stitt, Schmidt, Pierce, & Kipnis, 1983; Strodtbeck & Mann, 1956; Sturm, 1989). Nine investigations, however, reported no differences between men and women in task input (Bartol & Wortman, 1979; Chapman, 1975; Helmich, 1974; Hoffman & Maier, 1961; Jacobson & Effertz, 1974; Kerr & Sullaway, 1983; Maier, 1970; Wexley & Hunt, 1974; Wheelan, 1974).

(4)   Meta-analyses conducted by Wood (1987) and another by Eagly and Karau (1991) support differences in male vs. female interaction styles. These studies also concluded that men were typically more task oriented than women, who maintained more socially facilitative behaviors.

(5)   Twenty studies were located that investigated whether men or women in mixed or homogeneous groups contributed more maintenance statements. Sixteen reported that women contributed significantly more maintenance input than men (Bartol & Butterfield, 1976; Borgatta & Stimson, 1963; Ellis & McCallister, 1980; Eskilson & Wiley, 1976; Forsyth et al., 1985; Geis et al., 1984; Hare, 1976; Jago & Vroom, 1982; Lockheed & Hall, 1976; Mabry, 1985; Piliavin & Rosemann-Martin, 1978; Strodtbeck & Mann, 1956; Sturm, 1989; Tower, 1979; Wexley & Hunt, 1974; Wheelan, 1974). Only four studies reported no sex difference in maintenance input (Chapman, 1975; Helmich, 1974; Nemeth et al., 1976; Stitt et al., 1983).

(6)   Given the evidence, a general conclusion regarding sex differences has emerged. This conclusion is exemplified by a statement in a recent textbook on group dynamics. In that work, Forsyth (1990) states that "despite the many changes in perceptions of women and men during the years . . ., men still tend to be task oriented, whereas women are still friendlier and more personally oriented" (p. 245).

(7)   While Bales (1950, 1970) concluded that both task and maintenance input are necessary to adequate group functioning, leadership has been very consistently associated with task input as opposed to maintenance input (Aries, 1976; Eskilson & Wiley, 1976; Geis et al., 1985; Hare, 1976; Lockheed & Hall, 1976; Nemeth et al., 1976; Strodtbeck et al., 1957). This is thought to explain why men are more likely to be perceived as leaders in groups. Thus, differences between women and men in verbal contributions to group discussion have provided, albeit inadvertently, a scientific rationale for the continuing dearth of female leaders at all levels of American society. The small number of female leaders may not be due to prevailing sexist views. Rather, the behavior of women themselves can be viewed as causal. Given that such a conclusion has serious political and economic ramifications in the lives of real people, continuing study seems warranted.

(8)   While the presence of sex differences in the type and quantity of communication in same-sex and mixed-sex groups has gained wide acceptance, it may be that this conclusion is due to the methodologies employed rather than to actual differences between the sexes. The majority of studies in this area were based on observations of groups that met one time only. Studies that investigate types of verbal communication of men and women in groups that meet for longer time periods may conclude differently. Given what is known about the beginning phases of a group's development, and the issues the group experiences surrounding dependency and anxiety, it seems reasonable that the beginning time periods may be confounded by these central issues. Consequently, researchers' conclusions about the verbal behavior of men and women in short-lived groups may not be substantiated in groups that meet for longer periods of time. Extended interaction time could change members' experiences of gender. Brown (1979) suggests that socialization may modify views of sex role stereotypes. Eagly (1987) and Eagly and Wood (1982) suggest similar explanations for this change.

(9)   Since studies of the relationship of gender composition on patterns of verbal input over an extended period of time are nonexistent in the literature, and conclusions regarding the respective behavior of men and women in groups are based on limited samples of those behaviors, it seemed warranted to investigate groups which meet for longer time periods.

(10)   The purpose of this descriptive study, then, was to investigate the types of verbal contributions made by men and women over time in groups. Specifically, the research asked whether differences existed in the types of verbal input contributed by women and men in same-sex groups during progressive phases of group life.

Method

Setting and Participants

(11)   A Group Relations Conference held in 1988 provided the context for this study. The conference was designed to provide participants with the opportunity to study group and organizational dynamics experientially. The common task outlined in the conference brochure was "to explore group and organizational processes and issues encountered in the exercise of authority and responsibility as these affect the ability of men and women to work together." The conference was chosen as the context for this study since participation was voluntary, conference members were adults of both sexes, the conference design included the opportunity to study same-sex and mixed-sex groups, and groups met from a minimum of 4 1/2 hours to a maximum of 7 1/2 hours.

(12)   There were 27 active members who attended this four-day conference. Their ages ranged from 24 to 58 years. Members were administrators or professionals in business, government, education, health, ministry, social service, and/or graduate students in social sciences. Twenty-one members (14 women and 7 men) were participants. Six members (3 men and 3 women) comprised the conference staff. In this conference, all members and staff were middle-class white Americans of European extraction.

(13)   There were many different group events during the four days. This study, however, focused on three specific groups. An all-female group composed of the 14 female participants and 3 female staff, an all-male group of 7 male participants and 3 male staff, and a mixed-sex group containing 17 females and 10 males were used in this analysis. The homogeneous groups met for three sessions of 90 minutes each. The mixed-sex group met for four sessions of 90 minutes each. Sessions were spread out across the four days of the conference. The task of the groups was the same as the task outlined above.

Data Collection

(14)   Each group session was audiotaped. Next the tapes were transcribed verbatim. Transcripts identified speaker and content. To ensure accuracy, transcripts were rechecked by another researcher. Once the transcription process was accomplished, every complete thought in the transcripts was identified. Complete thoughts, the units of analysis in this study, are communications or indications that are understood as simple statements (Bales, 1970). There were a total of 3627 units in the three sessions of the women's group. The men's group total was 3941 and the mixed-group contained 3960 complete thoughts.

(15)   Two raters were trained in the use of a coding system that placed each complete thought into one of seven categories. Transcripts were divided into units and coded accordingly. Data were tabulated and condensed to facilitate analysis. Descriptive statistics and repeated measures multiple analysis of variance were used to analyze the obtained data.

(16)   The category system was based on the work of Bion (1961), and extended by Thelen (1954), and Stock and Thelen (1958). The seven categories of the Group Development Observation System are described and illustrated briefly here.

(17)   *Dependency Statements.* Dependency statements are those that show an inclination to conform with the dominant mood of the group, to proceed along established lines, and to follow suggestions made by the leader. Generally, dependency statements demonstrate a desire for direction from others or to seek approval from the leader. Statements can communicate tentativeness or vulnerability.

> What should we do next?
> We are not supposed to do it that way.
> The leader wants us to sit in these chairs.
> Are we doing a good job?
> Is it OK to do it this way?
> I don't know where we should go from here.
> I'm tired.

(18)   *Counterdependency Statements.* Counterdependency statements are those that assert independence from and rejection of leadership, authority, or a member's attempts to lead. These statements communicate in a direction away from formal authority, and suggest a new direction for the group. These statements may suggest that the group do something or support a position

that is counter to the leadership or established structure of the group.

> Let's do it our way for a change.
> The leader is useless.
> Who cares what he thinks?
> We are better trained than the leader.
> I will not do it that way.
> We can meet for 40 minutes instead of the usual hour.

(19)   *Fight Statements.* Fight statements are those that convey participation in a struggle to overcome someone or something, and imply argumentativeness, criticism, or aggression. Statements are confrontations, show disagreement, and support conflict. Direct challenges and accusations are fight statements.

> I don't agree with you.
> You have too much to say at these meetings.
> What makes you think you are so smart?
> Show me the evidence to support that ridiculous statement.
> Maybe you should try to be on time for a change.
> I can't accept your behavior.
> I want to see him *fry*.

(20)   *Flight Statements.* Flight statements are those that indicate avoidance of task, and confrontation. They may take form as jokes, fantasies, or hypotheticals. Simply, flight statements are any statements that are irrelevant to the task of the group. In this manner, statements may be true, accurate, and valuable in another group context, but have nothing to do with the task of the present group. Flight statements are dependent on the task of the group. In a group whose task is to develop a budget policy, the following statements would be flight statements.

> Did you see the game last night?
> On a brighter note, what are you doing this weekend?
> Did I tell you I was going on vacation?
> Suppose you had hired Tom before you hired Gary?
> Guess what happened on the way to work today.
> How are the kids?

(21)   *Pairing Statements.* Pairing statements are those that include expressions of warmth, friendship, support, or intimacy with others. These statements show solidarity, suggest agreement, assistance, or reward. Statements may take form as greetings, reflectives, or as simple acknowledgments that communicate that the speaker is being heard and understood. Pairing statements are similar to maintenance statements as outlined by Bales (1950).

> I agree with you.

> Can we help you to feel better about yourself today?
> We are really a great team.
> Do you know what I am saying?
> What I hear you saying is . . .
> I like your shoes.

(22)   *Counterpairing Statements.* Counterpairing statements are those that indicate an avoidance of intimacy and connection, and a desire to keep the discussion distant and intellectual. These statements communicate disconnection, withdrawal, or resistance to form a relationship.

> I am not following you today.
> What you are saying really bothers me.
> I don't like anyone in this group.
> I have more experience than anyone here.
> I can't say what I really think about this place.
> The sooner we end this discussion the better off we will be.
> I will not be able to help you because that is not my responsibility.

(23)   *Work Statements.* Work statements are those that represent purposeful, goal-directed activity and task-directed efforts. They are direct, reality bound, and problem solving. They represent attempts to understand and cognitize group processes, task, and structure, and are directly related to the task. The task of each group is defined before the group begins to interact. Therefore, discussion about an issue not defined as the group's task may meet the criteria of a work statement; however, the statement must be relevant to the task of the group as defined by its task. In a group whose task is to evaluate a client's misconduct, the following statements would be work statements:

> This employee works in the billing department.
> What is our policy on absenteeism?
> The procedure for dealing with this situation is outlined here.
> We can write an accurate evaluation with this information.
> We have until 11 o'clock to come up with a decision.
> The penalty for this behavior is termination.

Results

(24)   Data from the coding process were tabulated to answer the following question:

(25)   Do differences exist in the types of verbal input contributed by women and men in same-sex and mixed-sex groups during progressive phases of group life?

Table I. Percentage of Each Verbal Category by Group Type

Group category[a]		Time segment								
		1	2	3	4	5	6	7	8	9
M	D	6.2	7.8	8.5	5.3	5.1	10.7	8.6	5.4	3.8
W	D	7.7	10.1	4.7	6.4	3.9	4.9	8.0	4.8	5.8
Mx	D	9.5	13.4	9.6	9.7	9.7	4.2	6.6	2.4	5.8
Mx*	D	13.7	10.6	9.6	7.8	7.6	1.9	4.9	4.2	2.2
M	CD	1.9	5.8	5.0	3.6	0.7	0.4	7.9	2.6	0.3
W	CD	1.8	7.8	0.3	1.4	1.0	3.8	2.0	1.7	1.2
Mx	CD	7.9	14.4	6.7	1.6	2.7	1.1	7.0	0.3	1.2
Mx*	CD	5.3	12.7	1.8	2.5	5.3	2.4	1.1	0.0	0.2
M	Fi	1.0	7.4	0.3	4.8	2.0	4.9	1.7	9.7	13.8
W	Fi	1.6	6.6	5.9	1.6	4.7	0.4	4.0	4.4	4.4
Mx	Fi	3.2	7.3	3.2	10.4	6.0	12.6	5.3	19.1	0.7
Mx*	Fi	2.6	5.2	10.1	8.0	7.6	16.6	1.1	1.2	7.2
M	FL	50.4	24.9	39.2	36.0	44.4	4.4	32.8	15.7	37.2
W	FL	56.5	19.8	27.1	41.4	17.6	22.0	24.9	38.1	17.7
Mx	FL	30.2	16.5	14.2	24.1	34.5	4.8	30.6	34.1	36.0
Mx*	FL	28.6	13.2	23.9	28.1	22.9	30.1	54.7	49.9	29.6
M	P	14.9	19.9	15.0	13.2	21.1	19.1	18.9	16.7	15.3
W	P	18.4	12.3	20.6	17.4	20.7	20.6	15.1	7.8	10.2
Mx	P	10.3	13.6	27.8	12.3	16.8	13.2	14.5	8.5	0.8
Mx*	P	9.3	22.4	11.4	15.8	15.5	8.7	10.9	4.9	23.9
M	CP	0.3	4.0	0.0	3.2	5.1	6.8	6.9	4.5	4.4
W	CP	3.4	5.9	5.6	6.3	7.1	7.7	7.4	0.3	1.2
Mx	CP	4.0	2.1	3.2	7.0	4.7	8.1	2.4	0.0	0.0
Mx*	CP	0.9	1.3	13.1	6.4	2.5	0.0	0.0	7.2	3.1
M	W	23.3	28.8	30.4	33.0	20.2	51.6	21.7	44.0	24.3
W	W	9.1	36.3	32.4	24.0	42.9	35.9	37.1	42.5	58.8
Mx	W	24.6	25.6	30.6	30.2	18.3	52.4	28.8	27.3	33.8
Mx*	W	31.3	26.9	25.2	25.1	35.2	32.8	19.1	67.7	28.6

[a]Mx: 30-minute intervals; Mx*: 40-minute intervals.

Table II. Mean Number of Thought Units per Participant by Sex and Group Type

	Homogenous group		Mixed group	
	Mean	SD	Mean	SD
Male	6.10	5.40	2.50	2.50
Female	3.45	2.60	2.08	2.21

(26)   Of the 11,528 units coded, the percentage of unscorable units was 3.13%. These unscored units were either unintelligible or unsuitable for coding. Interrater reliability for the entire coding process averaged 0.93. The three 90-minute sessions (270 minutes total) of the men's and women's groups were each divided into 9 intervals of 30 minutes each. The four 90-minute sessions of the mixed group were divided into twelve 30-minute segments. Due to the differing length of the mixed group, it was necessary to also divide this group into nine intervals of 40 minutes each for certain analyses. This was done to facilitate statistical analysis and also to allow comparison of comparable stages in the groups' development.

(27)   The proportion of Dependency (D), Counterdependency (CD), Fight (Fi), Flight (Fl), Pairing (P), Counterpairing (CP), and Work (W) for each interval was tabulated for each of the three groups. Percentages are used in this analysis to facilitate description of the categories in relation to each other and to take into account the differences among the groups in total verbal units. Results are displayed in Table I.

Table III. Repeated Measures MANOVA on Large and Middle Groups by Sex, Size, Time Segment, and Verbal Category

	F	df	Significance[a]
Main effect			
Sex	1.71	1,25	ns
Size	27.88	1,25	.000[a]
Segment	.40	2,50	ns
Category	21.02	6,150	.000[a]
Two-way interactions			
Sex by size	5.82	1,25	.024[a]
Sex by segment	.38	2,50	ns
Sex by category	1.40	6,150	ns
Size by segment	1.15	2,50	ns
Size by category	14.30	6,150	.000[a]
Segment by category	1.88	12,300	.036[a]
Three-way interactions			
Sex by size by segment	.66	2,50	ns
Sex by size by category	1.25	12,300	ns
Size by segment by category	4.32	12,300	.000[a]
Four-way interactions			
Sex by size by segment by category	.98	12,300	ns

[a] $p \le .05$.

Table IV. Total Percentage of Each Verbal Category by Group Type

Group	D	CD	Fi	FL	P	CP	W
M	6.57	3.27	4.74	33.80	17.18	3.74	29.23
W	6.34	2.29	3.63	30.14	16.07	5.02	34.06
Mx	6.79	3.66	7.15	29.34	14.62	4.19	28.16

(28)   The total number of thought units per partici-pant was subjected to a repeated-measures multivariate analysis of variance (MANOVA). A four-way analysis of variance tested for main and interaction effects for Sex (Male or Female), Size (Large vs. Middle), Time Segment (I, II, or III), and Verbal Category (D, CD, P, CP, Fi, Fl, W).

(29)   A repeated-measures analysis of variance re-vealed no significant differences between the men's and women's group. Significant differences were noted be-tween the homogeneous groups and the heterogeneous group (see Tables II and III). Also, no differences were noted between the verbal behavior of women and men in the homogeneous groups vs. the mixed group. The differences between the same-sex groups and the mixed-sex group may be due to the fact that the mixed group is larger in size. Further support for this conclu-sion can be seen in the following *t*-test results. Men produced more verbal output in the smaller all-male group than they did in the larger mixed-sex group ($t = 3.28$, $df = 9$, $p = .01$). Similarly, women also produced more verbal output in the smaller all-female group than they did in the larger mixed-sex group ($t = 4.08$, $df = 16$, $p = .001$). No difference was found, however, be-tween the verbal output of women and men in the mixed-sex group ($t = .41$, $df = 25$, $p = .682$).

(30)   While no significant differences were found between the all-male and all-female group, the descrip-tive analysis proved informative. The pattern of male and female communication reported in previous studies suggests that females should have higher percentages overall of dependency and pairing statements. Pairing, in this coding system, is the equivalent of maintenance or social-emotional statements described in previous re-search. Males, on the other hand, should have a higher overall percentage of work statements. This prediction is not supported in this study (see Table IV).

(31)   It is of interest to note, however, that women do exceed men in the proportion of dependency state-ments in the first and second intervals of the same-sex groups (see Table I). They also have a higher propor-tion of pairing statements than men in the first interval.

Men have a much higher percentage of work statements than women in that first interval as well. Beyond the first interval, however, no consistent pattern emerges.

Discussion

(32)   The results of this descriptive study do not sup-port the prevailing view that the types of verbal contri-butions made by men and women in groups vary systematically. The percentages of the various catego-ries of verbal input do differ significantly between the mixed-sex group and the same-sex groups. However, it appears that those differences are due to group size rather than gender composition. The verbal contribu-tions of both men and women decrease in the larger mixed group. This finding is consistent with studies demonstrating that as size increases, the average group member's contribution decreases (Albanese & Van Fleet, 1985; Renzulli, Owen, & Callahan, 1974).

(33)   This study's results differ markedly from the majority of findings regarding the verbal behavior of men and women in group settings. However, as was mentioned earlier, most previous research did not look at the verbal input of men and women over time. In-stead, many studies have limited their analyses to one session of 30-60 minutes. If this study had employed a similar methodology, it, too, would be reporting that men are more task-oriented and women more maintenance-oriented in group discussions. During the first of the nine 30-minute intervals, the results of this study are consistent with the majority of previous re-search that supports task-oriented communication pat-terns for men and socioemotional communication patterns for women. However, after that first time pe-riod, no clear pattern is evident between the sexes and no significant differences were noted overall.

(34)   There are many reasons that may explain these two contrasting conclusions. Since the beginning phases of group development are characterized by is-sues of dependency where members are anxious and struggling to form, it seems reasonable that the begin-ning time periods of previously investigated groups may reflect the participants needs to control individual and

group anxiety. In this attempt, individuals respond in ways that are most familiar, and consequently assume traditional sex roles. Members in this initial period may be more responsive to personal attributes in relation to sociocultural roles of "male" and "female." Thus the initial anxiety of formation is managed by the participants' assumption of these socialized roles (Lockheed & Hall, 1976; Fennel, Barchas, Cohen, McMahon, & Hildebrand, 1978; Meeker & Weitzel-O'Neill, 1977; Thune, Manderscheid, & Silbergeld, 1980).

(35)   These differences may also be explained by the participants' response to status and situational demands rather than personal factors such as male and female. Members act and respond in ways that reflect expectations for normatively defined behavior. Members are immediately aware of gender, aware of the normative expectations associated with gender, and what is accepted and what is not. Given this awareness, compliance and noncompliance with these expectations is respectively rewarded or rebuked (Meeker & Weitzel-O'Neill, 1977).

(36)   The additional time period of the group's life could change members' experiences of gender. Brown (1979) suggests that socialization may modify views of sex role stereotypes. Members in this study engaged in a socializing process that may have modified sex role stereotypes, status, and expectations. As men and women experienced each other in roles that were not gender stereotyped, the expectations of sex-typed behavior became less apparent. Eagly (1987) and Eagly and Wood (1982) suggest similar explanations for this change.

(37)   Also, since a number of investigations were conducted in laboratory settings, the generalizability of such results to more naturally occurring groups could be questioned. The groups used in this study represented a temporary society, and not a laboratory setting. In experimental settings, sex differences are widely reported (Wood, 1987; Dobbins & Platz, 1986). A meta-analysis by Eagly and Johnson (1990) found male and female differences in laboratory settings, but concluded that female and male leadership styles did not differ in organizational field studies.

(38)   A possible confound between the effects of time and the effects of the type of participants studied presents a conceptual problem in this research. While this study cannot resolve this issue, it is prudent to address it so that future researchers may take it into account.

(39)   Previous research that investigated one-time meetings and short discussions by a random sample of undergraduates found task-maintenance sex differences. Other field research studies using samples of professional men and women have found smaller or no such sex differences. Therefore, are these differences accounted for by the length of time the participants interact, or are they due to the fact that in the population in general, as represented by undergraduates, sex differences exist? Are undergraduates more inclined to adhere to societal norms surrounding gender, or are they not yet experienced in more androgynous circumstances? Perhaps in a subpopulation of self-selected men and women who are professionals and managers by occupation, no such differences exist. In a parallel thought, are individuals who elect to take part in a university-sponsored group relations conference whose task is "to explore group and organizational processes . . . as these affect the ability of men and women to work together . . .," likewise unaffected by gender differences? This same subpopulation may never have differed even as undergraduates, or perhaps they differed as undergraduates and later, because of role requirements of their work positions, developed similar effective styles of task and socioemotional emphasis. The present study cannot address this confound because its participants were also professionals and managers.

(40)   Other possible confounds worth consideration concern real vs. statistical differences, as well as group size. The repeated-measures analysis of variance revealed no significant effect for Sex in the amount of contributions overall. However, significant differences were found for Size (Table III). The t test showed no significant difference between men and women in the mixed-sex group. Men, however, contributed an average of 6 thoughts each in the all-male group, compared to women who contributed only 3 1/2 each in the all-female group (Table II). Similarly, in the mixed-sex group, men averaged 2 1/2 thoughts, and women averaged only 2 thoughts. These differences were not statistically significant because sample size ($df = 1, 25$) was small. The group size variable can account for this effect. Speaking rates per person decrease as group size increases. The smallest group ($n = 10$) was the all-male group. The all-female group was larger ($n = 17$). Thus, while the differences in contributions in the same-sex groups could be a sex difference, it is more likely a group-size difference. The decreased difference in speaking rates between the sexes in the mixed group adds weight to this conclusion.

(41)   This has led the present authors to tentatively conclude that the results of previous research in this

area are due to the methodologies employed. Groups studied over longer periods of time yield very different findings. Of course, studies such as the present one are very time-consuming. This study, for example, has taken two years of concentrated effort due to the labor intensive nature of transcription and coding. However, before general conclusions are reached and taught as fact to a new generation of students, more intensive analyses are indicated. This is especially true in areas that are politically sensitive. In that spirit, the authors do not conclude that these findings are definitive. More studies of this type are needed to confirm or disconfirm these results.

References

Albanese, R., & Van Fleet, D. (1985). Rational behavior in groups: The free-riding tendency. *Academy of Management Review, 10,* 244-255.

Aries, E. (1976). Interaction patterns and themes of male, female, and mixed groups. *Small Group Behavior, 7,* 7-18.

Bales, R. F. (1950). *Interaction process analysis: A method for the study of small groups.* Chicago: The University of Chicago Press.

Bales, R. F. (1970). *Personality and interpersonal behavior.* New York: Holt, Rinehart and Winston.

Bartol, K. M., & Butterfield, D. A. (1976). Sex effects in evaluating leaders. *Journal of Applied Psychology, 61,* 446-454.

Bartol, K. M., & Wortman, M. S. (1979). Sex of leader and subordinate role stress: A field study. *Sex Roles, 5,* 513-518.

Bion, W. (1961). *Experiences in groups.* New York: Basic Books.

Borgatta, E., & Stimson, J. (1963). Sex differences in interaction characteristics. *Journal of Social Psychology, 60,* 89-100.

Brown, S. M. (1979). Male verses female leaders: A comparison of empirical studies. *Sex Roles, 5,* 595-611.

Chapman, J. B. (1975). Comparison of male and female leadership styles. *Academy of Management Journal, 18,* 645-650.

Crocker, J., & McGraw, K. M. (1984). What's good for the goose is not good for the gander. *American Behavioral Scientist Journal, 7,* 357-369.

Denmark, F. L. (1977). Styles of leadership. *Psychology of Women Quarterly, 2,* 99-113.

Dobbins, G. H., & Platz, S. J. (1986). Sex differences in leadership: How real are they? *Academy of Management Review, 11,* 118-127.

Eagly, A. H. (1987). *Sex differences in social behavior: A social-role interpretation.* Hillsdale, NJ: Lawrence Erlbaum Associates.

Eagly, A. H., & Johnson, B. T. (1990). Gender and leadership style: A meta-analysis. *Psychological Bulletin, 108,* 223-256.

Eagly, A. H., & Karau, S. J. (1991). Gender and the emergence of leaders: A meta-analysis. *Journal of Personality and Social Psychology, 60,* 685-710.

Eagly, A. H., & Wood, W. (1982). Inferred sex differences in status as a determinant of gender stereotypes about social influence. *Journal of Personality and Social Psychology, 43,* 915-928.

Ellis, D. G., & McCallister, L. (1980). Relational control sequences and sex-typed and androgynous groups. *Western Journal of Speech Communication, 44,* 35-49.

Eskilson, A., & Wiley, M. (1976). Sex composition and leadership in small groups. *Sociometry, 39,* 183-194.

Fennell, M. L., Barchas, P., Cohen, E., McMahon, A., & Hildebrand, P. (1978). An alternative perspective on sex differences in organizational settings: The process of legitimation. *Sex Roles, 4,* 589-604.

Forsyth, D. R. (1990). *Group dynamics.* (2nd ed.) Pacific Grove, CA: Brooks/Cole.

Forsyth, D. R., Schlenker, B., Leary, M. R., & McCowen, N. E. (1985). Self-presentational determinants of sex differences in leadership behavior. *Small Group Behavior, 16,* 197-210.

Geis, F. L., Boston, M. B., & Hoffman, N. (1985). Sex of authority role models and achievement by men and women: Leadership performance and recognition. *Journal of Personality and Social Psychology, 49,* 636-653.

Geis, F. L., Brown, V., Jennings, J., & Corrado-Taylor, D. (1984). Sex vs. status in sex-associated stereotypes. *Sex Roles, 11,* 771-785.

Greene, L. R., Morrison, T. L., & Tischler, N. G. (1981). Gender and authority: Effects on perception of small group co-leaders. *Small Group Behavior, 12,* 401-413.

Hare, A. P (1976). *Handbook of small group research* (2nd ed.). New York: The Free Press.

Helmich, D. C. (1974). Male and female presidents: Some implications of leadership styles. *Human Resource Management, 13,* 25-26.

Hoffman, L. R., & Maier, N. R. (1961). Sex differences, sex composition, and group problem solving. *Journal of Abnormal and Social Psychology, 63,* 453-456.

Jacobson, M. B., & Effertz, J. (1974). Sex roles and leadership perceptions of the leaders and the led. *Organizational Behavior and Human Performance, 12,* 383-396.

Jago, A. G., & Vroom, V. H. (1982). Sex differences in the incidence and evaluation of participative leader behavior. *Journal of Applied Psychology, 67,* 776-783.

Kerr, N. L., & Sullaway, M. (1983). Group sex composition and member motivation. *Sex Roles, 9,* 403-417.

Lockheed, M. (1975). The modification of female leadership behavior in the presence of males. *Research in Education.* ERIC Document Reproduction Service No. ED 106 742.

Lockheed, M. E., & Hall, K. (1976). Conceptualizing sex as a status characteristic: Applications to leadership training strategies. *Journal of Social Issues, 32,* 111-124.

Mabry, E. A. (1985). The effects of gender composition and task structure on small group interaction. *Small Group Behavior, 16,* 75-96.

Maier, N. (1970). Male versus female discussion leaders. *Personnel Psychology, 23,* 455-461.

Meeker, B. F., & Weitzel-O'Neill, P. A. (1977). Sex roles and interpersonal behavior in task-oriented groups. *American Sociological Review, 42,* 91-105.

Nemeth, C. J., Endicott, J., & Wachtler, J. (1976). From the 50's to the 70's: Women in jury deliberations. *Sociometry, 39,* 293-304.

Piliavin, J. A., & Rosemann-Martin, R. (1978). The effects of the sex composition of groups on style of social interaction. *Sex Roles, 4,* 281-295.

Renzulli, J., Owen, S., & Callahan, C. (1974). Fluency, flexibility and originality as a function of group size. *Journal of Creative Behavior, 8,* 107-113.

Stein, T., & Heller, T. (1983). The relationship of participation rates to leadership status: A meta-analysis. In Blumberg, H., Hare, A. P., Kent, V., & Davies, M. (eds.), *Small groups and social interaction* (Vol. 1). New York: John Wiley & Sons.

Stitt, C., Schmidt, S., Pierce, K., & Kipnis, D. (1983). Sex of leader, leader behavior and subordinate satisfaction. *Sex Roles, 9,* 31-42.

Stock, D., & Thelen, H. A. (1958). *Emotional dynamics and group culture.* New York: New York University Press.

Strodtbeck, F. L., James, R. M., & Hawkins, C. (1957). Social status in jury deliberations. *American Sociological Review, 22,* 713-719.

Strodtbeck, F. L., & Mann, R. D. (1956). Sex role differentiation in jury deliberation. *Sociometry, 19,* 3-11.

Sturm, M. (1989). *Communication patterns in gender homogeneous and heterogeneous groups.* Unpublished dissertation, Temple University, Philadelphia, PA.

Thelen, H. A. (1954). *Dynamics of groups at work.* Chicago: University of Chicago Press.

Thune, E. S., Manderscheid, R. W., & Silbergeld, S. (1980). Status or sex roles as determinants of interaction patterns in small mixed-groups. *The Journal of Social Psychology, 112,* 51-65.

Tower, B. (1979). *Communication patterns of women and men in same-sex and mixed-sex groups.* Unpublished paper, Women's Training and Support Program. 1407 North Front Street, Harrisburg, PA 17102.

Wexley, R. N., & Hunt, P. J. (1974). Male and female leaders: Comparison of performance and behavior patterns. *Psychological Reports, 35,* 867-872.

Wheelan, S. A. (1974). *Sex differences in the functioning of small groups.* Unpublished dissertation, The University of Wisconsin, Madison, WI.

Wood, W. (1987). Meta-analytic review of sex differences in group performance. *Psychological Bulletin, 102,* 53-71.

Factual Questions

1. What are the differences between task statements and social-emotional (maintenance) statements?

2. Of the 28 studies that reported on whether men or women contributed more task statements in small groups, how many concluded that men contributed more? How many concluded that women contributed more? How many concluded that there were no differences?

3. Of the 20 studies that reported on whether men or women contributed more maintenance statements in small groups, how many concluded that men

contributed more? How many concluded that women contributed more? How many concluded that there were no differences?

9. In which of the nine intervals did significant differences appear between the all-male and all-female groups? Describe those differences.

4. Why was the Group Relations Conference selected as the site for a small group study?

10. If this study had limited its observation of groups to one session of 30-60 minutes, what results would it be reporting?

5. How many men and women were in each of the three groups observed for this study? How long did each group meet?

Questions for Discussion

11. Does the introduction provide a clear notion of the research problem, the purpose of the research, and its significance?

6. What is the unit of analysis in this study?

12. Does the literature review seem relevant to the research problem?

7. What are the seven categories in the Group Development Observation System?

13. Is the number of groups studied sufficient? To what population would you generalize the results of this study?

8. Did significant differences exist between the all-female and all-male groups in the overall types of verbal output? Did significant differences exist in the overall types of verbal output for men and for women in the mixed-sex groups?

14. Is there enough information on the research instruments and procedures to allow you to replicate this study?

15. Do the seven categories of the Group Development Observation System represent distinct categories of communication?

16. Do the research instruments and procedures have adequate reliability and validity?

17. Does the analysis include sufficient statistical information? Are the statistics that are used appropriate?

18. Are the conclusions supported by and do they logically follow from the data that have been presented?

19. How do the authors explain why distinct male and female patterns appear during the first 30-60 minutes of group interaction but then disappear?

20. What changes in research design might resolve the confounds noted at the conclusion of the article?

21. Are the findings discussed in terms of their implications and/or practical significance?

Shyness and Sociability:
A Dangerous Combination for Illicit
Substance Use in Adolescent Males?

Randy M. Page

Researchers have hypothesized that behavioral problems are accentuated when a shy person wants to be with other people. This need to be with others — sociability — is a related but separate construct from shyness. The purpose of the present study was to examine the relationship of shyness and sociability to illicit substance use in a sample of 654 male high school students. It was found that, in general, shy male adolescents were significantly more likely to use illicit substances when compared to those who were not shy. Those who were shy and highly sociable were significantly more likely to use hallucinogenic substances than were those who were shy and low to moderate in sociability as well as those who were not shy. Although not significant, there was a trend toward more cocaine and marijuana use among those who were shy and highly sociable. The implications of these findings for those who work with adolescents are discussed.

(1)   According to Cheek and Buss (1981) shyness and sociability are separate constructs, rather than opposing extremes of a bipolar dimension. As a result, they develop independent measures of shyness and sociability. They define shyness as "the discomfort and inhibition that may occur in the presence of others" and sociability as a "preference for affiliation or need to be with people" (p.330). In their study, the two measures of shyness and sociability were negatively correlated ($r = -.30$), suggesting that the two constructs are related, but only moderately. A factor analysis of shyness and sociability items also revealed two distinct factors, indicating that shyness and sociability are separate personality factors.

(2)   As part of their study, Cheek and Buss had pairs of college women interact for five minutes. Shy subjects spent less time talking, averted their gaze more, and engaged in more self-manipulations that indicated nervousness (i.e., touching the body or face with one's hands). Briggs and Smith (1986) commented on this finding:

> . . . the case for separate measures of shyness and sociability was bolstered in that it was individuals scoring high on both shyness and sociability who were rated by observers as being the most interpersonally impaired. Apparently, the behavior problems associated with shyness are accentuated when the shy person also wants to be with other people. (p.55)

(3)   The purpose of the present study was to examine the relationship of shyness and sociability to illicit substance use among adolescent males.

Reprinted with permission from *Adolescence, 25*(100): 803-806. Copyright © 1990 by Libra Publishers, Inc.

Reprint requests to Randy M. Page, Ph.D., Division of Health, Physical Education, Recreation and Dance, University of Idaho, Moscow, Idaho 83843.

Method

(4)   A survey instrument consisting of measures of shyness, sociability, and illicit substance use in the past month was administered to 654 adolescent males during their health classes. These subjects represented ninth to twelfth graders from 14 senior high schools which comprised a representative sample of high schools in a western state. Over 90% of the subjects were white; the average age of respondents was 15.48 years (SD = 2.88).

Instrumentation

(5)   The shyness and sociability scales used in this study were those developed by Cheek and Buss (1981). They reported an alpha coefficient of .79 and a 90-day test-retest correlation of .74 for their shyness scale; no reliability information was provided concerning the sociability scale. See Cheek and Buss (1981) for further discussion of the properties and validation procedures for these scales.

(6)   Subjects also responded to questions which asked how many times they had used the following substances in the past month: cocaine; marijuana or hashish; and LSD, PCP, mescaline, or other hallucinogens. An index of illicit substance use was formed by summing the number of times a subject had used an illicit substance in the past month.

Data Analysis

(7)   Subjects scoring above the 70th percentile were placed in the shy group. Likewise, those scoring above the 70th percentile on the sociability scale were placed in the high-sociability group. Two-way ANOVA tests were computed to determine the main effects of shyness and sociability on illicit substance use. Interaction effects between shyness (unshy and shy) and sociability (low to moderate sociability and high sociability) also were computed.

Results

(8)   The main effects of shyness revealed significantly higher use of illicit substances among shy males than unshy males, with the exception of hallucinogenic substances (see Table 1). Significant shyness main effects were observed for cocaine, $F(1, 653) = 4.50$, $p = .0342$, and marijuana or hashish use, $F(1, 653) = 5.56$, $p = .0187$. In addition, the main effect of shyness on the illicit substance use index was significant, $F(1, 653) = 6.75$, $p = .0096$. The shyness main effect for hallucinogenic substances approached significance, $F(1, 653) = 3.05$, $p = .0812$.

(9)   None of the sociability main effects were significant. The only significant shyness by sociability interaction effect was for hallucinogenic substances, $F(1, 653) = 12.07$, $p = .0005$. However, an examination of the group means in Table 2 suggests that adolescent males in the high shyness–high sociability group were slightly more likely to use illicit substances than were the other groups.

Discussion

(10)   Shyness appears to be an important risk factor in illicit substance use among adolescent males. One explanation for this may be that shy males turn to proactive substances in an effort to alleviate their social discomfort and inhibition.

(11)   This study provides some evidence that the combination of shyness and high sociability increases the likelihood of illicit substance use among males. Within this sample, shyness and high sociability was found to be associated with increased use of hallucinogenic substances. There also was limited evidence suggesting that these two factors in combination may increase the risk of cocaine and marijuana use. These findings are consistent with research by Cheek and Buss (1981), that those who score high on both of these measures are the most interpersonally impaired. Perhaps the use of illicit drugs, as well as other adolescent problem behaviors, is a function of this form of impairment.

Table 1. Mean Illicit Substance Use — Shy versus Unshy (times used per month)

	Cocaine	Marijuana	Hallucinogens	Index
Shy	0.35	2.19	0.17	2.72
Unshy	0.10	0.90	0.06	1.06

n = 654

Table 2. Mean Illicit Substance Use — Shyness/Sociability Category (times used per month)

	Cocaine	Marijuana	Hallucinogens	Index
Shy and high sociability	0.40	3.40	0.64	4.44
Shy and low to moderate sociability	0.34	1.98	0.09	2.42
Unshy and high sociability	0.02	0.65	0.02	0.71
Unshy and low to moderate sociability	0.12	0.97	0.07	1.16

Shy and high sociability n = 25, Shy and low to moderate sociability n = 144, Unshy and high sociability n = 107, Unshy and low to moderate sociability n = 378

(12)   These findings have important implications for professionals who work with adolescents. It seems that early recognition and treatment of shyness, particularly when found in combination with high sociability, may be an important component of substance abuse prevention programs. Further, those who provide substance abuse treatment services to adolescents may also find it helpful to incorporate strategies that focus upon these personality factors. To date, these have largely been ignored as factors in the etiology, prevention, and treatment of substance abuse among adolescents and children.

(13)   Additional research, particularly among other adolescent groups, is needed to verify and extend these findings. It seems clear that shyness, and perhaps sociability, is associated with the use of illicit substances among adolescents. Future research should seek to define the role that these characteristics play in determining illicit substance use, and perhaps other adolescent problem behaviors as well.

References

Briggs, S. R., & Smith, T. G. (1986). The measurement of shyness. In W. H. Jones, J. M. Cheek, & S. R. Briggs (Eds.), *Shyness: Perspectives on research and treatment*. New York: Plenum Press.

Cheek, J. M., & Buss, A. H. (1981). Shyness and sociability. *Journal of Personality and Social Psychology, 41*, 330-339.

Factual Questions

1. How is shyness defined?

2. How is sociability defined?

3. What is the study's purpose?

4. How many research subjects were used?

5. What was the average age of the respondents?

6. How was the index of illicit substance use formed?

11. Does the introduction provide a clear notion of the research problem, the purpose of the research, and its significance?

7. Which subjects were classified as shy? Which subjects were placed in the high-sociability group?

12. Does the literature review seem relevant to the research problem?

8. Shy subjects were significantly more likely than non-shy subjects to use which illicit substances?

13. Is the number of research subjects sufficient? To what population would you generalize the results of this study?

9. Looking just at the effects of sociability, were there any illicit substances which high sociability subjects used significantly more often than non-high sociability subjects?

14. Is there enough information on the research instruments and procedures to allow you to replicate this study?

10. Subjects who were both shy and highly sociable were significantly more likely than other subjects to use which illicit substances?

15. Do the research instruments and procedures have adequate reliability and validity?

16. Does the analysis include sufficient statistical information? Are the statistics that are used appropriate?

17. Are the conclusions supported by and do they logically follow from the data that have been presented?

18. Since there is a statistical relationship between shyness and illicit substance use, can we be certain that shyness is the cause of the illicit substance use?

19. Are the findings discussed in terms of their implications and/or practical significance?

Notes:

Article 13

A Role Perception Study of School Social Work Practice

Marlys Staudt

A study conducted in an intermediary educational agency examined principals' and special education teachers' perceptions of actual and ideal performance of school social work tasks. Those services seen as provided most frequently are directed toward individuals. Although respondents want these services to continue, they also want more group work services. The study contained several recommendations, including one for the development of individualized building service plans and another on the development of a screening process for special education assessments.

(1)   Since the landmark study of Costin (1969), a number of national, state, and local studies have further clarified and determined the evolving role and current tasks of the school social worker (Alderson & Krishef, 1973; Chavkin, 1985; Lambert & Mullaly, 1982; Lee, 1987; Meares, 1977; Timberlake, Sabatino, & Hooper, 1982). Most of these studies have focused on how school social workers view their role. This research helps the profession define the current focus of school social work practice. Constable and Montgomery (1985) and Staudt and Craft (1983) described local studies of school staff who were asked for their perceptions of how school social workers function in their system. These latter studies also meet program evaluation needs and point the direction for needed program change or inservice development of the school social worker role. Input from educators and school social workers helps determine if and to what extent differences exist in role perception.

(2)   A summary of research completed to date indicates that school social workers focus on work with individual students, consultation, student group work, and activities related to teaming. Social workers do not often provide parent groups, teacher in-service or workshops, research, and other activities related to leadership or systems change. Yet, these activities are recommended as an effective services delivery model in meeting the needs of groups of students (Costin, 1975).

(3)   The purpose of the current study was to ascertain special education teachers', principals', and school social workers' perceptions of how frequently certain school social work services are provided and how effective they are.

Method

(4)   A questionnaire listing 19 school social work services was developed and sent to all principals and special education teachers who work in public and private schools that are served by an intermediary educational agency in Iowa. Respondents were asked to indicate the degree to which each service or task was provided and the degree to which they would like the service provided. The four possible responses were

Reprinted with permission from *Social Work, 36*(6): 496-498. Copyright © 1991 by National Association of Social Workers, Inc.

Marlys Staudt, MSW, is a Visiting Assistant Professor, University of Iowa, Iowa City, IA 52242.

0, never provided; 1, rarely provided; 2, sometimes provided; and 3, frequently provided. Respondents were also asked to rank six school social work services and to explain the role of the school social worker in the assessment process for special education placement. Special education teachers and principals were asked if they were satisfied with the quality and quantity of school social work services. Several open-ended questions were asked, and background information was obtained. All of the school social workers employed by the agency were asked to complete a similar questionnaire.

(5)   Fifty-five principals and 158 special education teachers received the questionnaire, and 32 principals (58 percent) and 98 teachers (61 percent) responded. One questionnaire was incomplete, and three were received too late to be included, so 126 were used for data analysis. The nine school social workers in the agency completed the questionnaire at a staff meeting. Thus, of 222 total questionnaires, 139 (63 percent) were returned.

Results

Actual and Ideal Frequency of Services

(6)   The three groups gave similar responses about which services they saw as provided most frequently. (Mean frequencies were computed for each service of each group.) The four tasks seen by all groups as provided most frequently were assessments for special education placement, participation in special education placement staffings, liaison services, and individual student consultation. Referral activities, counseling with students and parents about students' educational programs and needs, and crisis intervention were also seen as provided more frequently than other services.

(7)   Tasks rarely provided included program planning in the school and community, research activities, work with an entire class of students, teacher in-service, and parent groups. School social workers viewed student group work as provided more frequently than did teachers or principals, who viewed student group work as provided rarely. This was not atypical; for most services, school social workers saw themselves as providing the service more frequently than did teachers or principals. This may be because school social workers are assigned to more than one school and rated their overall service provision to all schools, whereas teachers and principals viewed service provision from the perspective of their own school. Although school social workers are involved in the identification and placement of special education students, neither they nor teachers see social

workers as actively involved in the development of the student's Individualized Educational Program (IEP).

(8)   Services wanted more frequently by teachers and principals were non-student-specific consultation (on groups of students or issues encountered on a regular basis), family counseling, group work, and parent counseling. Although principals see school social workers as more active in IEP planning than do either teachers or school social workers, all groups wanted more involvement of the social worker in this activity. Although student group work and parent counseling were wanted more frequently, parent groups were not rated as highly in terms of ideal frequency. Also, school social workers wanted to be more active in group work and non-student-specific consultation.

Priority Ranking

(9)   When asked to rank six services (student group work, individual counseling, consultation with teachers on individual students, teacher in-service, developing new services, and liaison activities), all groups ranked counseling, liaison, and consultation as the three services that are needed most to meet student needs. Although all groups wanted more group work, they also wanted a continued focus on the individual student. Despite time constraints, school social workers also viewed as priority those services that focused on individuals instead of group work.

Role in Assessment

(10)   In regard to assessment for special education placement, two choices were given on the questionnaire: (1) provide a complete social assessment on every child referred for possible special education placement, or (2) provide a complete social assessment only where social, behavioral, or emotional concerns are indicated. Eighteen percent of the special education teachers and 27 percent of the principals wanted a complete social assessment on every child referred for placement. None of the school social workers wanted a complete assessment if behavioral, social, or emotional concerns were not indicated. Several respondents wrote that social workers should do only what is legally required.

Discussion

(11)   Studies such as the one described are inexpensive to complete, do not require technical data analysis, and provide useful information to local school social work departments and education agencies. The agency in which this study was conducted examined and

modified the assessment process as a result of the findings. More screenings, consisting of reviewing files and contacting teachers, are now conducted, especially in third-year student reevaluations and referrals when only academic concerns exist. Focus is on those referrals where social or behavioral concerns exist, with emphasis on follow-through and participation in the development of these students' IEPs. A screening process also allows more time for the delivery of other requested services such as group work.

(12)   The results of the evaluative question directed toward educators indicated that 70 percent of teachers and 45 percent of principals were not satisfied with quantity of available school social work time. As a result, it was recommended that individual school social workers meet with teachers and principals at the beginning of the school year. School social workers perform many tasks, and not all of these can be performed or are even appropriate in certain schools. Obtaining teacher and principal input in the development of an individualized building service plan will help ascertain that student needs are being met. This can help ease the concern over quantity of service, because teachers and principals will know the amount of time available to their school and will have input with regard to the services that will be provided. Although in this study there was no discrepancy among groups as to the role of the school social worker, this process can help prevent and decrease tension resulting from different perceptions among groups regarding the role of the school social worker.

(13)   Social work is usually the one discipline in the school setting with the role of parent contact. Yet parent groups and parent counseling were not seen as provided frequently, and parent group work was not rated highly as an ideal service. However, special education identification and liaison work often do include work with parents. The results of this study agree with those of Kurtz and Barth (1989) in that respondents in the latter study ranked handicapping conditions as the most frequent reason for contact with parents, and they ranked parent groups, program development, and parent association as used less frequently as parent interventions in school-based and family-based student problems.

(14)   Apparently, school social work services in this intermediary educational agency are traditional — services are focused on the individual student. Also much time is spent in the identification of and staffing for special education students. However, respondents request other types of service, especially group work.

Conclusion

(15)   As early as mid-1970, Costin (1975) suggested a systems model approach to school social work. Evaluations would focus on how school and community conditions affect groups of students, and services would be developed to meet the needs of target groups. But Zielinski and Coolidge (1982) found that school administrators favor the traditional individual service delivery model over a systems approach. Perhaps school social workers and educators are concerned that individual needs will be overlooked in a systems approach. With the increasing number and intensity of social problems experienced by students in today's society, creative school social workers will work with educators to ensure that service delivery helps the greatest number of students in the most effective and efficient way.

References

Alderson, J. J., & Krishef, C. H. (1973). Another perspective on tasks in school social work. *Social Casework, 54,* 591-600.

Chavkin, N. F. (1985). School social work practice: A reappraisal. *Social Work in Education, 7,* 3-13.

Constable, R. T., & Montgomery, E. (1985). Perceptions of the school social worker's role. *Social Work in Education, 7,* 244-257.

Costin, L. B. (1969). An analysis of the tasks in school social work. *Social Service Review, 43,* 274-285.

Costin, L. B. (1975). School social work practice: A new model. *Social Work, 20,* 135-139.

Kurtz, D. P., & Barth, R. P. (1989). Parent involvement: Cornerstone of school social work practice. *Social Work, 34,* 407-413.

Lambert, C., & Mullaly, R. (1982). School social work: The congruence of task importance and level of effort. In R. T. Constable & J. P. Flynn (Eds.), *School social work: Practice and research perspectives* (pp. 72-84). Homewood, IL: Dorsey Press.

Lee, C. (1987). School social work in Louisiana: An analysis of practice. *Social Work, 32,* 442-444.

Meares, P. A. (1977). Analysis of tasks in school social work. *Social Work, 22,* 196-201.

Staudt, M. M., & Craft, J. L. (1983). School staff input in the evaluation of school social work practice. *Social Work in Education, 5,* 119-131.

Timberlake, E. M., Sabatino, C. A., & Hooper, S. N. (1982). School social work practice and P.L. 94-142. In R. T. Constable & J. P. Flynn (Eds.), *School social work: Practice and research perspectives* (pp. 271-281). Homewood, IL: Dorsey Press.

Zielinski, T., & Coolidge, J. (1982). Systems model of school social work: Barriers to implementation. In

Professional issues for social workers in schools: Conference proceedings (pp. 123-137). Silver Spring, MD: National Association of Social Workers.

Factual Questions

1. What was the title of Costin's landmark 1969 study?

2. What is the purpose of the research described in this article?

3. What percentage of questionnaires sent to principals were returned? to special education teachers? to school social workers?

4. What four tasks are performed most frequently by school social workers?

5. Did most of the survey respondents want social workers to do a complete assessment on every child referred for possible special education placement?

6. What advantages does the author note of studies such as this one?

7. Why does the author characterize social work services in this intermediary educational agency as traditional?

Questions for Discussion

8. Does the introduction provide a clear notion of the research problem, the purpose of the research, and its significance?

9. Does the literature review seem relevant to the research problem?

10. Is the number of research subjects sufficient? To what population would you generalize the results of this study?

11. Is there enough information on the research instruments and procedures to allow you to replicate this study?

12. Should there be information about the reliability and validity of the research instruments and procedures?

13. Does the analysis include sufficient statistical information? Are the statistics that are used appropriate?

14. Are the conclusions supported by and do they logically follow from the data that have been presented?

15. Are the findings discussed in terms of their implications and/or practical significance?

Notes:

Job Strain Among Police Officers: Gender Comparisons

Leanor Boulin Johnson
Arizona State University

The present study assessed the gender differences in job burnout among 457 male and 139 female police officers. While both male and female police showed moderately high degrees of burnout, they expressed it differently. Higher levels of emotional burnout were associated with females, while males showed higher levels of depersonalizing citizens. Controlling for tenure, the data suggest that gender differentials reflected the officers' gender role socialization rather than the women police officers' "newcomer" status.

(1)   The influx of women police officers into patrol duty began nearly twenty years ago. While several studies show that women police officers have performed their work effectively (Bloch and Anderson 1974; Sichel, Friedman, Quint, & Smith, 1978), the mental and emotional strains they experience as compared to their male counterparts are in need of further empirical investigation.

(2)   The reports by Wexler and Logan (1983), Martin (1980) and Pendergrass and Ostrove (1984) are among the few published empirical studies on stress among women police officers. The former study showed numerous job stressors which paralleled those experienced by male officers as well as stressors unique to women working in male-dominated jobs (e.g., negative attitudes of males/sexual harassment). However, Wexler and Logan (1983) did not focus on strain (i.e., stress consequences) nor did they directly measure male and female differences. In Martin's (1980) study, focus was given to women police officers and their perception of the males' attitudes and treatment of them. Again, lacking were direct male-female comparisons. Although Pendergrass and Ostrove (1984) compared the

responses of male and female officers on stress consequences, their utilization of scales to measure job stress and psychological consequences provided only limited insight into specific job strain differences among male and female officers. Finally, none of those studies took into account variations in stress consequences (i.e., job strain) across tenure levels. It is possible that reported male-female differences may be more a function of the "newcomer" status of women rather than gender-specific attributes (Silbert 1982).

(3)   In the present study, focus is given to specific mental and emotional strains experienced by male and female officers. After comparing males and females on various indicators of job strains, gender comparisons are made by job tenure.

Method

(4)   In 1983 over 700 police officers employed in two major Eastern cities were administered a 333 item questionnaire (topics included work experiences/satisfaction, work-family issues, social support, coping strategies, physical and mental health). For bureaucratic

reasons we were able to randomly sample in only one department. The present sample consists of 457 males (47 Blacks/410 Whites) and 139 females (39 Blacks/100 Whites). These officers represented those joining since 1970, when a substantial number of females entered the police force. The questionnaire reflected input from many sources, including an advisory panel, police ride-along experiences, workshops for police officers and their spouses, formal and informal interactions with ethnic minority and gender-based police organizations, over 60 intensive interviews with police officers and spouses, and pretesting in one rural and two urban departments.

(5)   While the instrument covered a wide range of topics, our present focus is with job strain. Several items considered to be indicators of job strain were selected in modified form from Maslach and Jackson's emotional exhaustion and depersonalization scales (1979). The two distinct clusters which emerged from our factor analysis were labeled Internal Burnout and External Burnout (Cronbach's alphas: .85 and .87 respectively). Internal Burnout items reflected feelings of being emotionally depleted by the job. External Burnout items indexed feelings of being emotionally hardened by the job and lacking compassion for citizens. Focus is

given to the specific items underlying these burnout scales (see Table 1). The response format for these items consisted of a 7-point Likert-type scale anchored at the end points with "agree" and "disagree."

Results

(6)   Table 1 reveals that only one of the five items significantly differentiated males and females on Internal Burnout. Females on the average were more likely to report that they felt fatigued when they awakened to face another day on the job. In contrast, External Burnout showed pervasive male-female differences. Males and females were found to be similar on only one of the six items. Interestingly, while both males and females worried that the job was hardening them emotionally, males were significantly more likely than females to report that working with people put a strain on them and that they treated citizens like impersonal objects or did not really care what happened to some citizens.

(7)   Given that females are relatively new to patrol duty and are generally younger than their fellow male officers, their lower rate of External Burnout may have resulted from less exposure to the stressors of working with citizens. Examining these items by tenure level

Table 1: Mental and Emotional Strain by Gender

	Male $\overline{X}$	Female $\overline{X}$
I. Internal Burnout		
a. I feel emotionally drained from my work.	4.1	4.1
b. I feel used up at the end of the workday.	4.3	4.4
c. I feel fatigued when I awake to face another day on the job.	3.7	3.9**
d. I feel burned out from my work.	3.4	3.3
e. I feel I am working too hard on my job.	3.3	3.1
II. External Burnout		
f. I treat some civilians as if they were impersonal objects.	3.8	2.9*
g. Working with people all day is really a strain for me.	2.9	2.6**
h. I have become more callous toward people since I took this job.	4.3	3.3*
i. I worry that this job is hardening me emotionally.	4.2	4.1
j. I don't really care what happens to some citizens.	4.1	2.7*
k. Working directly with people puts too much stress on me.	2.8	2.5**

*p < .01 Level
**p < .10 Level

The significant level refers to the differences between the means of males and females to the left of the asterisk(s).

provided partial insight into this possible explanation. Tenure was trichotomized into Low (1-3 years), Medium (4-7 years), and High (8 or more years) levels.

(8)   In part II of Table 2, all significant gender differences showed females lower on the External Burnout items. Four of the six External Burnout items showed significant male-female differences at the highest tenured level. In addition, significant gender differences persisted at every tenure level for each of two items (f, j): "I treat some civilians as if they were impersonal objects" and "I don't care what happens to some citizens." Oddly, item "h" ("I have become more callous toward people since I took this job") showed significant male-female differences only at the Medium tenure level.

(9)   In general, it appears that for this sample External Burnout is more characteristic of males. However, among females, it must not go unnoticed that higher tenure was associated with higher External Burnout, particularly when moving from Low to

Table 2. Mental and Emotional Strain by Gender and Tenure

	Tenure					
	Low		Medium		High	
	M	F	M	F	M	F
Mental/Emotional Strain	$\overline{X}$	$\overline{X}$	$\overline{X}$	$\overline{X}$	$\overline{X}$	$\overline{X}$
I. Internal Burnout						
a. I feel emotionally drained from my work.	3.8	3.9	4.2	4.2	4.2	4.6
b. I feel used up at the end of the workday.	3.9	4.1	4.3	4.7**	4.4	4.7
c. I feel fatigued when I awake to face another day on the job.	3.3	3.6	3.5	4.4*	4.0	4.3
d. I feel burned out from my work.	2.7	3.1**	3.3	3.4	3.8	3.9
e. I feel I am working too hard on my job.	3.0	2.9	3.3	3.5	3.3	3.1
II. External Burnout						
f. I treat some civilians as if they were impersonal objects.	3.7	2.8*	3.8	3.1*	3.8	2.9*
g. Working with people all day is really a strain for me.	2.7	2.7	2.9	2.8	3.1	2.4*
h. I have become more callous toward people since I took this job.	4.1	3.9	4.4	3.8**	4.7	4.4
i. I worry that this job is hardening me emotionally.	3.9	3.8	4.3	4.3	4.3	4.7
j. I don't really care what happens to some citizens.	4.0	2.6*	4.0	3.0*	4.1	2.7*
k. Working directly with people puts too much stress on me.	2.5	2.4	2.6	2.7	3.0	2.4**

*p < .01 Level   The significant level refers to the differences between the means of males and females to the left of the asterisk(s).

**p < .10 Level

Medium. On the other hand, after the seventh year there appears to be a trend towards lower levels of External Burnout among females, whereas for males their scores appear relatively stable or elevated.

(10)   When Internal Burnout is viewed by tenure level, one significant difference appeared between males and females at Low tenure (Table 2:Part I, d) and two occurred at the Medium level. Females were (a) more likely to feel used up at the end of the working day and (b) more likely to report that they felt fatigued when they awakened to face another day. Thus, two additional differences emerged as a result of taking tenure into consideration. Overall, it is clear that females tend to have higher Internal Burnout scores.

Conclusions

(11)   The data tend to support a moderately high degree of burnout in our sample of police officers. In general, for both males and females burnout scores were above the semantic scale mean of 3.5. However, it was clearly seen that burnout is expressed differently by gender. Females were more likely to report feelings of being drained and used up by their job; men were more likely to externalize the burnout by treating citizens like impersonal objects or becoming callous toward people. Gender differences persisted across tenure levels. These cross-sectional data suggest that greater exposure to the harshness of street life is not an adequate explanation for men's higher level of External Burnout. However, gender role socialization may offer partial insight.

(12)   In our interviews of female police officers, it was common to hear them speak about the compassion they felt they brought to the job because they were females or mothers. Some related to the citizens as if they were erring children in need of stern correction. Many felt that what they lacked in physical strength relative to males was compensated by their ability to relate to the people verbally and psychologically. As one woman officer stated,

> Some of the roughest guys see me as a mother rather than a police officer. I then talk to them as a son — I use it to my advantage. I'm able to use psychology to make them comply.

(13)   Several police women remarked that when a male perpetrator is arrested by a male officer the male ego is challenged — battle lines are immediately drawn. In contrast, many suspects find little challenge in fighting a woman. It was also noted that some male offenders comply because they assume that since the woman officer does not have the body strength, she is more likely to use the gun or they believe that women with guns are unpredictable. As Sherman (1975) has noted, women tend to have a "gentling" effect on potentially explosive situations.

(14)   Finally, a number of women police officers noted that early in their career males did not know whether to treat them as a lady or a police officer. One reported that

> I was just about to enter a dark alley to investigate a robbery in progress when my male back-up motioned for me to fall back. He said I might get hurt. I did not know whether to be flattered at his chivalry or angry at his lack of confidence in me!

(15)   These comments suggest that the reason why women's External Burnout remains relatively lower than men's at each tenure level is because their policing style or their status as women reduced the number of physical confrontations or harsh encounters relative to those experienced by their male colleagues. They may be shielded by their socialization and the social attributes assigned to women in our society.

(16)   The lower Internal Burnout on the part of males may simply be the result of their greater physical stamina and psychological readiness. Competitiveness, assertiveness, offensiveness, strength and a military regimentation are familiar themes in the male culture. Traditionally, these attributes have also been considered desirable within the police culture (Balkin 1988). While males already manifest these traits or find it natural to internalize them, females must make a conscious effort to adapt. In addition, the higher level of Internal Burnout among females may partly result from their constant struggle to be accepted in a male-dominated occupation (see Greene 1987). Wexler and Logan (1983) note that among the most common mentioned sources of stress for women police officers were those centered around their being women — the negative responses from their fellow male officers and threats to their self-esteem. Many police women feel that the constant pressure to prove themselves is frustrated by the realization that their best efforts and contributions go unnoticed by their fellow male colleagues (Balkin 1988). Thus, they are disillusioned and sometimes exhibit high levels of strain. For example, after numerous and unsuccessful efforts to gain acceptance, one member of our sample was so traumatized that she had to seek professional counseling. While the need for professional counseling may be expressed by only a few, certainly these anti-women experiences must contribute significantly to the

Internal Burnout of the vast majority of women officers (See Jacob 1987; Martin 1980).

(17)   In sum, unlike some reports which suggest that burnout is higher for female officers (See Pendergrass & Ostrove 1984; Silbert 1982), these present data show relatively high levels of burnout for both males and females. However, the quality of burnout differed by gender. The data suggest that perhaps males avoid Internal Burnout because they are better prepared for policing and experience group affirmation, and women avoid External Burnout by incorporating into their policing style the skills and attributes derived from traditional sex role socialization. A more precise quantification of these suggested conclusions will be possible if future empirical studies use larger female samples as well as longitudinal data to examine these two burnout types within the context of individual coping styles, job history, social experiences, work social support and group acceptance.

References

Balkin, Joseph. 1988. Why policemen don't like policewomen. *Journal of Police Science and Administration.* 16:29-36.

Bloch, Peter B. and Anderson, Deborah. 1974. *Policewomen on patrol: Final report.* Washington, D.C.: Police Foundation.

Greene, Robin L. 1987. Psychological support for women entering law enforcement: Police managerial use of psychology and psychologists, in More, H. W., & Unsinger, P. C. (Eds.) *Police managerial use of psychology and psychologists.* Illinois: Charles Thomas Publishers.

Jacobs, Pearl. 1987. How female police officers cope with a traditionally male position. *Sociology and Social Research* 72 (1):4-6.

Johnson, Leanor Boulin; Nieva, Veronica F.; and Wilson, Michael. 1985. *Police work-home stress study: Interim report.* (Winter). Maryland: Westat, Inc.

Maslach, C. and Jackson, S. E. 1979. "Burn-out Cops and Their Families." *Psychology Today* (May): 54-62.

Martin, Susan Ehrlich. 1980. *Breaking and entering: Police women on patrol.* Berkeley: University of California press.

Pendergrass, Virginia E. and Ostrove, Nancy M. 1984. Survey of stress in women in policing. *Journal of Police Science and Administration.* 12:303-309.

Sherman, L. J. 1975. Evaluation of police women on patrol in a suburban police department. *Journal of Police Science and Administration.* 3:434-438.

Sichel, Joyce; Friedman, Lucy N.; Quint, Janet C.; and Smith, Michael E. 1978. *Women on patrol: A pilot study of performance in New York City.* Washington, D.C.: Government Printing Office.

Silbert, M. H. 1982. Job stress and burnout of new police officers. *Police Chief.* 49:46-48.

Wexler, Judie Gaffin and Logan, Deana D. 1983. Sources of stress among women police officers. *Journal of Police Science and Administration*, 11 (1): 46-53.

Factual Questions

1. How many male police officers completed questionnaires used in the present study? how many female police officers?

2. The questionnaire used by the researchers was a result of input from which sources?

3. Items used to measure job strain were taken and then modified from what source?

4. Internal burnout corresponds to what? External burnout corresponds to what?

5. What answer format was used for the job strain items?

11. Does the introduction provide a clear notion of the research problem, the purpose of the research, and its significance?

6. Why did the author divide subjects by tenure level and then again examine gender differences by job strain?

12. Does the literature review seem relevant to the research problem?

7. Are there any significant differences between male and female officers with high tenure on the internal burnout items?

13. Is the number of research subjects sufficient? Is it a problem that there are more male subjects than female subjects?

8. At all tenure levels, significant differences between male and female officers on the external burnout items always show which gender having lower external burnout?

14. To what population would you generalize the results of this study?

9. How does the author explain female police officers' lower level of external burnout?

15. Is there enough information on the research instruments and procedures to allow you to replicate this study?

10. What does the author suggest as an explanation for male officers' lower level of internal burnout?

16. Do the research instruments and procedures have adequate reliability and validity?

17. Does the analysis include sufficient statistical information? Are the statistics that are used appropriate?

18. Are the conclusions supported by and do they logically follow from the data that have been presented?

19. Are the findings discussed in terms of their implications and/or practical significance?

20. In concluding, the author suggests that the present study's conclusions could be more precisely measured if future studies use longitudinal data. Why would that be an advantage over the cross-sectional data used in this study?

Notes:

Article 15

Leisure Time Use and Academic Correlates of Alcohol Abuse Among High School Students

James E. Pendorf
Psychiatry Service
VA Medical Center

High school students use of alcohol is examined in relation to leisure time use and attitudes toward school climate. Male and female students in grade 10 (n=115) and grade 12 (n=107) in a rural Pennsylvania high school were surveyed. Heavy use of alcohol correlated with participation in social and vocational activities. Heavy users enjoyed school and school subjects less, had greater potential for conflicts with teachers, and received lower grades. This study demonstrates heavy alcohol use bears a relationship to aspects of social and vocational behaviors and attitudes required for healthy and positive adolescent development. The results of this study cloud the generalized detrimental effects from high school students' heavy use of alcohol.

Introduction and Purpose

(1)   People drink alcohol for a variety of reasons which include recreation, social, and relaxation; some drink as an addiction (Blum, 1982; Murray & Stabenau, 1982). Alcohol is widely known to cause a variety of personal problems. It has been related to criminal behaviors (Matsunage, 1983; Hammond, 1978), accidents and employment absenteeism (APA, 1980; Quayle, 1983), and behavioral changes and relationship difficulties (Ray, 1983; McCrady, 1982).

(2)   Historically, studies on alcohol abuse have focused on adults. For example, studies have typically examined alcohol's relationship with driving skills and abilities (Nathan, 1983), employment issues (Knott & Beard, 1982), health (Feldman, 1982; Matsunage, 1983; APA, 1980), and psychological and behavioral factors (e.g., judgment and coordination) (Ray, 1983). Recent attention has focused on a wider population to include adolescents (Keys & Block, 1984; Gordon & McAlister, 1982; Johnston, O'Malley, & Bachman, 1984). Efforts have also been made to educate society, including adolescents, about the effects of alcohol, evidenced by such national groups as Mothers Against Drunk Driving (MADD) and Students Against Drunk Driving (SADD).

(3)   Adolescents' use of alcohol is becoming more problematic. Most adolescents drink alcohol before

Reprinted with permission from *Journal of Alcohol and Drug Education, 37*(2): 103-110. Copyright © 1992 by the Alcohol and Drug Problems Association of North America.

This study is based on the author's dissertation research.

Correspondence concerning this article should be sent to James E. Pendorf, Ph.D., Administrative Coordinator, Psychiatry Service, VA Medical Center, Lebanon, PA 17042.

leaving high school, and nearly 6% drink on a daily basis (Johnston et al., 1984). Over one-half of students are initiated to alcohol use before entering high school (Johnston, Bachman, O'Malley, 1982; Keys & Block, 1984; Lowman, 1981). It must be emphasized that alcohol by itself is seldom the only drug used by high school students (Johntson et al., 1984). Other drugs used include marijuana, cocaine, and hallucinogens, although with much less frequency (Johntson et al., 1984). However, alcohol is the drug first used, initiating the onset to this behavior and possible exposure to a wider availability of drugs. Subsequently, alcohol abuse is considered the major drug problem facing America's youth. (National Institute on Alcohol Abuse and Alcoholism, 1980)

(4)   Adolescents who are heavy users of alcohol are reported as less happy (Conger & Petersen, 1984), of lower expectations of the future (Gordon & McAlister, 1982), of lower grades (Conger & Petersen, 1984), of resisting or alienated from traditional adult values (Gordon & McAlister, 1982; Savickas, 1984), and personally dissatisfied and alienated (National Institute on Alcohol Abuse and Alcoholism, 1984). Such social and academic difficulties would be expected to interfere with important developmental tasks awaiting the adolescent. This importance is underscored by adolescence being a time of significant emotional and social growth, requiring the support of family and peers, and school achievement.

(5)   Tasks facing the adolescent are basically three fold: to learn important social skills (Conger & Petersen, 1984), to engage in self-discovery and identity development (Marcia, 1966; Super, Starishevsky, Matlin & Jordan, 1963), and to enter into vocational activity leading to future vocational choices (Walsh & Osipow, 1983; Vondracek & Lerner, 1982). For this, positive parental, peer and school influences are important for optimal development (Miller, 1974). These influences are found in the home, through use of leisure pursuits and at school. Leisure pursuits may include entertainment and social activities, studying, involvement in sports and religion, hobbies and related activities, and vocational activity. Students' attitudes toward school may be measured by achievement (grades); and attitudes held toward school, teachers, and course subjects. For many high school students the majority of their time is spent away from home, and certainly away from parents and adult figures. Most adolescents also consume alcohol away from home where critical developmental tasks occur.

(6)   The purpose of this study was to explore the relationship between high school students' use of alcohol, their use of leisure time, and their attitudes toward school climate. Because consequences of heavy alcohol use are associated with behaviors and attitudes detrimental to critical development associated with, and dependent upon, leisure pursuits — social and personal behaviors — and attitudes and behaviors associated with school involvement, it was predicted that heavy alcohol use would bear negative relationships with all these variables.

Method

Participants

(7)   A rural Pennsylvania high school was surveyed to examine the relationship between students' alcohol use and their attitudes toward their school climate, and their use of leisure time. Participants included 222 10th grade (n=115) and 12th grade (n=107) students. Students were predominately white, 15 to 19 years of age, and were in various curricula ranging from general to college and vocational studies. Data were collected at the beginning of the school year.

Questionnaire

(8)   Swisher's Primary Prevention Awareness, Attitude, and Usage Scales, Form 7 (Swisher, 1983), was used to collect data relative to the student's alcohol behaviors, attitudes, and values. The questionnaire contains 79 items and takes about 30 minutes to complete. It also assesses leisure time activities and attitudes held toward school, teachers, and subjects, and the respondent's grade point average (GPA).

(9)   Data were collected on a continuous scale for alcohol use. This ranges, for specific drugs used, from "never use," "used before," and use including, "once or twice per year," "once or twice per month," "once or twice per week," "once or twice per day," and "often, each day." Time use variables include Entertainment and Social Activities (movies, dating, parties, etc.), Academic Activities (homework, reading, school projects, etc.), Sports (any physical sports activity), Religious Activities, Extra-curricular Activities and Hobbies (school clubs, collecting stamps or coins, caring for pets, musical instruments, working on cars, etc.), and Vocational Activities (looking for a job or working part-time, etc.). These variables are also scored on a continuous scale of "never," "once or twice a year," "once or twice a month," "once or twice a week," "once or twice a day," and "many hours" a day. The Form 7 contains other items related to attitudes and values held

toward drug and alcohol behaviors. Only alcohol use frequency, leisure time, and school climate items were analyzed in this study.

(10)   A "lie item" consisting of a non-existent drug was included in the list of possible drugs ever having been used. If a student reported using this "drug" the student's entire testing was discarded. Only a very few tests were discarded for this reason of carelessness or dishonesty. Alpha reliability of the Swisher scale ranges from .63 to .74 on School Climate subscales and from .83 to .90 on Self Reported Drug and Alcohol Use. Good validity across the Form 7 subscales is also reported (Swisher, Shute, & Bibeau, 1984).

Procedure

(11)   Students and their parents were informed of the study and consent was obtained from all but a few parents. Teachers were instructed on test administration two weeks before testing. Uniform instructions were prepared for teachers to read to students. Data collection was conducted in homeroom classes to assure all students would be tested. Anonymity was assured to all participants, and at the end of testing participants could deposit their questionnaires in a stack in whatever order they wanted. The students not receiving parental approval to participate in the study waited in the school library under faculty supervision.

Results

(12)   Alcohol use was divided first by type of beverage (beer, wine, and hard liquor) then separated into "use" and "abuse." Students reporting use of any type of alcohol weekly or more often were classified as heavy users, or abusers. Scoring the Form 7 resulted in low scores corresponding with low alcohol use, less frequent leisure time commitment, negative attitudes toward school, school teachers, and school courses, and high grades. The sample size was nearly evenly distributed

between the grade 10 students (n=115) and grade 12 students (n=107) making nearly equivalent groups.

(13)   Table 1 illustrates how Time Use variables correlate with different types of alcohol use. Entertainment and social activities correlated with beer, wine, and hard liquor use. This demonstrates that these socially active adolescents are more involved in overall alcohol use. Time spent with school work correlates negatively with beer and hard liquor use meaning that heavier drinkers of these beverages spend less time with school homework, school projects, and/or reading. Participation in Sports activities is not correlated with alcohol use. Not surprisingly, youth reporting heavier alcohol use also report less involvement with religious activities. Hobbies and Extracurricular activities correlate negatively with beer use and wine use suggesting that beer and wine users, but not hard liquor users, are less involved with extracurricular school activities or hobbies. Involvement with vocational activities is positively correlated with the use of each beverage type. In other words youth who report more involvement with working, or who are at least looking for work, are heavier users of alcohol.

(14)   Table 2 represents how School Climate variables correlate with different types of alcohol use. Lower grade point averages are correlated with beer, wine, and hard liquor use as are negative feelings toward the enjoyment of school. Students' feelings toward teachers correlate negatively with alcohol use in all three forms suggesting that heavy drinkers hold low opinions of their teachers' helpfulness. Students' feelings about school subjects also correlate negatively with beer use and hard liquor use.

(15)   To summarize, heavy use of alcohol by high school students positively correlates with social and vocational involvement. In addition, heavy alcohol use correlates with less enjoyment of school or school

Table 1. Summary of Correlations with Time Use Variables

Measure	Entertainment & activities	School work	Sports	Religion	Hobbies & activities	Vocational activities
Beer	.28**	-.26**	-.02	-.23**	-.13*	.22**
Wine	.25**	-.12	.02	-.13*	-.13*	.17**
Hard liquor	.37**	-.24**	-.02	-.16*	-.09	.18**

*p < .05

**p < .01

Table 2. Summary of Correlations with School Climate Variables

Measure	Grade-point average	Enjoy school	Feel about teachers	Feel about subjects
Beer	.18**	-.29**	-.30**	-.17**
Wine	.13*	-.22**	-.17**	-.08
Hard Liquor	.21**	-.24**	-.29**	-.16

*p < .05

**p < .01

subjects. Heavy alcohol users have more negative feelings toward teachers and receive lower grades.

Discussion

(16)   This study addressed high school students' use of alcohol with different leisure time activity and school attitude variables. Limitations are that it was conducted in a rural setting, and that it did not assess racial or gender differences. There were no significant differences found between 10th and 12th grade students in their overall use of alcohol, yet heavy use of alcohol by 12th grade male participants was somewhat less than for the 10th grade males. Females' use of alcohol showed an increase between the 10th and 12th grade. This is not surprising since more adolescent females are using alcohol than before (Johnson et al., 1982; Johnson et al., 1984).

(17)   This study also found a positive relationship between alcohol use and social and vocational activities, suggesting that heavy users of alcohol are going out, dating, and attending movies and parties more, and are job searching and working part-time more than are light users. Surprisingly, heavy use of alcohol correlates with social and vocational activities, tasks critical to healthy adolescent development. Learning social skills, self-discovery, and entry into vocational activity, do not seem affected by heavy alcohol use. To the contrary, heavy use of alcohol may be more available in these settings. Certainly peer influence leads to alcohol use, while a vocational setting provides both funds and access to people to supply it. Thus, growth supportive activities — social and vocational — provide opportunity to obtain and use alcohol. However, heavy alcohol use correlates with lower grades, less enjoyment of school and school subjects, and a more negative view of teachers, that is, growth restrictive outcomes.

(18)   Positive post-high school and career outcomes result from establishing personal identity, learning social roles, vocational entry, and from good school work

(Vondracek & Schulenberg, 1984; Super, 1985). This study clouds allegations of generalized ill effects of alcohol abuse during the middle and late adolescent years during high school; heavy alcohol users were socially and vocationally oriented, but were not as well applied in school as were low alcohol users. Certainly follow-up studies need to be conducted to determine the strength, the magnitude, and even the direction of personal, social, and vocational choices made by students during their high school years.

(19)   Application of these results in any setting fostering vocational or academic growth among adolescents, or any setting treating adolescent alcohol problems, should be tempered with caution. While students who are socially active are also more inclined to abuse alcohol, the same group of students takes a dimmer view of school, school subjects, and school teachers. Perhaps this knowledge of contrast of growth supportive and growth restrictive adolescent alcohol use patterns could lend themselves to approaching high school students in alcohol use prevention, or in personal counseling settings. In any event, it may not be prudent for adults to suggest that alcohol use is entirely bad when adolescents know that it may indeed serve as an important springboard into self-discovery, acquiring friends, and acquiring self-esteem through social and entertainment channels. Such general "advice" from parents or adult figures may only serve to damage their own credibility, adding to the "generation gap" casually referred to when attitudinal differences prevail between generations.

References

American Psychiatric Association (1980). *Diagnostic and statistical manual of mental disorders* (3rd ed.). Washington, DC: Author.

Blum, K. (1982). Neurophysiological effects of alcohol. In E.M. Pattison & E. Kaufman (Eds.), *Encyclopedic handbook of alcoholism* (pp. 105-134). New York: Gardner.

Conger, J.J. & Petersen, A.C.(1984). *Adolescence and youth: Psychological development in a changing world* (3rd ed.). San Francisco: Harper & Row.

Feldman, E.B. (1982). Malnutrition in the alcoholic and related nutritional deficiencies. In E.M. Pattison & E. Kaufman (Eds.). *Encyclopedic handbook of alcoholism* (pp. 255-262). New York: Gardner.

Gordon, N.P. & McAlister, A.L. (1982). Adolescent drinking: Issues and research. In T. Coates (Ed.), *Promoting adolescent health: A dialogue on research and practice* (pp. 201-232). New York: Academic Press.

Hammond, R.L. (1978). *Almost all you ever wanted to know about alcohol but didn't know who to ask.* (Michigan Alcohol and Drug Information Foundation), Lansing, MI: Author.

Johnston, L.D., O'Malley, R.M., & Bachman, J.D. (1982). *Monitoring the future: Questionnaire responses from the nation's high school seniors, 1981.* Ann Arbor, MI: Institute for Social Research.

Johnston, L.D., O'Malley, R.M. & Bachman, J.D. (1984). *Highlights from drugs and American high school students, 1975-1983.* Rockville, MD: National Institute on Drug Abuse.

Keys, S. & Block, J. (1984). Prevalence and patterns of substance use among early adolescents. *Journal of Youth and Adolescence, 13,* 1-14.

Knott, D.H. & Beard, J.E. (1982). Effects of alcohol ingestion on the cardiovascular system. In E.M. Pattison & E. Kaufman (Eds.), *Encyclopedic handbook of alcoholism* (pp. 332-342). New York: Gardner.

Lowman, C. (1981). *Prevalence of alcohol use among U.S. senior high school students* (Facts for Planning No. 1, RP 0346). Rockville, MD: National Institute on Alcohol Abuse and Alcoholism.

Marcia, J.E. (1966). Development and validation of ego-identity status. *Journal of Personality and Social Psychology, 3,* 551-558.

Matsunage, S. (1983). The federal role in research, treatment, and prevention of alcoholism. *American Psychologist, 38,* 1111-1115.

McCrady, B.S. (1982). Marital dysfunction: Alcoholism and marriage. In E.M. Pattison & E. Kaufman (Eds.), *Encyclopedic handbook of alcoholism* (pp. 673-685). New York: Gardner.

Miller, D. (1974). *Adolescence: Psychology, psychopathology and psychotherapy.* New York: Aronson.

Murray, R.M. & Stabenau, J.R. (1982). Genetic factors in alcoholism predisposition. In E.M. Pattison & E. Kaufman (Eds.), *Encyclopedic handbook of alcoholism* (pp. 3-30). New York: Gardner.

Nathan, P.E. (1983). Failures in prevention: Why we can't prevent the devastating effect of alcoholism and drug abuse. *American Psychologist, 38(4),* 459-467.

National Institute on Alcohol Abuse and Alcoholism (1984). *Alcohol use and abuse among youth* (National Institute on Alcohol Abuse and Alcoholism Publication No. RP 0257). Rockville, MD: National Clearinghouse for Alcohol Information.

National Institute on Alcohol Abuse and Alcoholism (1980). *Alcohol and youth* (National Institute on Alcohol Abuse and Alcoholism Publication No. RP 0067). Rockville, MD: National Clearinghouse for Alcohol Information.

Quayle, D. (1983). American productivity: The devastating effect of alcoholism and drug abuse. *American Psychologist, 38,* 454-458.

Ray, O. (1983). *Drugs, society, and human behavior* (3rd). St. Louis: C.V. Mosby.

Savickas, M.L. (1984, June). Career maturity: The construct and its measurement. *The Vocational Guidance Quarterly, 33,* 222-231.

Super, D.E. (1985). Coming of age in Middletown: Careers in the making. *American Psychologist, 40(4),* 405-414.

Super, D.E., Starishevsky, R., Matlin, N. & Jordan, J.P. (1963). *Career development: Self-concept theory.* New York: Columbia University, Teachers College.

Swisher, J.D. (1983). *Primary prevention awareness, attitudes, and usage scales.* State College, PA: Database.

Swisher, J.D., Shute, R.E. & Bibeau, D. (1984, June). Assessing drug and alcohol abuse: An instrument for planning and evaluation. *Measurement and Evaluation in Counseling and Development, 17,* 91-97.

Vondracek, F.W. & Lerner, R.M. (1982). Vocational role development in adolescence. In B. Wolman (Ed.), *Handbook of developmental psychology* (pp. 602-614). Englewood Cliffs, NJ: Prentice-Hall.

Vondracek, F.W. & Schulenberg, J.E. (1984). Adolescence and careers. In R.M. Lerner & N. Galambos (Eds.), *Experiencing adolescents: A sourcebook for parents, teachers, and teens* (pp. 317-359). New York: Garland.

Walsh, W.B. & Osipow, S.H. (1983). *Handbook of vocational psychology: Vol 2, Applications.* Hillsdale, NJ: Erlbaum.

Factual Questions

1. Nearly what percentage of high school students consume alcohol on a daily basis?

2. What is the purpose of this study?

3. How many students participated in this study?

4. What was the high school from which the subjects came?

5. What is the nature of the "lie item" used in the study?

6. What happened to the data gathered from a student if the "lie item" indicated the student lied?

7. Who administered the survey to students and where was it administered?

8. How did beer use correlate with entertainment and social activities, school work, and sports?

Questions for Discussion

11. Does the introduction provide a clear notion of the research problem, the purpose of the research, and its significance?

12. Does the literature review seem relevant to the research problem?

13. Is the number of research subjects sufficient? To what population would you generalize the results of this study?

14. Is there enough information on the research instruments and procedures to allow you to replicate this study?

15. Do the research instruments and procedures have adequate reliability and validity?

16. Does the analysis include sufficient statistical information? Are the statistics that are used appropriate?

17. Are the conclusions supported by and do they logically follow from the data that have been presented?

18. Are the findings discussed in terms of their implications and/or practical significance?

19. The author notes that the study did not explore gender differences. How might gender differences in alcohol use, leisure activities, and school attitudes be examined?

Notes:

A Comparison of Four Income Groups on Perceptions About Welfare

Connie Lizotte Spreadbury

The focus of this study is twofold: (1) to examine perceptions on three positive and three negative statements about welfare, and (2) to compare the perceptions of the poor and the nonpoor toward welfare. Data for the study were collected as part of a larger 1986 General Social Survey by the National Opinion Research Center (NORC). The research sample for this study consisted of 1346 respondents who had answered the question about their family income for 1986. In general, all four income categories agreed with all of the statements. That is, the poor and the nonpoor shared the same perceptions of welfare. For example, the poor were as likely as the nonpoor to agree that welfare helps prevent hunger and starvation and that it encourages young women to have babies before marriage. Although there was some difference between the poor and the other income groups on some of the statements, it was more of a degree rather than a difference in perception. For example, the poor were less likely to agree that welfare would make people work less and more likely to agree that it would help people get on their feet. The poor were also more likely to agree that welfare helps keep marriages together and less likely to agree that it discourages young women who get pregnant from marrying the father of the child.

Introduction

(1)   In recent years there has been a considerable body of research that has refocused America's attention on poverty. Most of the research about poor people has focused on such characteristics as age, family structure, and ethnic background (Backley, 1988; Bane, 1986; Danziger et al., 1986; Ellwood and Summers, 1986; Institute for Research on Poverty, 1987-88; National Research Council, 1989; U.S. Bureau of the Census, 1980, 1981a, 1981b, 1983, 1987, 1989). Many recent studies indicate that poverty, neglected in the 1970s, is once again growing in the United States (Bowen and Pizer, 1987; Levy, 1987; McGeary and Lynn, 1988; National Research Council, 1989; Porter, 1989). Only one study has researched the attitudes of the American public toward the welfare system (AuClaire, 1984), and no study has compared the attitudes of the poor versus nonpoor toward the welfare system.

(2)   The focus of this study is twofold: (1) to examine the respondents' perceptions of welfare, and (2) to compare the perceptions of four family income groups toward welfare. The hypotheses were that (1) respondents have mixed perceptions of welfare, and (2) that the poor have the same perceptions of welfare as the nonpoor.

Reprinted with permission from *Family Perspective, 24*(4): 411–418. Copyright © 1990 by Brigham Young University.

Connie Lizotte Spreadbury is a professor in the Department of Sociology, Stephen F. Austin State University, Nacogdoches, TX 75962.

Attitudes Toward Poverty and Welfare

(3)   Although many people are concerned that poverty is growing in America, they often feel that the poor are largely to blame for their own poverty. They maintain that the poor consist of the unemployed, who are responsible for their condition because they choose not to work. If they could be persuaded to work for a living, or were forced to take jobs, poverty could be eliminated (Ellwood, 1988; Feagin, 1975; Levitan et al., 1989; National Research Council, 1987; Working Seminar on Family and American Welfare Policy, 1987). This perception is not accurate, however. In 1985, 33 million people were classified as living below the official poverty line. Of these, 12.5 million (38%) were children under 18, 3.5 million (11%) were over 65, 3.5 million (11%) were female heads of households with children under 18 and no husband present, 3.25 million (10%) were ill or disabled, 2.6 million (8%) were going to school, and 7.5 million (23%) worked either full or part time in the previous year, but their wages were not sufficient to elevate them above the poverty threshold (U.S. Bureau of the Census, 1987). Nearly half of these recipients are either too young or too old to work. Of the remainder, Matza and Miller (1976) found that only two-thirds of the poor who are eligible for welfare, apply for welfare. Prager (1988) claims that 25% of American families use the welfare system at some time or other, but that the assistance needed is for short periods only.

(4)   Many people also believe that welfare families are loaded with children, they have more children to get more money, and that most of the children are illegitimate (Edelman, 1987; Garfinkel and McLanahan, 1986; Johnson et al., 1988; Miller, 1989). The facts are that welfare families have an average of 2.2 children (U.S. Department of Health, Education and Welfare, 1972), and less than half of them are illegitimate. For example, 55% of the mothers receiving AFDC are divorced or separated, and 38% have never been married (Garfinkel and McLanahan, 1986; Sidel, 1986; U.S. Bureau of the Census, 1981b).

(5)   Many people also believe that once a family goes on welfare, it will remain on welfare forever. Evidence indicates that half of the families on welfare receive assistance for less than two years (Duncan, 1984; U.S. Department of Health, Education and Welfare, 1972), although black female heads of households remain on public assistance twice as long as white female heads of households. The median length of time for black female heads is 45.2 months compared to 21.6 months for white female heads (Rank, 1988).

(6)   Studies indicate that once peoples' beliefs about the causes of poverty and their attitudes toward welfare are formed, they do not change over time, even when it becomes clearly evident that the social structure rather than individual characteristics is causing the poverty. A nationwide survey showed that most people attribute the causes of poverty to the poor themselves rather than to the social structure; 55% of respondents in one study said that lack of effort by the poor is a very important cause of poverty, and 58% said that lack of thrift and proper money management are significant causes of poverty (Feagin, 1975). These attitudes did not change in the 1970s when the country underwent "stagflation" and recession and many people lost their jobs and had to accept public assistance (Kluegel, 1987; Levitan and Shapiro, 1987; Shapiro, 1989; U.S. Bureau of the Census, 1989).

(7)   Studies also indicate that the poor share many of the attitudes and goals of the middle class. For example, research has found that the poor and nonpoor share a willingness to work; the differences are that the poor lack confidence in their ability to succeed and accept welfare as a necessity caused by chronic unemployment or underemployment (Duncan, 1984; Ellwood, 1988; Goodwin, 1973).

Data, Sample, and Measures

(8)   Data for the study were collected as part of a larger 1986 General Social Survey by the National Opinion Research Center (NORC). Each survey was an independently drawn sample of English-speaking persons 18 years of age or over, living in noninstitutional arrangements within the United States. Each of 1470 respondents selected at random was interviewed for about one and a half hours, but the research sample for this study consisted of only the 1346 respondents who stated their family income for 1986. The research sample was 89% white, 54% female, and 77% had at least a high school education, which is similar to the total sample population.

Dependent and Independent Variables

(9)   The dependent variable is perception of welfare. To measure this variable, respondents were asked to 1 = strongly disagree, 2 = disagree, 3 = agree, or 4 = strongly agree with three positive statements and three negative statements about welfare. The positive statements were as follows: "Welfare helps prevent hunger and starvation." "Welfare helps people get on their feet when facing difficult situations such as unemployment, a divorce or a death in the family." "Welfare helps keep

marriages together in times of financial problems." The three negative statements were as follows: "Welfare makes people work less than they would if there wasn't a welfare system." "Welfare encourages young women to have babies before marriage." "Welfare discourages young women who get pregnant from marrying the father of the child."

(10)   The independent variable is family income, which was divided into 1 = $0-$10,000 (poor), 2 = $10,001-$20,000 (working class), 3 = $20,001-$40,000 (lower middle class), 4 = $40,001-$60,000 (middle class). This placed 299 (22%) respondents in the $0-$10,000 category, 314 (23%) in the $10,001-$20,000, 481 (36%) in the $20,001-$40,000, and 252 (19%) in the $40,001-$60,000. The $10,000 was selected as the poverty level for this study because 33% of American households have a net worth of less than $10,000 (including checking and savings accounts, vehicles, and all other assets except regular income) (U.S. Bureau of the Census, 1980, 1987).

(11)   Analysis of variance is used to determine the nature of relationships between the independent variable of four different categories of family income and the dependent variable of perception of welfare. Although the categories are not of equal intervals, the assumption was made that some degree of interval data existed among the family income categories and the degree of agreement or disagreement on the attitude items. Therefore, analysis of variance statistics are used to find the means and the significance levels. A mean of 2.5 or more is considered to show agreement with the statement since that is the midpoint of the continuum.

Findings

(12)   The nature of the relationship between family income and perception of welfare is presented in table 1. Hypothesis 1 is confirmed: Respondents in all four categories agreed with all three positive statements about welfare as well as all three negative statements about welfare. They agreed that welfare helps prevent hunger and starvation, that it helps people get on their feet, that it helps keep marriages together, that it makes people work less, that it encourages young women to have babies before marriage, that it discourages young women who get pregnant from marrying the father of the child.

(13)   The second hypothesis is partially confirmed. On the first statement, there are no significant differences among the four income categories in terms of welfare helping prevent hunger and starvation. All four

groups strongly agreed. On the second statement, the three lower-income categories have higher means on the perception that welfare helps people get on their feet. The difference is significant at the .05 level. On the third statement, the two lower-income groups are more likely to agree that welfare helps keep marriages together. The difference is significant at the .05 level. On the fourth statement, the lowest income group is less likely to agree that welfare makes people work less. The means increase with each income category, and the difference is significant at the .01 level. On the fifth statement, there are no significant differences among the four income categories in terms of welfare encouraging young women to have babies before marriage; all four groups agree. On the last statement, the two lower-income groups are less likely to agree that welfare discourages young women who get pregnant from marrying the father of the child. The difference is significant at the .05 level.

Conclusions and Discussion

(14)   The focus of this study was twofold: (1) to examine respondents' perceptions of welfare, and (2) to compare the perceptions of four family income groups on welfare. In general, all four income categories agreed with all three positive statements: that welfare helps prevent hunger and starvation, that it helps people get on their feet, that it helps keep marriages together.

(15)   It is not surprising that most respondents agreed that welfare helps prevent hunger and starvation since that is the underlying premise of the program and the agency has been effective in promoting that image. We can make the assumption that people are willing to pay taxes for a welfare system that keeps people from going hungry, helps them get on their feet, and helps save their marriages.

(16)   In general, all four income categories also agreed with all three negative statements: that welfare makes people work less, encourages women to have babies before marriage, and discourages young women who get pregnant from marrying the father of the child. The idea that welfare makes people work less is particularly strong in this study. We have to make some assumptions about what "works less" means to the recipients. It is assumed that all four income groups perceive the system as encouraging welfare recipients to work less (i.e., that if they lose their jobs, they can go on welfare and take their time about finding another job; that if they have no present job and are willing to live on low government payments, there are no incentives to make them go out and find a job to get off

Table 1. A Comparison of Four Income Groups on Perceptions About Welfare

Percep-tion Item	Poor 0– 10,000		Working 10,001– 20,000		Lower Middle 20,001– 40,000		Middle 40,001– 60,000			
	X̄	SD	X̄	SD	X̄	SD	X̄	SD	F	Sig
Welfare: Helps Pre-vent Hunger and Starvation	3.08 (295)	.52	3.04 (313)	.54	3.01 (478)	.57	2.99 (252)	.59	1.56	.197
Helps People Get on Their Feet	2.95 (297)	.59	2.97 (312)	.62	2.97 (476)	.61	2.83 (251)	.63	3.22	.022*
Helps Keep People's Marriages Together	2.64 (282)	.64	2.61 (309)	.65	2.57 (470)	.72	2.46 (244)	.66	3.40	.017*
Makes Peo-ple Work Less	3.00 (291)	.78	3.13 (312)	.71	3.21 (478)	.71	3.30 (250)	.64	8.64	.000**
Encourages Young Women to Have Babies Before Marriage	2.68 (283)	.86	2.75 (308)	.86	2.83 (470)	.81	2.82 (249)	.80	2.16	.090
Discour-ages Preg-nant Young Women from Marrying the Father of the Child	2.65 (278)	.76	2.63 (302)	.73	2.77 (464)	.74	2.72 (244)	.70	2.64	.047*

*$p < .05$

**$p < .01$

public assistance). We can further assume that when the public responds negatively to the concept of public assistance, it is because of perceptions like these (i.e., the American public may not be willing to contribute to a system that is perceived as counterproductive for the society).

(17)   If departments of human services desire more support from the American public, they will have to provide evidence that will dispel these negative perceptions. For example, it will be necessary to provide statistics that indicate that the marriage rate for young women on welfare who get pregnant is the same as it is for the rest of the population; that women on welfare have the same number of babies as young women who are not on welfare; and that people on welfare continue to look for work, and once off welfare, are as productive as people who have never been on welfare.

(18)   The second hypothesis proposed that the poor share the same perceptions of welfare as the nonpoor. The findings support the hypothesis. The poor in the study agreed with all six statements — the only differences from the nonpoor were in the degrees of agreement. For two statements there was no difference: the poor were as likely as the nonpoor to agree that welfare helps prevent hunger and starvation and that it encourages young women to have babies before marriage.

(19)   There were some differences in perceptions between the poor and the other income groups on four statements. The poor were less likely to agree that welfare would make people work less and more likely to agree that it would help people get on their feet. These differences in perception may be explained in that people in the low-income group know that they are not lazy — just having trouble, and when their period of difficulty is over, they anticipate that they will find work again. The middle class may be too far removed from the poor to "see" the recipients applying for work or interviewing for jobs.

(20)   The poor were also more likely to agree that welfare helps keep marriages together and less likely to agree that it discourages young women who get pregnant from marrying the father of the child. Again, the poor are in a better position to realize that welfare assistance for an additional child is not sufficient to support that child. The poor may also be in a better position to know that although there are not enough available men to marry in the lower class, some women will choose to have children anyway; or they may choose not to marry the father of their child who has no prospects for a job or an income himself. She can support her child herself. But should she leave her baby at home while she works, often for minimum pay? The poor may decide that the mother should remain at home with her child; the middle class, on the other hand, who are attempting to be "super mom" and are combining and balancing marriage, parenthood and jobs may have less sympathy for that attitude.

(21)   Regardless of the reasons for the perceptions, it is clear from this study that the poor share many of the same perceptions of welfare as other people. Because the poor are blamed for their condition, a stigma is attached to poverty and particularly to those who receive welfare or some other form of government assistance. These prejudices against welfare recipients have made it difficult to establish effective programs to help the poor. It is clear that if we are to change the perceptions of the public toward welfare, we must change the perceptions of the poor as well as the nonpoor. If they have the same negative perception of themselves as others do, it is understandable that a third of the people eligible for assistance do not apply for it (Matza and Miller, 1976).

References

AuClaire, P. A.
1984   "Public attitudes toward social welfare expenditures." Social Work 29: 139-144.

Backley, P. R.
1988   "Explaining relative income of low-income families in U.S. cities." Social Science Quarterly 69:835-852.

Bane, M. J.
1986   "Household composition and poverty." Pp. 209-231 in S. H. Danziger and D. H. Weinberg (eds.), Fighting Poverty: What Works and What Doesn't. Cambridge, MA: Harvard University Press.

Bowen, J. L. and Pizer, H. F.
1987   Living Hungry in America. New York, NY: New American Library.

Danziger, S. H., Haveman, R. H. and Plotnick, R. D.
1986   "Antipoverty policy: effects on the poor and the nonpoor." Pp. 50-77 in S. H. Danziger and D. H. Weinberg (eds.), Fighting Poverty: What Works and What Doesn't. Cambridge, MA: Harvard University Press.

Duncan, G. J.
1984   Years of Poverty, Years of Plenty: The Changing Economic Fortunes of American Workers and Families. Ann Arbor, MI: Institute for Social Research.

Edelman, M. W.
1987   Families in Peril: An Agency for Social Change. Cambridge, MA: Harvard University Press.

Ellwood, D. T.
1988   Poor Support: Poverty in the American Family. New York, NY: Basic Books.

Ellwood, D. T. and Summers, L. H.
1986   "Poverty in America: is welfare the answer or the problem?" Pp. 78-105 in S. H. Danziger and D. H. Weinberg (eds.), Fighting Poverty: What Works and What Doesn't. Cambridge, MA: Harvard University Press.

Feagin, J.
1975   Subordinating the Poor: Welfare and American Beliefs. Englewood Cliffs, NJ: Prentice-Hall.

Garfinkel, I. and McLanahan, S.
1986   Single Mothers and Their Children: A New American Dilemma. Lanham, MD: University Press of America.

Goodwin, L.
1973   Do the Poor Want to Work? Washington, DC: Brackens Institution.

Institute for Research on Poverty
1987–1988 "Tracking the homeless." Focus (Winter): 20-24.

Johnson, C. M., Sum, A. M. and Weill, J. D.
 1988 Vanishing Dreams: The Growing Economic Plight of America's Young Families. Washington, DC: Children's Defense Fund.

Kluegel, J. R.
 1987 "Macro-economic problems, belief about the poor and attitudes toward welfare spending." Social Problems 34:82-99.

Levitan, S. A., Mangum, G. L. and Pines, M. W.
 1989 A Proper Inheritance: Investing in the Self-Sufficiency of Poor Families. Washington, DC: Center for Social Policy Studies.

Levitan, S. A. and Shapiro, I.
 1987 Working But Poor: America's Contradiction. Baltimore, MD: Johns Hopkins University Press.

Levy, F.
 1987 Dollars and Dreams: The Changing American Income Distribution. Ithaca, NY: Cornell University Press.

Matza, D. and Miller, H.
 1976 "Poverty and proletariat." Pp. 655-656 in Robert K. Merton and Robert Nisbet (eds.), Contemporary Social Problems (4th ed.). New York: Harcourt Brace Jovanovich.

McGeary, M. and Lynn, L. E.
 1988 Urban Change and Poverty. Washington DC: National Academy Press.

Miller, G., ed.
 1989 Giving Children a Chance: The Case for More Effective National Policies. Lanham, MD: University Press of America.

National Research Council
 1987 Risking the Future: Adolescent Sexuality, Pregnancy, and Childbearing. Washington, DC: National Academy Press.
 1989 A Common Destiny: Blacks and American Society. Washington, DC: National Academy Press.

Porter, K. H.
 1989 Poverty in Rural America. Washington, DC: Center on Budget and Policy Priorities.

Prager, C. A. L.
 1988 "Poverty in North America: losing ground." Canadian Public Policy 14: 52-65.

Rank, M. R.
 1988 "Racial differences in length of welfare use." Social Forces 66:1080-1101.

Shapiro, I.
 1989 Laboring for Less: Working But Poor in Rural America. Washington, DC: Center on Budget and Policy Priorities.

Sidel, R.
 1986 Women and Children Last: The Plight of Poor Women in Affluent America. New York, NY: Penguin Books.

U.S. Bureau of the Census
 1980 "Money income and poverty status: 1980." Washington DC: U.S. Government Printing Office.
 1981a "Characteristics of the population below the poverty level: 1980." Washington DC: U.S. Government Printing Office, p.6.
 1981b Statistical Abstract of the United States: 1981 Washington DC: U.S. Bureau of the Census, p. 156.
 1983 Statistical Abstract of the United States: 1982-83. Washington DC: U.S. Bureau of the Census, p. 429.
 1987 Statistical Abstract of the United States: 1986. Washington DC: U.S. Bureau of the Census.
 1989 "Money income and poverty status in the United States: 1988 ." Washington, DC: Government Printing Office.

U. S. Department of Health, Education and Welfare
 1972 "Welfare myths vs. facts." Washington, DC: U.S. Government Printing Office.

Working Seminar on Family and American Welfare Policy
 1987 The New Consensus on Family and Welfare: A Community of Self-Reliance. Lanham, MD: University Press of America.

Factual Questions

1. How does the present research differ from the study published by AuClaire in 1984?

2. What hypotheses does the author propose?

3. What percentage of the persons living below the poverty line in 1985 were children?

4. Why does this study use only 1346 of the 1470 respondents who participated in the 1986 General Social Survey?

5. What percentage of the sample was female?

6. What were the three positive statements to which respondents were to indicate the extent of their agreement or disagreement?

7. What was the highest family income a person could have and still be classified as poor? What percentage of the sample was classified as poor?

8. A majority of the respondents in which income groups agreed with the statement that welfare makes people work less?

9. On which of the six statements were there significant differences among the four income groups on the average level of agreement?

Questions for Discussion

10. Does the introduction provide a clear notion of the research problem, the purpose of the research, and its significance?

11. Does the literature review seem relevant to the research problem?

12. Are the stated hypotheses reasonable? Do they appear to reasonably follow from the review of the literature?

13. Is the number of research subjects sufficient? To what population would you generalize the results of this study?

14. Is there enough information on the research instruments and procedures to allow you to replicate this study?

15. Should there be information about the reliability and validity of the research instruments and procedures?

16. Does the analysis include sufficient statistical information? Are the statistics that are used appropriate?

17. Are the conclusions supported by and do they logically follow from the data that have been presented?

18. Are the findings discussed in terms of their implications and/or practical significance?

Article 17

Age and White Racial Attitudes:
National Surveys, 1972–1989

David E. Jorgenson
Christabel B. Jorgenson
Southwest Texas State University

The responses of white adults to three questions concerning race relations from national surveys (1972-1989) were examined. The questions, which served as the major dependent variables, refer to interracial marriage, open housing, and the election of a black for president of the United States. The responses to these questions were analyzed in terms of four age groups. The issues addressed by this research include: Are there statistically significant differences in the responses among the four age groups regarding the racial questions? Do these differences remain significant or do they change over time? How are the differences among age groups explained?

The results indicated significant differences in the percentage responses among the four age groups in the cross-sectional analysis for each year from 1972-1989. These differences remained rather stable over a 15- and 16-year span, although there was a slight shift in attitudes overall. It is proposed that racial attitudes were developed in the formative years, especially in late adolescence and young adulthood and remained rather constant through time. This explanation corresponds to Mannheim's (1952) idea that we are creatures of the culture and become affected by the "spirit of the time."

(1)   Although age has been studied in relationship to medicine, physiology, and psychology, the social issue of race relations has received minimal attention in reference to age. Some researchers have addressed the issue of whether attitudes change as people grow older (Cutler and Kaufman 1975; Cutler, Lentz, Muha and Riter 1980; Foner 1974; Glenn 1974, 1981; Riley and Foner 1968). In the use of cross-sectional data, differences in attitudes by different age groups led to the assumption by some that growing old was accompanied by a resistance to change and an increase in rigidity and conservatism regarding political and social issues (Cutler and Kaufman 1975; Riley and Foner 1968).

(2)   With the availability of archival data spanning long periods of time, this inference has been challenged. Cutler et al. (1980), using survey data spanning a 12-year period, demonstrated that the aging process did not lead to greater conservatism and attitudinal rigidity relative to the abortion issue. There was little variation among the birth cohorts, and the older cohorts were no more rigid than the younger ones. Other studies also challenged the belief that the aging process brings about change, especially changes in attitude that may differ from the population in general (Foner 1974; Glenn 1974; Willits, Bealer and Crider, 1977).

Reprinted with permission from *Sociological Spectrum, 12*: 21-34. Copyright © 1992 by Taylor & Francis, Inc.

An earlier version of this article was presented at the annual meeting of the American Sociological Association, Washington, DC, August, 1990.

(3)   Are there differences in racial attitudes among different age groups? Do these differences between age groups change over time? How are these differences in attitudes by age groups explained? This article addresses these questions.

(4)   Time and events affect the lives of those generations that experience them. Clausen (1986) stated: "Even in relatively stable, traditional societies, each generation has its unique themes and problems" (p. 7). Today we face different kinds of challenges and situations than our parents and grandparents faced. The social and technological changes that occurred during their early years may have had a profound impact on their life course. Specific events such as World War II or the Great Depression may have had such a profound impact on the lives of the people experiencing them that they carried or will carry these effects with them throughout their lives (Foner, 1986).

(5)   In a unique study of collective memories by various age groups, Schuman and Scott (1989) demonstrated the profound effects that major events had in the lives of the generations who experienced them. They asked a probability sample of Americans, 18 years of age and older, to name a national or world event occurring within the last 50 years that they considered to be of special importance. The results indicated that age groups of people named those events that corresponded most closely to the time period of their adolescence or young adulthood. With all of the noteworthy events that have happened since, it was World War II that ranked highest among the older ages who experienced the war during their adolescence or young adult years. The Vietnam War and the assassination of President John F. Kennedy were mentioned by those who experienced these events during that period of their lives. The national and world events considered most important to other age groups also related to the time frame of their adolescence and young adulthood.

(6)   Mannheim (1952) spoke about the uniqueness of each generation of people who through their experiences develop a distinctive *Zeitgeist* or "spirit of the time" that they carried with them through their life course. In addition to being creatures of culture, they are creatures of their time and for Mannheim the most profound time seemed to be in adolescence and early adulthood. Whereas some psychologists may stress the importance of early childhood in personality formation, Mannheim contends late adolescence and young

adulthood are the formative years. This is especially true in relation to the impact of social and political events, as these are the years when issues become more clearly defined and meaningful.

(7)   In continuity theory we find emphasis on personality formation of the early years that continues throughout the life cycle with relatively little change (Neugarten 1968). Adjustments or lack of them during the middle and later years is explained by a core personality, which is formed early in life. In this paper we contend that attitudes relative to social issues are formed in the early years but are most profoundly affected in the time of adolescence and young adulthood. During this period the issues such as race relations will have more meaning both experientially and cognitively. It is hypothesized that when responding to questions of race relations, there will be statistically significant differences among four age groups of white U.S. adults in terms of percentage of positive responses. It is expected that there will be a larger percentage of younger age groups responding positively than older age groups. It is further hypothesized that the percentage differences among the four age groups will remain significant for each year over a 15- to 16-year span and that there will be a slight improvement in attitudes overall.

(8)   Research has shown a trend toward more positive attitudes by white samples (Carlson and Iovini 1985; Schuman, Steeh and Bobo 1985). Schuman et al. (1985) summarized the trends in white racial attitudes by examining results of surveys conducted by the National Opinion Research Center (NORC), Gallup, and the Institute of Social Research (ISR). Examining surveys that dated back to the mid-1940s and extending to the mid-1980s, they concluded that there was a trend in more positive attitudes among white citizens relative to interracial marriage, integrated neighborhoods, and the election of a black president. These studies did not, however, take into account the percentage differences in attitudes that exist among age groups.

Method

Sample

(9)   The data for this research were obtained from 16 general social surveys (1972-1978, 1980, 1982-1989) from the NORC (Davis and Smith 1989).[1] The responses of white adult U.S. residents to three questions pertaining to racial attitudes were examined.

---

[1] Surveys were not conducted by the NORC in 1979 and 1981. The reasons for these omissions are unknown to authors.

TABLE 1.
Number of Possible Respondents by Birth Cohort and Age for Each Survey Year, 1972 to 1989

Birth cohort	1972 Age	N	1973 Age	N	1974 Age	N	1975 Age	N	1976 Age	N	1977 Age	N	1978 Age	N	1980 Age	N
-1918	54+	431	55+	396	56+	390	57+	379	58+	399	59+	331	60+	320	62+	304
1919–1930	42–53	315	43–54	260	44–55	253	45–56	241	46–57	229	47–58	277	48–59	249	50–61	219
1931–1942	30–41	270	31–42	297	32–43	269	33–44	271	34–45	269	34–46	284	36–47	245	38–49	224
1943–1954	18–29	332	19–30	349	20–31	366	21–32	360	22–33	370	23–34	410	24–35	410	26–37	381
Total		1348		1302		1278		1251		1267		1228		1224		1128

Birth cohort	1982 Age	N	1983 Age	N	1984 Age	N	1985 Age	N	1986 Age	N	1987 Age	N	1988 Age	N	1989 Age	N
-1918	64+	285	65+	248	66+	210	67+	227	68+	203	69+	177	70+	183	71+	165
1919–1930	52–63	235	53–64	238	54–65	198	55–66	221	56–67	194	57–68	197	58–69	207	59–70	202
1931–1942	40–51	208	41–52	225	42–53	191	43–54	223	44–55	190	45–56	220	46–57	137	47–58	203
1943–1954	28–39	330	29–40	382	30–41	327	31–42	330	32–43	328	33–44	312	34–45	330	34–46	316
Total		1058		1093		926		1001		915		906		857		886

The three questions were included in most of the surveys but none of the three was included in all 16 surveys.

(10)   Block quota sampling was used in the 1972, 1973, and 1974 surveys and for half of the 1975 and 1976 surveys. In half of the 1975 and 1976, and in all of the 1977, 1978, and 1980-1989, full probability sampling was used (Davis and Smith, 1989).[2] Table 1 shows the actual number of possible respondents for each age group for each of the 15 years.

Variables

(11)   The focus of this study was on racial attitudes of white adults from 1972 to 1989, using age groups as the major independent variable. Four age groups with age ranges of 12 years (with the exception of those born 1918 and earlier) were used for the entire 16-year span. Beginning with the year 1972, these age groups are: (1) 1918 and earlier (54 years and over); (2) 1919-1930 (42 to 53 years); (3) 1931-1942 (30 to 41 years); and (4) 1943-1954 (18 to 29 years).

(12)   The three racial attitude questions constitute the dependent variables. These questions were selected among several racial attitude questions because they appeared to represent important personal and social issues around which race relations have revolved in this country. The three questions were:

1. "Do you think there should be laws against marriages between blacks and whites?" The responses were coded as 0 = yes, 1 = no.
2. "Suppose there is a communitywide vote on the general housing issue. There are two possible laws to vote on. Which law would you vote for?
   a. One law says that a homeowner can decide for himself who to sell his house to, even if he prefers not to sell to blacks.
   b. The second law says that a homeowner cannot refuse to sell to someone because of their race or color." Agreement to *a* is coded as 0 and agreement to *b* is coded as 1.

3. "If your party nominated a black for president, would you vote for him if he were qualified for the job?" Responses were coded as 1 = yes, 0 = no. The average number of responses by all four age groups for each of these questions was Q1 = 1,072 Q2 = 1,090 Q3 = 1,103. These numbers compare to an average total possible response for all 16 years of 1,104.

Procedure

(13)   The trend in racial attitudes as depicted by these three questions was first examined using the entire sample of white respondents for each of these appropriate years. The trend in racial attitudes for each age group was then examined for each of the questions, tracing the changes in percentages from 1972-1989. An analysis of variance was computed to determine if the differences among these age groups were significant.

(14)   The changing sex ratio from early adulthood to old age may produce a bias if females hold different attitudes than males relative to the racial questions. We compared the response differences between males and females for each group for each survey year and for each question. Out of the 140 comparisons only 16 (11%) produced statistically significant differences between males and females relative to the racial questions. Following Glenn (1981), we did not control for sex ratio in our analysis.

Results

(15)   The first question concerns attitudes toward interracial marriage: "Do you think there should be laws against marriages between blacks and whites?" In Figure 1 the percentage of the general sample who responded "no" to that question (those in favor of allowing interracial marriage) changed from 60.7% in 1972 to 76.8% in 1989. Figure 2 shows that when age groups are considered there is little variation from 1972-1989, and there is a significant difference among the age groups relative to this question in each survey year ($p < .05$). The difference between the oldest and youngest in 1972 was 33.3% and 31.1% in 1989. The

---

[2]The block quota method used in the early 1970s was a multistage area probability sample at the block or segment level. At the block level, the quota method was used based on sex, age, and employment status. Half of the 1975 and 1976 samples and those in the following years were full probability samples. The primary sampling units (PSUs) employed are standard metropolitan statistical areas (SMSAs) or nonmetropolitan counties selected in NORC's master sample. These SMSAs and counties were stratified by region, age, and race before selection. At the second stage the units of selection were block groups (BGs) and enumeration districts (EDs), which were stratified according to race and income before selection. The third stage was blocks where selections were made with probabilities proportional to size. Where there were no blocks, measures of size were obtained by field counting. At the block or segment level, the interviewer begins at the first dwelling unit from the northwest corner and proceeds in a specified direction until the quotas have been filled. The quotas call for the exact proportion of men and women in that census tract with the additional requirement that there be the proper proportion of employed and unemployed women and there be the proper proportion of men over and under 35 years of age in that location (Davis and Smith 1989, Appendix A).

smallest percentage favoring interracial marriage is found in the oldest age group and the largest percentage is found in the youngest group. The percentage agreeing with the statement "that a homeowner cannot refuse to sell to someone because of their race or color" for the general sample is displayed in Figure 3 and for each of the age groups in Figure 4. There is a trend in favorable attitudes for the general sample, where in 1973 34.8% agreed with the statement, whereas in 1989 57.9% agreed. When examining the trends by age groups (Figure 4), there is a slight upward trend for each group with upward and downward turns for the three oldest groups from the mid-1980s. Again there is a statistically significant difference among all age groups with the oldest having the smallest percentage favoring open housing and the youngest showing the largest favorable percentage. These differences for each group for each year are also significant ($p < .05$) with a difference between the oldest and youngest in 1973 (25%) and in 1989 (24.7%).

(16)   Again, the third question was: "If your party nominated a black for president, would you vote for him if he were qualified for the job?" The percentage of the general white sample answering this question in the affirmative appears in Figure 5. There was a slight overall increase from 1972-1989 with 73.8% responding positively in 1972, and 81% in 1989, even though there was a downward turn from 1986-1989. The trends of the age groups in Figure 6 show very little change with greater variation among the oldest group. The differences although slight, between the youngest and oldest groups are statistically significant ($p < .05$) with a difference between the oldest and youngest in 1972 (20.4%) and in 1989 (10.9%).

Discussion

(17)   We hypothesized that when comparing the percentages of positive responses to three race relations questions, there would be statistically significant

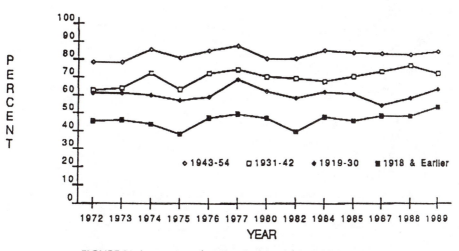

FIGURE 1. General sample favoring interracial marriage.

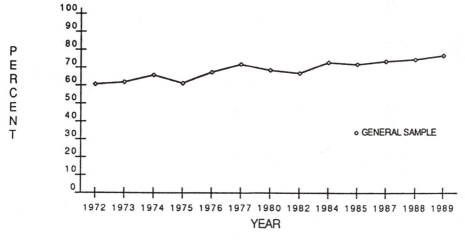

FIGURE 2. Age groups favoring interracial marriage.

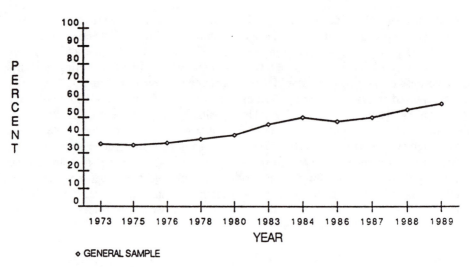

FIGURE 3. General sample favoring open housing.

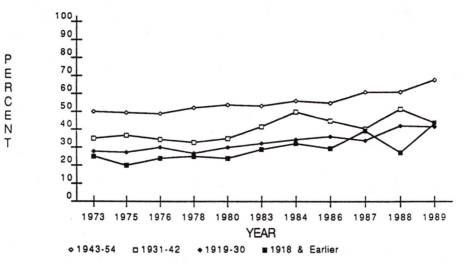

FIGURE 4. Age groups favoring open housing.

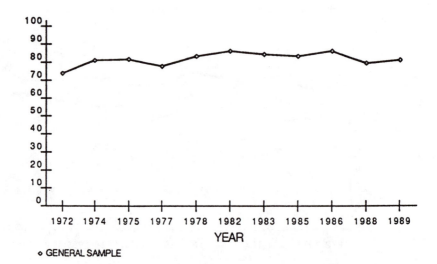

FIGURE 5. General sample favoring a black for president.

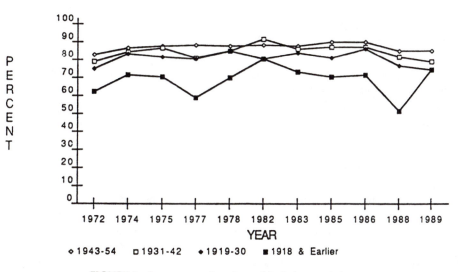

FIGURE 6. Age groups favoring a black for president.

differences among age groups of U.S. white adults. We further hypothesized that these differences would be observed through the survey years. Finally, we hypothesized that there would be a slight improvement in racial attitudes over the 16-year span.

(18)   The results of this research appear to support these hypotheses. When examining the responses of the four age groups to three race relations questions, the percentage differences in positive responses were statistically significant, with the younger age groups more positive in their attitudes than the older age groups. The differences among the four groups were statistically significant for each of the survey years. The most noticeable differences were related to the questions of interracial marriage and open housing. The differences among the groups in reference to the question of a black president were slight for the three youngest groups. A much smaller percentage of the oldest group answered affirmatively. This research demonstrates that there was a slight improvement in racial attitudes when observing the increase in the percent of positive responses over the 16-year period for both the general sample and for each age group.

(19)   Glenn (1981) suggested that other information should be included in one's analysis of the changes that may be observed among age groups over time. A changing social structure and climate might be responsible for some of the change. In examining interracial marriage during the survey time periods, there was an increase from .7% in 1970 to 1.5% in 1987 of all marriages. In actual numbers this was a change from 310,000 interracial marriages out of 44,597,000 total marriages to

799,000 interracial marriages out of 52,286,000 total marriages.

(20)   When examining other changes during this time period among the white sample in this study, it was found that the level of education increased. The percentage of the whites who had more than a high school education rose from 32.2% in 1973 to 45.1% in 1989 — a 12.9% increase. From the same sample, it was found that church attendance by blacks to white churches increased from 34% in 1978 to 40% in 1989.

(21)   There was evidence of counter trends among this sample of white adults. Responding to a political scale of liberalism and conservatism, 28.9% of the white sample laid claim to a liberal political philosophy in 1974, and in 1989 only 26.6% made this claim. By the same token in 1973, 23.8% of the white sample identified with religious fundamentalism but 28.9% in 1989 — an increase of more than 5%.

(22)   This additional evidence — increase in interracial marriage, increase in level of education, increase in blacks attending white churches — may partly explain the trend toward a more positive atmosphere for race relations. Yet, the increase in political conservatism and religious fundamentalism may also help to explain why the change was not greater than it was.

(23)   The differences among the age groups can be explained partly by the socialization process. Each age group experiences a different "spirit of the times" with regard to race relations. Although much of this experience and training occurred during the formative years of childhood, late adolescence and early adulthood were

age periods when probably much of their thinking became crystallized with regard to race relations.

(24)   The 1918 and earlier age group experienced a time during these formative years when racial segregation prevailed. Interracial marriage was outlawed in most states and considered by many a violation of much higher laws. The right to vote for blacks was not a consideration, and electing a black for president was probably not among their wildest dreams. Attitudes about race relations were formed, if not clarified, and acted on in this sociocultural climate; they were carried onward through the years that followed and have prevailed for many people to this day (Parrillo 1990).

(25)   The 1919-1930 age group may have found in its formative years of late adolescence and early adulthood a racial climate that was beginning to change. Many in this group entered the military and served during World War II. Although there was some evidence of a breakdown of racial barriers, segregation was widespread even in the military. Some in this age group were affected by the 1954 Supreme Court decision of *Brown v. Board of Education*. Although there was still segregation in neighborhoods, and laws against interracial marriage, the sociocultural climate of the times may have been more positive from the climate of the times experienced by the previous age group.

(26)   Members of the age group born between 1931 and 1942 found themselves in their formative years of late adolescence and early adulthood at the beginning of other changes. As with the earlier age group, many went through the *Brown v. Board of Education* Supreme Court decision and were affected by a national climate that helped elect President John F. Kennedy, a strong advocate of civil rights. Yet, it was the next age group, born between 1943 and 1954, that perhaps was most affected by changes in civil rights activities during their formative years of late adolescence and early adulthood. Not only did they witness the enactment of civil rights legislation, some of which included the breakdown of racial barriers of public accommodations and the educational system, but also many of them were participants in the civil rights movement. Certainly, the atmosphere in race relations was far different from earlier times.

(27)   Each age group in this study, passing through the formative years of late adolescence and early adulthood, experienced a unique sociocultural climate of race relations and, for the most part, was affected by it. They carried with them through the ensuing years the consequences of these earlier experiences and observations.

With each generation, the climate may not only have been different but, with each birth period, somewhat improved — at least regarding the issues of interracial marriage, open housing, and a black for president. If the trend continues as it has, the onset of each new age group and the passing of each older age group should bring about an improved general climate of race relations in this country.

References

Carlson, James M. and Joseph Iovini. 1985. "The Transmission of Racial Attitudes from Fathers to Sons: A Study of Blacks and Whites." *Adolescence* 20:233-237.

Clausen, J. A. 1986. *The Life Course: A Sociological Perspective*. Englewood Cliffs, New Jersey: Prentice-Hall.

Cutler, Stephen J., Sally Ann Lentz, Michael J. Muha and Robert N. Riter. 1980. "Aging and Conservatism: Cohort Changes in Attitudes About Legalized Abortion." *Journal of Gerontology* 35:115-123.

Cutler, S. J. and R. L. Kaufman. 1975. "Cohort Changes in Political Attitudes: Tolerance of Ideological Nonconformity." *Public Opinion Quarterly* 39:69-81.

Davis, James and Tom W. Smith. 1989. *General Social Surveys, 1972-1989*. Chicago: National Opinion Research Center.

Foner, A. 1974. "Age Stratification and Age Conflict in Political Life." *American Sociological Review* 39:187-196.

Foner, A. 1986. *Aging and Old Age: New Perspectives*. Englewood Cliffs, New Jersey: Prentice-Hall.

Glenn, N. D. 1974. "Aging and Conservatism." *Annal of the American Academy of Political and Social Science* 415:176-186.

Glenn, N. D. 1981. "Age, Birth Cohorts, and Drinking: An Illustration of the Hazards of Inferring Effects from Cohort Data." *Journal of Gerontology* 36:362-369.

Mannheim, Karl. 1952. "The Problem of Generations." Pp. 276-322 in *Essays on the Sociology of Knowledge*, by Karl Mannheim. London: Routledge and Kegal-Paul.

Neugarten, Bernice. 1968. *Middle Age and Aging*. Chicago: University of Chicago Press.

Parrillo, V. N. 1990. *Strangers to These Shores: Race and Ethnic Relations in America* (3rd ed). New York: Macmillan.

Riley, M. W. and A. Foner. 1968. *Aging and Society: An Inventory of Research Findings*. New York: Russell Sage.

Schuman, H. and J. Scott. 1989. "Generations and Collective Memories." *American Sociological Review* 54:359-381.

Schuman, H., C. Steeh and Lawrence Bobo. 1985. *Racial Attitudes in America: Trends and Interpretations*. Cambridge, MA: Harvard University Press.

Willits, F. K., R. C. Bealer and D. M. Crider. 1977. "Changes in Individual Attitudes Toward Traditional Mortality: A 24-Year Follow-up Study." *Journal of Gerontology* 32:681-688.

Factual Questions

1. When asked to name a national or world event of special importance, a person is most likely to name an event which occurred during what period of that person's life?

2. What does *zeitgeist* mean?

3. What hypotheses do the authors state?

4. What are the four age groups, as defined by birth date, being compared?

5. What is the third racial attitude question used to form the dependent variable?

6. What was the average total number of responses by all four age groups for questions one, two, and three?

7. Why could a changing sex ratio from early adulthood to old age produce a bias in the results?

8. Why did the researchers not control for sex ratio in their analysis?

9. What percentage of the general sample responded "no" to the question "Do you think there should be laws against marriages between blacks and whites?" in 1972? in 1989?

10. How many percentage points difference was there between the percentage of the oldest group and the percentage of the youngest group responding "no" to the question "Do you think there should be laws against marriages between blacks and whites?" in 1972? in 1989?

11. Are all of the researchers' hypotheses supported by the data?

16. None of the three racial attitude questions was asked in every one of the years being studied. Is this a problem?

Questions for Discussion

17. Is there enough information on the research instruments and procedures to allow you to replicate this study?

12. Does the introduction provide a clear notion of the research problem, the purpose of the research, and its significance?

18. Should there be information about the reliability and validity of the research instruments and procedures?

13. Does the literature review seem relevant to the research problem?

19. Does the analysis include sufficient statistical information? Are the statistics that are used appropriate?

14. Are the stated hypotheses reasonable? Do they appear to reasonably follow from the review of the literature?

20. Are the conclusions supported by and do they logically follow from the data that have been presented?

15. Is the number of research subjects sufficient? To what population would you generalize the results of this study?

21. Are the findings discussed in terms of their implications and/or practical significance?

Article 18

A Measure of Risk Taking for Young Adolescents: Reliability and Validity Assessments

Cheryl S. Alexander
Johns Hopkins School of Hygiene and Public Health
Young J. Kim
Johns Hopkins School of Hygiene and Public Health
Margaret Ensminger
Johns Hopkins School of Hygiene and Public Health
Karin E. Johnson
Salisbury State University
B. Jill Smith
Johns Hopkins School of Hygiene and Public Health
Lawrence J. Dolan
Johns Hopkins School of Hygiene and Public Health

Researchers often define adolescent risk taking in terms of individual behaviors such as alcohol and drug use, early sexual activity, and reckless driving. It is not clear whether these behaviors defined by adults as "risky" have the same meaning for adolescents. This paper describes the development and preliminary testing of an instrument to assess risk taking among young adolescents. The six item scale was constructed by asking small groups of eighth grade boys and girls to describe "things that teenagers your age do for excitement or thrills." The measure was then used in a longitudinal study of 758 young adolescents from three rural counties in Maryland. The scale shows good reliability, as indicated by coefficient alpha and factor analyses. Eighth-grade scores on the scale are associated with the initiation of sexual activity and substance use in ninth grade among virgins and nonusers of alcohol, marijuana, cocaine and pills in eighth grade.

Reprinted with permission from *Journal of Youth and Adolescence, 19*(6): 559-569. Copyright © 1990 by Plenum Publishing Corporation.
Received January 10, 1990; accepted July 21, 1990

Introduction

(1)   Adolescence is generally considered as a time of risk taking. The major causes of death and disability for youth 15-19 years of age, motor vehicle injuries, other accidental injuries, suicide, and homicide, are rooted in behaviors that carry social and health risks (National Center for Health Statistics, 1984). Other behaviors such as sexual intercourse without protection against pregnancy or sexually transmitted diseases or driving when intoxicated have been offered as evidence of a risk taking propensity among teens (White and Johnson, 1988; Byrne and Fisher, 1983). For the most part, researchers have used individual behaviors to define adolescent risk taking. It is not clear whether behaviors defined by adults as "risky" carry the same connotation for young people. For example, driving fast may be viewed as risky by adults but the sign of a good driver by young adolescents. Risk taking may best be defined within the adolescent's own social context.

(2)   In this paper, we review two major theoretical approaches to the conceptualization and measurement of risk taking behavior during adolescence. We describe the development and preliminary testing of an instrument to assess risk taking among young adolescents.

Theoretical Approaches to Risk Taking

(3)   Jessor's (Jessor and Jessor, 1977) theory of problem behavior suggests that drinking, marijuana use, delinquency, and early sexual intercourse constitute a syndrome of behaviors that deviate from societal norms for adolescents. The onset of these behaviors is preceded by a psychosocial pattern of unconventional attitudes and perceptions. Studies of high school- and college-age populations indicate that adolescents who place a lower value on academic achievement and have lower self-esteem, greater tolerance of deviance, less religiosity, and a greater attachment to the positive aspects of problem behaviors are more likely to initiate those behaviors than those who do not share their perceptions (Jessor, 1983). Engagement in any one problem behavior increases one's susceptibility to engage in others.

(4)   Jessor's construct stresses the cognitive aspects of risk taking. Adolescents who are prone to engage in risky behaviors are characterized by a set of shared attitudes, perceptions, and values about themselves and society. A second perspective focuses on the emotional components of risk taking, that is, taking risks for pleasure and excitement. Zuckerman (1984) and his colleagues, in their studies of stimulus-seeking be-havior, developed an instrument to assess individual differences in optimal stimulation. The Sensation Seeking Scale differentiates individuals with strong needs for stimulation and arousal from those with fewer stimulus needs. In general, individuals with high sensation-seeking scores are uninhibited, nonconforming, and impulsive and have high needs for independence and change (Zuckerman and Link, 1968). In a series of studies using college students and young adults, individuals scoring high on sensation seeking reported more varied patterns of drug use and sexual activity than low-scoring individuals (Zuckerman et al., 1972).

(5)   The Sensation Seeking Scale was developed and tested using college students. Items reflect the experiences and activities of young adults. Our development of a risk-taking scale for young adolescents is based on both models and incorporates items on thrill seeking and involvement in deviant acts within the context of a population of 13-14 year olds.

Methods

Design

(6)   A longitudinal cohort design was used to examine the antecedents of health-compromising behaviors among rural adolescents. Health-compromising behaviors are defined as those behaviors initiated during the adolescent years that have long-term health and social consequences. These behaviors include tobacco, alcohol, and other drug use and early unprotected sexual intercourse. A cohort of rural students was surveyed annually over a 3-year period from eighth to tenth grade. Participants had their heights and weights measured and completed an assessment of their own pubertal development in each of the study years. In ninth grade, parents of participating students were interviewed about their perceptions of their adolescent's health and behavior, about their educational expectations for their youngster, and about family characteristics and family functioning. Information on standardized test scores and grades from eighth to tenth grades were obtained from school records. Analyses presented in this paper are based on data from the first 2 years of the 3-year study.

Sample

(7)   All eighth-grade students enrolled in seven public schools in 1986-1987 in three rural counties in Maryland were invited to participate. The decision to include all students was based on the size of the schools

and school officials' concerns about selecting some students and not others. Local advisory boards were created in each county to review survey materials and to monitor the administration of the study. Letters were sent to parents and students inviting participation. A few small but vocal groups in two of the counties objected to questions that asked students about their sexual experiences. Parent refusal rates in those two counties ranged from 20 to 35%.

(8)   The study sample of 758 eighth graders represented 64% of the total eligible population. The race and gender composition and California Cognitive Skills Test scores of participants did not differ significantly from distribution for the total cohort of eighth grade students. In ninth grade, 120 students were added to the study. These young people represented students who had transferred into the school systems or whose parents agreed to have them participate in high school. In this paper, we have used the total sample of students in the eighth and ninth grades as well as a subsample of panel students for whom we have *both* eighth- and ninth-grade information.

Measure of Risk Taking

(9)   The measure of risk taking was constructed using small focus groups of 8 to 10 students. Each group contained only males or females. These focus groups were part of the pilot testing of the questionnaire. Thirty-five students from a school not included in the study agreed to talk with the investigators about their health concerns and the kinds of behaviors engaged in by students in their school. They also agreed to complete the questionnaire and provide feedback regarding the clarity and appropriateness of items for rural adolescents. Students were asked to describe "things that teenagers your age do for excitement or thrills." Although there was overlap in what males and females reported as risking behaviors, boys focused on more daring physical feats such as racing a dirt bike and walking across a bridge rail, while girls were more likely to indicate disobedience or rule breaking. Suggestions were recorded and then collapsed into six items representing those common themes that the students agreed signaled risk taking. Students were asked about frequency categories for the risk-taking items. A three-level ordinal response scale was selected (Never, Once or Twice, and Several Times). An overall risk-taking score was computed by summing over the six items. Possible scores ranged from 6 to 18.

Results

(10)   Table I shows the frequency distributions of items at each time period. Items involving physical feats such as racing on a bike or boat show a decline in the percentage of students who report frequent involvement; on the other hand, more students at time 2 reported having ridden with a dangerous driver at least once. Such shifts would be expected as students move into high school and have greater exposure to older students.

Reliability

(11)   The internal consistency of the Adolescent Risk Taking Scale (ARTS) was assessed at each time period. Table II shows the item-to-total correlations and the alpha coefficients for the scale in eighth and ninth grade. Coefficients of .78 and .80 for a six-item scale indicate good internal consistency. Item-to-total correlations remain relatively stable over the 1-year period.

Shifts in Item Responses

(12)   Internal consistency assessments at each time period do not take into consideration shifts in individual item responses over the two time periods. To examine item response patterns, we first compared the distribution of responses to each of the six risk-taking items for students who remained in the study over the 1-year period ($n = 661$) with those who dropped out in ninth grade ($n = 97$) and those students who joined the study in ninth grade ($n = 120$). No significant differences in the response distributions between stayers and either dropouts or joiners were noted. We then examined the responses of the stayers or panel students. Overall, students were consistent in their reporting of individual items from eighth to ninth grade, with between 53 and 73% of the adolescents giving the same response each year (Table III). Rule breaking showed the greatest movement, while stealing exhibited the greatest stability. This may reflect the relative ambiguity of the items. Stealing is relatively unambiguous while rule breaking is more subjective and is open to different sets of rules at different times. Daring and racing on a bike or boat showed downward movement. In contrast, 25% of the students gave more frequent reports of riding with a dangerous driver in ninth grade. These shifts are indicative of the changing social context of young adolescents as they move from pedal to motor vehicles. Kappa statistic percentages range from 26 to 34, indicating moderate agreement. Note that stealing, the item showing the greatest stability over the 1-year period, had one

Table I. Percentage Distribution of Responses to Risk-Taking Items in Eighth and Ninth Grades[a]

Item	8th grade			9th grade		
	Never	Once or twice	Several times	Never	Once or twice	Several times
Race on a bike or boat (Raced)	52.4	21.5	26.1	58.9	21.5	19.6
Did something risky or dangerous on a dare (Dare)	40.3	33.6	26.1	40.2	40.9	18.9
Broke a rule that your parents set for you just for the thrill of seeing if you could get away with it (Broke Rule)	37.9	35.3	26.8	37.1	40.2	22.7
Stole or shoplifted (Steal)	76.8	15.1	8.1	77.7	15.7	6.6
Slipped out at night while your parents thought you were asleep (Sneaked Out)	70.8	18.3	10.9	68.5	22.0	9.4
Willingly ridden in a car with someone you knew was a dangerous driver (Dangerous Driver)	64.6	22.0	13.4	57.0	28.3	14.7

[a]Eighth grade, $n = 758$; ninth grade, $n = 781$.

Table II. Item-Total Correlations and Alpha Coefficient[a] of Risk-Taking Items

Item	Coefficient	
	8th grade	9th grade
Raced	.44	.35
Dare	.62	.59
Broke Rule	.56	.60
Steal	.46	.49
Sneaked Out	.54	.53
Dangerous Driver	.54	.61
Alpha	.78	.80
Sample size	732	761

[a]Standardized item alphas.

of the lower Kappa values. This value is a direct result of the item having both high observed agreement and high expected agreement.

(13)   Factor analyses using principal-components analyses were performed at each time period. As seen in Table IV, findings indicate a unifactorial structure for risk-taking items in both eighth and ninth grades. Items show fairly strong loadings ranging from .524 to .767. The amount of variance in the matrix explained by the single factor is moderate but respectable. The analysis offers support for the unidimensionality of risk taking.

(14)   Since we suspected that there might be gender differences in risk taking, a second series of factor analyses was conducted separately for males and females in eighth and ninth grades. In eighth grade, a single factor emerged for both girls and boys, with similar factor loadings for both groups (data not shown). In ninth grade, two factors were extracted for girls and one factor for boys. For girls, racing on a dirt bike or boat loaded on the second factor (.7385), with the remaining five items loading on the first factor. This suggests that

Table III. Percentage Shifts in Responses to Risk-Taking Items from Eighth to Ninth Grade

	Item (%)[a]					
Response	Raced	Dare	Broke Rule	Steal	Sneaked Out	Dangerous Driver
Remained same[b]	60	57	53	73	67	60
Moved up	16	19	23	13	18	25
Moved down	24	24	24	14	15	15
Kappa (%)[c]	32	34	28	27	28	26

[a]Response categories are 1 = never, 2 = once or twice, and 3 = several times.

[b]For each item, remained same represents students who gave the same response in both eighth and ninth grade.

[c]Kappa statistic calculated $\kappa = \dfrac{\text{(Observed agreement – expected agreement)}}{\text{(1 – expected agreement)}}$.

daring behavior is viewed differently from delinquent acts as girls mature.

Validity

(15)   Thus far, we have assessed the reliability of the risk-taking scale and examined its structural properties. Some preliminary analyses have been conducted to address validity issues.

(16)   Risk-taking items were factor analyzed along with a five-item anger scale as an indicator of construct validity. Anger was chosen because we wanted to see if risk-taking behaviors could be differentiated from expressions of hostility. In eighth grade, risk items and anger items loaded on separate factors (Table V). Anger items continued to load on a single factor in ninth grade (Factor II in Table V); however, two distinct factors underlined the risk-taking data (Factor I and Factor III in Table V). Factor I is defined principally by items representing antisocial behaviors (i.e., stealing, sneaking out, and riding with a dangerous driver). Physical feats (i.e., racing on a bike or boat and taking a dare) load on Factor III, with rule breaking loading similarly on Factors I and III. Perceptions of risky behaviors in ninth grade become differentiated into thrill seeking and deviant behaviors in the presence of another construct, anger, with rule breaking as the ambiguous indicator.

(17)   Analyses were conducted to investigate the predictive validity of risk taking by examining the extent to which eighth-grade scores were associated with the initiation of behaviors that often serve as indicators of risk taking in the ninth grade. Five substances and

two measures of sexual behaviors were identified. For substances such as cigarettes, alcohol, and pills where prior experimentation was reported by most eighth graders, 30-day use served as the indicator of health-compromising behaviors. For infrequently reported substances (i.e., marijuana and cocaine), a lifetime categorization was selected. Sexual intercourse was treated in two different ways. First, we examined the association

Table IV. Factor Loadings[a] of Risk-Taking Items

	8th grade		9th grade	
Item	Factor	h	Factor	h
1. Raced	.596	.353	.524	.324
2. Dare	.767	.588	.742	.612
3. Broke Rule	.730	.533	.719	.499
4. Steal	.631	.398	.639	.397
5. Sneaked Out	.705	.497	.688	.434
6. Dangerous Driver	.702	.493	.737	.529
Eigenvalue	2.86		2.76	
Percentage of variance	47.80		46.10	

[a]Extracted factors using principal-components analysis.

Table V. Factor Loadings of Risk-Taking and Anger Items

Item	8th grade Factor			9th grade Factor			
	I	II	h	I	II	III	h
Raced	.610	.080	.379	.035	.087	.770	.602
Dare	.736	.197	.581	.274	.220	.689	.599
Broke Rule	.684	.189	.504	.453	.188	.499	.490
Steal	.625	.096	.400	.735	.106	.019	.553
Sneaked Out	.714	.053	.512	.651	.107	.330	.425
Dangerous Driver	.677	.183	.492	.592	.145	.395	.527
Stay Angry	.057	.580	.342	-.035	.630	.186	.433
Hit Someone	.203	.651	.466	.230	.689	.084	.535
Yell at People	.109	.745	.568	.185	.760	.061	.616
Lose Temper	.059	.829	.691	.077	.865	.089	.705
Get into Fights	.355	.619	.510	.286	.666	.139	.546
Eigenvalue	3.80	1.64		4.90	1.78	1.28	
Percentage of variance	34.60	14.90		32.70	11.90	8.60	

Table VI. Associations Between Eighth-Grade Risk-Taking Scores and Ninth-Grade Behaviors

9th-grade behavior	8th-grade risk taking			χ^2	Significance
	Upper 25%	Mid 50%	Lower 25%		
% ever had sexual intercourse[a] (n = 297)	55.9	36.2	25.7	16.47	$p < .000$
% not using contraceptive (n = 285)	8.7	6.3	6.1	0.43	ns
% ever used cocaine (n = 619)	11.7	5.6	1.5	18.13	$p < .000$
% ever used marijuana (n = 212)	32.0	22.1	5.4	38.74	$p < .000$
% smoked cigarettes in past 30 days (n = 237)	32.8	28.4	26.2	0.86	ns
% drank alcohol in past 30 days (n = 176)	72.2	47.4	40.4	6.28	$p < .04$
% used pills in past 30 days (n = 596)	18.7	4.7	2.0	40.80	$p < .000$

[a]Sample size equals the number of students who reported no sexual intercourse or cocaine, marijuana, cigarette, alcohol, or pill used in the eighth grade.

between risk taking in the eighth grade and the transition to sexual intercourse in ninth grade among eighth-grade virgins. Second, we assessed the relationship between prior risk-taking status in eighth grade and sexual intercourse without the use of contraceptive methods in ninth grade. In this analysis, we considered sexual intercourse without protection as a health-compromising behavior rather than sexual intercourse per se. The decision to use quartiles to categorize risk-taking responses was based both on the distribution of responses and on the desire to examine ninth-grade behavioral transitions along a continuum of risk taking.

(18)   The subsample for these analyses was students who reported no involvement in the seven behaviors in eighth grade. Table VI shows associations between categories of risk taking in eighth grade and ninth-grade behaviors. As seen in the table, five of the seven behaviors demonstrate significant associations with eighth-grade risk-taking scores. Approximately 56% of the students who had eighth-grade risk-taking scores in the upper 25% of the distribution became sexually active in ninth grade, as compared with 26% of the students who were in the lower 25% of risk taking. A similar pattern is seen for the transition to alcohol, cocaine, marijuana, and pill use. Initiation of cigarette smoking and contraceptive use were not related to the risk-taking scale.

(19)   Analyses were conducted to determine if there were gender differences in the correlations between risk taking and health-compromising behaviors (data not shown). Patterns for boys and girls were similar and did not differ significantly from findings for the total sample.

Discussion

(20)   This paper describes a risk taking measure that is based on adolescents' reports of deviant and thrill-seeking behaviors. Young adolescents described both physically daring events and rule breaking as risky behaviors. The clustering of both types of items within a single factor clearly indicates that delinquent and physically daring behaviors are perceived similarly. Petty theft, sneaking out at night, and other forms of rule breaking may be addressing adolescent needs for excitement and arousal more than rebellion or the adoption of unconventional attitudes. Although more needs to be learned about the meaning ascribed to risky behaviors by adolescents, it is clear that young people can articulate a series of behaviors that they view as risky.

(21)   The six-item scale appears reliable and has some demonstrated predictive validity over a 1-year period. Those eighth-grade adolescents who score higher on the risk-taking scale were more likely to initiate sexual activity and substance use in ninth grade than those who scored lower. It also was distinct from a scale of hostile behavior.

(22)   As young people mature, the risk-taking construct may become more complex, reflecting the changing social context of adolescent experiences and a wider variety of behaviors. Some behaviors, like daring, may loose their risky quality as development proceeds and other behaviors take their place. Lewis and Lewis (1984) found that among a sample of fifth-eighth graders, daring behaviors occurred more frequently among eighth graders. In this study, the frequency of daring behaviors decline from eighth to ninth grade. It may be, however, that individuals who engaged in daring feats in eighth grade are the same adolescents who take chances in sports or who drive recklessly in high school. In our own longitudinal study, we will be examining the internal consistency of scores over 3 years and the predictive power of eighth-grade risk taking for tenth-grade behaviors, including reports of injuries, school dropout, and HIV-risking behaviors.

(23)   In this study, the transition from virginity to nonvirginity was associated with reported thrill-seeking and deviant behaviors in eighth grade, while contraceptive practice was not. For young adolescents, the use of contraceptives requires the execution of a variety of behaviors (i.e., accessing contraceptives, negotiating with a partner) that depend on sophisticated communication, problem solving, and planning skills. Risk taking per se may play less of a role.

(24)   The Adolescent Risk Taking Scale was developed using adolescents who live in rural communities. Some items, such as racing on a bike or boat, may not be appropriate for young people in urban areas. Other items like stealing have more general applicability. This scale should be piloted before use with urban or suburban populations.

(25)   Risk taking is an important concept in studies of adolescent behavior. Its measurement is often confined to behaviors that are defined by adults as risky such as use of alcohol or drugs and early sexual intercourse. For researchers and policy makers interested in the antecedents of problem or health-compromising behaviors, a measure of risk-taking orientation is potentially useful in identifying young people who are likely

to initiate drug and alcohol use or engage in sexual intercourse in their early teenage years.

References

Byrne, D., and Fisher, W. (eds.) (1983) *Adolescents, Sex and Contraception*, Erlbaum, Hillsdale, NJ.

Jessor, R. (1983). Adolescent development and behavioral health. In Matarazzo, J. (ed.), *Behavioral Health: A Handbook of Health Enhancement and Disease Prevention*, Wiley, New York.

Jessor, R., and Jessor, S. (1977). *Problem Behavior and Psychosocial Development: A Longitudinal Study of Youth*, Academic Press, New York.

Lewis, C., and Lewis, M. (1984). Peer pressure and risk-taking behaviors in children. *Am. J. Pub. Health* 74: 580-584.

National Center for Health Statistics (1984). Public Health Service, U.S. Department of Health and Human Services Publication No. (PHS) 85-1232, Government Printing Office, Washington, DC.

Zuckerman, M. (1984). Sensation seeking: A comparative approach to a human trait. *Behav. Brain Sci.* 7: 413-471.

Zuckerman, M., and Link, K. (1968). Construct validity for the sensation seeking scale. *J. Consult. Clin. Psychol.* 32: 420-426.

Zuckerman, M., Bone, R., Neary, R., Mangelsdoff, D., and Brustman, B. (1972). What is the sensation seeker? Personality trait and experience correlates of the sensation seeking scales. *J. Consult. Clin. Psychol.* 32: 420-426.

Factual Questions

1. What example do the authors use of a behavior which adults may view as risky but adolescents may view otherwise?

2. The Sensation Seeking Scale was developed and tested using what type of students?

3. In which specific health-compromising behaviors are the authors interested?

4. What is the purpose of the local advisory boards?

5. What types of questions in the study raised objections from some parents?

6. What evidence do we have that the eighth grade students who did not participate in the study were not substantially different from the eighth grade students who did participate?

7. The 35 students who participated in the focus groups were asked what question to get them to name risky behaviors?

8. The measure of risk taking developed by the authors consists of how many items? What answer categories do these items have?

9. On which risk-taking item were students most likely to give the same answer in ninth grade they gave in eighth grade?

10. Eighth-grade risk-taking behavior was associated with which five ninth-grade behaviors?

Questions for Discussion

11. Does the introduction provide a clear notion of the research problem, the purpose of the research, and its significance?

12. Does the literature review seem relevant to the research problem?

13. Why did the authors feel the Sensation Seeking Scale developed by Zuckerman and colleagues was not an adequate measure of adolescent risk taking?

14. Is the number of research subjects sufficient? To what population would you generalize the results of this study?

15. Is there enough information on the research instruments and procedures to allow you to replicate this study?

16. Do the research instruments and procedures have adequate reliability and validity?

17. Does the analysis include sufficient statistical information? Are the statistics that are used appropriate?

18. Are the conclusions supported by and do they logically follow from the data that have been presented?

19. Why does the ability to differentiate between risk-taking behavior and hostile behavior support the validity of the authors' adolescent risk-taking scale?

20. Are the findings discussed in terms of their implications and/or practical significance?

21. Why does the association between eighth-grade risk-taking behavior and ninth-grade health-compromising behavior support the validity of the authors' adolescent risk-taking scale?

Article 19

Adolescent Dress, Part II: A Qualitative Study of Suburban High School Students

Joanne B. Eicher
Suzanne Baizerman
John Michelman

Through observation and interviews of high school students, the role of dress in a nonpsychiatric population was explored in order to provide data complementary to the first phase of a larger research project. Adolescent dress was examined in relation to three dimensions of the self: the public, private, and secret self. Due to the age of subjects and the length of contact with the interviewer, results provided most information about the public self, particularly descriptions of social types — categories based on appearance and behavior. These types included a modal, or "average," type and more extreme types including "punks," "freaks" and "nerds." Extreme social types appeared to offer valuable reference points for "average" adolescents in the development of their individual identities.

(1)　　This paper reports findings on the second phase of a larger study of adolescent dress. The first phase studied dress and body markings of adolescent psychiatric patients (Michelman, Eicher, & Michelman, 1991). In the second phase, the goal was to place these findings in a broader context and generate comparative data on adolescents in the general population, not in psychiatric treatment. To assess adolescents' perceptions, a qualitative study of dress, including body markings, utilized participant observation and interviews with a nonrandom sample of eleven students.

(2)　　As with the work in phase one, Stone's (1962) symbolic interaction approach to appearance and the self guided the theoretical orientation. In Stone's framework, appearance is a critical dimension of communication, almost always preceding verbal transactions. In addition, Stone proposed that appearance is important in formulating the self, especially in early development. Appearance establishes identity when an individual projects his or her "program" (loosely interpreted as one's social roles of gender, age, and occupation) to others. In turn, the self is validated or challenged when the program is "reviewed" by others.

Reprinted with permission from *Adolescence, 26*(103): 679-686. Copyright © 1991 by Libra Publishers, Inc.
Minnesota Agricultural Experiment Station Publication No. 18-008.

"Adolescent Dress, Part I: Dress and Body Markings of Psychiatric Outpatients and Inpatients" appeared in *Adolescence,* Vol. 26, No. 102, Summer 1991.

Suzanne Baizerman, Ph.D., and John Michelman, M.D., University of Minnesota.

Reprint requests to Joanne B. Eicher, Ph.D., Professor, Design, Housing, and Apparel, University of Minnesota, 240 McNeal Hall, 1985 Buford Avenue, St. Paul, Minnesota 55108.

(3)   Eicher's (1981) typology of dress and the public, private, and secret self also was utilized. The *public self* pertains to an individual's formal social roles, the *private self* to relationships with close friends or family in informal settings, and the *secret self* to secluded or intimate settings and fantasy. This study is based on the premise that these aspects of self are socially developed, governed by cultural systems of meaning shared by participants. Further, insight into these cultural systems of meaning will lead to greater understanding of how an individual uses dress in the development of the self and in communicating identity.

(4)   The ideas of Stone and Eicher were translated into questions posed to the adolescent psychiatric patients in phase one, and the high school students in phase two. In phase one, both male and female outpatients and inpatients shared information, even intimate details, about dress and body markings relating to the private and secret self in the course of clinical treatment (Michelman & Michelman, 1986; Michelman, Eicher, & Michelman, 1991). Because the clinical research highlighted the need for comparative data on the dress of adolescents not under psychiatric treatment, phase two was devised (1) to explore more fully the social context of adolescent dress from the perspective of the adolescent, and (2) to relate these findings to the three domains of dress and the self.

Method

(5)   The research site was the only public high school serving a small city of 42,000 people on the edge of a large metropolitan area in the upper midwest, the same location as Michelman et al.'s clinical study. It is one of the largest public high schools in the state, well-known for its athletic programs.

(6)   Past studies of adolescent dress have largely used survey research methods. Of these, many have focused on social variables, such as acceptance, participation, popularity, leadership, and conformity in relation to dress. Others have focused on personality variables or on the adolescent as consumer, studying selection, acquisition, care, and use of clothing. In general, such studies used conceptual models developed by researchers to study relatively large numbers of individuals, and focused on dress and what we term the public self. (An exception is a study by Hethorn (1987) that included quantitative responses to presentation of visual images, supplemented by observation and interviews with a selected number of students.)

(7)   Survey methods did not seem appropriate for generating data relevant to dress and the public, private, and secret self. Instead, qualitative research methods consisting of observation and in-depth interviews were selected. Preliminary observations were conducted over a period of two months in 10th-grade classes, and interviews were conducted with teachers. From two required English classes, a nonrandom sample of students was selected by the researcher in consultation with the teachers. Students were approached as research collaborators during classroom descriptions of the project. A list of twenty students who had potential for being productive informants — representing a range of observed appearance types — yielded eleven informants. In order to allow a more informal exchange (analogous to the clinical setting of the child psychiatrist), and in a setting not associated with school, interviews were conducted in the students' homes. To reinforce the notion of the student as informant, the interviewer sat adjacent to the student so that both could read the research instrument as the interviewer recorded the student's responses. As in Michelman et al.'s clinical study, students were extremely cooperative and willing to serve as research collaborators. Interviews lasted from forty-five minutes to two hours.

(8)   The interview schedule contained both structured and open-ended questions. Structured questions about shopping patterns and financing of clothing purchases provided an opportunity to establish rapport with the teenagers prior to open-ended questions. Examples were: "Where do your clothes come from?" and "How do you decide what to wear?" Each had a checklist of choices provided.

(9)   Of the less structured questions, many derived from Michelman et al.'s clinical study. Examples were: "Do you dress to emphasize something about yourself?" and "Do you dress to hide something about yourself?" Others included: "Is there anyone whose clothes and appearance you admire (such as another kid at school or a celebrity)?" "Some people say that people communicate through the way they dress. Do you think that you try to communicate messages to others with your clothes?" "If you are trying to communicate through your dress, how well do others understand the message of your clothes?" "Do you have any clothes that you wear only in private or secret?" "Do you have any tattoos? Do you ever make designs or marks on your skin?" Additional, less structured questions were devised especially for this project: "In your school, how do the most popular kids dress?" "In your school, are there different groups of kids that have names? (Some students have used descriptions like druggies, preppies,

jocks.) If so, what are the different groups? What is their appearance like?" "Are you part of any of these groups?" "Were you ever a member of another of these groups?" "Would you want to be a member of a different group than you are now?"

Results

(10)   Observations and interviews indicated that the three dimensions of self were evident, with the secret self less prominent (at least in a one-session interview). For the adolescents in our sample, the public self featured most prominently in their responses. The school is an arena of high social intensity characterized by both formal and informal relationships. In apparent contrast to the adult world, the differentiation between public and private self does not seem as marked. Consequently, school clothing that we observed and that the students reported wearing was said to be worn for most social occasions in and out of school. Thus, public and private self do not generally seem to be distinguished by dress in this student population. Since the students' select dress for public use, our discussion centers on dress for the public self.

(11)   Shared meaning systems relating to the public self were revealed most clearly in student classifications of the dress of social types at school. Twenty descriptive categories were used, some serving as synonyms for broader categories. There was variation in the number of social types mentioned by each student, ranging between four and seven. Although social types were distinct from one another, the adolescents in our sample did not always agree on the criteria for membership in the categories. "Jocks," "freaks," "preppies," "nerds," and "punks" were mentioned most frequently.

(12)   Jocks were mentioned by all eleven students, and there was a greater core of similarity in descriptions of them as compared to other social types. Jocks encompassed both genders in this school, where athletics plays such a prominent role. Descriptions of male and female jocks typically included athletic clothing, such as letter jackets and jerseys, and casual items of dress. One informant called male jocks "mesh men," a reference to the fabric from which athletic jerseys are made. A male described jock dress as "nice jeans like Guess, gym shoes, and nice sweaters with brand names." One female respondent used the term "jockette" to refer to the female counterpart to the jock, emphasizing their expensive clothes. Another emphasized "pretty makeup, hair spray." Short haircuts were commonly mentioned for male jocks.

(13)   Consensus existed about nerds, a contrasting social type. The emphasis was on out-of-style clothes:

> Flood pants that come up too high, totally out of style.

> Ugly sweaters that look like their parents' choice, or hand-me-downs.

(14)   One student commented: "They're in a different world. Like striped shirts that don't match." Descriptions omitted reference to features common to other groups, such as black clothing, name brands, and athletic attire. Unkempt hair was another characteristic of nerds:

> They have messy hair.

> They don't comb their hair.

> Their hair looks like they don't care.

(15)   There was similarity in the descriptions of dress worn by punks and freaks, probably because both represent a visibly extreme social type that appears to be associated with rebellion. In addition, each category stimulated extensive responses from the students, including some spontaneous remarks about drug and alcohol use.

(16)   Punks were mentioned by ten of the eleven informants. Some descriptions focused on distinctive makeup and hairstyles:

> Their hair is all different. They have different-colored dyed hair.

> They wear strange makeup. One takes other people's hair and ties it to her hair. Another has shaved eyebrows, then draws zig-zag eyebrows. They look very pale.

(17)   Other respondents noted male and female differences: "The boys wear their hair shaved on one side and spiked up." Female punks "wear eye shadow out into points." In terms of dress, black clothing and leather items figured prominently. One student described punk boys as wearing "black leather with things hanging off, T-shirts with beer advertisements, black army boots, jeans with holes." Another student spoke of punks' "shredded clothes." Still another noted: "They wear black; also high boots with silver chains, T-shirts with peace signs on them, different symbols, too."

(18)   Nine of the eleven commented on the category "freaks." Black and leather clothing and T-shirts associated with music groups, especially "heavy metal" groups, appeared frequently in descriptions: "They wear black—everything. Leather boots and coats." Another respondent commented:

> They wear black leather. Jackets of black leather, black ripped up jeans. They wear hanging-cross earrings. They're a totally separate group.

When hair was mentioned, it was identified as long for boys, teased or unkempt for girls. A characteristic that distinguished punks from freaks seemed to be the coloring and shaping of hair among the punks.

(19)   Preppie seemed to be a category in transition, with contradictions in informants' observations. Some informants described preppies as wearing "expensive, nice clothes": "The boys wear ... brands like Guess, Genera, and Girbaud jeans. Some Esprit." In contrast, another said that male preppies "don't wear name brands; they're not fashionable." Another student described preppies as "well-ironed." As in the case of nerds, respondents mentioned neither leather nor black clothing in association with preppies. Makeup and hairstyles produced few remarks.

(20)   Highly visible social types like the nerds, punks, and freaks appeared with very low frequency at the school if we judge by (1) observations in a variety of classrooms, lunchrooms, and hallways over a six-month period, and (2) review of the school yearbook. Based on observations in the general school population, dress was unisex and homogeneous: loose tops and jeans or pants for males and females. This casual look was seen by one teacher as pointing to the school's emphasis on and reputation for athletes. Some differentiation in hairdos distinguished males from females more than did apparel. However, hair length alone did not differentiate, except for the very longest on females or the very shortest on males. Footwear was mostly athletic shoes, with a few students in flats or other leather shoes such as short boots. Jewelry was not used extensively, except occasionally earrings. Students dressing in this homogeneous manner can be categorized as modal or "average."

(21)   Visual analysis of head and shoulder portraits in the yearbook for tenth through twelfth graders supports the observations of homogeneity of appearance: shirts, blouses, or sweaters for the upper garment, and carefully managed hairdos for both males and females. The absence of forms of dress that would be characteristic of extreme social types may have several explanations. First, few students wear extreme forms of dress on a daily basis. Second, even those students who wear extreme forms may elect to conform to modal forms of dress for school pictures — voluntarily or under parental or school authorities' pressure. A third explanation may be that extreme social types choose not to have their photograph taken for the yearbook.

(22)   Subsequent interview data corroborated observations and expanded our understanding of modal dress. Highly visible social types seemed to represent extremes, against which what students termed "average," "regular," or "ordinary" persons were contrasted. This latter type was most often the way the informant saw his or her own dress. "They dress the way I do . . . what's in, what they like, casual." Another respondent called them "in-betweens": "Not a jock, not a nerd. They wear what they want."

(23)   We hypothesized that the jocks were a hypernormal social type, and were frequently referred to when students described the popular kids at their school. For example:

> The smart ones . . . they're the dream dates. You can't feel neutral about a jock. Some girls really want to date them. Punk girls usually hate them.

Another girl described what she termed the "elegant prom queen cheerleader," a kind of female analog to the "superjock."

(24)   Students emphasized the potential to change membership, indicating that both forms of dress and dress categories were ephemeral and capable of flux. This potential was dramatically illustrated by one informant, who coined the term "frock" — between a freak and a jock — to describe another social type, a category into which he put himself.

(25)   Questions in phase two, as in phase one, were designed to assess dress and the secret self. Most significantly, when queried about body marking and tattoos, the students in our sample, in contrast to the clinical population in phase one, seemed surprised and even embarrassed by the question and gave few responses. Thus the two populations were distinguished by this index of the secret self.

Conclusions

(26)   Data on the social context of adolescent dress led to students' descriptions of distinctly different social types based on appearance and behavior. Various social types, including the modal or "average" type, where the casual, comfortable, unisex look dominated, were identified. Within this complex system, there was a hierarchical aspect of fluctuating dress categories. Categories seemed to serve as temporary anchors or reference points for the average or "mainstream" adolescent in developing identity. Extreme forms of dress associated with the categories of "punk" and "freak" provided significant, provocative contrasts to the more modal ones. Other types of dress represented almost unattainable social categories, such as supernormal jocks, jockettes, and "elegant prom queen cheerleaders," or completely undesirable categories, such as nerds.

(27)   This loose hierarchy was suggested by analysis of respondents' comments. All categories outside the modal or normal ones stimulated respondents' thoughts on who they were and who they were not. Some respondents indicated that they might want to appear in one of the extreme forms of dress or as a jock or preppie. For example, one student indicated a yearning to deviate from the normal when he said that he would like to be a "punker," but his family — his parents and older brothers — would not approve. However, none of the respondents indicated a desire to dress like a nerd.

(28)   Collecting qualitative data provided us with the subtle distinctions and variations in students' perceptions of a particular world of dress, relating primarily to the public self at one specific high school. As in phase one of this project, students were extremely cooperative and willing to serve as research collaborators. However, as a result of phase two, we concluded that exploring more fully the private self, and especially the secret self, requires more prolonged and intensive contact with informants than was afforded in this research. Nevertheless, there were certain similarities between the two phases of research. Males and females, whether in psychiatric care or not, were conscious of their own dress and that of others, and distinguished groups by their dress.

(29)   A clearer understanding of the relevance of dress categories for adolescents, including the meaning of dress within the context of a given school, has implications for teachers and others working with adolescents in youth agencies and clinical settings. Caution must be exercised when one hears about the existence of certain social types. Their numbers may be small and the boundaries between categories not always clear. In spite of the furor created by the more extreme dress forms of certain social types, we suggest that these extremes play an important role in the development of "normal" adolescents — as a reference point against which they symbolically assess and make decisions about themselves.

References

Eicher, J. B. (1981). Influence of changing resources on clothing, textiles and the quality of life: Dressing for reality, fun and fantasy. *ACPTC Proceedings* (Central Region), St. Louis, Missouri.

Eicher, J. B., & Kelley, E. A., with Wass, B. M. (1981). Birds of a feather. In G. B. Sproles (Ed.), *Contemporary perspectives of fashion.* Minneapolis, MN: Burgess Publishing Co.

Hethorn, J. L. (1987). *Adolescent appearance: Some issues impacting change in acceptability.* Unpublished doctoral dissertation, University of Minnesota.

Michelman, J. D., Eicher, J. B., & Michelman, S. O. (1991). Adolescent dress, Part I: Dress and body markings of psychiatric outpatients and inpatients. *Adolescence, 26* (102), 375-386.

Michelman, S. O., & Michelman, J. D. (1986). Public, private and secret self: A multidisciplinary approach to the study of dress and body markings. *ACPTC Proceedings* (National Meeting).

Stone, G. P. (1962). Appearance and the self. In A. M. Rose (Ed.), *Human behavior and social processes: An interactionist approach.* New York: Houghton Mifflin.

Factual Questions

1. This article is titled "Adolescent Dress, Part II . . ." With what type of adolescents did "Adolescent Dress, Part I . . ." deal?

2. Why did the initial research reported in "Adolescent Dress, Part I . . ." lead the authors to the research reported in "Adolescent Dress, Part II . . ."?

3. What data-gathering methods were used in this qualitative study?

4. Past studies of adolescent dress primarily used which research method?

5. How were the informants selected?

6. Why were interviews conducted at home rather than at school?

7. What technique was used to reinforce the notion that these students were informants and not just interview subjects?

8. What is an example of a structured question used in this study?

9. What is an example of an open-ended question used in this study?

10. What five distinctive (not average) categories of students and student dress were mentioned frequently by informants?

11. Why would a study of adolescent dress that used just yearbook pictures be misleading?

12. How did the informants typically describe their own pattern of dress?

Questions for Discussion

13. Does the introduction provide a clear notion of the research problem, the purpose of the research, and its significance?

14. Does the literature review seem relevant to the research problem?

15. Is the number of informants sufficient? To what population would you generalize the results of this study?

16. Is there enough information on the research instruments and procedures to allow you to replicate this study?

17. Should there be information about the reliability and validity of the research instruments and procedures?

18. Does the analysis include sufficient statistical information?

19. Are the conclusions supported by and do they logically follow from the data that have been presented?

20. The authors indicate limited success in gathering information about dress as it affects/expresses the secret self. What might be required to gather such information?

21. What kinds of information did this qualitative study obtain that a quantitative study would not have been able to obtain?

22. Are the findings discussed in terms of their implications and/or practical significance?

Notes:

Article 20

Rats and Bunnies:
Core Kids in an American Mall

George H. Lewis

Although adolescents use shopping malls as important places of congregation, very little attention has been paid to this phenomenon by social scientists. This paper reports on a qualitative, interview-based study of adolescents in a New England shopping mall. Regular, day-to-day frequenters ($N = 23$) were identified and interviewed extensively over a six-week period in 1988. These "core kids" exhibited a good deal of alienation from both family and school, and used the mall as a neutral ground on which to create a fragile but mutually supportive community of kind.

(1)   Over the past three decades, the shopping mall has evolved into a sort of civic center for many suburban, middle-class Americans. More than just central locations for shopping, these covered and climate-controlled monoliths have become meeting places — easily reachable and safe spots in which many activities only marginally related to the economics of the stores take place. Cultural events are staged by outside groups acting in cooperation with mall management. Leisure activities are offered, from video arcades to ice-skating rinks. Fast-food shops, fashion shows, and petting zoos abound. This mix of recreation, leisure, and community facilities with retail outlets is an effort to make the mall a focal point for community life (Kowinski, 1985). In addition, and to some extent because of the reputation a mall can build within a community, it becomes a social magnet, drawing others inside its walls — people who come not to buy or participate in the staged events, but out of curiosity, to meet friends, to hang out and pass the time in its controlled and temperate environment.

(2)   One such group to whom the mall appeals are adolescents. Many younger children are happily dropped off there during the day on weekends in the winter and any day of the week during summer vacation by their parents, with enough change for the video games and lunch at a fast-food stand. Older teenagers arrive by themselves or, more typically, in small groups, to hang out and see their friends. One remarked to an interviewer, "If you don't have a car to go cruising in, you cruise the mall" (Green, 1982, p. 67). As Anthony (1985) reported, young people spend a great deal of their time hanging out in malls. In her study of a suburban Los Angeles shopping mall, she found that a large proportion of her sample visited the mall at least once a week, with an average stay being from 3 to 5 hours.

(3)   Although the popular press has looked at this phenomenon to some extent, the shopping mall as a contemporary center of adolescent activity has received little attention from social scientists. Indeed, in his extensive empirical overview of American youth in the

Reprinted with permission from *Adolescence, 24*(96): 881-889. Copyright 1989 © by Libra Publishers, Inc.

Reprint requests to George H. Lewis, Professor, Sociology Department, University of the Pacific, Stockton, California 95211.

The author served as Director of Research for this study. Interviews were conducted by the author; SALT staff members Pamela Wood and Hugh French; and Brett Jenks, Julie Maurer, Harry Brown, and Amy Schnerr. SALT Center is located in Kennebunkport, Maine.

1980s, in which he discusses community, school, work, and the place of media in the lives of young people, Starr (1986) fails even to mention the shopping mall as a locus of social interaction. In a literature review of the major social science journals that deal with youth and adolescence, I found only one empirical study (Anthony, 1985) of shopping mall activity reported in the last seven years. And yet it must be clear to even the casual observer that the mall has become a focal point around which a good deal of suburban, middle-class adolescent behavior is based.

The Present Study: New England Mall

(4)   This study focused on adolescent social behavior and use patterns in a large New England shopping mall. This particular mall was begun seventeen years ago and has evolved, changed, and grown for nearly two decades. Thus it is a permanent cultural fixture in the eyes of the adolescents who frequent it. To them, it has always been there. This mall is extremely well-known, and is regionally popular. In fact, it draws customers from all over the state, from adjoining states, and even from the bordering Canadian province. It boasts of being the largest mall "north of Boston."

(5)   Five years ago, a major new wing was added, as large as the original mall and connected to it by a short, enclosed promenade. Shops in the new wing are more flashy in appearance — boutiques, T-shirt stores, record and video shops and, occupying the most space, the fast-food court with its many take-out stands. The older wing, in contrast, is more heavily weighted toward more established stores—men's and women's clothing, banks, professional offices, stationery and book stores. The old mall has three sunken circular "conversation pits" with benches for short-term sitting; the new mall has the food court, with modern wire and metal chairs and tables arranged around large potted plants. The old mall has a wooden gazebo, an information desk, and bulletin board; the new mall has a video arcade. The old mall has few security personnel in evidence; the new mall has security people walking relatively regular beats. In all, there are over 250 shops in the mall, 22 food outlets, a video arcade, three movie theaters, and five major (anchor) department stores.

(6)   In general, adolescents spend nearly all their time in the new wing of the mall, congregating around the video arcade and the food court when they are sitting, and moving through and around the various shops in groups of two or three when they are "cruising." The old mall is perceived by them as "boring"—a place where adults shop and where the elderly congregate.

Psychologically, from the adolescent perspective, the old mall is not defined as their "territory," and thus they do not frequent it except perhaps as a convenient short-cut to or from the parking lot.

(7)   Data for this study are qualitative in nature and consist of a series of unstructured interviews conducted by a team of researchers over a period of six weeks in June and July 1988. These interviews are one portion of a research effort undertaken by the SALT Center for Field Studies in examining various facets of the impact of mass culture on contemporary life.

(8)   What the research team was especially interested in was social groupings and behavior in the mall. In this case, did adolescents congregate on any regular basis? Was the mall a place where peer groups could develop and grow, where a sense of common culture—or even community—could be found? Or, was the mall just another place to go, to be part of a crowd of like-minded strangers, to hang out (perhaps with a friend) when you were both bored and looking for some action?

(9)   With this in mind, the team spent many hours observing behavior in the mall, looking for and identifying "regulars" for interview purposes. These youths, the ones who showed up day after day (the criterion was at least four times a week), who spent most of their time interacting with others, and who were familiar to the custodians and security personnel, were interviewed by team members, some on as many as five occasions over the six-week period of research. These 23 young people, identified as the "core kids," the ones who defined the new mall as their turf and hung out there day after day, were the focus of the research effort. The many other youths who frequented the mall on a less regular basis, or who came with their parents for shopping purposes, were not included in the study, even though short interviews were conducted with some of them for comparative purposes.

Core Kids: Conversations in the Mall

(10)   Calling themselves "mall rats" (males) and "mall bunnies" (females), the teenagers congregate in the new wing of the mall, the largest number of them arriving in the late afternoon. They wander around the different shops, playing video games in the arcade, smoking cigarettes, showing off their latest hairstyles, makeup and clothing, and waiting for something — anything — to happen. Most of them stay until nine-thirty or ten, when the stores close and the mall shuts down.

(11)   Derick (the names of all teenagers have been changed), age 15, his hands jammed into the pockets of his frayed cutoff jeans, admits that the mall is "a place to go before I have to go to work. I only work right across the street. I have nowhere else to hang out. Most of my friends hang out here."

(12)   Looking at the arcade further down this wing of the mall, he gestures toward it with a quick nod of his head. "Go over there to play video games. Spend all my money. I don't like spending all my money, but it's there." He shrugs. "Fuck it."

(13)   Standing near Derick in the small knot of teenagers, Ed, 16, takes a long, slow drag on his cigarette and exhales out of the corner of his mouth. "I just started coming on almost a daily basis last year because it was something to do," he says. "You can come here anytime. It's pretty good, but if we didn't have anything, anywhere to go, you know, we'd probably get into a lot more trouble, so it kind of works out. It's something to do and it kind of keeps you out of trouble."

(14)   Nodding toward his friends, Ed goes on to explain the social networking that takes place in the mall. "I met all these people here. I've met lots of other people, too. One place where you can always find someone. If you know somebody, they know somebody else, they'll probably see 'em here, and you'll know them, then they'll know someone who is walking around and you know that person. So when you come here, you kind of build on people."

(15)   For some teenagers, a great deal of time is spent networking in the mall. It is, for them, practically a second home. Tammy, age 14, says, "I used to come here every Saturday from eleven in the morning to nine-thirty at night, and just walk around with my friends, like Gina here, just walk around and check out the guys. Now, most of my friends I meet here at the mall. I try to come out every day, if I can."

(16)   When the strip becomes tiresome after roaming from shop to shop, playing video games, or cruising, they usually migrate to the food court. There they sit, talk, bum change, smoke cigarettes, and try to avoid the attention of the security people since most of the activities they are engaged in will inevitably attract it.

(17)   The group gathers around a table, some standing, others sitting and talking. One of the girls breaks from her conversation to announce that Bob is coming.

Bob has been kicked out of the mall for boisterous behavior and is not allowed in for another two months.

(18)   "Just about all of us have gotten kicked out at one time or another," Tony says matter-of-factly. "I was sitting down without anything to eat once, and like I didn't know the policy and he said, 'Move,' and I go, 'Why?' I ran my mouth a little too much. What I basically did was stand up for myself, but he didn't like that, so he just booted me for a couple months. Actually, I'm not supposed to be even in here. He said he's kicked me out forever, but I mean like I changed my hairstyle so he doesn't recognize me anymore."

(19)   Ed nods. "I changed mine and I changed my jacket. I used to wear a big leather jacket. I used to wear that all the time. That gave me away. But I've started wearing this jacket now with all my KISS pins on. And as long as I don't act up or do anything, they don't really care. See, I like it here so much I have to come back."

(20)   Liz, 15, discusses relationships with the security guards in general. "Somedays they can really get on us and other days they just won't come, and like we'll be sitting down at the table and on busy days or on days they're not in a really good mood, they'll come over and tell us to move."

(21)   "They have no respect for mall rats," adds Caulder, 14, standing on the edge of the group. "It's just days like that they can be real dinks."

(22)   And yet the harassment by the security guards is easily borne, especially when changing one's clothing or haircut often can be enough to erase their identity. Such treatment is much better, for most of them, than what they could expect if they were to hang around any public places outside of the mall. This relatively light scrutiny by the security guards also allows some adolescents to get away with minor drug transactions, especially when the mall is crowded.

(23)   "Other than Dark Harbor [a boardwalk/amusement park area 20 miles down the coast], which is just like, 'deal it out on the streets,' I mean you can get just about anything out here — pot, acid, hash, right here on Saturdays, when it is crowded."

(24)   "If you know the right people, you can pick up anything."

(25)   "And we pretty much know everybody here."

(26)   For some teenagers, the mall — with or without drugs — is an escape from home or school. Heather, 16, explains that she goes there "to get away from home, get away from problems because I can't stay at home. Because my mom's always on my case when she's not off partying with her boyfriend. And that dude's bad news, really. They bother me. So I come to the mall." Slouching in her seat, she flips open the top of her red Marlboro box and counts her cigarettes. "School is no better. I got through a year of school, and they still put me through the next grade even if I'm failing. I don't care about partying. I just want to get through school. Get out."

(27)   For Tiffany, the mall has become a second home. At the age of thirteen, she lives with Tony and one other mall friend. "My mom kicked me out when I was eleven," she says with an edge of anger in her voice. "She's a bitch. I call her every day and she's just . . ." Tiffany stops short, shaking her head and rolling her eyes.

(28)   "I started going to foster homes and everything, and I just quit. Now, I'm in state custody and I just . . ." She stops again, laughing nervously and blushing. "Sorry about that," she says, apologizing to her friends, seeming to imply that she has become too personal, too emotional. Abruptly, she continues. "I don't do anything that they want me to do." She lets out a quick triumphant laugh.

(29)   "I swear to God if they came up to me and dragged me where I didn't want to go, I'd beat the crap right out of them. I would kill 'em. I got 'em twisted around my little finger. They don't mess with me," she growls, as she clenches her teeth and curls her small fist, pounding it lightly on the table.

(30)   Tony leans back and shakes his head slightly to part his long hair from his face. "I left home and I quit school and moved from, like, hotel to hotel for awhile with a Navy buddy, and that wasn't a really good situation because we were getting kicked out of hotels and motels. We didn't have any money. Didn't have anywhere to go. So we went up to the Beach [Pine Beach, a town 40 miles up the coast, where there are employment opportunities in a large shipyard] and when I went up there it's like there's a Burger King and an auto parts store and a Shop and Save and it's like . . . there was no mall. I was real glad to get back down here because it was, like up there, it was boring the hell out of me."

Discussion: Alienation and Peer Support in the Mall

(31)   Unlike Anthony (1985), who interviewed a larger random sample of youth in a California mall and found only 4% who went to the mall every day, our more focused sample of "regular" mall rats and bunnies was far more likely to visit daily. These 23 "core kids" make up a fairly tightly integrated social group, with about a quarter of them employed at least part-time in the fast-food shops in the mall. Around this core there move others, whose patterns of belonging are less regular — possibly three visits a week at the maximum, usually fewer. But even these young people try to make it to the mall to hang out at least once a week.

(32)   Most of the core kids (91%) go to the mall to be with their friends, as opposed to just 42% of Anthony's larger, random sample. Their social lives revolve around the mall. Most arrive by midafternoon and stay until it closes at ten. They eat at the fast-food outlets (or get under-the-counter handouts from those of their group who do work at these places). Most of them, with the exception of purchasing their food and, mainly for the younger ones, playing the video arcade, spend almost no money at the mall, a finding which coincides with what Anthony found in the California mall. For these youths, the records, clothes, and videos purchased by the many young people who visit the mall for shopping purposes are not easily affordable, and there has developed almost a norm against the purchase of shiny, new media material from the mall.

(33)   For many of the core kids, like Tiffany, Heather, Derick, and Tony, the mall offers a form of much-needed peer support. Their home and school experiences, filled with personal rejections, institutional indifference, and abuses of power as means of control, create the classic conditions for alienation (Calabrese, 1987; Gallette, 1987). That these youths would exhibit very low social involvement outside of their mall world, have obvious difficulty in conforming to bureaucratic and institutional rules and conditions, and have somewhat negative self-images as well as fairly high levels of hostility against the outside world, should come as no great surprise.

(34)   These themes of alienation seem to weave a common web of understanding around most of the mall rats and bunnies. Taken together, they comprise a mutual social support system of alienated young persons. Rat put it well when he said, "Sometimes, if I couldn't work out here and be with my friends, like, I don't know if I could make it. My dad's, ah, real fucked, if you know what I mean. He's always out of control and

stuff. So I try to stay out of his way. And *school*," he laughs and shakes his hair. "Like I've been kicked out three times, man. For nothing. Just talk. It's boring, man. I'm not ever going back there. I don't give a shit what my dad says. Let him blow, man."

(35)   Tina adds, "We're all just good friends here. We give each other space, which we need, I guess. We do kid around a lot, but basically we don't hit on each other. That's what we came here to get away from."

(36)   As Calabrese (1987) has stated, youths operating under these conditions "find alienation a way of life. They are left with few alternatives because society and its organizations do little to reduce their at-risk nature. Adolescents have responded by developing their own culture" (p. 935). This culture, at least as it appears in the New England mall, is one that seems to provide a sense of democratic friendship and belonging, while allowing for a great deal of individual self-expression and exploration of personal identity. This culture, forged from shifting networks of peer relationships, appears to be a somewhat unstable social system and one that rests almost entirely in present time and revolves around present circumstances. Personal pasts are, for the most part, only briefly sketched in. They are seldom spoken about and appear not to be a part of the shared mall culture in anything but a very general sense.

(37)   Then, too, adolescents grow up and, for the most part, drift out of the mall culture as they are drawn socially, sexually, and economically into the adult world that has, until they come of age, so effectively excluded them. This fluidity and change in social relationships is one more uncertain part of the teenage years which, for mall rats and bunnies, is also characterized by a lingering malaise concerning the world outside their fragile community — a malaise in which jealousy, mistrust, and despair are the prominent features. As Tony says, "We are the mall rats. We are the mall. What the fuck else can I say?"

Conclusion

(38)   The mall, it seems, acts as a social magnet, drawing adolescents to its safe and socially neutral territory. Especially for middle-class youths with unresolved problems and difficult social situations at home and school, it offers a "third ground," a place where congregation is possible and hassles are minimal. As one security guard explained, "We aren't allowed to harass the kids, and I know they got to hang out

somewhere. I was a kid once myself. But they've got to keep moving, not block up access to shops or the food service area. And if they get too loud, we have to clear them out."

(39)   The small core group of mall rats and bunnies are mall regulars. These young people hang out there nearly every day, usually from midafternoon until closing time. Several of them, in addition, work in the mall's fast-food stands, providing some minimal amount of cash for themselves, as well as an introduction to the world of adult work. In addition, they can and do provide others in the core group with "junk food" snacks, which allows for longer periods of hanging out.

(40)   The culture of these regulars centers around present-day concerns and is caught up to a great extent with mass-media images, idols, and sounds. These kids dress, talk, and act like the kids they see on MTV and in the teen movies. They discuss issues of importance in the commercial youth culture—Madonna's new hairstyle, Bruce Springsteen's divorce, Eddie Murphy's new routine. By mutual consent, they each "cover" for the others' deficiencies in self-image, validating their mutual appropriations of mass-mediated roles, clothes, expressions, and physical moves.

(41)   And underneath, holding this frail community together, is their recognition of the themes of alienation in each other — alienation from family, school, the whole adult middle-class community that shuts them out. There is anger there, and hostility. And there is also a good deal of despair, masked cunningly by the glittering neon and commercial pop in which the mall rats and bunnies so easily wrap themselves, as the adults of the community, entrapped by the economic lure of the mall, rush hurriedly by, eyes averted, feet tapping and echoing on endless, tiled floors.

References

Anthony, K. H. (1985). The shopping mall: A teenage hangout. *Adolescence, 20*(78), 307-312.

Calabrese, R. L. (1987). Adolescence: A growth period conducive to alienation. *Adolescence, 22*(88), 929-938.

Gallette, L. C. (1987). Children in maritally violent families: A look at family dynamics. *Youth and Society, 19*(2), 117-133.

Green, B. (1982). Fifteen: Young men cruising shopping malls. *Esquire, 98*, 67-73.

Kowinski, W. (1985). *The malling of America*. New York: Morrow.

Starr, J. (1986). American youth in the 1980's. *Youth and Society, 17*(4), 323-345.

Factual Questions

1. How many empirical studies of shopping mall activity appeared in major social science journals in the seven years prior to this study?

2. How many different persons conducted interviews for this research?

3. This study of core kids is based on the study of how many youths?

4. The interviews for this study were conducted over how long a period of time?

5. What were the requirements for a youth to be considered a "regular" by the researcher?

6. Were some subjects interviewed on more than one occasion?

7. If the interviewers were interested in the core kids, why did they conduct short interviews with non-core kids?

8. What is the difference between a mall rat and a mall bunny?

9. What proportion of the core kids are employed, at least part-time, in the mall?

10. How does the author's methodology differ from the methodology used by Anthony (1985)?

Questions for Discussion

11. Does the introduction provide a clear notion of the research problem, the purpose of the research, and its significance?

12. Does the literature review seem relevant to the research problem?

13. Is the number of core kids studied sufficient? To what population would you generalize the results of this study?

14. Is there enough information on the research instruments and procedures to allow you to replicate this study?

15. What purpose, if any, does the description of the mall's stores and physical layout serve?

16. What purpose, if any, do the quotations from the core kids serve?

17. Should there be information about the reliability and validity of the research instruments and procedures?

18. Does the analysis include sufficient statistical information?

19. Are the conclusions supported by and do they logically follow from the data that have been presented?

20. Are the findings discussed in terms of their implications and/or practical significance?

Notes:

Paramedic Performances

C. Eddie Palmer
The University of Southwestern Louisiana

Based upon immersion into the work culture of city emergency medical systems, this qualitative study of paramedics and emergency medical technicians identifies seven generic audiences before which emergency health care is provided. Interactions between audience members and paramedics are described. It is hoped that a more conceptually complete understanding of the occupational milieu of paramedics will be provided by this study and that such an understanding will lead to mutually beneficial interactions between paramedics and members of the audiences that are involved in the drama of pre-hospital emergency medical care. Also, this study is intended as an addition to the growing body of literature on "street work" and can be used as a datum for future comparative research efforts.

Introduction

(1)   Emergency medical systems (hereafter EMS), designed to supply prehospital emergency care to patients by paraprofessionals, are recent additions to the medical repertoire of the United States. In the mid 1960s, funeral homes were operating nearly one-half the available ambulance services in this country. Only three percent of ambulance services were operated by hospitals, and these had only minimally trained personnel, inadequate equipment, and little staff and community support (Jackson 1979, p. 11). These emergency workers attempted to get to the scene of an emergency as soon as possible and to quickly transport the patient(s) to the nearest hospital, possibly administering first aid en route. The outdated Cadillac hearse, staffed by untrained volunteers, may still be operative in a few remote areas of the country, but it has largely disappeared as a mode of emergency medical care. State and federal legislation, community awareness, and pioneering individuals in medical and hospital organizations have significantly influenced the EMS "movement." According to Mannon (1981, p. 5):

> Today all fifty of the United States have minimum standards that must be met in regard to the ambulances used in emergency work — their communication system, size, medical supplies and equipment — and the personnel who staff the ambulances must pass certain certification requirements . . . . Those with life threatening illnesses or injuries have a far greater chance to survive today than they would have a decade ago.

(2)   The last twenty years, therefore, have seen not only great improvements in the response to traumatic injury and illness, but have, from a sociological standpoint, generated a number of new occupational specialties. One specialty recently acknowledged in the sociological literature is the advanced emergency medical technician — the paramedic (Oldham 1979; Mannon 1981; Metz 1981; Palmer 1983). In an attempt to add to the growing literature on emergency medical systems and the actions involved in providing the public

Reprinted with permission from *Sociological Spectrum,9:211-225*. Copyright 1989 © by Taylor & Francis, Inc.

Request reprints from C. Eddie Palmer, Department of Sociology and Anthropology, University of Southwestern Louisiana, Lafayette, LA 70504-0198.

with much needed pre-hospital care and treatment, the present undertaking explores the dramaturgical aspects of the work roles of paramedics by examining interactions they have with various audiences. Many sociologists, notably Goffman (1959) and Lofland (1976), have documented the importance of audiences in the development of impression management strategies and performances. Earlier works dealing with medical environments (Douglas 1969; Roth 1972; Coombs and Powers 1975; Emerson and Pollner 1976; Richard 1986) demonstrated that the audience can have a definite effect on the type of medical care afforded individuals in various medical settings. Manning and Van Maanen (1978) particularly demonstrate the effect of audiences on police officers as they do their work "in the streets." These studies appear to be guided by the suggestion that "sociology should penetrate more deeply into the personal and social drama of work . . ." thereby allowing us to learn "more about social processes in general" (Hughes 1958, p. 48; 1972, p. 106).

(3)   An investigation of the interactions of paramedics with others particularly reveals the "social drama of work." Paramedics constitute a nascent occupational group not fully understood by the public, the medical community, or even the patients they transport. Being a new part of the sociomedical scene, the rights, duties, and legal authority of emergency medical workers have yet to be fully articulated and their positions yet to be clearly defined. Thus, paramedics are still having to "prove themselves" and frequently encounter situations in which neither medical training, medical protocol, agency policy, nor past performances fully guide their actions.

(4)   The paramedic essentially occupies a mutable occupational status which changes from that of an almost complete "authority" at the scene of a traumatic injury to one of an "assistant" once in contact with "medical control" (the radio room of the emergency department of the receiving hospital). As an extension of the physician's authority and medical expertise, "control" can give and withhold permission for paramedics to begin medical treatment. Paramedics must deal frequently with such status changes and role ambiguities (elevation of authority at the scene and deflation at the emergency room) and with multiple audiences with different expectations about "proper" social and medical responses. Such complexity and mutability produce a need for paramedics to construct their own brand of social and physical control over their work world. They do this by a variety of performances before significant audiences in several "negotiation contexts" (Strauss 1978). Managing people, therefore, becomes a

central feature of the work of the paramedic and is fraught with all the problems (and rewards) of those forced to negotiate their positions (and worth) with others in interactions of an "emergent" nature (see Maines 1982; Sugrue 1982). The current research attempts to provide a more conceptually complete description of interaction patterns between actors caught in the web of emergency medical situations.

Methodology

(5)   Data for this article were gathered by a variety of qualitative research techniques. These include participant observation, direct observation, informal interviews, formally scheduled interviews, conversations, inspection of written documents, listening to official radio communications, and a general "immersion" into the work culture of the paramedic. At this writing, such immersion consists of (1) the logging of approximately 510 hours with EMS personnel; (2) spending approximately 100 additional hours attending Emergency Medical Technician (hereafter EMT) School, and completing hospital rotations for state certification as an Emergency Medical Technician (a status obtained in March, 1981, and maintained until December, 1986); (3) making 91 emergency "runs" with EMS workers; (4) becoming certified by the State Department of Health as an EMT Lecturer; (5) lecturing to EMT students on ethics and the development of human skills; and (6) being transmitted to a hospital as a patient (in December, 1983) by EMS personnel under study.

(6)   Most data for this study were collected between June, 1980, and December, 1981. The field research was completed in July, 1984, but some data have been collected as late as June, 1988. Most data come from the informal interaction between the author and EMS personnel during the course of making emergency "runs," 65 of which resulted in a patient or patients being transported to an emergency room of a hospital, while 26 runs ended with no person being transported. While on these runs I observed all facets of the work of EMS personnel and on most occasions assisted in providing emergency care to patients. Such assistance included taking vital signs, bandaging, extrication, "bagmasking," helping in cardiopulmonary resuscitation (CPR) efforts, controlling patients and bystanders, "packaging" patients (sometimes placing them on long spine boards and attaching cervical collars) and loading and unloading persons at hospital emergency rooms. Rapport was established to the point of being given a uniform and badge and being considered "one of us" by most members of the EMS staff. All personnel were made aware of the research project and were given

assurances of anonymity. Notes were taken in the presence of the workers. A tape recorder was used in some interviews and for documenting some conversations. Field notes were polished on the scene during slack times and were often checked for validity by asking participants for clarification of comments and accuracy of recorded notes. Thus, data are qualitative in nature and were gathered in an ethnographic tradition aimed toward understanding how EMS workers negotiate reality and "make sense" of their work worlds (see Handel 1982).

Audiences

(7)   There are at least seven generic audiences before which the EMT performs. These are: (1) patients, (2) patients' families, (3) bystanders, (4) riders, (5) peers, (6) the media, and (7) the emergency room (hereafter ER) staff. Even though the nature of the patient's injury and the general condition of the patient may call for a particular action protocol, the evaluation of audiences by paramedics and the actions of audience members definitely have an effect on the general demeanor of paramedics and affect the level and type of medical care provided to patients.

Patients

(8)   The primary audience confronted by paramedics is composed of the patients themselves. Patients are handled, prompted, packaged, examined, questioned, treated, and transported by paramedics. Keeping in mind that paramedics like to work on people who need *emergency* service and devalue "nonessential calls" (Metz 1981, p. 116), their performances are affected by the type of patient involved. The severely injured child, for example, will elicit much more tender loving emergency care than will an old, drunk, dirty, belligerent "belly acher" who is a member of an ethnic group disliked by the particular paramedic.

(9)   Paramedics are taught to perform before their patients. A statement in the textbook used in the EMT class attended by the author (American Academy of Orthopaedic Surgeons 1977, pp. 4-5) contends that:

Although the EMT cannot be expected to know the underlying factors that might trigger abnormal emotional responses, he must quickly and calmly appraise the actions of the patient and of relatives and bystanders and gain the confidence and cooperation of all involved. Courtesy, proper tone of voice, sincere concern, and efficient action in examination and the administration of care will go far to allay anxiety, fear, and insecurity. Reassurance rather than abrupt dismissal, chiding, or accusation will engender confidence and cooperation.

(10)   On the street this ideal perspective on courtesy, sincere concern, and reassurance is sometimes difficult to affect. Some patients are hostile, will not listen to or cooperate with the paramedic and are frightened, in some cases, to the point of hysteria. "Some patients make us act mean with them," one EMT said. Continuing attempts at reassurance will sometimes pay off in getting a patient to cooperate and sometimes it will not. On one run, for example, a man had been shot in an attempt to foil a robbery of money involved in a motel poker game. The unsuccessful attempt had left the patient with a bullet wound and an expressed sense of extreme fear. The patient screamed, "I'm so scared! I could have been killed! I don't know why I jumped him (the robber). I'm so scared, so scared that I could be dead." This hysterical condition did not abate on the way to the hospital and we wheeled him into the ER in his frantic state. En route, the paramedic attending him had used all the calming, placating, and reassuring techniques in his medical inventory and finally shrugged it off. We listened to the ranting all the way to the ER.

(11)   On another occasion when a young female "pitched a fit," hyperventilated, and acted as if she were having a seizure ("boyfriend left her," according to a relative) the paramedics worked with her for approximately twenty minutes before giving up and leaving the building. During the "fit" the paramedic had used calming tones and commands such as, "We can't help you if you won't cooperate," and "Calm down now. Slow your breathing. Breathe slow for me, we just want to help." When we walked out of the building the same paramedic said, "That hysterical bitch!" "But you were so nice," I said. "Not on the inside," he replied and slammed the door of the ambulance. On another occasion we ran on an elderly black man who had been (allegedly) hit by a car. We treated him with kid gloves and packaged him neatly for transport, all the while listening to jeers from young black men who said: "Shit, Man. Old (name) is just drunk. You don't know nothing. You dudes don't know shit." When we were en route to the ER one paramedic slipped in an eight track tape of soothing music. Looking at me and referring to the music the paramedic said, "It makes you forget the kind of slime we're hauling back there."

(12)   One interesting finding of this research regards a conceptualization used and understood by paramedics

to be a MDS (Mexican Distress Syndrome) or AMDS (Acute Mexican Distress Syndrome). Street wisdom of the paramedics indicates that Mexican patients, particularly males, are much more expressive and vocal about even minor injuries or illnesses. As one EMT related to me, "They got this macho thing, you know, and when they let down they really let down. They take on like they were dying, and everybody in the family and up and down the block comes screaming." This discovery is in keeping with the previous finding of Roth (1972, p. 840) that medical personnel, unless explicitly discouraged from doing so, "will apply the evaluations of social worth common to their culture and will modify their services with respect to those evaluations . . . ." Similarly, Papper's (1978, p. 166) frequently quoted piece states explicitly that race may lead to a patient being labeled undesirable. Evidence that the AMDS evaluation is group-held rather than idiosyncratic is found in the fact that it has been reduced to a commonly understood abbreviation (MDS or AMDS) used in a fashion similar to other radio "10" codes or signals. When the dispatcher reports to the unit that the call may be an "AMDS" call, the diligence of the crew may vary significantly from those calls considered more worthy of their attention.

(13)   On some calls the paramedics are "pros" and display the textbook tact advocated by EMS educators. When patients are "playacting" or when they are uncooperative, the paramedic will usually "stay cool" until in the back of the ambulance and then "level" with the patient by using a more harsh tone and/or giving the patient an ultimatum such as, "You lie still or I'm going to have to make you, and you ain't going to like the way I do it." (However, no persons were observed to be physically abused by a paramedic upon being placed in the ambulance. Some fighting and scuffling with patients and bystanders occurred, but mainly by members of one crew. In some cases, police officers handcuff resistive and abusive patients before they are transported, and they remain in that uncomfortable state until they arrive at the ER. In these situations police authority supersedes that of paramedics.)

(14)   On one occasion an EMT was observed trying to keep a patient who was drunk (and possibly overdosed) from falling asleep en route to the hospital. "Talk to me," the EMT commanded. When she did not, he pinched her on the arm. When she still did not respond (this was after ammonia capsules had been used), he vigorously pinched her on the neck. At this, she angrily yelled, "Don't pinch me! Don't ever pinch me again." He replied, "I won't if you answer my ques-

tions, but if you don't answer my questions I'll keep pinching you."

(15)   These few cases illustrate that part of the street work of paramedics involves varying levels of performance depending on the characteristics of the patient audience and on the degree of concealment afforded by the microecological boundaries of the ambulance (see Zurcher 1979, for the general characteristics of such "encapsulated travel"). Most of the time the stern voice used inside the ambulance is sufficient to "control" the uncooperative patient. Only on occasion will a patient have to be physically restrained, and only on one occasion was a patient heard to ask for a paramedic's name and badge number for purposes of complaining about rough treatment.

Patient's Family Members

(16)   Family members (out of ignorance, anxiety, fear, or hysteria) can represent a real problem for paramedics. Family members may also interfere with the attempts made to provide emergency care to a patient. ("Everybody's a medic," one EMT told me.) Once we ran on an attempted suicide (by hanging). When we arrived the wife of the victim rushed out and yelled, "He needs oxygen. Bring the oxygen!" When we entered the apartment (passing a gauntlet of cops and curious apartment dwellers), she said, "I've been doing his chest, he just needs oxygen." The patient was in respiratory arrest and the EMT opened an airway and started "bagging" (ventilating with a bag mask) over the shouts and objections of the wife. When the EMT on the radio to ER could not hear due to the noise in the room, he said, "Lady, why don't you set down and shut up! I've done this a few times and I know what I'm doing. Just get out of here." The wife responded, "You can't tell me where to get. This is my kitchen you know." "Just get out of our way," the EMT said. About that time someone came into the kitchen and escorted the wife into the living room and we proceeded to treat the patient. (He walked out of the hospital the next morning.)

(17)   Another EMT told me that upon being told to "Hurry it up and get him out of here," he responded, "Look lady. I don't do this for grins." "That was enough to shut her up," he said. Frequently family members want to ride in the ambulance with the patient. This is not allowed except in certain circumstances, such as when the family member does not have any other means of transportation or when a parent wishes to accompany a child. Usually they are told the name and location of the receiving hospital (if they

have not designated it themselves) and are asked to meet their relatives at the emergency room. Often family members follow the ambulance to the ER in their own vehicles. Sometimes family members have been involved in physical altercations with the patient and are detained by police officers or are transported to jail.

(18)   Most of the time, however, the family members involved are the ones who summoned the ambulance and are extremely helpful and deferential to the paramedics. They assist in providing information about the patient and direct the ambulance to the hospital and doctor used by the patient and provide other useful services as requested by the paramedics.

Bystanders

(19)   "People like to see blood and gore," one EMT said. "It's just human nature to want to see what's going on and to be as close to it as possible," said another. Curious bystanders can get in the way of providing care to a patient and can take on a milling crowd character in some situations. While most bystanders are "just curious" and even helpful if called upon, some are problematic. Some may jeer at the EMTs and distract them from their jobs and some may have to be pushed or held back when a patient is being loaded into the ambulance. In these situations police officers are essential (if available, they run on all calls answered by EMS except "medical" cases).

(20)   In one racially mixed neighborhood we ran on a shooting and by the time we arrived a crowd had gathered. Even though the victim (a 17 year old female) had been dead for a few minutes when we got there, the neighbors chided us for not arriving sooner and entering the house more quickly with rescue equipment. Being on a narrow street, traffic was jammed and squad cars had a difficult time getting to the scene. This situation escalated into a potentially troublesome racial event and was not helped when a late arriving brother of the victim tried to break past a female police officer to enter the house. One of the EMTs grabbed the man and shoved him off a small porch and then pushed him into the fender of a parked car.

Riders

(21)   Because new EMTs and paramedics have to get "field experience" before they can be certified by the State Health Department, EMTs at city EMS are scheduled to take these "riders" with them when answering calls. For the EMT trainee, the experienced EMT is an on-site teacher and supervisor and must "sign off" the

runs (on special forms supplied to the trainee). When several classes are in session and several "special skills" trainees need to ride with preceptors (qualified paramedics), the stations and the ambulances can get crowded.

(22)   In my EMT class the primary instructor talked about the paramedics we would be riding with in very favorable terms. During one lecture he said, "If you're in a situation where a paramedic can teach you something, you have made a friend. They will be glad to show you anything they can." While some paramedics take a professional interest in showing the novices a "thing or two about ambulance work," not all paramedics were helpful to EMT trainees. Some trainees complained of being left at the station rather than being taken on a run and others complained of rudeness and a flippant attitude on the part of the paramedics. Other trainees said they felt they were "just in the way" and others said they never did feel "comfortable" around the station, out on a run or in the ER. While basically helpful and professional, some EMTs used the presence of the trainees as an opportunity to "strut their stuff" and to impress the trainee or kid them for their lack of experience or willingness to tackle certain tasks. A statement made by a physician to a group of paramedics and special skills EMTs at a recertification lecture indicates the general attitude adopted by paramedics toward trainees. According to the doctor, "EMTs are entry level jobs and you must help them. They're not very sophisticated. You practitioners are going to have to push them along. Pat them on the head, kick their rears, but help them. They see the laceration and forget the cervical spine (injury)."

Peers

(23)   The role of partner is very important in EMS work (see Mannon 1981, pp. 50-63, for a detailed description of the role of partner in an urban ambulance organization). Crews form cliques and evaluate peers on the basis of the degree of expertise demonstrated in the field. An EMT might make a snide comment about the lack of driving ability of another EMT or about how peer A is still a "hot dog" ("getting off" on the blood and guts, lights and siren, and uniform and badge) or about how so and so cannot start an I.V. without trying several times. Some paramedics provide positive role models ("He's the best in the business!") and others negative ones ("I'd call a taxi before I'd let them carry me to the hospital."). Basically, EMTs perform in such a manner as to impress each other with their technical abilities and their willingness to pull their share of the various loads encountered. Palmer (1983, pp. 172-179)

identifies the following roles of paramedics and EMTs: (1) medical authority figure, (2) lifesaver, (3) information specialist, and (4) partner. As co-workers, paramedics perform these roles and carry out a variety of tasks attendant to specific medical and social situations. It is thought that paramedics develop a "working personality" (see Skolnick 1975, for the articulation of factors creating a working personality of police officers) influenced by evaluations of co-workers and other audiences. Information supplied directly and indirectly by audiences creates part of the feedback loop found in most symbolic interaction. Information supplied by co-workers forms an integral component of the overall performance of paramedics and becomes influential in affecting their occupational identities.

Media

(24)   "Look there! We made the six o'clock news on the wreck. Look. Did you see me gettin' in the back of the unit?" This type of conversation is fairly common around the stations and reflects societal as well as individual interest in emergencies. One comment was, "We have egos. We like to see ourselves on the T.V." Another said, "This whole job is an ego trip and the media helps us a lot." At one disaster drill covered by several local television stations and newspaper reporters, however, the presence of the media added an element of frustration because they captured the general confusion of the drill. One field supervisor said, "Damn. All the media in town was here." When asked by a paramedic participating in the drill, "What went wrong?" the supervisor said angrily, "You want me to list them in order?"

(25)   The media, particularly T.V., document the actual operation of emergency procedures as well as serving as a vehicle for carrying public service announcements for EMS. The public image of EMS is directly tied to the amount and type of coverage provided by the media. As there is a media hotline fed into the dispatch center, there is a degree of symbiotic cooperation experienced between EMS and the media. Dispatchers assist in this "PR" work by talking to media personnel when they phone and ask for the specifics of calls heard over radio scanners. One past dispatcher "got fed up" with the media people calling him about runs and told them to "go to hell." "We lost a lot of good PR when he did that. We're just now getting back in with them," one EMT stated.

ER Staff

(26)   "Some docs are good, some ain't worth shit," proclaimed one EMT. Another said, "You'll never find a doc who doesn't have some animosity towards us. Because we're doing their job and we haven't gone the long years of schooling they have. You don't have to go to school for twelve years to recognize a heart attack.... We're destroying the mystique of doctors as healers, with the magic touch in their fingers." Another stated, "Aloof doctors are bad. I like one who is not condescending and looks at us with some respect regarding our knowledge . . . you have to watch your attitude. I know I've made some situations worse because I get angry."

(27)   Physicians at some hospitals are still leery about the skills and capabilities of EMTs and are not very cooperative about "giving orders" over the radio. Some are most trusting and, while "standing orders" do not technically exist, these doctors are more willing to let the EMT start the medical protocols utilized in emergency procedures.

(28)   ER nurses basically get along with the EMTs and assist them in their chores and engage in ER horseplay with them. Some nurses, in some situations, are a bit hostile to the EMTs for being on their turf and for being physically "in the way" when work is hectic. "They've done their job. Why don't they just get on out of the way," one nurse was overheard to say about the EMT crew in the ER. Issues needing further study involve the status differentials extant between EMTs and nurses. Nurses have to train for longer periods of time and may feel somewhat threatened by paramedics who perform (often in view of physicians) many of the duties once exclusively reserved for nurses. In many situations it is apparent that paramedic training is more mechanical and designed for the "short haul" where nurse training is more theoretical and designed for the long term-care of the patient. Such differences in perspectives may produce contexts for disagreement. The ER experience, however, cements bonds between nurses and EMTs. Such bonds allow them to be cooperative in many of their joint endeavors and generally positive in their evaluations of each other. They often sided with each other when confronted with angry or uncooperative patients, family members, or physicians and were observed to engage in several social events together ("bar hopping," picnicking, barbecuing, et cetera). This interaction produces an occupational subculture of EMS personnel and provides some protection and power to EMS workers.

Summary and Conclusions

(29)   This qualitative study of paramedics and emergency medical technicians reveals that they perform before several significant audiences: patients, patients' families, bystanders, riders, peers, the media and the emergency room staff. Interaction with these audiences affects the medical and social demeanor of paramedics and serves to create public images of this nascent occupational group. From a sociological standpoint, paramedics are to be seen as participants in a social drama of work wherein negotiations about emergencies as well as about self-concepts become standard fare within the occupational milieu.

(30)   Research by Graham (1981) and Hammer et al. (1986) demonstrates that paramedics experience elevated amounts of occupational stress and that stress is related to making critical medical errors in the field. Paramedics in the Hammer et al. (1986, p. 50) study, when compared to general hospital employees, "showed significantly higher levels of organizational stress, job dissatisfaction, and negative patient attitudes." It is thought that identifying audiences significant to paramedics (and describing interaction patterns and negotiations between audience members and role incumbents) will increase our understanding of the social dynamics that go into the production of emergency health care. It is hoped that an understanding of the social conditions under which paramedics perform will allow analysts of stress to more fully comprehend the occupational strains experienced by emergency health care providers. Such an understanding will increase our ability to assist paramedics and their audiences to more effectively engage in mutually beneficial behavior during life-and-death situations.

References

American Academy of Orthopaedic Surgeons. 1977. *Emergency Care and Transportation of the Sick and Injured*. Menasha, Wisconsin: Banta.

Coombs, R.H. and P.S. Powers. 1975. "Socialization for Death: The Physician's Role." *Urban Life* 4:250-271.

Douglas, D.J. 1969. "Occupational and Therapeutic Contingencies of Ambulance Services in Metropolitan Areas." Ph.D. diss. University of California.

Emerson, Robert M. and Melvin Pollner. 1976. "Dirty Work Designations: Their Features and Consequences in a Psychiatric Setting." *Social Problems* 23:241-254.

Goffman, Erving. 1959. *The Presentation of Self in Everyday Life*. Englewood Cliffs, New Jersey: Prentice-Hall.

Graham, Nancy K. 1981. "Done In, Fed Up, Burned Out." *Journal of Emergency Medical Services* (January):24-29.

Hammer, Jeffrey S., James J. Matthews, John S. Lyons and Nancy J. Johnson. 1986. "Occupational Stress Within the Paramedic Profession: An Initial Report of Stress Levels Compared to Hospital Employees." *Annals of Emergency Medicine* 15:45-48.

Handel, Warren. 1982. *Ethnomethodology: How People Make Sense*. Englewood Cliffs, New Jersey: Prentice-Hall.

Hughes, Everett C. 1972. "The Study of Occupations." Pp. 106-120 in *The Social Dimensions of Work*, edited by Clifton D. Bryant. Englewood Cliffs, New Jersey: Prentice-Hall.

_____. 1958. *Men and Their Work*. Glencoe, Illinois: Free Press.

Jackson, Francis C. 1979. "Accidental Injury — The Problem and the Initiatives." Pp. 1-20 in *Trauma in Pregnancy*, edited by Herbert J. Buchsbaum. Philadelphia: Saunders.

Lofland, John. 1976. *Doing Social Life: The Qualitative Study of Human Interaction in Natural Settings*. New York: Wiley.

Maines, David R. 1982. "In Search of Mesostructure: Studies in the Negotiated Order." *Urban Life* 11:267-279.

Manning, Peter K. and John Van Maanen (eds.). 1978. *Policing: A View from the Streets*. Santa Monica, California: Goodyear.

Mannon, James M. 1981. *Emergency Encounters: A Study of an Urban Ambulance Service*. Port Washington, New York: Kennikat.

Metz, Donald L. 1981. *Running Hot: Structure and Stress in Ambulance Work*. Cambridge: Abt Books.

Oldham, Jack. 1979. "Social Control of Voluntary Work Activity: The Gift Horse Syndrome." *Sociology of Work and Occupations* 6:379-403.

Palmer, C. Eddie. 1983. " 'Trauma Junkies' and Street Work: Occupational Behavior of Paramedics and Emergency Medical Technicians." *Urban Life* 12:162-183.

Papper, Solomon. 1978. "The Undesirable Patient." Pp. 166-168 in *Dominant Issues in Medical Sociology*, edited by Howard D. Schwartz and Cary S. Kart. Reading, Massachusetts: Addison-Wesley.

Richard, Michel P. 1986. "Goffman Revisited: Relatives vs. Administrators in Nursing Homes." *Qualitative Sociology* 9:321-338.

Roth, Julius A. 1972. "Some Contingencies of the Moral Evaluation and Control of Clientele: The Case of the Hospital Emergency Service." *American Journal of Sociology* 77:839-856.

Skolnick, Jerome H. 1975. *Justice Without Trial: Law Enforcement in Democratic Society*. 2nd ed. New York: Wiley.

Strauss, Anselm. 1978. *Negotiations*. San Francisco: Jossey-Bass.

Sugrue, Noreen M. 1982. "Emotions as Property and Context for Negotiation." *Urban Life* 11:280-292.

Zurcher, Louis A., Jr. 1979. "The Airline Passenger: Protection of Self in an Encapsulated Group." *Qualitative Sociology* 1:77-99.

Factual Questions

1. A dramaturgical approach such as the one employed in this article emphasizes the interactions between actors and whom?

2. What type of qualitative research techniques were used by the author for this article?

3. Were EMS staff aware that the author was doing research?

4. How did the author maintain as complete a set of field notes as possible?

5. What are the seven generic audiences before whom EMTs perform?

Questions for Discussion

6. Does the introduction provide a clear notion of the research problem, the purpose of the research, and its significance?

7. Does the literature review seem relevant to the research problem?

8. Are the length of observation and the variety of situations observed adequate? To what population would you generalize the results of this study?

9. Is there enough information on the research instruments and procedures to allow you to replicate this study?

10. Should there be information about the reliability and validity of the research instruments and procedures?

11. Does the analysis include sufficient statistical information?

12. Are the conclusions supported by and do they logically follow from the data that have been presented?

13. What kinds of information did this qualitative study obtain that a quantitative study would not have been able to obtain?

14. Are the findings discussed in terms of their implications and/or practical significance?

Notes:

Article 22

College Students Use Implicit Personality Theory Instead of Safer Sex

Sunyna S. Williams
State University of New York College at Buffalo
Diane L. Kimble, Nancy H. Covell, Laura H. Weiss,
Kimberly J. Newton, and Jeffrey D. Fisher
University of Connecticut
William A. Fisher
University of Western Ontario

Many college students engage in high levels of unsafe sexual behavior that puts them at risk for HIV infection. To better understand the dynamics underlying college students' unsafe behavior, focus group discussions were conducted with 308 students (146 men and 162 women). The results showed that, instead of consistently using condoms, many college students use implicit personality theories to judge the riskiness of potential sexual partners. Specifically, partners whom college students know and like are not perceived to be risky, even if what students know about these individuals is irrelevant to HIV status. The students determine the riskiness of partners they do not know well based on superficial characteristics that are also generally unrelated to HIV status. Therefore, AIDS prevention interventions for college students must expose the ineffectiveness of the students' use of implicit personality theories to determine potential partners' riskiness, and the "know your partner" safer sex guideline should be abandoned.

(1)   Health experts are increasingly concerned about HIV infection among college students because students are continuing to engage in high levels of unsafe sexual behavior that puts them at risk for infection (Miller, Turner, & Moses, 1990). J. D. Fisher and W. A. Fisher (1990) found that 72% of college students had been sexually active during the previous year; of those who had been sexually active, 75% had not always used condoms during sexual intercourse and 44% had had two or more partners. Other surveys (e.g., Abler & Sedlacek, 1989; DeBuono, Zinner, Daamen, & McCormack, 1990; Fisher & Misovich, 1991) have obtained similar results.

Reprinted with permission from *Journal of Applied Social Psychology, 22*(12): 921-933. Copyright © 1992 by V. H. Winston & Son, Inc. All rights reserved.

Preparation of this article was supported by National Institute of Mental Health grant MH46224 to Jeffrey D. Fisher and William A. Fisher. We are grateful to William R. Lenderking and Stephen J. Misovich for moderating the male-only groups and to Kelly A. Hooper and Stephen J. Misovich for their assistance in analyzing audiotapes of the discussions. We also thank two anonymous reviewers for their helpful comments on an earlier draft.

Correspondence concerning this article should be addressed to Sunyna S. Williams, Department of Psychology, State University of New York College at Buffalo, Buffalo, NY 14222.

(2)   There is evidence that there are already appreciable levels of HIV seroprevalence among college students. An American College Health Association study (Gayle et al., 1990) found that 1 in 500 college student blood samples was HIV+. There was substantial variability among the universities sampled, and because these blood samples are now 3 years old, the incidence of HIV seropositivity may have increased substantially in the interim. Moreover, according to the General Accounting Office/Human Resources Department (1990), the number of AIDS cases among people in their twenties increased 41% during 1989. Because of the long latency period between HIV infection and the development of AIDS, many of those who developed AIDS in their twenties were probably infected through unsafe sexual behavior during their teens or early twenties, which is the average age for college students.

(3)   In order to reduce the amount of unsafe sex exhibited by many college students, it is necessary to understand the dynamics associated with their unsafe sexual behavior. While there is a great deal of quantitative research documenting the incidence of risky sexual behavior among students (e.g., Abler & Sedlacek, 1989; DeBuono et al., 1990; Fisher & Fisher, 1990; Fisher & Misovich, 1991), much less work has been directed at identifying the reasons underlying college students' unsafe sex and the conditions under which it occurs. Nevertheless, such research, which can best be performed using qualitative methods (see Fisher & Fisher, 1992), is necessary both to develop conceptualizations of college students' unsafe sexual practices and to design interventions to change these practices (Manning, Balson, Barenberg, & Moore, 1989; Parker & Carballo, 1990). To address this need, the present study attempted to gain a better understanding of the dynamics underlying college students' unsafe sexual behavior.

Method

Overview

(4)   This research employed focus group techniques to explore the dynamics of heterosexual college students' safer and unsafe sexual behavior. Focus groups, which are often used to facilitate understanding of the psychological underpinnings of behavior (Basch, 1987; Nix, Pasteur, & Servance, 1988) and can also be used to corroborate quantitative findings (Parker & Carballo, 1990; Stewart & Shamdasani, 1990), provide an appropriate means to perform such an analysis.

Furthermore, the feasibility of using this technique in the area of sexual behavior and AIDS risk reduction research has been demonstrated by studies conducted with lower income African American women and teenage girls (Fullilove, Fullilove, Haynes, & Gross, 1990), African American teenage boys (Nix et al., 1988), and gay men (Offir, Williams, Fisher, & Fisher, 1991).

(5)   In the current research, groups of four to eight college students were asked to discuss their safer and unsafe sexual behavior and their reasons for engaging in those behaviors, as well as the contexts within which safer and unsafe sex occurred. Both same-sex (male-only and female-only) and mixed-sex focus groups were conducted to ensure breadth of results. That is, although mixed-sex groups may have more mundane realism, in that members of both sexes are present, it is possible that college students may disclose more in same-sex groups.[1]

(6)   In addition, both types of groups were conducted because the two types of groups had different purposes. The same-sex groups (in which the discussions lasted about 2 hours) were run solely for the purpose of exploring the dynamics of college students' safer and unsafe sexual behavior. However, the mixed-sex groups (in which the discussions lasted about 1 hour) were conducted for another purpose as well; they were conducted to perform a quantitative analysis to determine the consequences for impression formation of an individual taking a pro- or anti-AIDS prevention stance during the focus group discussion. This latter data will not be addressed here.

Subjects

(7)   The subjects were 308 University of Connecticut undergraduate students (146 men and 162 women) who were recruited both through an advertisement in the campus newspaper and through the university subject pool to ensure a representative sample. The individuals received either $10 or course experimental credits for their participation. Based on focus group availability, the subjects were assigned to same- or mixed-sex groups of four to eight subjects each. Only previously unacquainted people were assigned to the same group, and there were at least two men and two women assigned to each mixed-sex group. Overall, there were 169 subjects (80 men and 89 women) in 25 mixed-sex groups, 66 men in 13 male-only groups, and 73 women in 13 female-only groups.[2]

---

[1] In the present research, differences in focus group discussion content among mixed-sex, male-only, and female-only groups were minimal. Therefore, the results for the same- and mixed-sex groups were combined.

Procedure

(8)   The protocols for the focus group discussions were developed in accordance with established guidelines for focus group research (Basch, 1987; Krueger, 1988). The discussion sessions were conducted by trained moderators who followed a prepared, semistructured outline. The moderators for the mixed-sex groups were female, whereas those for the same-sex groups were of the same sex as the group members. The participants and the moderator were seated comfortably in a circle, and a multidirectional microphone was used to record the session.

(9)   Before the discussion began, the subjects were asked to read and sign an informed consent form. They were told that the discussion was being audiotaped for later review by the research team, but were assured that their responses were confidential. It was also stressed that the purpose of the discussion was to find out what college students think and feel about sex and AIDS and that subjects should state their opinions whether or not they agreed with other group members. Furthermore, the participants were told that they did not have to answer any questions that made them uncomfortable and that they could withdraw from the study at any point without loss of either monetary remuneration or experimental credit.

(10)   After brief self-introductions, the discussion began. The questions focused on situations in which the participants may have had or refused to have unsafe sex, the number and types of sexual relationships the participants had experienced, what methods of sexual protection the participants currently used and why, what they liked and disliked about using condoms, and whether the participants thought that AIDS was a concern for college students. These questions were designed to tap the students' reasons for engaging in unsafe sexual behavior.

Results and Discussion

Data Analysis

(11)   Because focus group data is collected in group settings, it is inappropriate to analyze the data by conducting frequency counts of responses within fixed content categories (Basch, 1987; Krueger, 1988). Instead,

focus group discussions should be analyzed using a systematic process to extract and interpret descriptive statements from audiotapes or transcripts (Krueger, 1988). Basch suggests analyzing such data by creating categories of ideas to generate themes and backing these themes with illustrative quotes from the discussion participants. The data analytic procedures for the present study followed the above guidelines. Focus group discussion audiotapes were analyzed by having several research assistants listen to each tape. Only viewpoints raised in the majority of groups and by more than one person in the group were considered. Each listener generated several perceived themes and extracted descriptive statements and quotes in support of those themes. The research assistants then discussed their individual findings with one another in order to develop consensually validated conclusions.

Findings

(12)   The results from these analysis techniques are presented in four subsections which deal with (a) how students make judgments of the riskiness of their sexual partners, (b) their assessments of their own personal risk, (c) their reasons for specific incidents of unsafe sex, and (d) their beliefs about condoms. These four subsections represent the major categories of findings. As noted above, these categories originated from what the subjects said, rather than from the protocol questions per se. In other words, the categories were data-driven. Because the categories were data-driven and so few subjects were abstinent or practiced noninsertive sex (only 13% of those in the mixed-sex groups had abstained from insertive sex during the previous year), the results emphasize condom use as the primary AIDS prevention method.

(13)   *Judgments of the riskiness of sexual partners.* The data strongly indicated that our respondents appeared to have a well-developed and generally accepted set of ideas regarding which potential sexual partners are risky for HIV infection and which are not. We found consistently that partners whom students *know* and *like* (including monogamous partners who have not been tested for HIV infection) are perceived as *not* being risky. One subject summed up this view by saying, "When you get to know the person . . . as soon as you begin trusting the person . . . you don't really have to use a condom." In effect, such partners appeared to be

---

[2] AIDS risk behavior data that was collected only on subjects in the mixed-sex focus groups suggests that those in our sample were engaging in high levels of unsafe sexual behavior comparable to those found in other college student samples (e.g., Abler & Sedlacek, 1989; DeBuono et al., 1990; Fisher & Fisher, 1990; Fisher & Misovich, 1991). Specifically, 87% of those in the mixed-sex sample had been sexually active during the previous year. Of those who had been sexually active, 67% had not always used condoms during sexual intercourse (although only 23% had ever had an HIV blood test), 57% had had two or more sexual partners, and 14% had had anal sex.

considered not to be risky, regardless of the objective safeness or unsafeness of their past or present sexual behavior, and actual HIV status was almost never known. As one man said, "I knew my partner really well before we had sex, so I didn't have to worry about her sexual history." These and many other similar statements make it clear that students do not use condoms with partners whom they know and like.

(14)   Our impression is that the tendency for students not to practice safer sex with partners they know and like (and whom they invariably trust) is based on their reluctance to link risk or disease with loving or caring. As one student put it, "Because I love her . . . it's kind of hard to think that [about AIDS]." Furthermore, it is our impression that students generally do not have sex at all with people they do not like. Interestingly, therefore, the only situation in which students are likely to use condoms is with partners they feel they do not know well enough to eschew condom use.

(15)   When judging the riskiness of previously unknown potential partners, our focus group data indicated that students often seem to rely on simple rules to label someone as risky for HIV infection (and therefore, to decide either to use a condom or not to have sex with that person). They tend to assume that risky people are those who dress provocatively, whom one met in bars, who were older than most college students, who are from large cities, or who are overly anxious for sex. As one student explained, "If they're . . . 24, they've been around 6 more years than someone . . . who's 18. . . . If they're dressed up like a slut . . . they're usually a slut." Another subject summed up this reliance on superficial cues by saying, "If I [were] in the bar-hopping, New York scene and meeting stray women . . . then I'd worry about getting AIDS." In addition to using the above cues, many men appear to perceive women they have just met who use oral contraceptives to be risky. As one man said, "You don't want to trust someone who just went on the pill." Offir et al. (1991) found a similar reliance on superficial cues in judging the riskiness of potential partners among gay men.

(16)   Because of their confidence in their abilities to assess a partner's riskiness, most subjects indicated that they would only consider using condoms during sex with partners they feel they do not know well enough and whom they perceive might be risky. A typical response was, "If you just met them, you use a condom. . . if it's long-term, you aren't going to worry." Therefore, the subjects sometimes indicated that they would use condoms at the beginning of a relationship, before they feel that they knew the partner sufficiently. One subject

explained, "It's important [to use condoms] for . . . either one-night stands or the beginning of relationships where you just really don't know enough about the person yet." Another summed up the prevailing view by saying, "At first you should use a condom. Then, once you get to know her, you should discuss other means of birth control." The students reported that once they feel that they know their partners, usually in ways unrelated to HIV status, they almost invariably cease using condoms. A typical response was, "I'm mostly using the pill since my relationship, but if it's a new partner . . . [I would] definitely use a condom." When asked what he would need to know about a partner to decide to stop using condoms, one man said he would want to "know how she lives, know her friends, [talk] to her about her life."

(17)   From these findings, it is clear that college students appear to judge the riskiness of sexual partners based on characteristics that are not related objectively to HIV status specifically, whether they know and like the partner and whether a previously unknown partner has certain superficial traits. Perceived relationships among characteristics, such as the perception that a partner whom one knows or who is from a small town is not risky, are called implicit personality theories (e.g., Schneider, Hastorf, & Ellsworth, 1979). Clearly, college students are using an implicit personality theory to determine the riskiness of sexual partners, rather than consistently practicing safer sex.

(18)   Implicit personality theories are often adaptive, even if they are not entirely accurate, because they allow people to interpret their social world. However, the use of an implicit personality theory for ascertaining a partner's AIDS risk is extremely unreliable and potentially fatal. Because the only way to accurately determine someone's AIDS risk is through knowledge of that person's HIV status, the use of any other cues to assess risk will often provide a dangerous, false sense of security. Therefore, health education efforts to reduce AIDS risk behavior among college students (and perhaps others as well) must expose the ineffectiveness of their use of implicit personality theories to assess the riskiness of partners or potential partners. Furthermore, it must be emphasized that, in the absence of specific knowledge regarding the partner's HIV status, knowing one's partner and being monogamous do not constitute safer sex.

(19)   Ironically, one of the safer sex guidelines that has been widely promoted in many large circulation pamphlets such as the Surgeon General's Report on Acquired Immune Deficiency Syndrome (U.S. Department

of Heath and Human Services, 1986) is the exhortation to "know your partner." Although this guideline is intended to refer to knowing one's partner's sexual history (and, of course, acting on that knowledge), college students, and probably many others as well, appear to have misinterpreted it. In effect, they are using the guideline to strengthen their beliefs that they are not being unsafe if they know their partners, even if the ways in which they know them are entirely irrelevant to AIDS risk. Furthermore, even if one does consider one's partner's sexual history, it is dangerous to infer a negative HIV status from a nonpromiscuous sexual history. Clearly, the "know your partner" guideline has backfired and should be abandoned.

(20)   Even less cryptic safer sex guidelines such as the advice to "take precautions whenever you have sex outside a long-term monogamous relationship" (e.g., American College Health Association, 1987) create problems. College students seem to misinterpret such advice to mean that monogamy itself constitutes safer sex, even serial monogamy in the absence of objective knowledge regarding one's partner's HIV status. Therefore, students often appear to be using such advice to bolster their beliefs that they need to use condoms only with partners whom they do not know. Unfortunately, pamphlets containing the "know your partner" and "take precautions outside a long-term monogamous relationship" guidelines are still being distributed.

(21)   *Assessments of personal risk.* While they judge their partners' riskiness based on implicit personality theories, our respondents do not generally seem to consider themselves to be at risk for HIV infection, regardless of whether or not they engage in safer sex. For example, one subject said, "I'm not involved with one-night stands, so I don't worry about it [AIDS] too much." Another said, "I'd worry if I [currently] had multiple partners." Some do not even feel that AIDS should be a concern on a college campus. As one subject summed it up, "Personally, I'm not really worried about AIDS on this campus. . . . I'd be willing to bet that there aren't too many cases outside homosexuals."

(22)   However, even those who may feel that AIDS should be a concern on campus do not seem to feel personally vulnerable because they do not really believe that heterosexual college students are at risk. As one student said, "I don't know anybody [who has] AIDS, I've never seen anybody [who has] AIDS, I'm not gay, and it seems, regardless [of] what the facts are . . . like it's mostly gay guys that get it." Another explained, "I've always felt that it wasn't something that was going to affect me. . . .   It happened to drug users and it

happened to gay people, but it would never happen to me." Clearly, most students perceive themselves to be very socially distant from the typical person with AIDS. According to Weinstein (1980, 1988), the greater the perceived social distance between oneself and the typical victim of a particular misfortune, the less personally vulnerable one will feel to that misfortune, regardless of objective risk.

(23)   The major practical implication of this finding is that AIDS prevention efforts must emphasize students' personal vulnerability to HIV infection. To increase perceived vulnerability, students may need to be confronted with cases of heterosexually transmitted HIV infection among college students. In addition, one could present students with statistics regarding the alarming incidence of sexually transmitted diseases (STDs) and unwanted pregnancy on their own campuses, coupled with the reminder that AIDS is transmitted in the same way. This could be followed by a personal risk audit to emphasize that the students are engaging in behavior that puts them at risk for HIV/AIDS.

(24)   For most of our respondents, the risk of pregnancy is far more salient than the risk of AIDS or other STD. In this context, a typical response among those who use condoms was, "I use condoms . . . for birth control. That's what I'm worried about." Another subject admitted, "I think more about pregnancy than I do about it [AIDS]." Because their primary concern is pregnancy, most students are not likely to use condoms in the context of a relationship if the female partner is on the pill. As one man said, "Before she was on the pill, we used condoms; now we don't." A woman explained, "I know that if I'm on it [the pill] that I tend to think less. . . [about] protection against disease." Unfortunately, use of oral contraceptives appears to be antithetical to condom use. Therefore, AIDS prevention interventions must highlight the fact that the pill does not provide protection from HIV infection or other STD, and campus health professionals should advise individuals who receive prescriptions for oral contraceptives to use condoms as well.

(25)   *Reasons for incidents of unsafe sex.* Because most college students do not really believe that they are at risk for HIV infection, many often engage in sexual behavior that they acknowledge is objectively unsafe. There are two major reasons our respondents gave for engaging in specific instances of unsafe sex.

(26)   One of the most frequently mentioned reasons for engaging in unsafe behavior was alcohol impairment. One frank response was, "I guess there . . . [are]

episodes where you get really, really [drunk], and things happen, and you forget about consequences." Another student said, "Most times, yes, I use a rubber, but it's happened that I didn't use anything when I [was drunk]." College students need to be taught techniques to prevent the unsafe combination of sex and alcohol intoxication. For example, students could be encouraged to choose not to drink or to drink less when they anticipate the possibility of having sex. Alternatively, if they are drunk or anticipate becoming drunk, they could be encouraged to ask friends to not allow them to leave a social event with a potential sexual partner.

(27)   Another frequently mentioned reason for being unsafe is overwhelming lust. As one student admitted, "There's been a couple of times . . . that you do give in because it's like *the moment*." Another explained that, "In the heat of the moment you don't think about it [AIDS]." It must be emphasized to college students that, if they make condom use habitual and they carry condoms with them, they will be far less likely to forget to use them in the heat of passion. Offir et al. (1991) found the same tendency among gay men to attribute specific incidents of unsafe sex to passion.

(28)   *Beliefs about condoms.* In order for college students to use condoms consistently, regardless of the temptations offered by particular situations or their beliefs about their partners' riskiness, they must have positive feelings about condom use. Unfortunately, students reported almost unanimously that they do not like using condoms and believe that using them interferes with their enjoyment of sex. One subject summed up this view by saying, "I think condoms really suck . . . . When I finally thought about maybe getting AIDS I began to pseudo [sometimes] use them. I don't like them, though."

(29)   Overall, college students reported feeling that condoms are unpleasant to use, primarily because they decrease sensation and spontaneity. A typical response was, "I don't like condoms at all. I hate them. I can tell the difference, and I don't like it." More specifically, one subject explained, "I can't stand — the spontaneity — how it's ruined, and the smell of condoms . . . makes me sick." Even students who reported always using condoms often reported not especially enjoying them. Furthermore, many students reported feeling that condoms are inconvenient, because one must remember to buy them and have them available. As one subject explained, "You get sick of taking a condom everywhere; it's a real hassle." Clearly, college students need to be taught ways to be more comfortable with condom use and to have pleasurable sex with condoms. Offir et al.

(1991) found that gay men expressed a similarly strong dislike of condoms.

(30)   In addition to feeling that condoms are unpleasant to use, many students seem to feel that the use of condoms has undesirable social implications. Many respondents indicated that requesting that a condom be used may imply that one distrusts one's partner; that is, that one believes the partner has been promiscuous or will not be monogamous. One subject summed up this view by saying, "If it's someone [with whom] I have to use a condom, it's someone I don't trust." Furthermore, discussing condom use prior to having sex with someone for the first time might imply that one expected to have sex, which might be perceived as socially inappropriate. As one subject put it, "[If] I was going to have sex and I pulled out a condom, it would look bad." These findings suggest that AIDS prevention interventions should seek to alter perceived social norms regarding condom use, so that requesting condom use would not carry undesirable implications regarding one's trust of one's partner or one's social appropriateness (cf. Fisher, 1988).

Conclusions

(31)   The main theme that emerged from the results was that college students' judgments of a particular partner's riskiness are not based on the relevant objective criterion of HIV status. Instead, students use an implicit personality theory to determine a partner's riskiness. In addition, students do not believe that they themselves are at risk for HIV infection. Therefore, they often engage in behavior that is unsafe, because they do not perceive the need for using condoms (which they do not like), except when having sex with a partner whom they feel they do not know well enough and perceive may be risky. Future research should confirm these qualitative findings with more rigorous quantitative methods. For example, one could experimentally examine the influence of various characteristics of a stimulus person on subject judgments of the riskiness of that person for transmitting HIV. Finally, the main findings of this study have several practical implications for AIDS prevention with college students, which have been discussed throughout the *Findings* section. In conclusion, college students need to understand that they are vulnerable to HIV infection and can drastically reduce their HIV risk by abandoning their biased judgments of partners' riskiness and, instead, engaging in pleasurable safer sex.

References

Abler, R. M., & Sedlacek, W. E. (1989). Freshman sexual attitudes and behaviors over a 15-year period. *Journal of College Student Development*, **30**, 201-209.

American College Health Association (1987). *Making sex safer*. Rockville, MD: Author.

Basch, C. E. (1987). Focus group interview: An underutilized research technique for improving theory and practice in health education. *Health Education Quarterly*, **14**, 411-448.

DeBuono, B. A., Zinner, S. H., Daamen, M., & McCormack, W. M. (1990). Sexual behavior of college women in 1975, 1986, and 1989. *The New England Journal of Medicine*, **322**, 821-825.

Fisher, J. D. (1988). Possible effects of reference group-based social influence on AIDS-risk behavior and AIDS prevention. *American Psychologist* **43**, 914-920.

Fisher, J. D., & Fisher, W. A. (1990). [College student predictive study of AIDS risk reduction]. Unpublished raw data.

Fisher, J. D., & Fisher, W. A. (1992). Changing AIDS-risk behavior. *Psychological Bulletin*, **111**, 455-474.

Fisher, J. D., & Misovich, S. J. (1991). *1990 Technical report on undergraduate students' AIDS-preventive behavior, AIDS-knowledge, and fear of AIDS*. Storrs, CT: University of Connecticut, Department of Psychology.

Fullilove, M. T., Fullilove, R. E., Haynes, K., & Gross, S. (1990). Black women and AIDS prevention: A view towards understanding the gender rules. *The Journal of Sex Research*, **27**, 47-64.

Gayle, H. D., Keeling, R. P., Garcia-Tunon, M., Kilbourne, B. W., Narkunas, J. P., Ingram, F. R., Rogers, M. F., & Curran, J. W. (1990). Prevalence of the human immunodeficiency virus among college students. *The New England Journal of Medicine*, **323**, 1538-1541.

General Accounting Office/Human Resources Department (1990). *AIDS education: Public school programs require more student information and teacher training* (GAO/HRD Publication No. 90-103).

Krueger, R. A. (1988). *Focus groups: A practical guide for applied research*. Newbury Park, CA: Sage.

Manning, D., Balson, P. M., Barenberg, N., & Moore, T. M. (1989). Susceptibility to AIDS: What college students do and don't believe. *Journal of American College Health*, **38**, 67-73.

Miller, H. G., Turner, C. F., & Moses, L. E. (Eds.). (1990). *AIDS: The second decade*. Washington, DC: National Academy.

Nix, L. M., Pasteur, A. B., & Servance, M. A. (1988). A focus group study of sexually active Black male teenagers. *Adolescence, 23*, 741-751.

Offir, J. T., Williams, S. S., Fisher, W. A., & Fisher, J. D. (1991, June). *Possible reasons for inconsistent AIDS prevention and relapse behavior among gay men*. Paper presented at the meeting of the American Psychological Society, Washington, DC.

Parker, R. G., & Carballo, M. (1990). Qualitative research on homosexual and bisexual behavior relevant to HIV/AIDS. *The Journal of Sex Research*, **27**, 497-525.

Schneider, D. J., Hastorf, A. H., & Ellsworth, P. C. (1979). *Person perception* (2nd ed.). Reading, MA: Addison-Wesley.

Stewart, D. W., & Shamdasani, P. N. (1990). *Focus groups: Theory and practice*. Newbury Park, CA: Sage.

U.S. Department of Health and Human Services (1986). *Surgeon General's report on acquired immune deficiency syndrome*. Rockville, MD: Author.

Weinstein, N. D. (1980). Unrealistic optimism about future life events. *Journal of Personality and Social Psychology*, **39**, 806-820.

Weinstein, N. D. (1988, July). *Perceptions of personal susceptibility to harm*. Paper presented at the Psychological Approaches to the Prevention of Acquired Immune Deficiency Syndrome conference at the University of Vermont, Burlington, VT.

Factual Questions

1. Since college students' sexual behavior has already been studied using quantitative measures, why is qualitative research on the subject still needed?

2. Individual focus groups consisted of how many subjects?

3. What advantage might same-sex groups have for this research?

4. How many research subjects were used and how were they selected?

5. What directions were given to subjects before discussion began?

6. How was the data from the focus group discussions analyzed?

7. What do the authors mean in paragraph 12 when they state that the categories in which their findings will be discussed are data-driven?

8. What are the four categories in which the authors discuss their findings?

9. What are implicit personality theories?

Questions for Discussion

10. Does the introduction provide a clear notion of the research problem, the purpose of the research, and its significance?

11. Does the literature review seem relevant to the research problem?

12. Is the number of research subjects sufficient? To what population would you generalize the results of this study?

13. Is there enough information on the research instruments and procedures to allow you to replicate this study?

14. Should there be more information about the reliability and validity of the research instruments and procedures?

15. Does the analysis include sufficient statistical information?

16. Are the conclusions supported by and do they logically follow from the data that have been presented?

17. Are the findings discussed in terms of their implications and/or practical significance?

Notes:

Effect of Server Introduction on Restaurant Tipping

Kimberly Garrity
Douglas Degelman
Southern California College

The effect of a server introducing herself by name on restaurant tipping was investigated. Forty-two, 2-person dining parties were randomly assigned to either a name or a no name introduction condition. The use of a buffet brunch reduced contact between server and diners and held bill size constant. Results indicated that having the server introduce herself by name resulted in a significantly higher tipping rate (23.4%) than when the server did not introduce herself by name (15.0%), $p < .001$. Tipping rate also was affected by method of payment, with diners who charged the meal having a higher rate (22.6%) than those paying cash (15.9%), $p < .001$. The findings suggest the importance of initial server-diner interactions. Possible alternative explanations and suggestions for future research are provided.

(1)   Empirical research on restaurant tipping has tended to focus either on characteristics of the dining party, such as gender, number in the party, method of payment, and alcohol consumption (Crusco & Wetzel, 1984; Cunningham, 1979; Freeman, Walker, Borden, & Latane, 1975; May, 1978; Stillman & Hensley, 1980), or on characteristics of the server, such as attractiveness, dress, or gender (Lynn & Latane, 1984; May, 1978; Stillman & Hensley, 1980).

(2)   Very little research has addressed the potentially important role of server-diner interactions on tipping. It has been shown that when a server physically touches a diner it has a significant effect on tipping rate (Crusco & Wetzel, 1984; Stephen & Zweigenhaft, 1986), as does the number of nontask server visits (May, 1978). Although employees perceive a relationship between service rendered and earnings (Bennett, 1983; Shamir, 1983), several studies have found the quality of the service rendered to be unrelated to tipping rate both in a restaurant setting (Lynn & Latane, 1984; May, 1978) and in a taxi setting (Davis, 1959; Karen, 1962).

(3)   One aspect of the server-diner interaction which has not been empirically studied is the initial contact of the server and diners. In a classic work on the restaurant industry, Whyte (1948) suggests that it is

Reprinted with permission from *Journal of Applied Social Psychology*, 20(2): 168-172. Copyright © 1990 by V.H. Winston & Son, Inc. All rights reserved.

This research was submitted by the first author in partial fulfillment of course requirement in Experimental Psychology at Southern California College. The second author served as research adviser and course instructor. The authors wish to thank the management of Charley Brown's of Huntington Beach for their cooperation and members of the Spring, 1988 Experimental Psychology class at Southern California College for their assistance.

Correspondence concerning this article should be sent to Douglas Degelman, Department of Psychology, Southern California College, 55 Fair Drive, Costa Mesa, CA 92626.

the responsibility of the server to "seize the initiative in customer relations — to set the pattern for the relationship. This she does by the things she does, the things she says, the way she uses her voice, and the expression on her face" (pp. 110-111). Since characteristics of the initial contact have been shown to have an impact on other social situations, such as the counselor-client relationship (Angle & Goodyear, 1984), it is possible that various elements of the initial contact between server and diners could significantly affect tipping behavior.

(4)   The purpose of the present study was to systematically examine the effect of server introduction (name introduction or no name introduction) on tipping behavior. Method of payment (cash or charge) also was recorded to allow an additional test of an earlier finding that diners who charge tip more than those who pay cash (May, 1978).

Method

Subjects

(5)   Forty-two, 2-person parties eating Sunday brunch at Charley Brown's Restaurant in Huntington Beach, California on April 10 and 17, 1988 were used as subjects.

Setting and Procedure

(6)   Sunday brunch at Charley Brown's is a buffet at which the diners serve themselves. The bill for each 2-person party was $23.21. The server used in this study was a 22-year-old female who had been in her current position for approximately 4 years.

(7)   Twenty-one dining parties were randomly assigned to each of two interaction conditions. In both conditions, the server approached the diners, smiled, and greeted them. In the name condition, the server said, "Good morning. My name is Kim, and I will be serving you this morning. Have you ever been to Charley Brown's for brunch before?" In the no name condition, the same greeting was used omitting, "My name is Kim."

(8)   After making sure that the diners understood that the brunch was a buffet, the server's responsibility was to respond to special requests (e.g., silverware, sauces, etc.) and to provide beverages. When the diners were finished with their brunch, the server presented the bill, saying, "I'll take that as soon as you're ready." One dining party in the name condition was excluded from the analysis because the server discovered that she

had served them before. One dining party in the no name condition was excluded from the analysis because one of the diners asked the server what her name was.

Results

(9)   Since a preliminary analysis of the data revealed no significant effects of day of testing across conditions, the data were collapsed across day of testing. Amount tipped was used in a 2 (introduction condition) x 2 (method of payment) analysis of variance. Diners in the name introduction condition left significantly larger tips (M = $5.44, SD = $1.75) than those in the no name introduction condition (M = $3.49, SD = $1.13), $F(1,36)$ = 24.02, $p < .001$. With the constant bill amount of $23.21, tipping rate for the diners in the name introduction condition was 23.4%, while for the diners in the no name introduction condition the tipping rate was 15.0%.

(10)   Diners charging their brunch left substantially larger tips (M = $5.24, SD = $1.84) than those paying cash (M = $3.68, SD = $1.29), $F(1,36)$ = 15.35, $p < .001$. The tipping rate for diners charging brunch was 22.6%, while for diners paying cash, the tipping rate was 15.9%. There was no statistically significant interaction between introduction condition and method of payment, $F(1,36)$ = 0.707, $p > .10$.

(11)   The major finding of this study was that having the server identify herself by name resulted in a large, statistically significant effect on tipping behavior. At least two explanations for this effect exist. First, it is possible that server identification provided a social cue to the diners about the "class" of the restaurant, which created an atmosphere in which larger tips were perceived as being expected (see Snyder & Monson, 1975; Snyder & Swann, 1976). An alternative explanation of the findings of this study are provided by Latane's (1981) Social Impact Theory. To the extent that the manipulation of server name introduction affects the salience or strength of the social source (the server), the theory would predict larger tips when the server introduces herself by name than when she does not do so.

(12)   The server in the present study was necessarily aware of the experimental condition of each dining party. Although a minimized contact approach was used in this study (Rosenthal, 1976, p. 374), it is suggested that future research on server identification consider having the maitre d' give the server's name to the diners. This would further reduce the likelihood of experimenter effects.

(13)   The effects of other initial contact variables on tipping remain to be determined. As Whyte (1948) has suggested, the nonverbal behavior of the server (including facial expressions, posture, and eye contact) as well as the server's verbal behavior during the initial contact (content and length of the verbalization) are deserving of further study.

(14)   It also remains for further research to examine the effects of server introduction on tipping in other types of restaurants, with other servers, different party sizes, different meal arrangements, and so forth. Finally, restaurants represent only one of many settings in which tipping is prevalent. Further research in other settings is necessary to identify the extent to which the findings of the present study can be generalized.

References

Angle, S.S., & Goodyear, R.K. (1984). Perceptions of counselor qualities: Impact of subjects' self-concepts, counselor gender, and counselor introductions. *Journal of Counseling Psychology*, **31**, 577-580.

Bennett, H.L. (1983). Remembering drink orders: The memory skills of cocktail waitresses. *Human Learning: Journal of Practical Research & Applications*, **2**, 157-169.

Crusco, A.H., & Wetzel, C.G. (1984). The midas touch: The effects of interpersonal touch on restaurant tipping. *Personality and Social Psychology Bulletin*, **10**, 512-517.

Cunningham, M.R. (1979). Weather, mood, and helping behavior: Quasi-experiments with the sunshine samaritan. *Journal of Personality and Social Psychology*, **37**, 1947-1956.

Davis, F.S. (1959). The cab driver and his fare: Facets of a fleeting relationship. *American Journal of Sociology*, **65**, 158-165.

Freeman, S., Walker, M., Borden, R., & Latane, B. (1975). Diffusion of responsibility and restaurant tipping: Cheaper by the bunch. *Personality and Social Psychology Bulletin*, **1**, 584-587.

Karen, R. (1962). Some factors affecting tipping. *Sociology and Social Research*, **47**, 68-74.

Latane, B. (1981). The psychology of social impact. *American Psychologist*, **36**, 343-356.

Lynn, M. (1988). The effects of alcohol consumption on restaurant tipping. *Personality and Social Psychology Bulletin*, **14**, 87-91.

Lynn, M., & Latane, B. (1984). The psychology of restaurant tipping. *Journal of Applied Social Psychology*, **14**, 549-561.

May, J.M. (1978). *Tip or treat: A study of factors affecting tipping behavior*. Unpublished master's thesis, Loyola University of Chicago.

Rosenthal, R. (1976). *Experimenter effects in behavioral research*. New York: Irvington Publishers, Inc.

Shamir, B. (1983). A note on tipping and employee perceptions and attitudes. *Journal of Occupational Psychology*, **56**, 255-259.

Snyder, M., & Monson, T.C. (1975). Persons, situations, and the control of social behavior. *Journal of Personality and Social Psychology*, **32**, 637-644.

Snyder, M., & Swann, W.B. (1976). When actions reflect attitudes: The politics of impression management. *Journal of Personality and Social Psychology*, **34**, 1034-1042.

Stephen, R., & Zweigenhaft, R.L. (1986). The effect on tipping of a waitress touching male and female customers. *The Journal of Social Psychology*, **126**, 141-142.

Stillman, J.W., & Hensley, W.E. (1980). She wore a flower in her hair: The effect of ornamentation on nonverbal communication. *Journal of Applied Communication Research*, **1**, 31-39.

Whyte, W.F. (1948). *Human relations in the restaurant industry*. New York: McGraw-Hill Book Company.

Factual Questions

1. The relationship between restaurant tipping and what characteristics of the server have already been studied?

2. Previous research has found what relationship exists between the quality of service rendered and the rate at which customers tip?

3. How does this study of restaurant tipping differ from studies of restaurant tipping that have already been done?

4. How was it determined whether a couple would be in the name or no name condition?

5. What was the difference between the way the server introduced herself in the name condition and in the no name condition?

6. How many two-person parties were used as subjects?

7. Why were two couples excluded from the analysis?

8. What were the average tips given by couples in the name condition and in the no name condition?

9. What was the major finding of this study?

10. What other initial contact variables do the authors suggest might be studied to determine their effect on tipping?

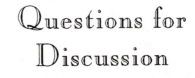

Questions for Discussion

11. Does the introduction provide a clear notion of the research problem, the purpose of the research, and its significance?

12. Does the literature review seem relevant to the research problem?

13. Is the number of research subjects sufficient? To what population would you generalize the results of this study?

14. Is there enough information on the research instruments and procedures to allow you to replicate this study?

15. Should there be information about the reliability and validity of the research instruments and procedures?

16. What possible problem results from the fact that the server was aware of the experimental condition of each dining party?

17. Does the analysis include sufficient statistical information? Are the statistics that are used appropriate?

18. Are the conclusions supported by and do they logically follow from the data that have been presented?

19. Are the findings discussed in terms of their implications and/or practical significance?

Notes:

The Communicative Function of Minimal Responses in Everyday Conversation

Mark Bennett
Jan Jarvis
Roehampton Institute, England

Investigators of linguistic devices such as minimal responses have assumed their function, neglecting to examine the matter empirically. This study introduces a technique enabling the identification of the function of such responses. With stereophonic recordings of conversation between two people, it was possible to delete minimal responses from an original recording. Eighty British students heard either an original recording or an edited version in which minimal responses had been deleted and were asked to make judgments about various aspects of the interaction. Results indicate minimal responses served to denote agreement and to suggest a context of informality.

(1)   Minimal responses are alternatively known as "assent terms" (Schegloff, 1972), "accompaniment signals" (Kendon, 1967), or "back channels" (Roger & Nesshoever, 1987). Utterances, such as *mmmm, hmm,* and *yeah* are presented by a listener during or immediately following the other's speech (Coates, 1986; Hirschmann, 1974). Without exception, sociolinguistic research has shown that women in Western societies use minimal responses significantly more often than men do (see Coates for a review).

(2)   Although unanimity exists concerning the greater use of minimal responses by women, the pragmatic functions that researchers attribute to this device are various. Coates (1986) asserts that minimal responses "are a way of indicating the listener's positive attention to the speaker" (p. 99). However, Schegloff's (1972) use of the term "assent term" implies that this device functions to indicate agreement. Roger and Nesshoever (1987) make the more general suggestion that women's use of minimal responses "supports the view that women use a more empathic interactional style than men do" (p. 253). Maltz and Borker (1982) argued that minimal responses "have significantly different meanings for men and women" (p. 202); specifically, they maintain that "for women a minimal response . . . simply means something like, 'I'm listening to you; please continue,'" whereas "for men it has a

The Journal of Social Psychology, 131(4): 519-523. Reprinted with permission of the Helen Dwight Reid Educational Foundation. Published by Heldref Publications, 1319 Eighteenth St., N.W., Washington, D.C. 20036-1802. Copyright © 1991.

Order of authorship is alphabetical and does not denote seniority.

We thank Jennifer Coates for her enthusiastic discussion of the research, Malcolm Hibberd for assistance in computing, and Chris Dewberry for helpful comments on an earlier version of the article.

Requests for reprints should be sent to Mark Bennett, Department of Psychology, University of Dundee, Dundee DD1 4HN Scotland.

Received November 27, 1990.

somewhat stronger meaning such as, 'I agree with you' or at least 'I follow your argument so far' " (p. 202).

(3)   The fact that there are multiple interpretations of the function of minimal response is itself problematic and necessitates more detailed inquiry into the matter so that some clarification might be provided. However, an altogether more troubling aspect of this issue concerns the methodology used by previous researchers: Judgments about the communicative function of minimal responses (and other similar devices) have been based only on researchers' personal judgments. For example, Maltz and Borker (1982) state candidly that their claims are "based on our attempts to understand personal experience" (p. 202). Kendon's (1967) conclusions were reached through the interpreting of transcripts of conversation, and he asserts on this basis that minimal responses that "coincide approximately with the ending of each of [the speaker's] points or statements do no more than indicate that [the listener] is still 'with' [the speaker]" (p. 89). Others — for example, Schegloff (1972) and Coates (1986) — adopt the same approach. Although such an approach goes beyond an appeal to personal experience, it is nevertheless founded ultimately on the researcher's personal judgment.

(4)   By relying on personal judgment alone, we propose that, in addition to the functions ascribed previously by researchers, minimal responses may play a role in signaling, among other things, informality, politeness, and liking. Equally, one might even make the case that their meaning is *indexical* (Garfinkel, 1967): It may always depend on particular features of the specific context rather than on any invariant principle. However, instead of perpetuating this sort of unlicensed conjecture, this study draws attention to the need for empirically based description, clearly a requirement to establish what minimal responses mean to laypersons rather than to social scientists.

Method

Subjects and Procedure

(5)   Eighty British undergraduate students (40 men, 40 women), drawn from a broad range of disciplines, participated in this study. Their ages ranged from 19 to 25 years, with a mean of 21 years.

(6)   All subjects listened to a tape recording of a 4-min conversation between two women, who were alone in a room and who had been told that they were free to talk about anything. In light of Weimann's

(1981) finding that laboratory recording techniques have little impact on behavior after the first 2 minutes, the initial 2 minutes of the recording were not used in the study. The conversation was not gender related, and it covered issues concerned with delinquency, social attitudes, and discipline. The original recording was made stereophonically: Each speaker was recorded via her own microphone on only one channel, allowing the subsequent deletion of all minimal responses from the conversation. Operationally, this procedure involved the removal from the original recording of all cases of the following types of utterance produced by a listener: *"mmm," "hmm," "yeah,"* and *"aha."*

(7)   Subjects were assigned to Condition 1 (original recording; i.e., with minimal responses) or Condition 2 (edited recording; i.e., without minimal responses). Equal numbers of men and women were in each condition. Subjects participated in small groups of about 10-15 people. Before hearing the tape recording, they were instructed to listen not only to what the speakers were saying but also to the speakers' manner and attitude toward each other. They were told that both speakers were undergraduate students. The tape recording was played only once.

(8)   Immediately after the presentation of the tape recording, subjects were presented with a questionnaire that requested judgments concerning the interaction. On a 7-point bipolar scale, they indicated their perceptions on the following dimensions: formal-informal; stilted-fluent; interested-uninterested (speakers' interest in the conversation); polite-impolite; agreement-disagreement between speakers; listening closely-not listening at all; speakers knew each other well-speakers did not know each other well; and speakers strongly liked each other-speakers strongly disliked each other. In summary, the experiment involved a 2 x 2 x 8 (Condition x Sex x Question Type) design, with the latter as a repeated factor.

Results

(9)   A multivariate analysis of variance (MANOVA) was computed. No effects of gender were obtained, nor were there any interaction effects. However, two significant effects of condition were noted. First, the conversation was judged to be significantly more formal in Condition 2 than in Condition 1: $F(1, 76) = 5.41$, $p < .05$; $M = 4.27$ and 5.00 for Conditions 1 and 2, respectively. In addition, a highly significant difference was found on the agreement dimension. In particular, the speakers were judged to be more in agreement in Condition 1 than in Condition 2: $F(1, 76)$

= 8.71, $p < .005$; $M = 4.33$ and 3.55 for Conditions 1 and 2, respectively.

Discussion

(10)   The results suggest that minimal responses had two main functions: to signal agreement and to indicate a context of informality. The former finding clearly bears out the assumption implicit in Schegloff's (1972) reference to minimal responses as "assent terms." The latter finding was relatively less expected, having no obvious relation to any of the functions proposed previously by researchers.

(11)   No evidence was provided for the contention of Kendon (1967) and Coates (1986) that minimal responses indicate the listener's attention to the speaker. On the strength of this finding, we suggest that attention is indicated both by the nonverbal responses (e.g., head nods, smiles) that typically accompany minimal responses and by the appropriateness of the content of responses to a speaker's remarks. However, this conjecture awaits empirical scrutiny.

(12)   Contrary to Maltz and Borker's (1982) assertion that for women minimal responses indicate attention, whereas for men they indicate agreement, the men and women in this study appeared to interpret minimal responses in the same manner. This is incompatible with Maltz and Borker's strong claim that men and women occupy different sociolinguistic subcultures. It also permits the rejection of their proposal that, "the fact that women use these responses more often than men is in part simply that women are listening more often than men are agreeing" (1982, p. 202).

(13)   We concede, however, that the absence of gender differences with respect to perceived function may be culturally specific: Maltz and Borker conducted their study in the United States, whereas this study was conducted in England. Nevertheless, the finding does leave open the question of why the gender difference in the use of minimal responses exists. Do women feel that it is necessary to signal agreement more often than men do, or is their concern with fostering informality? And why should these features of interaction be more important to them than to men? Clearly, many questions remain to be answered.

(14)   Our findings may reflect the most general functions of the minimal response; future research may well demonstrate the need for qualifications to the observations made here. Possibly, in requesting general judgments of the interaction, we may have neglected a disjunction between the role of minimal responses in conveying overall impressions and in communicating information at highly local points in interaction. Thus, future research might profitably examine function at a more microscopic level, looking at interpretations of particular minimal responses; it is conceivable that particular types of minimal response at particular junctures of conversation do signal attention, as has been suggested previously by researchers. In addition, the meaning of minimal responses may be dependent on the nature of the relationship between speakers, particularly their relative status (Giles, 1984). This study has only examined the meaning in the context of an encounter involving equals.

(15)   Notwithstanding the provisos provided, these findings represent a first step in the more rigorous clarification of the function of devices such as minimal responses. We suggest that the deletion technique used here lends itself readily to the investigation of many other devices, such as tag questions (". . ., isn't it?" Coates, 1986), and hedges (e.g., "you know," "kind of," and " just"; Fishman, 1980).

References

Coates, J. (1986). *Women, men and language.* New York: Longman.

Fishman, P. (1980). Conversation insecurity. In H. Giles, W. P. Robinson, & P. M. Smith (Eds.), *Language: Social psychological perspectives* (pp. 127-132). Oxford, England: Pergamon Press.

Garfinkel, H. (1967). *Studies in ethnomethodology.* Englewood Cliffs, NJ: Prentice Hall.

Giles, H. (Ed.). The dynamics of speech accommodation. *International Journal of the Sociology of Language, 46,* (Special issue).

Hirschmann, L. (1974, July) Analysis of supportive & assertive behaviour in conversations. Paper presented at Linguistic Society of America meeting.

Kendon, A. (1967). Some functions of gaze-direction in social interaction. *Acta Psychologica, 26,* 22-47.

Maltz, D. N., & Borker, R. A. (1982). A cultural approach to male-female miscommunication. In J. Gumperz (Ed.), *Language and social identity* (pp. 195-216). Cambridge, England: Cambridge University Press.

Roger, D., & Nesshoever, W. (1987). Individual differences in dyadic conversation strategies: A further study. *British Journal of Social Psychology, 26,* 247-255.

Schegloff, E. (1972). Sequencing in conversational openings. In J. Gumperz & D. Hymes (Eds.),

Directions in sociolinguistics (pp. 346-380). New York: Holt Rinehart.

Weimann, J. M. (1981). Effects of laboratory videotaping procedures on selected conversation behaviors. *Human Communication Research, 7,* 302-311.

6. How did condition 1 and condition 2 differ?

Factual Questions

1. What are three examples of minimal responses?

7. What were the seven dimensions on which subjects were asked to describe the taped conversation?

8. Were there any significant differences in the answers given by men and by women?

2. What functions have previous researchers attributed to minimal responses in conversation?

9. What two functions do the authors conclude minimal responses have?

3. What methodologies have previous researchers used to determine the functions of minimal responses in conversation?

10. How do the results contradict Maltz and Borker's (1982) assertion that for women minimal responses indicate attention whereas for men they indicate agreement?

4. How many research subjects were used and who were they?

5. Weimann (1981) reported that laboratory recording techniques have no impact on behavior after how long?

Questions for Discussion

11. Does the introduction provide a clear notion of the research problem, the purpose of the research, and its significance?

12. Does the literature review seem relevant to the research problem?

13. Is the number of research subjects sufficient? To what population would you generalize the results of this study?

14. Is there enough information on the research instruments and procedures to allow you to replicate this study?

15. Should there be information about the reliability and validity of the research instruments and procedures?

16. Does this research test the conclusion of other researchers that women use minimal responses more often than men?

17. Does the analysis include sufficient statistical information? Are the statistics that are used appropriate?

18. Are the conclusions supported by and do they logically follow from the data that have been presented?

19. Are the findings discussed in terms of their implications and/or practical significance?

Notes:

Article 25

The Influence of Affirmative Action on Perceptions of a Beneficiary's Qualifications

Russel J. Summers
Saint Mary's University

Relative to females, males tended to discount the qualifications of a woman promoted into management. However, the male-female difference was dependent upon the promoting organization's Affirmative Action environment. There were no differences between males and females when females thought that the organization promoting the woman had an Affirmative Action program in place. Under these circumstances females behaved as males in discounting the woman's qualifications. In contrast, females who thought that the organization promoting the woman was anti-Affirmative Action augmented the woman's qualifications. The interpretation of this is that these women viewed the organization's anti-Affirmative Action position as an inhibitory factor that could only have been overcome on the basis of the promoted woman possessing the necessary qualifications. Results are interpreted in relation to practical implications for Affirmative Action programs.

(1)   As women have become more actively involved as members of the work force, governments have enacted legislation (e.g., Title VII of the Civil Rights Act) to prohibit sexual discrimination in selection, promotion, and other personnel decisions. The goal of this legislation is to provide women with equal and fair access to employment and career opportunities. In addition, to make up for past discrimination and to increase the employment opportunities for women (as well as other targeted groups), governments have also promoted Affirmative Action programs.

(2)   Affirmative Action may go beyond simply ensuring that women have equal and fair access to employment opportunities. Instead, Affirmative Action may act to provide women with a degree of preferential treatment (Kleiman & Faley, 1988). For instance, organizations may target recruitment efforts at females, develop special selection procedures, as well as set goals and timetables to increase the participation of women within the organization. However, in spite of the noble social goals of Affirmative Action, a woman who benefits from a decision that favors her because she

Reprinted with permission from *Journal of Applied Social Psychology*, 21(15): 1265-1276. Copyright © 1991 by V. H. Winston & Son, Inc. All rights reserved.

The author would like to thank Shripad Pendse, Terry Wagar and an anonymous reviewer for their comments and suggestions on the manuscript. He would also like to thank his research assistants Gary Dukeshire and Sandy Falconer for their assistance with the investigation. An earlier version of the paper was presented at the Academy of Management meeting in Washington, DC in the summer of 1989. This research was supported by a Saint Mary's University Senate research grant.

Correspondence concerning this article should be addressed to Dr. Russel J. Summers, Department of Management, St. Mary's University, Halifax, Nova Scotia, Canada B3H 3C3.

is a female, as may occur with an Affirmative Action program, may suffer on various accounts. For example, in a field study, women who felt that they obtained a managerial position because they were female experienced a number of negative reactions (Chacko, 1982). Specifically, these women reported lower satisfaction with their work, less satisfaction with their supervisor and co-workers, greater role conflict and role ambiguity, and less commitment to their organizations. Comparable results were obtained in a laboratory study that examined how women viewed themselves after they were selected into leadership roles on the basis of their sex as opposed to merit (Heilman, Simon, & Repper, 1987). Results indicated that women who felt that they had been made leaders based on their sex developed negative reactions in relation to several aspects of their experience. For instance, these women devalued their success as leaders, downgraded their leadership abilities, and were less interested in engaging the leadership role in the future. Thus, both studies found that women who felt they had been placed in leadership positions on the basis of their sex experienced negative outcomes in regard to their self-perceptions and their reactions to their work situations.

(3)   Research also indicates that observers' perceptions and judgments of a woman may be influenced when they think that a decision in her favor has been based on her sex. For example, when information indicated that female managers had secured their position because of legal requirements to place more women in the position, the job the women held was devalued and viewed as less interesting by others (Heilman & Herlihy, 1984). Similarly, Jacobson and Koch (1977) examined the effect of leader selection method on male subordinates' assessments of the performance of female leaders. It was found that when gender was the basis for appointing a woman as the leader male subordinates blamed the woman more for failure and gave her less credit for success. In contrast, when male subordinates thought the woman was made leader because of her qualifications, she was blamed less for failure and given more credit for success.

(4)   Therefore, evidence indicates that decisions that favor a woman because she is female (i.e., as with Affirmative Action) can have negative effects on two accounts. First, the woman herself may respond negatively to the situation in terms of her self-perceptions and in terms of her relationship with her work environment (cf., Chacko, 1982; Heilman, Simon, & Repper, 1987). In addition, there may be undesirable consequences in terms of how the woman's job and her performance are evaluated by others (cf., Heilman &

Herlihy, 1984; Jacobson & Koch, 1977). These studies represent important preliminary steps toward an understanding of the implications of Affirmative Action programs. The purpose of the present investigation was to extend our understanding of Affirmative Action by further examining the influence of Affirmative Action on peoples' perceptions of women who benefit from Affirmative Action. In particular, the primary focus of the investigation was to examine the influence of an organization's Affirmative Action position (pro- versus anti-Affirmative Action) on people's perceptions of the qualifications of a woman promoted into a managerial position.

(5)   Perceptions of a manager's qualifications are important because how those in the managerial role are perceived may determine the extent to which their subordinates view them as leaders. For instance, when people are told that a person is the leader of a group that has performed poorly they form a "poor-leader" label for the person (Lord, Binning, Rush, & Thomas, 1978). This label is then used as a heuristic in perceiving the leader's behavior such that actions are interpreted and recalled in accordance with the label. This process can have important consequences in regard to subordinates' willingness to accept the influence of a leader. In a similar manner, perceptions of a manager's qualifications may determine whether a subordinate is willing to accept a manager's input. For instance, perceptions of a manager's qualifications would have an influence on the extent to which the manager could rely on legitimate and expert power (French & Raven, 1959). If a manager was seen to be unqualified he/she may have these power bases undermined which could seriously limit the person's ability to exercise influence over subordinates.

(6)   In relation to an organization's Affirmative Action position the problem that arises concerns how the Affirmative Action environment influences peoples' perceptions of the qualifications of a promoted woman. Two possibilities exist, both of which rely on attribution principles. One aspect of attribution principles concerns attempts to explain an event which has two possible causes. When this occurs the influence of any one of the causes may be discounted because of the presence of the other (Kelley, 1972, 1973). Thus, in relation to a personnel decision to promote a woman, one explanation for the event is that the woman possesses the necessary qualifications. In the absence of an alternative explanation this cause would stand as the primary reason for a decision in favor of the woman. However, an Affirmative Action program represents an alternative cause of a pro-female decision. As a result, the presence of an

Affirmative Action program may encourage people to discount a woman's qualifications.

(7)   On the other hand, in the case of an anti-Affirmative Action organization, attribution principles suggest that a promoted woman's qualifications may be augmented (Kelley, 1972, 1973). Augmentation of a cause's influence takes place when an outcome of the cause occurs in the presence of an inhibiting factor. In such circumstances the presence of the inhibiting factor results in an amplification of the influence of the cause. Thus, an organization's anti-Affirmative Action position may be interpreted as an inhibitory influence such that a promotion for a woman results in estimates of her qualifications being enhanced.

(8)   A second research issue addressed by the investigation concerned whether males and females would view a woman's qualifications for promotion differently. To begin, the stereotype of a woman (e.g., passive, sensitive) contradicts the stereotype of a manager which tends to reflect masculine characteristics (e.g., analytic, competitive) (Schein, 1973, 1975). However, the willingness to use stereotypes is a function of the degree of familiarity and similarity between the actor and the observer (Taylor, 1982). Essentially, those with less in common with the actor will be more likely to use a stereotype for making judgments about the person. Therefore, as members of the out-group, males should be more likely to view a woman using the traditional, feminine stereotype. As a result males may be less favorable in their judgments of a woman's qualifications for a management position. Conversely, females should identify more with another woman and be less likely to use a stereotypic frame of reference in making judgments of her qualifications.

(9)   Therefore, the issues addressed by the present investigation concerned whether peoples' judgments of a promoted woman's qualifications were influenced by (a) an organization's Affirmative Action environment and (b) the sex of the person making the judgments.

Methods

Participants and Procedures

(10)   One hundred and twelve undergraduate students from an East Coast university participated. Most of the students were enrolled in personnel management courses in the faculty of commerce. The students were a mix of regular undergraduates and continuing-education students who were enrolled in courses for upgrading. Fifty-seven participants were females and 55

were males. The participants' ages ranged from 17 years to 43 years with a mean of 22.13 years. The mean years of work experience was 3.70.

(11)   Groups of up to 10 people were solicited to participate in a study concerning information gathering and decision making in relation to personnel issues in organizational settings. At the beginning of an experimental session participants were told that they would be considering a promotion issue and be given background information for both the company and the female candidate involved as well as the results of an assessment report for the candidate. When the participants had finished reviewing this information they were given the results of the promotion decision. After reviewing the promotion information participants completed a questionnaire that asked them to recall the information they had received. Participants were not allowed to reconsider any material after deciding to move on to the next set of materials or the questionnaire. Finally, when all the participants in a session were finished they were debriefed and dismissed.

Stimulus Materials

(12)   The information concerning the company detailed various aspects of the organization (e.g., involvement in community activities, labor-management relations, etc.). However, there were two different versions of this description. One version contained information indicating that the organization had willingly adopted an Affirmative Action program to comply with government regulations. The second version indicated that the organization had refused to adopt an Affirmative Action program to comply with government regulations. This manipulation was used to establish perceptions of a pro- versus anti-Affirmative Action organization. Twenty-four females and 25 males received information describing the pro-Affirmative Action organization whereas 33 females and 30 males received information describing the organization as anti-Affirmative Action.

(13)   The information concerning the woman being considered for promotion was the same for all participants. The information outlined the woman's university education, her work experience, and her history with her present employer. The assessment report provided information describing the woman's achievement orientation, intellectual functioning, and interpersonal orientation. The assessment report was deliberately constructed to be ambiguous concerning the woman's qualifications. This was accomplished by providing information that was both favorable and unfavorable. For

example, information concerning an interview conducted as part of the assessment suggested that the woman was earnest and keen (i.e., favorable information) but at the same time somewhat guarded concerning the expression of her feelings (i.e., unfavorable information). Thus the report was equivocal in that it did not clearly describe the woman as qualified or unqualified.

(14) Finally, participants were provided with information concerning the decision in favor of promoting the woman. For the pro-Affirmative Action condition participants were given an excerpt from the company's newsletter wherein the announcement by the company president was cited along with a reiteration of the company's support of Affirmative Action. For the anti-Affirmative Action condition the president's announcement included a statement concerning the company's commitment to ensure that men and women are treated equally.

Measures

(15) The dependent measure and manipulation check were imbedded in the questionnaire that participants completed after reviewing the stimulus material. The questionnaire consisted of a 30-item, multiple-choice recall questionnaire. Most of the questions asked participants to recall information that was not central to the study's purpose. For example, questions asked about the number of people employed by the company, the name of the woman's first employer, the woman's age, etc. For each question there were four possible answers, a, b, c, and d, with the last choice (i.e., answer d) always "no information given" for all questions.

(16) The dependent measure was constructed from the answers selected for nine key questions. These questions asked participants to recall information from the assessment report and concerned the woman's qualifications for the managerial position. For these questions if participants did not select answer "d" (i.e., no information given) they had to select an answer that was either neutral, favorable (i.e., qualified), or unfavorable (i.e., unqualified) in relation to a person's suitability for a managerial position.[1] The dependent measure was constructed by dividing the total number of favorable answers selected by the total number of favorable and unfavorable answers selected. When multiplied by 100 this ratio provided a measure of participants' perceptions of the candidate's qualifications. With this measure higher scores (e.g., 100%) meant that more favorable answers were selected whereas lower scores (e.g., 10%) meant more unfavorable answers were selected. However, because the information provided was ambiguous an estimate of 50% qualified would have most accurately reflected the equivalence of the information outlining the woman's qualifications. Therefore, scores below 50% indicated that the woman's qualifications had been discounted and scores exceeding 50% indicated that the woman's qualifications had been augmented.

(17) Finally, one question asked participants to recall the information concerning the organization's Affirmative Action situation. This question served as a manipulation check to ensure that participants had noted this information.

Research Design

(18) The experimental protocol generated a 2 X 2 completely crossed experimental design. The

Table 1. Regression Analysis for Judgments of the Woman's Qualifications

Source of variance	Increment in R^2	F increment
Organization's AA position (A)	.01	1.07
Judge sex (B)	.04	3.95*
A X B	.04	4.00*

Note: AA = Affirmative Action. Variables were effect coded for the analysis.
*$p < .05$.

[1] The favorability of these answers was determined using a panel of five neutral judges. The judges were instructed to consider each answer to each question in relation to whether it contained information that was favorable, unfavorable, or neutral in relation to a person's qualifications for being a manager. Judges indicated their evaluation of each answer by writing either a "+ ," "- ," or "0" beside the answer to signify whether they felt it was favorable, unfavorable, or neutral, respectively. A response was considered favorable, unfavorable, or neutral if it was evaluated the same way by at least three of the five judges.

Table 2. Duncan's Comparison of Means

anti-AA organization		pro-AA organization	
Females	Males	Females	Males
58.19$_a$	43.47$_b$	46.17$_b$	47.02$_b$

Note: AA = Affirmative Action. Duncan's test was performed using harmonic means based on the *ns* for all groups. Means with different subscripts differ significantly at *p < .05.*

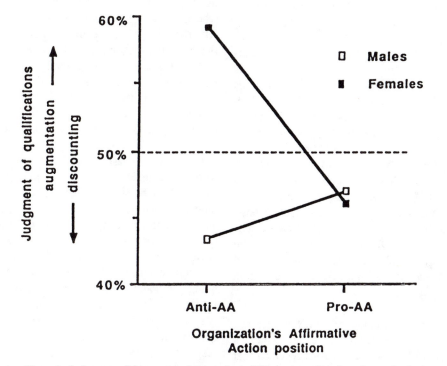

Figure 1. Judgments of the promoted woman's qualifications as a function of organization's Affirmative Action position and judge sex.

experimental factors were participants' sex (male versus female) and organizational position concerning Affirmative Action (pro-Affirmative Action vs. anti-Affirmative Action).

Results

Manipulation Check

(19) Participants' accuracy in recalling the company's Affirmative Action position was assessed before their data was included in the analysis. Errors in recalling this information resulted in nine participants' being eliminated from the anti-Affirmative Action condition and five participants' being eliminated from the pro-Affirmative Action condition. As a result the pro-Affirmative Action condition involved 24 males and 20 females and the anti-Affirmative Action condition involved 28 males and 26 females.

Judgment of Qualifications

(20) To assess their judgments of the woman's suitability for the management promotion, participants'

perceptions of her qualifications were regressed on the organization's Affirmative Action position, the participant's sex, and the interaction of these two factors (see Table 1).[2] In relation to the effect of the organization's Affirmative Action position the means were in the predicted direction. When the organization was pro-Affirmative Action the woman was judged to be less qualified ($M = 46.62\%$). Conversely, when the organization was anti-Affirmative Action participants recalled more favorable information and the woman was judged to be more qualified ($M = 51.04\%$). However, although these results are suggestive, the difference between the groups was nonsignificant. Therefore, there was no evidence to indicate that either discounting or augmentation occurred on the basis of the organization's Affirmative Action position.

(21)   In contrast, the sex of the judge did have an effect on estimates of the woman's qualifications. This was due to the tendency of males to judge the woman as less qualified ($M = 45.11\%$) and the tendency of females to judge the woman as more qualified ($M = 53.53\%$). This provides support for the suggestion that males would discount a woman's qualifications. Thus, males may have viewed the woman in terms of stereotypic, feminine characteristics which conflicted with traditional notions of what is necessary for a manager. However, the interpretation of this effect must be postponed in light of the significant interaction effect indicating that males' and females' judgments of the woman's qualifications depended upon whether or not the organization was pro- or anti-Affirmative Action (see Table 1 and Figure 1).

(22)   To examine the interaction effect a post hoc comparison of means was performed using Duncan's range test (see Table 2). The comparisons revealed that the anomalous group consisted of females who thought the woman had been promoted by an organization that was anti-Affirmative Action. Relative to the other three groups these females judged the woman to be more qualified; by comparison, all of the other groups judged the woman to be less than 50% qualified (see Table 2). Thus, an organization's Affirmative Action environment did influence judgments of a promoted woman's qualifications but the effect depended on the sex of the person making the judgment.

Discussion

(23)   Aspects of the results suggest that both discounting and augmentation processes were operating. First, both groups of males and those females who thought the woman had been promoted in a pro-Affirmative Action organization judged the woman to be less than 50% qualified for the promotion. Given that the information provided was equivalently favorable and unfavorable, and therefore implied at least 50% qualified, these three groups appear to have discounted the woman's qualifications. Males may have discounted the woman's qualifications on the basis of an inclination to consider females in terms of a traditionally feminine stereotype. On the other hand, females who thought the woman had been promoted in a pro-Affirmative Action organization may have discounted the woman's qualifications because of the presence of the Affirmative Action program. These females may have viewed the Affirmative Action program as an alternative explanation for the woman's promotion and thereby given the woman less credit in terms of her qualifications as a cause of her promotion.

(24)   In contrast to the other three groups the woman's qualifications seem to have been augmented by females who thought that the woman had been promoted in an anti-Affirmative Action organization. These females judged the woman to be more than 50% qualified. In this case the organization's anti-Affirmative Action position may have been viewed as an inhibitory factor that would prevent a woman from being promoted. Thus, it may have been reasoned that in this sort of environment a promotion would have only occurred if the woman possessed the necessary qualifications. In addition, as women themselves, these respondents may have been more sensitive to the possibility that, relative to a man, a woman would have greater obstacles to overcome in order to succeed in a managerial position (see Powell, Posner, & Schmidt, 1984). In contrast, the men in this condition may have been unable to relate to the obstacles that a woman would face in attempting to succeed as a manager. Thus, without being able to relate to the obstacles that would inhibit success for the woman, males' judgments may have been more a function of a stereotypic notion of women. Since this would have been incongruent with the stereotypic view of the requirements of a management position, the woman was perceived to be less qualified.

---

[2] Note that in recalling the woman's qualifications participants rarely selected the "no information given" answer (mean frequency for this response = 1.02).

(25)   The results have practical implications in regard to enhancing the career opportunities of groups targeted by Affirmative Action. One of the consequences of establishing an Affirmative Action program is that the program's existence may involve a considerable degree of fanfare in order to publicize the program. For example, it has been suggested that an organization should advertise its Affirmative Action program through in-house publications, and special educational sessions (cf., Piche, 1987). However, it may be unwise to explicitly present personnel decisions as being due to the program. This may create a dilemma because it may encourage the idea that those who benefit from the program have received aid for the needy (i.e., the unqualified). Instead, it may be wiser for organizations to adopt and enact an Affirmative Action program but avoid placing undue emphasis on personnel decisions associated with the program. In other words, if a member of a target group is hired or promoted within the context of an Affirmative Action program avoid emphasizing the role of the program by emphasizing the person's accomplishments and qualifications. By following this strategy it may be possible to avoid having co-workers and other organizational members discount the credentials of program beneficiaries. This strategy would also be advocated because of the possibility of augmentation processes. In the present investigation augmentation occurred when the organization was anti-Affirmative Action. However, it is possible that similar effects would occur if an organization simply avoided focusing attention on an Affirmative Action program as a cause of decisions. This would serve to ensure that actions taken to enhance the opportunities of target group members will pay benefits for them in terms of employment opportunities as well as how they are perceived by others. That is, the beneficiaries of the program may have their qualifications augmented if the program is not presented as the reason for decisions in their favor. Therefore, regardless of the attributional processes there may be compelling reasons for organizations to adopt Affirmative Action without explicitly linking their decisions to the program.

(26)   In regard to the interpretation of the results a preliminary analysis compared the responses of traditional students (i.e., full-time undergraduate student, n = 41) and continuing-education students (i.e., part-time student, employed, n = 57). This comparison found no differences in the perceptions of the two groups, $F(1,96)$ = .27, p = .60. Therefore, it is unnecessary to qualify the results in terms of generalizability and possible differences between "real people" and undergraduate students as subjects. However, it is important to be cautious in interpreting the results because of the limited magnitude of the effects observed. Therefore, although the results are interesting from an empirical perspective the practical implications are uncertain. However, in real-life organizations where there is competition for a limited number of career opportunities and people have vested interests in personnel decisions the effects may be more pronounced and the practical consequences may be significant. Finally, a further qualification that should be noted concerns the fact that the information outlining the woman's qualifications was ambiguous. Portraying the woman as 50% qualified was necessary for the purposes of the experiment and the detection of augmentation and discounting effects. However, in an actual work situation the woman being promoted would more than likely be well qualified. It remains to be determined if the results of the present investigation would be obtained if the information provided described the woman as well qualified.

References

Chacko, T. I. (1982). Woman and equal employment opportunity: Some unintended effects. *Journal of Applied Psychology*, **67**, 119-123.

French, J. R. P., & Raven, B. (1959). The bases of social power. In D. Cartwright (Ed.), *Studies in social power*. Ann Arbor, MI: Institute for Social Research.

Heilman, M. E., Simon, M. C., & Repper, D. P. (1987). Intentionally favored, unintentionally harmed? Impact of sex-based preferential selection of self-evaluations. *Journal of Applied Psychology*, **72**, 62-68.

Heilman, M., & Herlihy, J. M. (1984). Affirmative action, negative reaction? Some moderating conditions. *Organizational Behavior and Human Performance*, **33**, 204-213.

Jacobson, M. B., & Koch, W. (1977). Women as leaders: Performance evaluation as a function of method of leader selection. *Organizational Behavior and Human Performance*, **20**, 149-157.

Kelley, H. H. (1972). Causal schemata and the attribution process. In E. Jones, D. Kanouse, H. Kelley, R. Nisbett, S. Valins, & B. Weiner (Eds.), *Attribution: Perceiving the causes of behavior*. Morristown, NJ: General Learning Press.

Kelley, H. H. (1973). The processes of causal attribution. *American Psychologist*, **28**, 107-128.

Kleiman, L. S., & Faley, R. H. (1988). Voluntary Affirmative Action and preferential treatment: Legal and research implications. *Personnel Psychology*, **41**, 481-496.

Lord, R. G., Binning, J. F., Rush, M. C., & Thomas, J. (1978). The effect of performance cues and leader behavior on questionnaire ratings of leadership behavior. *Organization Behavior and Human Performance*, **21**, 27-39.

Piche, L. (1987). Employment equity at Canadian National Railways: Initiatives and proactive measures. In S. L. Dolan & R. S. Schuler (Eds.), *Canadian readings in personnel and human resource management*. New York: West Publishing Co.

Powell, G. N., Posner, B. Z., & Schmidt, W. H. (1984). Sex effects in managerial value systems. *Human Relations*, **37**, 909-921.

Schein, V. E. (1973). The relationship between sex-role stereotypes and requisite management characteristics. *Journal of Applied Psychology*, **57**, 95-100.

Schein, V. E. (1975). Relationship between sex-role stereotypes and requisite management characteristics among female managers. *Journal of Applied Psychology*, **60**, 340-344.

Taylor, S. E. (1982). A categorization approach to stereotyping. In D. L. Hamilton (Ed.), *Cognitive process in stereotyping and intergroup behavior*. Hillsdale, NJ: Lawrence Erlbaum Press.

Factual Questions

1. How many research subjects were used and who were they?

2. What is the range of ages of the subjects?

3. How did the two versions of the description of the organization differ?

4. In what way was the assessment report on the female job candidate ambiguous?

5. How were subjects informed of the company's decision to promote the woman?

6. How was the subject's assessment of the female candidate's ability measured?

7. How did the author check to make sure that subjects remembered the affirmative action information about the organization, and what happened if the subject did not remember the organization's affirmative action status?

8. How did the interaction between subject's sex and the organization's affirmative action stance affect the subject's assessment of the candidate's ability?

9. What is the basis for the author's claim that the results are not limited to just undergraduate student populations?

Questions for Discussion

10. Does the introduction provide a clear notion of the research problem, the purpose of the research, and its significance?

11. Does the literature review seem relevant to the research problem?

12. Is the number of research subjects sufficient? Is the author's claim that the results are not limited to undergraduate populations justified?

13. Is there enough information on the research instruments and procedures to allow you to replicate this study?

14. Should there be more information about the reliability and validity of the research instruments and procedures?

15. Does the analysis include sufficient statistical information? Are the statistics that are used appropriate?

16. Are the conclusions supported by and do they logically follow from the data that have been presented?

17. Are the findings discussed in terms of their implications and/or practical significance?

Notes:

An Evaluation of Parental Assessment of the Big Brothers/Big Sisters Program in New York City

Peter Frecknall
Alan Luks

This study used a self-report survey to assess parents' impressions of the impact of the Big Brothers/Big Sisters program on their children. Parents rated program success on each of seven outcome variables (school attendance, grades, getting along with family members, getting along with friends, self-esteem, staying out of trouble, and being more responsible), and two program variables (frequency of contact and length of time in program). While children were rated by their parents as benefiting significantly from the program, children's frequency of contact did not have a significant effect on the outcome measures. However, a trend of increased success with greater time spent in the program was found. Frequency of contact between parents and Big Brothers/Big Sisters was positively correlated with reported success.

(1)   A considerable body of evidence suggests that social support is a critical factor in individual adjustment and health, both physical and psychological (Kelly, 1979; Lazarus & Folkman, 1984; Antonovsky, 1987). Although primary social networks such as families and close friends provide an effective buffer between individuals and significant stress or adversity (Gottlieb, 1983), organized, professional assistance can also provide meaningful support to individuals, especially single mothers (Taylor, 1982; Dobson, 1981; Camera & Resnick, 1987; Barry, 1979). This study is the first formal attempt to gather data about the New York City Big Brothers/Big Sisters program.

(2)   Big Brothers/Big Sisters of New York, the founding chapter of the international program, was created in 1904 to provide positive role models, friendship, and guidance to high-risk children of single parents. The program specifically seeks to address the problems of truancy, delinquency, poor school performance, and low self-esteem among its target population. Big Brothers/Big Sisters of America is now the fastest growing volunteer family service network in the country. It has over 450 affiliates in the United States and Canada.

(3)   Big Brothers/Big Sisters of New York City currently serves over 1,000 children annually, matching 6- to 18-year-olds with same-sex adult volunteers on a one-to-one basis. Volunteers are screened, selected, and supervised by master's level social workers, and receive preservice training and ongoing group supervision for the duration of their volunteer period with the program. Volunteers are asked for a minimum two-year

Reprinted with permission from *Adolescence, 27*(107): 715-718. Copyright © 1992 by Libra Publishers, Inc.

Reprint requests to Peter Frecknall, Ph.D., New York University, Department of Communications, 239 Greene Street, New York, New York 10003.

commitment, but are encouraged to keep their Little Brother/Little Sister until the child turns 18 or leaves the program.

(4)   Previous studies (Campbell, 1985; Stocks, 1980) have found Big Brothers/Big Sisters programs to be effective in reducing court referrals and raising the self-esteem of Little Brothers and Little Sisters and in improving social support for single parents whose children participate in the program. This paper presents the results of the first formal attempt to gather data about the effectiveness of the New York City Big Brothers/Big Sisters program.

Method

Survey Instrument

(5)   The survey instrument used was a two-page questionnaire which measured parents' assessment of their children's length of time in the program, frequency of contact with their Big Brother/Big Sister, and their own frequency of contact with the Big Brother/Big Sister (program variables). The survey also asked parents to subjectively rate how much, if at all, the program had helped their children on the following seven outcome measures: school attendance, grades, getting along with family members, getting along with friends, self-esteem, staying out of trouble, and being more responsible. There was additional space at the end of the instrument for parents' comments. The data sought in this survey was not intended to be entirely objective; all answers were based on self-report.

(6)   The questionnaire was mailed in July 1990 to approximately 135 heads of household, of which 76 were returned with a minimum of follow-up (one phone call). This constitutes a return rate of approximately 56%, which is substantially higher than the 10%-15% return rate usually expected from mail surveys.

Results

Demographic Profile

(7)   The majority of children in the study were male, comprising 69% of the sample; females made up 30%, with missing data for 1% (gender not reported). The average length of time in program was 1 year 9 months. The average number of in-person contacts per child was 2.6 per month, with telephone contacts averaging 3.25 per month. Total combined contacts averaged 5.85 per month. The average combined frequency of contact with parents was 3.25 times per month.

Outcome Measures

(8)   A majority of the parents said that their children were improved in some aspect of their attitudes or behavior since enrollment in the program. An average of 63% reported that their children were "greatly improved"; the breakdown by individual outcome measure was: school attendance, 49%; school grades, 47%; getting along with family members, 55%; getting along with friends, 70%; self-esteem, 83%; staying out of trouble, 58%; being more responsible, 60%. An average of 14% reported "some improvement." Of those whose *parents* reported success, 72% were male and 28% were female.

Program Variables

(9)   A trend of increased success with greater time spent in the program (up to 3 years) was found. Reported success ranged from 69% for children in the program for 1-2 years to 90% for children in the program for 2-3 years.

(10)   An analysis of the relationship between reported success and frequency of children's contact was inconclusive: 77% of the parents whose children had frequent contact (once or more every two weeks) and 76% of those whose children had less contact (less than once every two weeks) reported success in the program.

(11)   Reported success and frequency of parental contact with Big Brothers/Big Sisters were strongly related, with 85% of the parents who had frequent contact reporting success as compared with only 65% of the parents who had infrequent contact. Parents' comments were generally positive (83%), with the remaining 17% being neutral.

Conclusion

(12)   This study has provided preliminary information about the nature of the New York City Little Brother/Little Sister population, an evaluation of the overall effectiveness of the program, and an assessment of its effectiveness in particular areas. It is clear, according to the parents who responded to the survey, that the Big Brothers/Big Sisters program works for their children. It is also apparent that the more contact parents have with Big Brothers/Big Sisters, the more they feel that the program is effective. It is anticipated from trends observed in these results that stronger conclusions would be available from a larger sample.

(13)   A number of questions are raised by this study: Are parental reports accurate reflections of improvement? Is such improvement taking place for those whose parents did not respond to the survey? Has such improvement taken place among non-Little Brothers/Little Sisters in similar communities? Is the reported improvement due to any one factor or set of factors in the Big Brothers/Big Sisters program, such as length of time in program, or to preenrollment family status? Is the Big Brothers/Big Sisters program particularly effective in specific areas, such as grades or self-esteem? These questions highlight the necessity of further research during this time of great need on the part of urban youth.

References

Antonovsky, A. (1987). *Unraveling the mystery of health.* San Francisco: Jossey-Bass.

Barry, A. (1979). A research project on successful single-parent families. *The American Journal of Family Therapy, 7,* 65-75.

Camera, K., & Resnick, G. (1987). Long term effects of divorce on children: A developmental vulnerability mode. *American Journal of Orthopsychiatry, 57*(4), 286-292.

Campbell, E. (1985). Social support for single mothers: A study of Big Brothers/Big Sisters. *Canadian Journal of Mental Health, 4*(1), 81-87.

Dobson, A. (1981). The social reinforcement network of the single mother: Its relationship to adjustment. *Dissertation Abstracts International, 41,* 3879.

Gottlieb, B. (1983). Social support as a focus for integrative research in psychology. *American Psychologist, 38,* 278-287.

Kelly, J. G. (1979). Creating power and reducing constraints. In S. Cooper & W. F. Hodges (Eds.), *The field of community mental health consultation.* New York: Human Sciences Press.

Lazarus, R., & Folkman, S. (1984). *Stress, appraisal and coping in human organizations.* New York: Spring Publishing Co.

Stocks, B. C. (1980). *Father-absence in boys with Big Brothers: Problems vs. remedy.* Unpublished Master's Thesis, University of Windsor.

Taylor, L. (1982). The effects of a non-related adult friend on children of divorce. *Journal of Divorce, 5*(4), 67-76.

Factual Questions

1. What specific problems does the Big Brothers/Big Sisters program address?

2. How old are the children who participate in the Big Brothers/Big Sisters program?

3. What two characteristics of the child's participation in the Big Brothers/Big Sisters program were measured? What seven outcomes were measured?

4. From whom did the researchers obtain information about the child's participation in the program and the program's outcomes?

5. How many parents were sent questionnaires?

6. If a parent did not initially return the mailed questionnaire, what did the researchers do?

7. How does the study's return rate compare to the usual return rate for mailed questionnaires?

8. On the average, how many times per month did the Big Brothers/Big Sisters personally visit and telephone the Little Brothers/Little Sisters?

9. For which outcome did there appear to be the greatest improvement?

10. How did the success rate of children in the program one to two years compare to the success rate of children in the program two to three years?

Questions for Discussion

11. Does the introduction provide a clear notion of the research problem, the purpose of the research, and its significance?

12. Does the literature review seem relevant to the research problem?

13. Is the number of research subjects sufficient? To what population would you generalize the results of this study?

14. Is there enough information on the research instruments and procedures to allow you to replicate this study?

15. Should there be information about the reliability and validity of the research instruments and procedures?

16. What do the authors mean in paragraph five when they state that "the data sought in this study was not intended to be entirely objective . . . "?

17. What, if any, bias is introduced into the study by gathering information about a child's participation in the program and their program outcomes from the child's parent? What other ways could this information be gathered? What would be the

advantages and disadvantages of those alternative methods?

18. The authors talk about reported success in paragraphs 8 through 11. How was reported success measured?

19. Does the analysis include sufficient statistical information? Are the statistics that are used appropriate?

20. Are the conclusions supported by and do they logically follow from the data that have been presented?

21. In paragraph nine the authors note a trend of increased success with greater time spent in the program. Are there alternative explanations for why the average success of children in the program two to three years was greater than the average success of children in the program just one to two years?

22. Are the findings discussed in terms of their implications and/or practical significance?

23. Why do the authors state in paragraph 12 that "It is anticipated from trends observed in these results that stronger conclusions would be available from a larger sample."?

Notes:

Enhancement of Attitudes Toward Handicapped Children Through Social Interactions

Marva K. Newberry
Thomas S. Parish
Kansas State University

Boy Scouts ($N = 225$) and Girl Scouts ($N = 251$) were surveyed on the Personal Attribute Inventory for Children (Parish & Taylor, 1978a, 1978b) regarding their attitudes toward various handicapping conditions, before and after treatment. Approximately half of these scouts were randomly assigned to six weekly meetings during which they were able to interact socially and directly with a child exhibiting the handicap in question. Scouts who had experienced these social interactions, as compared to their control group counterparts, demonstrated significantly more positive attitudes toward four of the five handicapping conditions to which they had been exposed. Specifically, mentally retarded, physically disabled, deaf or hearing impaired, and blind or partially sighted — but *not* learning disabled — were evaluated more favorably by nonhandicapped children if they had been directly involved in social interactions with individuals exhibiting these handicaps.

(1)   There have been conflicting results regarding the impact of mainstreaming procedures (Abramson, 1980; Budoff & Gottlieg, 1976; Parish & Copeland, 1978; Parish, Dyck, & Kappes, 1979; Ritter, 1978). One wonders why placing children into "least restrictive" environments has not been consistently successful, particularly in terms of increasing positive attitudes toward handicapped children. Gallagher and Crowder (1957), Getzels and Jackson (1960), and Kurtzman (1967) all proposed that children with any exceptionality will be less well accepted because of their handicaps, despite the integration strategies used by teachers in the classroom. Another possibility is that handicapped and nonhandicapped children lack the opportunity to interact and become more familiar with one another.

(2)   Scout troop meetings, more than regular classroom scenes, may provide an environment in which ongoing social contacts are more likely the rule than the exception. We attempted to determine whether such social interactions between handicapped and nonhandicapped children in open scout troop meetings foster more positive attitudes toward handicapped children by their nonhandicapped counterparts.

The Journal of Social Psychology, 127(1): 59-62. Reprinted with permission of the Helen Dwight Reid Educational Foundation. Published by Heldref Publications, 1319 Eighteenth St., N.W., Washington, D.C. 20036-1802. Copyright © 1987.

Requests for reprints should be sent to Thomas S. Parish, Department of Administration & Foundations, Kansas State University, Manhattan, KS 66506.

Received September 2, 1986

Method

(3)   Subjects were 8- to 11-year-old scouts (225 males, 251 females) who voluntarily participated in the study. The names of these children were placed in a box at an organizational meeting, drawn out one at a time, and placed in 10 troops with the first name drawn going into the troop with the lowest troop number, the second name into the next higher, and so forth. Two groups of the 10 dealt with one of the following areas of exceptionality as a target stimulus:

1. Mentally retarded
2. Physically handicapped
3. Deaf or hearing impaired
4. Blind or partially sighted
5. Learning disabled

(4)   For six weeks during the regular school year, during 1-hr meetings, five of these groups (the treatment groups) were exposed to, and socially interacted with, a child exhibiting the stigmata of the handicap to which the group was assigned. These interactions were not formally arranged and did not involve discussions concerning causes, treatments, or incidence. Interactions occurred as the children worked and spoke together. No other contact, formal or otherwise, was promoted between the handicapped and nonhandicapped participants outside these 1-hr weekly meetings.

(5)   The scouts in both the treatment and control groups were administered the Personal Attribute Inventory for Children (Parish & Taylor, 1978a, 1978b) before the start of these weekly meetings and at their conclusion. This inventory consists of 48 adjectives (24 positive and 24 negative). The respondent is asked to check exactly 15 adjectives that are most like the target group (e.g., mentally retarded children) in question.

Results

(6)   Pretest and posttest attitude scores on the Personal Attribute Inventory for Children were analyzed using five 2x2 analyses of covariance. The pretest scores served as the covariate and the posttest scores served as the criterion or dependent variable. These analyses of variance revealed that four of the five treatment groups adopted significantly more favorable attitudes than their control group counterparts concerning the handicap to which they were exposed: for mentally retarded, $F (1, 113) = 43.57$, $p < .0001$; $M_T = 6.37$, $M_C = 4.42$; for physically handicapped, $F (1, 89) = 67.76$, $p < .0001$; $M_T = 7.64$, $M_C = 4.67$; for deaf or hearing impaired, $F (1, 75) = 22.44$, $p < .0001$; $M_T = 6.43$ $M_C = $ 5.00; for blind or partially sighted, $F (1, 69) = 20.84$, $p < .0001$; $M_T = 5.92$, $M_C = 4.76$; but not for learning disabled, $F (1, 104) = .66$, $p > .05$; $M_T = 4.79$ vs. $M_C = 4.57$ There were no significant sex of subject main effects nor Treatment x Sex of Subject interaction effects found, regardless of the area of exceptionality investigated.

Discussion

(7)   Social interactions between handicapped and nonhandicapped children during scout troop meetings served to enhance evaluations of four out of five areas of exceptionality by the latter group of individuals. Findings show that when handicaps are relatively apparent, direct social contacts between such groups of children can foster more favorable attitudes in nonhandicapped children toward the handicapped. When handicaps are not so apparent (e.g., as with learning disabled), increased acceptance by nonhandicapped children may not be prompted by direct social contacts. Such an ex post facto explanation for these findings possesses a high degree of face validity.

References

Abramson, M. (1980). Implications of mainstreaming: A challenge for special education. In L. Mann & D. Sabatino (Eds.), *The fourth review of special education* (pp. 315-340). New York: Grune and Stratton.

Budoff, M., & Gottlieb, J. (1976). Special class mainstreamed: A study of an aptitude (learning potential) X treatment interaction. *American Journal of Mental Deficiency, 81*, 1-11.

Gallagher, J., & Crowder, T. (1957). The adjustment of gifted children in the regular classrooms. *Exceptional Children, 23*, 306-309.

Getzels, J., & Jackson, P. (1960). A study of giftedness: A multidimensional approach. *On the gifted student* (Cooperative Research Monograph No. 2, pp. 1-18). Washington, DC: U.S. Government Printing Office.

Kurtzman, K. (1967). A study of school attitudes, peer acceptance, and personality of creative adolescents. *Exceptional Children, 34*, 157-162.

Parish, T., & Copeland, T. (1978). Teachers' and students' attitudes in mainstreamed classrooms. *Psychological Reports, 43*, 54.

Parish, T., Dyck, N., & Kappes, B. (1979). Stereotypes concerning normal and handicapped children. *Journal of Psychology, 102*, 63-70.

Parish, T., & Taylor, J. (1978a). The Personal Attribute Inventory for Children: A report on its validity and reliability as a self-concept scale. *Educational and Psychological Measurement, 38*, 565-569.

Parish, T., & Taylor, J. (1978b). A further report on the validity and reliability of the Personal Attribute Inventory for Children. *Educational and Psychological Measurement, 38*, 1225-1228.

Ritter, D. (1978). Surviving in the regular classroom: A follow-up of mainstreamed children with learning disabilities. *Journal of School Psychology, 16*, 253-256.

Factual Questions

1. The authors suggest that scout troop meetings differ from regular classroom scenes in what way?

2. How were the 476 scouts who participated in the study selected?

3. How were the scouts assigned to groups?

4. The handicapped children represented five areas of exceptionality. What were they?

5. For how long did the scouts in the treatment groups interact with the handicapped children?

6. Persons who complete the Personal Attribute Inventory for Children are asked to do what?

7. What is the dependent variable in this study?

8. In paragraph six we are told that the mean for the treatment group (M_T) was 6.37. On exactly what did the subjects in the treatment group have a mean of 6.37?

9. For which handicaps did the treatment groups have significantly higher posttest scores than their corresponding control groups?

10. On which of the handicapping conditions was there a significant difference between the responses of girls and boys?

11. How do the authors explain the failure of social interactions to make a significant difference in attitudes toward children with learning disabilities?

Questions for Discussion

12. Does the introduction provide a clear notion of the research problem, the purpose of the research, and its significance?

13. Does the literature review seem relevant to the research problem?

14. Is the number of research subjects sufficient? To what population would you generalize the results of this study?

15. Rather than using five separate control groups, could the authors have used just a single control group?

16. Is there enough information on the research instruments and procedures to allow you to replicate this study?

17. Should there be information about the reliability and validity of the research instruments and procedures?

18. Does the analysis include sufficient statistical information? Are the statistics that are used appropriate?

19. Are the conclusions supported by and do they logically follow from the data that have been presented?

20. Are the findings discussed in terms of their implications and/or practical significance?

21. Explain the final sentence of the article: "Such an ex post facto explanation for the findings possesses a high degree of face validity."

Article 28

The Effects of a Sunday Liquor Sales Ban on DUI Arrests

Jan Ligon
Bruce A. Thyer
University of Georgia

A Sunday ban on the sales of alcohol was examined in terms of its effects on the incidence of arrests for driving while intoxicated. Both visual and statistical analysis supported the contention that the sales ban was effective in reducing the incidence of DUIs. These results illustrate a further extension of behavior analysis to the evaluation of public policy.

Introduction and Statement of the Problem

(1)   One very serious public health problem is that of individuals who drive motor vehicles after consuming alcoholic beverages. During 1988 over 20,000 of the approximately 60,000 persons killed in motor vehicle accidents had been drinking (U.S. Bureau of the Census, 1988). During 1986 over 1.4 million arrests were made for driving under the influence of alcohol (DUI), and the data indicate that drinking drivers aged 20–29 were implicated in 66–75% of the accidents involving fatal crashes (Voas & Williams, 1986). For drivers under the age of 20 who were killed, between 25 to 33% had been drinking. Overall, the National Highway Traffic Safety Administration reports that 40% of drivers and pedestrians killed in automobile accidents in 1987 were legally intoxicated (c.f. Tyson, 1988).

(2)   A number of social policy efforts have been made to reduce the adverse effects of alcohol abuse, including drinking and driving. Such policy may be manifested through a variety of contingency manipulations including taxation intended to render drinking prohibitively expensive, distribution policies regulating the wholesale and retail sales of alcohol, regulating the methods used to market liquor (e.g., abolishing television advertisements), the outright prohibition of the manufacture, sales or distribution of alcohol (e.g., the 18th amendment), altering the legal age at which one is permitted to purchase alcohol, and vigorous law enforcement campaigns.

(3)   Empirical analyses of the effectiveness of social policies intended to deter alcohol use or abuse are rare, relative to the efforts made to construct and enforce such regulations. The studies which have been conducted often do not support certain measures. For example, it has been determined that prohibiting the advertising of alcoholic beverages does little to deter the consumption of liquor (Smart, 1988).

Reprinted with permission from *Journal of Alcohol and Drug Education, 38*(2): 33-40. Copyright © 1993 by the Alcohol and Drug Problems Association of North America.

Please address correspondence to: Bruce A. Thyer, School of Social Work, University of Georgia, Athens, Georgia 30602.

Portions of this research were presented at the annual meeting of the Association for Behavior Analysis, May, 1989. The authors gratefully acknowledge the statistical consultation of J. Timothy Stocks and the helpfulness of officials in the Athens' Police Department.

(4)   A common approach to reduce the abuse of alcohol is to simply restrict the public's ability to purchase intoxicating beverages. This may be accomplished through city or county bans on the sales of liquor, prohibiting the sale of liquor by the drink, or more temperately, by prohibiting 'Happy Hours' or restricting the hours during which alcohol may be sold. A number of studies have shown that increasing the hours or days during which alcohol may be sold causes the incidence of DUIs to increase (e.g. Smith, 1978, 1988). The converse is not necessarily true: when Norway implemented Saturday closings of liquor stores ". . . it was not possible to prove any clear effects of Saturday closings upon drunken drivers" (c.f. Laurence, Snortum & Zimring, 1988, p. 185). The introduction of selling liquor by the drink in North Carolina was found to significantly increase the number of police-reported, alcohol-related accidents (Blose & Holder, 1987). The banning (for a two-year period) of 'Happy Hours' in Canada had a clear effect on reducing the incidence of DUIs (Smart & Adlaf, 1986), whereas the effects on DUIs of strikes by liquor store employees in Canada, Norway and Finland which resulted in the closure of sales outlets seemed negligible (c.f. Laurence et al., 1988).

(5)   To date, the published studies evaluating the restriction of the availability of liquor as a means of reducing the incidence of DUIs have employed conventional group research designs. The effectiveness of these social policies remains equivocal. We now report a further such study which employed data presented in a time-series design and graphically interpreted, as well as analyzed using inferential statistics, in order to shed further light on the potential value of social policies which restrict the availability of alcohol, in terms of their effects on the incidence of DUIs.

Method

Selling and Social Policy

(6)   Athens, Georgia is located about 70 miles northeast of Atlanta and has a population of about 43,000 people. The entire population of Clarke County, which includes Athens is estimated to be 79,000. Athens may be described as a college town, and is the home of the main campus of the University of Georgia, which has an enrollment of approximately 27,000 students.

(7)   The Athens City Code (City of Athens, 1987) regulates the sale of alcoholic beverages under Code 6-3-5 which authorizes four classes of liquor sales license. These licenses slightly vary in terms of the hours during which alcohol is permitted to be sold, but no license allows the sale of liquor between 11:45 p.m. on Saturday and 7:00 a.m. on Monday. This restriction is subsequently referred to as the Sunday Blue Law and it applies to all alcohol sales outlets, including taverns, hotels, restaurants, liquor stores and dance clubs.

Target Behavior

(8)   The target behavior in this study was the incidence of DUI arrests awarded by Athens' police for the two-year period from March, 1986 through February, 1988. The police department provided us with detailed statistical output regarding the numbers of DUI-related arrests issued by hour of the day, and day of the week, for each month over the study. Information on the daily frequency of DUI citations was not available, only that tabulated by days of the week. For example, we could examine the incidence of DUIs for all Sundays or all Mondays, etc. for any given month, but not for one particular Sunday or Monday of a given month. Data on police staffing patterns on the various days of the week for the two-year period covered in this study were not made available to us.

Design and Procedures

(9)   To tabulate the numbers of DUI arrests, we defined a 'day' as the 12-hour period covering 6:00 p.m. on one day until 6:00 a.m. the following day. For example, the data recorded as Saturday's DUIs represents the arrests which occurred from 6:00 p.m. on Saturday evening through 6:00 a.m. Sunday morning. The 'Sunday' data covers 6:00 p.m. Sunday evening through 6:00 a.m. Monday morning. This procedure avoided potential carry over effects of late Saturday night drinkers being counted as a 'Sunday' DUI, which would obscure any potential effects of the Blue Law.

(10)   We aggregated these daily DUI tabulations to obtain the total numbers and percentages of DUIs issued over all Sundays, Mondays, etc. for the two-year period. We also plotted the data in the form of an alternating treatments design (Barlow & Hersen, 1984), connecting the data obtained for Sundays on one line, and that for the other six days of the week on the other line.

Results

(11)   The aggregated daily frequency of DUI arrests made by members of the Athens' Police Department for the stipulated two-year period is presented in Table 1. The incidence of DUIs was lowest for Sundays. An

overall chi-square analysis performed on the data for the daily frequency of DUIs for all seven days of the week found an overall main effect which was statistically significant at the .001 level suggesting that the pattern of DUI arrests across the seven days is not reasonably attributable to random factors.

(12)   To further examine these daily differences, multiple chi-square analyses were calculated, corrected for the number of tests performed by using a comparison-wise alpha level of .0025, which yielded a family-wise alpha level of .05. The results of these day-by-day comparisons are presented in Table 2. The frequency of the DUI arrests made on Sundays were statistically significantly lower than for every other day of the week, except Monday. These results are consistent with the contention that the Sunday Blue Law reduces the incidence of DUI arrests. Although the Sunday-Monday difference is not statistically different, given the conservative nature of our statistical analysis, the fact that over the two-year period Mondays accounted for 6% of the DUIs (N = 73) versus Sunday's 3% (N = 41) argues in favor of the effectiveness of the social policy restricting liquor sales.

(13)   A visual presentation of a six-month portion of the data is presented in Figure 1, which displays the frequency of DUI arrests for Sundays versus the other six days of the week, formatted in the form of an alternating treatments design. The Sunday data are clearly discernable through visual inspection alone, relative to the other days, providing further evidence that the Sunday

Table 1. The Cumulative Daily Incidence and Percentages of DUI Citations Awarded by the Athens Police Department from March, 1986 through February, 1988

Day of Week	Total DUIs Awarded	Relative Percentage of DUIs Awarded
Sunday	41	3%
Monday	73	6%
Tuesday	144	11%
Wednesday	176	14%
Thursday	201	16%
Friday	349	27%
Saturday	288	23%

ban on the sale of alcohol had a practical impact on reducing DUI arrests.

Discussion

(14)   These data lend themselves to several interpretations. One explanation is that the Sunday ban on the sales of alcohol is effective in reducing the incidence of DUI arrests. The results of both the statistical and visual analyses lend themselves to this contention in an unambiguous manner. However, several limitations preclude an uncritical acceptance of this conclusion. It would have been desirable to document with data the equivalence of police staffing patterns for each day of

Table 2. Day-by-Day Comparison of the Incidence of DUI Citations in Athens, Georgia from March, 1986 through February, 1988*

	SUN	MON	TUE	WED	THUR	FRI
MON	(8.9) .003*	—				
TUE	(57.3) .001	(23.2) .001	—			
WED	(84.0) .001	(42.6) .001	(3.2) .07**	—		
THU	(105.8) .001	(59.8) .001	(9.4) .002	(1.7) .19**	—	
FRI	(243.2) .001	(180.5) .001	(85.2) .002	(57.0) .001	(39.8) .001	—
SAT	(185.3) .001	(128.0) .001	(48.0) .001	(27.0) .001	(15.5) .001	(5.8) .01**

*[These analyses involved multiple Chi-Squares computed using a comparison-wise alpha level of .0025, to yield a family-wise alpha of .05. Accordingly, alpha levels above .0025 are not significantly different.]
**Not statistically significant.

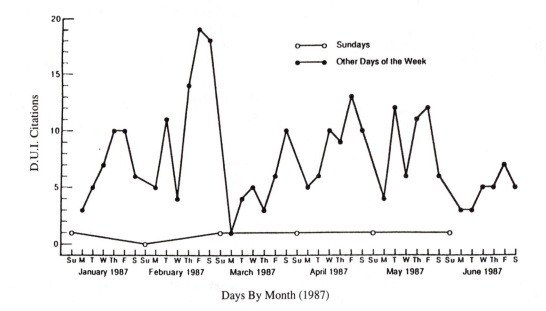

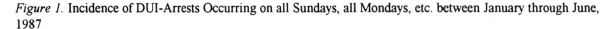

Figure 1. Incidence of DUI-Arrests Occurring on all Sundays, all Mondays, etc. between January through June, 1987

the week. In the absence of such documentation it is possible that the results reflect fewer police officers patrolling on Sundays. Our inability, despite vigorous efforts, to obtain staffing data illustrates one difficulty in the conduct of field research in natural settings.

(15)   It would have been desirable to track the daily incidence of DUIs in a parallel community which did not ban the sale of alcohol on Sundays. Such data would serve the function of a baseline or comparison group, as was aptly employed in the naturalistic study by McSweeny (1978). The Sunday 'dip' could be a phenomenon which would occur regardless of the Blue Law. Data from a parallel community could have helped rule out this explanation. The low incidence of DUIs on Mondays argues against the contention that the Sunday rate is purely a function of a weekend reduction in drinking.

(16)   Conceptually, we believe that the contrived manipulation of the availability of alcohol through Blue Laws as described in the present study may be viewed as the alteration of so-called 'setting events,' complex environmental stimuli which may have profound effects on behavior despite being temporally distant from the comportment they affect. Kantor (1959, p. 95) described one example of setting events as ". . . the presence or absence of certain environing objects (which) clearly

influence the occurrence or non-occurrence of interbehavior." Wahler and Fox (1981) further describe Kantor's view of "setting factors as those 'immediate circumstances' that influenced which of the various stimulus-response relationships (already built up through past organism-environment interactions) would occur" (p. 329). Clearly the presence of open liquor stores and taverns serves as a setting event for a complex chain of operant and respondent behavior which often culminates in driving while intoxicated.

(17)   This report illustrates the application of behavior analytic principles to the evaluation of an existing social policy. Like most such inquiries the results and interpretations are not without their flaws. This is inherent in field research where the experimental introduction and removal of independent variables is not feasible. Pending replication, the results of the present investigation suggest that one behavior analytic strategy which is effective in reducing the incidence of DUI-related arrests is to restrict the sales of alcoholic beverages on selected days of the week. The political repercussions of such city ordinances are not inconsiderable, but then the aversive societal and personal consequences of drunk driving may require equally drastic measures.

References

Barlow, D.H. & Hersen, M. (1984). *Single-case experimental designs: Strategies for studying behavior change* (second edition). New York: Pergamon.

Blose, J. & Holder, H. (1987). Public availability of distilled spirits: Structural and reported consumption changes associated with liquor-by-the-drink. *Journal of Studies on Alcohol, 48*, 371-379.

City of Athens (1987). *The code of the city of Athens, Georgia.* Tallahassee, FL: Municipal Code Corporation.

Kantor, J.R. (1959). *Interbehavioral psychology.* Granville, OH: Principia Press.

Laurence, M., Snortum, J., & Zimring, F. (1988). *Social control of the drinking driver.* Chicago, IL: The University of Chicago Press.

McSweeny, A.J. (1978). Effects of response cost on the behavior of a million persons: Charging for directory assistance in Cincinnati. *Journal of Applied Behavior Analysis, 11*, 47-51.

Smart, R. (1988). Does alcohol advertising affect overall consumption? A review of empirical studies. *Journal of Studies on Alcohol, 49*, 314-323.

Smart, R. & Adlaf, E. (1986). Banning happy hours: The impact on drinking and impaired-driving charges in Ontario, Canada. *Journal of Studies on Alcohol, 47*, 256-258.

Smith, D. (1978). Impact on traffic safety of Sunday alcohol sales in Perth, Western Australia. *Journal of Studies on Alcohol, 39*, 1302-1304.

Smith, D. (1988). Effect of traffic accidents on introducing flexible hotel trading hours in Tasmania, Australia. *British Journal of Addiction, 83*, 219-222.

Tyson, R. (1988, August, 3). Study: Education beats tough sobriety laws. *USA Today*, p. 3A.

U.S. Bureau of the Census (1989). *Statistical abstract of the United States: 1988* (108th edition). Washington, DC: U.S. Government Printing Office.

Voas, R. & Williams, A. (1986). Age difference of arrested and crash-involved drinking drivers. *Journal of Studies on Alcohol, 47*, 244-248.

Wahler, R.G. & Fox, J.J. (1981). Setting events in applied behavior analysis: Toward a conceptual and methodological expansion. *Journal of Applied Behavior Analysis, 14*, 327-338.

Factual Questions

1. What are some of the ways governments have tried to reduce the adverse effects of alcohol abuse?

2. It is noted in paragraph three that prohibiting the advertising of alcoholic beverages does little to deter the consumption of alcohol. What is the name of the article on which the authors base this statement?

3. What university is located in Athens, Georgia?

4. What was the target behavior in this study?

5. For this study, a day goes from what time to what time?

6. Which days of the week had the lowest and the highest incidences of DUI arrests?

7. Why did the researchers want data on police staffing patterns?

8. Why would data from a parallel community which did not ban the sale of alcohol on Sunday have been useful?

Questions for Discussion

9. Does the introduction provide a clear notion of the research problem, the purpose of the research, and its significance?

10. Does the literature review seem relevant to the research problem?

11. Is the two-year observation period sufficiently long? To what population would you generalize the results of this study?

12. Why might the Athens Police Department be reluctant to release information about police staffing patterns?

13. Is there enough information on the research instruments and procedures to allow you to replicate this study?

14. Should there be information about the reliability and validity of the research instruments and procedures?

15. Does the analysis include sufficient statistical information? Are the statistics that are used appropriate?

16. Are the conclusions supported by and do they logically follow from the data that have been presented?

17. Are the findings discussed in terms of their implications and/or practical significance?

Article 29

HIV Education for Probation Officers: An Implementation and Evaluation Program

Arthur J. Lurigio
John Petraitis
Bruce Johnson

This article describes the implementation and evaluation of an HIV education seminar for adult probation officers (POs) in Cook County (Chicago). The seminar consisted of medical and legal topics and was presented by an experienced educator. Pre- and postseminar measures of effectiveness were examined. Results showed a significant increase in participants' knowledge about HIV and a significant decrease in their fear of HIV. Suggestions are offered regarding the future implementation of HIV seminars for POs.

(1)　　HIV disease is perhaps the most profound health crisis our nation will ever face. It is caused by the human immunodeficiency virus (HIV), which renders the immune system incapable of combating a variety of opportunistic infections, diseases, and cancers. HIV also can directly attack the central nervous system, resulting in neurologic complications (Institutes of Medicine 1988). Acquired immune deficiency syndrome (AIDS) is the end point of a broad spectrum of clinical manifestations of HIV infection. An estimated 1 million Americans are presently afflicted with the virus (Cowley 1990). To date, more than 100,000 AIDS cases have appeared in the United States, and more than 60,000 Americans have died from AIDS-defining illnesses (Centers for Disease Control 1989). The avenues for HIV transmission are both clearly identified and

Reprinted with permission from *Crime and Delinquency, 37*(1): 125-134. Copyright © 1991 by Sage Publications, Inc.

Arthur J. Lurigio: Assistant Professor, Department of Criminal Justice, Loyola University and Research Associate, Center for Urban Affairs and Policy Research, Northwestern University. John Petraitis: Department of Psychology, Loyola University. Bruce Johnson: Research Assistant, Center for Urban Affairs and Policy Research, Northwestern University.

This study was supported by a grant from the State Justice Institute (#SJI-88-040) and by a grant from the Cook County Board of Commissioners. The opinions expressed in this article are the authors' and do not necessarily reflect the views of the Institute or the Cook County Board. We would like to thank Chief Judge Harry G. Comerford of the Cook County Circuit Court and Chief John J. Robinson of the Cook County Adult Probation Department for their support on our project. We could not have accomplished the effort without the expertise and cooperation of Adrienne Bellamy of the Adult Probation Department and Lois Lydens, formerly of Northwestern University, who helped with the logistics of program implementation, and Lynn Diller of the Adult Probation Department who scheduled the seminars and provided technical assistance. We also acknowledge the superlative performance of our AIDS educator, Dr. Gene Griffin of Northwestern University. Finally, we thank all the probation officers who participated in the sessions. Requests for reprints should be sent to Dr. Arthur J. Lurigio, Department of Criminal Justice, Loyola University of Chicago, 820 N. Michigan Ave., Chicago, IL 60611.

very limited. Transmission occurs through unprotected sexual intercourse, injections or infusions of infected blood or blood products (e.g., during transfusions and needle sharing among intravenous drug users), and from infected mother to unborn offspring (Friedland and Klein 1987). African-Americans and Hispanics are disproportionately affected by HIV (Jaffe 1990).

(2)   No cure or vaccine for HIV disease is currently available. Most persons with AIDS (PWAs) die within 2 years of diagnosis (Centers for Disease Control 1989). However, recent evidence suggests that the HIV-related decline in immunity can be retarded through the prophylactic use of zidovudine (AZT), and that some symptoms of AIDS-defining illnesses (e.g., pneumocystis carinii pneumonia) can be ameliorated through the use of other medications (e.g., pentamidine; Mills and Masur 1990). Early intervention is crucial. Until HIV is eradicated, education remains the single most effective weapon against the proliferation of the virus (Fineberg 1988). Education is not only essential for those at risk to contract HIV, but also for professionals who may have occupational contact with persons at risk. Probation officers (POs) are one such group of professionals. This article describes the implementation and evaluation of a HIV education program for POs in a large urban setting: Cook County, Illinois (Chicago).

HIV Education for POs

(3)   HIV education for probation officers is important for several reasons. POs are likely to interact with HIV-infected individuals during work activities. Criminal offenders, in general, have a demographic profile matching the profile of groups with the highest prevalence of HIV: They are predominately young, poor, minority males (Hunt 1989; Joint Subcommittee on AIDS in the Criminal Justice System 1989). The incidence of HIV in the offender population is estimated to be five or six times greater than the incidence in the general population (Hennessey forthcoming). In New York State and City correctional facilities, for example, AIDS is the leading cause of death for both male and female inmates (Joint Subcommittee on AIDS 1989). Many offenders are at serious risk for HIV largely because of their history of intravenous drug use. Intravenous drug users (IVDUs) are one of the fastest growing segments of the population with HIV disease (Cowley 1990). The Drug Use Forecasting Study revealed that a significant proportion of offenders were using injectable drugs at the time of arrest (National Institute of Justice 1990). IVDUs have extremely low survival rates for HIV disease due to poor health practices and inadequate medical care (Joint Subcommittee on AIDS 1989).

(4)   In a survey of Cook County Criminal Court judges, Lurigio, Petraitis, and Johnson (1990) found that 76% reported contact, while on the bench, with an avowed or known HIV-infected offender. Keeping pace with local HIV statistics (Chicago Department of Health 1990), the likelihood in Cook County of adjudicating an individual with the disease has increased substantially since the survey was conducted. Moreover, judges' information about offenders' HIV-status frequently was based on self-reports, which would yield a gross underestimate of seroprevalence. Hence Cook County POs can be fairly confident that persons with HIV disease will appear on their caseloads.

(5)   HIV education will prepare POs to respond properly to situations when universal precautions may be necessary (e.g., cleaning blood spills and vomitus and avoiding needle sticks). Outside the medical domain and its allied fields, occupational exposure is uncommon. According to Hammett (1988), no cases of job-related contagion have been documented among criminal justice personnel. Although occupational exposure is rare, fear of HIV is commonplace. Lurigio (1989) found that more than 80% of Illinois probation and detention workers revealed that they would feel at least "somewhat uncomfortable" supervising a confirmed or suspected HIV-antibody-positive offender. There have been instances of criminal justice personnel declining to perform their duties due to fear of HIV contraction (Hammett 1988). In a well-publicized case in Minnesota, for example, a corrections officer refused to search inmates believed to be HIV-infected (Takas and Hammett 1989). Probation departments can avoid any liability associated with occupational exposure if they demonstrate that their staff have been properly educated about HIV (Hennessey forthcoming). Furthermore, education is a basic prerequisite to the adoption of HIV workplace policies in criminal justice. As noted by the Joint Subcommittee on AIDS in the Criminal Justice System (1989), HIV education is "the essential foundation of all other policy developments" (p. 4).

(6)   Education also will equip POs to become more effective case managers. The most obvious benefit is that it will prepare them to be HIV educators themselves. Because they have access to individuals who are at greater risk for contraction and who are not likely to be privy to messages about precautions, POs can contribute to public health efforts to stem the spread of HIV (Lurigio, Gudenberg, and Spica 1988), and can join the "front lines" in battling the HIV epidemic (Joint Subcommittee on AIDS 1989). In addition, HIV education will assist officers to become more sensitive to the medical, social, and psychological sequelae of HIV

disease. With knowledge of the concomitants of HIV, POs can serve as HIV service brokers, client advocates, and counselors. Finally, education will place officers in a more informed position to request modifications in probation orders that match the ever-changing health conditions of infected persons on their caseloads.

Method

Participants

(7)   The HIV seminar was conducted at the Cook County Adult Probation Department in Chicago. POs (N = 254) were asked to participate in the seminar as part of their continuing education requirement. A total of 234 officers (92%) attended. More than half of the POs were male (58%), and the vast majority were either White (58%) or African American (33%). On the average, participants were 40 years old and had worked in the probation field for 8 years.

Procedure

(8)   The department's training coordinator scheduled officers in groups of 15 to 40. Two sessions were held each day for one work week — 1 in the morning and 1 in the afternoon — for a total of 10 sessions. An experienced educator presented the seminar. He was a clinical psychologist and a public defender in the Cook County court system, and had conducted several HIV seminars for criminal justice personnel. The seminar lasted approximately 2 hours and consisted of lectures, slides, videotapes, and handouts. The educator covered a wide range of topics on the medical and legal aspects of HIV. Medical topics included the symptoms and causes of HIV, how HIV is and is not transmitted, and current statistics on the prevalence of AIDS in Chicago, Cook County, and the United States. A brief videotape described the psychological problems that arise when working with HIV-infected clients and ways of coping with the fear of occupational contact. Legal topics included mandatory HIV testing, the confidentiality and the release of information on an offender's HIV status, state and federal regulations prohibiting discrimination against PWAs, and insurance for HIV-infected persons and PWAs. In addition, the educator informed officers about the Adult Probation Department's interim policies on the treatment of employees and probationers with HIV, and on the confidentiality of HIV-related case materials. He also informed them about clinical, legal, and social services for PWAs in Cook County. The educator encouraged participants to ask questions and to share their work experiences involving HIV-infected persons and PWAs.

(9)   At the end of each session, probation officers were given a resource manual containing (a) a written description of the Cook County Adult Probation Department's interim AIDS policy; (b) statistics on the prevalence of AIDS in Chicago by community area; (c) articles about HIV and intravenous drug use, the transmission of HIV, and the use of precautionary measures and protective equipment to prevent the spread of HIV; and (d) a booklet entitled *100 Questions and Answers about AIDS* prepared by the National Sheriffs' Association.

(10)   We asked participants to complete questionnaires immediately before and after the seminars. The preseminar survey assessed medical and legal knowledge about HIV and fear of HIV. Medical knowledge was measured by nine true-false questions about who can contract HIV (e.g., only gay persons), how HIV is spread (e.g., through needle sharing), and how people can protect themselves from infection (e.g., by sterilizing intravenous needles with bleach). Legal knowledge was measured by three true-false questions about Illinois statutes on mandatory HIV testing and the federal laws prohibiting discrimination against PWAs. Each participant was assigned a preseminar score on medical knowledge (ranging from 0 to 9 correct) and on legal knowledge (ranging from 0 to 3 correct).

(11)   Officers described their fear of HIV on four, 4-point scales measuring (a) how worried they are about becoming infected, (b) how frequently they thought about becoming infected, (c) how much of a risk they believed HIV poses for probation officers, and (d) how uncomfortable they would feel around a PWA. Higher scores indicated greater fear or concern about HIV. The intercorrelations between the scales were highly significant (all $ps < .001$) and in the expected directions. Hence we combined responses by computing a mean fear score for each participant.

(12)   When the seminar was completed, officers again answered the 12-item true-false questionnaire and the four fear-of-HIV scales. We compared knowledge and mean fear scores before and after the sessions to measure the seminar's effectiveness. Participants also were asked to rate the overall quality of the seminar and how important and helpful different aspects would be for their daily work activities. Finally, participants were asked to select topics they would like expanded in future HIV education sessions, to indicate how many HIV-infected persons and PWAs they have on their caseloads, and to recommend probation policies on HIV.

Table 1. Relative Frequencies (%) and Mean Ratings of the Helpfulness of Lecture and Lecture Suplements to Daily Work Activities

Seminar Components	Not Helpful (0)	Somewhat Helpful (1)	Helpful (2)	Very Helpful (3)	Mean
General presentation	5.2	22.9	46.3	25.5	1.92
Printed handouts	3.5	25.7	40.4	30.4	1.98
Slides	3.1	28.8	50.7	17.5	1.83
Video	8.7	30.7	41.6	19.0	1.71

Results

Occupational Contact With HIV-Infected Persons

(13)   Nearly 60% of the probation officers reported that they presently are supervising a known HIV-infected offender. Half of these participants reported that they had between 1 and 3 infected offenders on their caseloads, 5% had between 4 and 6 infected offenders, and 2% had more than 10 infected offenders.

Ratings of the Seminar

(14)   Overall, 93% of the officers gave the seminar either an "excellent" rating (52%) or "good" rating (41%). Only 6% gave the seminar a "fair" rating, and less than 1% gave it a "poor" rating. Almost three quarters of the participants (72%) indicated the seminar would be "very helpful" or "helpful" in their interactions with probationers. When asked to rate the helpfulness of the supplementary materials, 72% rated the handouts as "very helpful" or "helpful," 68% rated the slides as "very helpful" or "helpful," and 61% rated the video as "very helpful" or "helpful" (see Table 1 for helpfulness ratings).

(15)   Participants also were asked to rate the importance of the various seminar topics to their daily work activities. Table 2 shows these ratings. Services for PWAs and HIV-related legal topics were given higher importance ratings than were topics covering the medical and psychological aspects of HIV and the department's policy and procedural guidelines on HIV. Ratings of importance were inconsistent with officers' recommendations for expanding topics in subsequent HIV education sessions (see Table 2). For example, although medical and psychological issues were rated relatively low on importance, high percentages of participants indicated that they wanted to hear more about these topics in a future HIV seminar.

Evaluating Seminar Effectiveness

(16)   *Preseminar knowledge.* Table 3 presents the percentages of probation officers correctly answering each of the knowledge questions before and after the seminar. As shown, participants' preseminar medical knowledge was overall quite high. For example, nearly all of the officers (more than 98%) knew that HIV is not just a gay person's disease, that the risk of HIV increases with multiple sex partners, and that HIV can be transmitted from mother to fetus. Much lower percentages of officers, however, knew that most PWAs die

Table 2. Mean Ratings of the Importance of Lecture Topics to Daily Work Activities and Percentage of Respondents Who Want to See the Topic Expanded

Seminar Components	Mean Rating of Importance	Percentage Wanting Expanded Coverage
HIV services	2.22	47
Legal aspects	2.14	52
Psychological consequences	2.06	49
HIV policy	2.06	39
Medical Aspects	2.04	55

Table 3. Percentage of Probation Officers Giving the Correct Responses at the Pretest and Posttest

	Pretest	Posttest
Medical Knowledge		
Only gay people get HIV. (F)	99	99
A person can be infected with HIV for years before having symptoms. (T)	97	98
Most patients die within 5 years of being diagnosed with AIDS. (T)	58	69
HIV is present in large quantities in saliva, tears, and urine. (F)	78	85
Having multiple sexual partners increases the risk of being infected with HIV. (T)	99	99
A person cannot get HIV from just one exposure. (F)	87	80
A person can get HIV from giving blood. (F)	68	68
A woman can transmit HIV to her child during pregnancy or birth. (T)	98	99
Using bleach on shared needles will kill HIV. (T)	<u>58</u>	<u>82</u>
Medical knowledge average	82	87
Legal knowledge		
It is not legal for a judge to mandate HIV testing for those convicted of possession of hypodermic needles. (F)	41	72
Persons with AIDS are protected under federal antidiscrimination laws. (T)	79	96
It is legal to mandate HIV testing for persons convicted on prostitution. (T)	<u>38</u>	<u>90</u>
Legal knowledge average	52	86
Combined knowledge average	75	86

NOTE: (T) and (F) indicate whether a "true" response or a "false" response was the correct answer.

within 2 years of diagnosis and that bleach can be used on infected needles to kill HIV.

(17)   Probation officers' legal knowledge was overall much lower than their medical knowledge. For example, less than half of the participants knew that judges are authorized by statute to order mandatory HIV tests for offenders convicted of prostitution or possession of hypodermic needles.[1]

(18)   *Postseminar knowledge.* Results demonstrated that the seminar was successful in increasing subjects' preseminar medical and legal knowledge about HIV. A comparison of pre- and postseminar scores revealed that medical knowledge increased significantly from a pretest mean of 82% correct to a posttest mean of 87% correct [$t(232) = 4.57$, $p < .001$], and that legal knowledge

increased significantly from a pretest mean of 52% correct to a posttest mean of 86% correct [$t(231) = 14.45$, $p < .001$].

(19)   *Fear of HIV.* The seminar not only increased knowledge scores but also decreased fear of HIV. Although participants reported a minimal level of fear before the seminar (pretest $M = 1.11$), they reported a significantly lower level of fear after the seminar (posttest $M = 1.07$) [$t(228) = 2.14$, $p < .05$].

Discussion

(20)   The present findings reveal that a single educational seminar is an effective tool for increasing POs' knowledge about HIV and diminishing their fears of the disease. More research is needed to determine whether

the benefits of the session are longer term. A follow-up study of 6 months to 1 year is required to test the duration of impact. Another fundamental aspect to consider is whether the program actually alters PO behavior: Do educated officers remain more confident and less fearful when assessing and supervising infected clients? Are they better able to access services for PWAs? Are they more responsive to the needs of HIV-infected probationers? These are a subset of questions to be addressed in a future investigation. We offer some suggestions for the implementation of HIV seminars in probation (cf. Lurigio, Petraitis, and Johnson 1990).

(21)   Although it is imperative to include both medical and legal topics, the HIV curriculum should tip the balance in favor of legal issues: They are more complicated and protean, and bear more directly on probation officers' day-to-day activities. Because knowledge about HIV is continually advancing, refresher courses should be held at least annually (see Griffin, Lurigio, and Johnson this issue). At the conclusion of each seminar, officers should be given supplementary educational materials that will speak to their on-the-job concerns and remind them of fundamental HIV issues. By the same token, educators should stay accessible to probation officers: They can continue to answer POS' questions, alleviate their fears, and underscore the important points from training.

(22)   Education sessions should involve lectures and open discussions. The latter will help to engage POs in the seminar. Educators should be ready to field thorny questions about the origins of HIV and the controversies and myths surrounding the disease. Openly discussing erroneous beliefs will enable POs to disabuse their clients of HIV misconceptions that block testing, prevention, and treatment efforts. Finally, the content of the seminar must be tied explicitly to department policies and procedures. Educators should establish the relevancy of their materials to the assessment, monitoring, and referral of HIV-infected probationers.

Note

[1] Within the months following the seminar the Federal District Court ruled as unconstitutional the Illinois statute that allowed judges to mandate HIV testing. Although the State of Illinois is appealing that verdict, mandatory testing is currently illegal in Illinois.

References

Centers for Disease Control. 1989. "Update, AIDS-United States, 1981-1988." *Morbidity and Mortality Weekly Report* 38:229.

Chicago Department of Health. 1990. *Monthly AIDS Report*. June. Chicago, IL: Author.

Cowley, Geoffrey. 1990. "AIDS: The Next Ten Years." *Newsweek,* June 25, pp. 20-27.

Fineberg, Harold V. 1988. "Education to prevent AIDS: Prospects and Obstacles." *Science* 239:592-96.

Friedland, Gerald H. and Robert S. Klein. 1987. "Transmission of the Human Immunodeficiency Virus." *New England Journal of Medicine* 317:1125-35.

Griffin, Eugene, Arthur L. Lurigio, and Bruce Johnson. 1991. "HIV Policy for Probation Departments." *Crime and Delinquency* 37:36-47.

Hammett, Theodore M. 1988. *AIDS in Correctional Facilities: Issues and Options, Third Edition.* Washington, DC: National Institute of Justice.

Hennessey, Michael J. Forthcoming. "AIDS: The Legal Issues." In *AIDS and Community Corrections: The Development of Effective Policies,* edited by Arthur J. Lurigio, Gad J. Bensinger, and Anna T. Laszlo. Chicago, IL: Loyola University Press.

Hunt, Dana. 1989. *AIDS in Probation and Parole.* Washington, DC: National Institute of Justice.

Institutes of Medicine. 1988. *Confronting AIDS: Update 1988.* Washington, DC: National Academy Press.

Jaffe, Harold W. 1990. "The Medical Facts about AIDS." Pp. 7-26 in *AIDS and the Courts,* edited by Clark C. Abt and Kathleen M. Hardy. Cambridge, MA: Abt Books.

Joint Subcommittee on AIDS in the Criminal Justice System. 1989. *AIDS and the Criminal Justice System: A Final Report and Recommendations.* New York: Author.

Lurigio, Arthur J. 1989. "Practitioners' Views on AIDS in Probation and Detention." *Federal Probation* 53: 16-24.

Lurigio, Arthur J., Karl A. Gudenberg, and Arthur F. Spica. 1988. "Working with AIDS Cases on Probation." *Perspectives* 12:101-5.

Lurigio, Arthur J., John M. Petraitis, and Bruce Johnson. 1990. "The Cook County Experience: Assessing Education for Judges." *Judges Journal* 29:31-44.

Mills, John and Henry Masur. 1990. "AIDS-related Infections." *Scientific American,* August, pp. 50-59.

National Institute of Justice. 1990. *Drug Use Forecasting Annual Report—1989.* Washington, DC: National Institute of Justice/Bureau of Justice Assistance.

Takas, Marianne and Theodore M. Hammett. 1989. *Legal Issues Affecting Offenders and Staff.* Washington, DC: National Institute of Justice.

Factual Questions

1. PWA stands for what?

2. What percentage of those officers asked to participate in the HIV seminar attended? Why was the attendance level so good?

3. What was the total number of probation officers attending HIV seminars for this study? How many probation officers attended an HIV seminar at one time?

4. How were medical knowledge and legal knowledge about HIV measured?

5. What percentage of officers indicated the seminar would be helpful or very helpful in their interactions with probationers?

6. Which two seminar topics were judged by the officers to be most important?

7. Did the seminar significantly increase officers' medical knowledge and legal knowledge about HIV?

8. Did the seminar significantly reduce officers' fear of HIV?

9. When do the researchers suggest follow-up studies should be done to test the duration of the seminar's impact?

Questions for Discussion

10. Does the introduction provide a clear notion of the research problem, the purpose of the research, and its significance?

11. Does the literature review seem relevant to the research problem?

12. What use to the reader is knowing the demographic characteristics of the probation officers who attended the seminar?

13. Is the number of research subjects sufficient? To what population would you generalize the results of this study?

14. Is there enough information on the research instruments and procedures to allow you to replicate this study?

15. What was the reason for combining the four "fear of HIV" answers into a single score?

16. Do the research instruments and procedures have adequate reliability and validity?

17. Does the analysis include sufficient statistical information? Are the statistics that are used appropriate?

18. Are the conclusions supported by and do they logically follow from the data that have been presented?

19. Are the findings discussed in terms of their implications and/or practical significance?

20. In your opinion, did the seminar bring about enough change in officers' medical knowledge, legal knowledge, and fear of HIV to warrant its continuation?

Drug and Alcohol Prevention Project for Sixth Graders: First-Year Findings

Karole J. Kreutter
Herbert Gewirtz
Joan E. Davenny
Carol Love

Data gathered in this study are the first-year results of a three-year program evaluation for a drug and alcohol prevention project. One hundred fifty-two 6th graders made up the target group which received instruction using Botvin's life skills training curriculum. Sixty-four additional subjects made up a control group which received no treatment. Both groups were pre- and posttested on the following variables: knowledge about and attitudes toward substances, self-concept, passivity, and locus of control. Results indicated that the program had a significant positive impact on the target subjects' passivity, knowledge about drugs and alcohol, and self-image.

(1)   In the mid-1960s, as public concern about adolescent drug use became serious, many communities initiated prevention programs with the focus on increasing information about and establishing appropriate attitudes toward substance abuse. While these programs may have achieved these goals, the literature indicates that they were minimally effective in changing actual drug use behavior (Schaps, DiBartolo, Moskowitz, Palley, & Churgin, 1981; Second Report of the National Commission on Marijuana and Drug Abuse, 1973; Cabinet Committee on Drug Abuse Prevention, 1977). In fact, Swisher, Crawford, Goldstein, and Yura (1971) found a negative relationship between knowledge and actual usage, suggesting that programs which are solely informational can lead to more liberal attitudes and a corresponding tendency toward abuse. Not only were the positive results of these programs limited, but Dembo (1979) suggested that most utilized inadequate evaluation procedures.

(2)   The next generation of programs was oriented toward a more social-psychological model, and was thought to be more promising (Schaps et al., 1981; Battjes, 1985). This model assumes, in part, that substance use occurs within a context of social pressures, and therefore suggests an approach that familiarizes students with the major social influences on their behavior and teaches them strategies for resisting these pressures. Battjes (1985) described an effective education program designed to promote self-esteem,

Reprinted with permission from *Adolescence, 26*(102): 287-293. Copyright © 1991 by Libra Publishers, Inc.

This research was partially funded by a grant from the State of Connecticut Department of Children and Youth Services.

Herbert Gewirtz and Joan E. Davenny, Child Guidance Clinic for Central Connecticut.

Carol Love, Meriden Youth Service Bureau.

Reprint requests to Karole J. Kreutter, Ph.D., Child Guidance Clinic for Central Connecticut, 117 Lincoln Street, Meriden, Connecticut 06450.

successful interpersonal relationships, and adequate decision-making skills. However, in order for such prevention programs to be successful, the influence of peers has to be taken into account since it is the best single predictor of substance abuse (Ensminger, Brown, & Kellam, 1984; Newcomb & Bentler, 1985; Kandel, Kessler, & Margulies, 1978; Hansen, Malotte, Collins, & Fielding, 1987; Marcos, Baker, & Johnson, 1986; Budd, Eiser, Morgan, & Gammage, 1985; McKinnon & Johnson, 1986; Thorne & DeBlassie, 1985; Jessor, 1975; Hamburg, Kraemer, & Jahnke, 1975). Teenagers are the most vulnerable to involvement with drugs, beginning as early as age 13 or 14 (Segal, 1986) when, developmentally, parents are gradually replaced by peers as the predominant source of influence. This suggests that when there is more bonding to peers, as opposed to family and school, there is increased vulnerability to substance use. In looking for ways to combat this peer factor, researchers (Jurich & Polson, 1984; Dignan, Steckler, Block, Howard, & Cosby, 1985; Dignan, Block, Steckler, & Cosby, 1986; Steffenhagen, 1980; Kaplan, 1980) focused on such variables as locus of control and self-esteem, believing that they are related to resistance to peer influence.

(3)　　The newer models employ multicomponent approaches designed to establish social-psychological deterrents via skills building and the fostering of personal competence (Schinke, Gilchrist, Snow, & Schilling, 1985). One such approach was developed by Botvin and Eng (1982) (see also Botvin, Baker, Renick, Filazzola & Botvin, 1984; Botvin, Eng, & Williams, 1980). Using their life skills training approach with 8th, 9th, and 10th graders, they found that the program reduced cigarette smoking and increased resistance to smoking. Their studies also examined the effect of the curriculum on personality variables, such as social anxiety, locus of control, self-image, influenceability, and need for acceptance. The results varied as a function of grade, though knowledge increased for all grades. The program had a similar effect on the smoking behavior of 7th graders (Botvin & Eng, 1982), and results suggested that there was increased knowledge about smoking and advertising as well as a reduction in social anxiety and influenceability. Applying this curriculum to substance abuse, Botvin et al. (1984) found that it had a positive impact on drinking and marijuana use in 7th graders; they also obtained positive results for attitudes and knowledge.

(4)　　The present research employed Botvin's (1981) life skills training curriculum with 6th graders as a means of studying its effect on knowledge and attitudes toward substance abuse, self-concept, assertiveness, and

locus of control. Sixth graders were selected because there is considerable data to suggest that 13 and 14 are peak ages for beginning involvement with substance use (Segal, 1986).

Method

Subjects

(5)　　A total of 216 6th-grade parochial school students participated. One hundred fifty-two subjects from the Meriden-Wallingford, Connecticut, area made up the target group, and 64 subjects from parochial schools in Waterbury, Plainville, and New Haven, Connecticut, made up the control population. The control subjects were selected from areas thought to be roughly equivalent in demographics to those of the target group.

Materials

(6)　　Botvin's (1981) life skills training curriculum was presented to each class in the target group during 18 training sessions. All subjects in the study were administered the following measures as pretests and posttests: the Piers-Harris Children's Self-Concept Scale (Piers, 1977); a knowledge survey developed by the authors (based on Botvin's curriculum); the Nowicki-Strickland Personal Reaction Survey (locus of control-children) (Nowicki & Strickland, 1973); an informal drug and alcohol attitude scale developed by the authors; and the Children's Assertive Behavior Scale (Michelson & Wood, 1982).

Procedure

(7)　　All subjects in the study were given the pretest measures. The target subjects then participated in the curriculum presentation while the controls received no treatment. All of the training sessions were conducted by a single trainer, and at the end of the curriculum, all subjects were administered the posttests. Mean scores for self-concept, knowledge, passivity, and locus of control were calculated and compared using t tests. Gain scores for these variables were computed and compared using t tests as well. No comparisons were completed on the attitude scale due to the fact that all of the subjects in the study scored exceptionally high on the pretest. A simple yes-or-no format was utilized in the development of the scale, which did not offer a broader range of responses as would a Likert-type scale.

Table 1. Comparison of Pretest and Posttest Means for Target and Control Subjects

Variable	Target Subjects		Control Subjects	
	Pretest	Posttest	Pretest	Posttest
Self-Concept	55.69	61.09*	58.78	60.86
Knowledge (# of errors)	16.71	13.07**	16.27	16.31
Passivity	6.20	4.91***	5.95	6.36
Locus of Control	14.74	14.33	15.03	14.78

*t = 8.44; p < .001
**t = 11.14; p < .001
***t = 3.83; p < .001

Results

(8)　To see if the curriculum impacted on the target subjects, comparisons were made between the pre- and posttest scores on the measures of self-concept, knowledge, assertiveness (scored for passivity), and locus of control. Similarly, pre- and posttest results for control subjects were compared (see Table 1).

(9)　The significant difference between the pre- and posttest self-concept scores for the target group suggests that the curriculum had a significant positive impact on the self-esteem variable. Similarly, the significant decrease in the number of incorrect items on the knowledge survey for the target subjects indicates that the program increased their knowledge about drugs and alcohol. On the assertiveness measure, there was a significant decrease in passivity for target subjects. There

and passivity. The difference between the two groups on the locus of control variable was not significant. These findings are consistent with those cited in Table 1.

Discussion

(11)　The results of this study suggest that the current program had a significant positive impact on 6th graders' passivity, knowledge about drugs and alcohol, and self-concept. This is consistent with Botvin et al.'s (1984) findings.

(12)　A single trainer presented the curriculum to all target subjects so that there would be consistency in the presentations. This individual was not part of the educational system nor was she familiar to the students. The ultimate plan in the project involves training regular classroom teachers to present the curriculum and run booster sessions. It will be important to monitor the

Table 2. Comparison of Gain Scores for Target and Control Subjects

Variable	Target Subjects	Control Subjects	t Score
Self-Concept	5.41	2.08	2.67 (p < .008)
Knowledge	3.64	.05	6.39 (p < .001)
Passivity	1.38	-.41	-2.98 (p < .003)
Locus of Control	.41	.25	.23 (N.S.)

was no change for target subjects on the locus of control scale. No changes were noted on any of the variables for the control subjects.

(10)　Gain scores were computed for both the target and control groups on these same measures so that the groups could be compared on the basis of the amount of change that had taken place from pretest to posttest (see Table 2). There were significant differences between the target and control subjects for self-concept, knowledge,

results as the instructor changes from an unfamiliar presenter to a more familiar classroom figure.

(13)　The present study is part of a three-year intensive program evaluation. In addition to initial training for target groups, booster sessions will be held at specified time intervals, and the progress of youngsters on variables examined in this study will continue to be monitored. An alternative scale for measuring attitudes toward drugs and alcohol will be employed so that this variable can be measured more accurately. Additionally, a parent-involvement component will be added to the project to see if results improve by increasing parental knowledge and support.

References

Battjes, R.J. (1985). Prevention of adolescent drug abuse. *International Journal of Addictions, 20,* 1113-1134.

Botvin, G.J. (1981). *Life skills training: Teacher's manual.* New York: Smithfield Press.

Botvin, G.J., Baker, E., Renick, N.L., Filazzola, A.D., & Botvin, E.M. (1984). A cognitive behavioral approach to substance abuse prevention. *Addictive Behaviors, 9,* 137-147.

Botvin, G.J., & Eng, A. (1982). The efficacy of a multicomponent approach to the prevention of cigarette smoking. *Preventive Medicine, 11,* 199-211.

Botvin, G.J., Eng, A., & Williams, C.L. (1980). Preventing the onset of cigarette smoking through life skills training. *Preventive Medicine, 9,* 135-143.

Budd, R.J., Eiser, J.R., Morgan, M., & Gammage, P. (1985). The personal characteristics and life-style of the young drinker: The results of a survey of British adolescents. *Drug and Alcohol Dependence, 16,* 144-157.

Cabinet Committee on Drug Abuse Prevention. (1977). *Treatment and rehabilitation recommendations for future federal activities in drug abuse prevention.* Washington, DC: U.S. Government Printing Office.

Dembo, R. (1979). Substance abuse programming and research: A partnership in need of improvement. *Journal of Drug Education, 9,* 189-208.

Dignan, M.B., Block, G.D., Steckler, A., & Cosby, M. (1986). Evaluation of North Carolina risk reduction program for smoking and alcohol. *Journal of School Health, 55,* 103-106.

Dignan, M.B., Steckler, A., Block, G.D., Howard, G., & Cosby, M. (1985). Prevalence of health risk behavior among seventh grade students in North Carolina. *Southern Medical Journal, 79,* 295-303.

Ensminger, M.E., Brown, C.H., & Kellam, S.G. (1984). Sex differences in antecedents of substance use among adolescents. *Journal of Social Issues, 38,* 25-42.

Hamburg, B.A., Kraemer, H.C., & Jahnke, W. (1975). A hierarchy of drug use in adolescence: Behavioral and attitudinal correlates of substantial drug use. *American Journal of Psychiatry, 133,* 1155-1163.

Hansen, W.B., Malotte, K.C., Collins, L., & Fielding, J.E. (1987). Dimensions and psychosocial correlates of adolescent alcohol use. *Journal of Alcohol and Drug Education, 32,* 19-31.

Jessor, R. (1975). *Predicting time of onset of marijuana use: A developmental study of high school youth.* Publication No. 160, Institute of Behavioral Science, University of Colorado.

Jurich, A.P., & Polson, C.J. (1984). Reasons for drug use: Comparison of drug users and abusers. *Psychological Reports, 55,* 371-378.

Kandel, D.B., Kessler, R.C., & Margulies, R.Z. (1978). Antecedents of adolescent initiation into stages of drug use: A developmental analysis. *Journal of Youth and Adolescence, 7,* 13-40.

Kaplan, H.B. (1980, March). Self esteem and self derogation theory of drug abuse. In *Theories on drug abuse: Selected contemporary perspectives* (NIDA Research Monograph Series No. 30). Rockville, MD: U.S. Dept. of Health and Human Services.

Marcos, A.C., Baker, S.J., & Johnson, R.E. (1986). Test of a bonding/association theory of adolescent drug use. *Social Forces, 65,* 135-161.

McKinnon, D.J., & Johnson, T. (1986). Alcohol and drug use among "street" adolescents. *Addictive Behavior, 11,* 201-205.

Michelson, L., & Wood, R. (1982). Development and psychometric properties of the Children's Assertive Behavior Scale. *Journal of Behavioral Assessment, 4,* 32-44.

Newcomb, M.D., & Bentler, P.M. (1985). Substance use and ethnicity: Differential impact of peer and adult models. *Journal of Psychology, 120,* 83-95.

Nowicki, S., Jr., & Strickland, B.R. (1973). Locus of Control Scale for Children. *Journal of Consulting and Clinical Psychology, 20,* 148-154.

Piers, E.V. (1977). *The Piers-Harris Children's Self-Concept Scale.* Nashville, TN: Counselor Recordings and Tests.

Schaps, E., DiBartolo, R., Moskowitz, J., Palley, C.S., & Churgin, S. (1981, Winter). A review of 127 drug abuse prevention program evaluations. *Journal of Drug Issues,* pp. 17-43.

Schinke, S.P., Gilchrist, L.D., Snow, W.H., & Schilling, R.F., II. (1985). Skills building methods to prevent smoking by adolescents. *Journal of Adolescent Health Care, 6,* 439-444.

Second Report of the National Commission on Marijuana and Drug Abuse. (1973). *Drug use in America: Problem in perspective.* Washington, DC: U.S. Government Printing Office.

Segal, B. (1986). Age and first experience with psychoactive drugs. *International Journal of the Addictions, 21,* 1285-1306.

Steffenhagen, R.A. (1980, March). Self esteem theory of drug abuse. In *Theories on drug abuse: Selected contemporary perspectives.* (NIDA Research

Monograph No. 30). Rockville, MD: U.S. Dept. of Health and Human Services.

Swisher, J.D., Crawford, J., Goldstein, R., & Yura, M. (1971, October). Drug education: Pushing or preventing. *Peabody Journal of Education*, pp. 68-75.

Thorne, C.R., & DeBlassie, R.R. (1985). Adolescent substance abuse. *Adolescence*, 20 (78), 335-347.

Factual Questions

1. How did the second generation of drug abuse prevention programs differ from the first generation?

2. What drug abuse prevention program is being evaluated in this study?

3. Why did the authors choose to study sixth graders?

4. How many children were in the target group and in the control group?

5. What measures were used for both the pretest and the posttest?

6. Why did the researchers not test to see if the drug abuse prevention program significantly changed students' attitudes toward drugs?

7. On which of the four outcome measures tested were there significant differences in the target group's pretest and posttest scores?

8. What are gain scores and why were they computed?

9. Were the results from the analysis of gain scores consistent with the results from the analysis of pretest and posttest scores?

10. What do the researchers intend to do in the remaining two years of this evaluation project?

Questions for Discussion

11. Does the introduction provide a clear notion of the research problem, the purpose of the research, and its significance?

12. Does the literature review seem relevant to the research problem?

13. Why did the authors seek control group subjects who were similar in demographic characteristics to the target group subjects?

14. Is the number of research subjects sufficient? To what population would you generalize the results of this study?

15. Is there enough information on the research instruments and procedures to allow you to replicate this study?

16. Should there be information about the reliability and validity of the research instruments and procedures?

17. Does the analysis include sufficient statistical information? Are the statistics that are used appropriate?

18. Are the conclusions supported by and do they logically follow from the data that have been presented?

19. Are the findings discussed in terms of their implications and/or practical significance?

20. If the ultimate plan is to have classroom teachers present the drug abuse prevention program, why did the researchers use a non-teacher to present the program in this research?

Article 31

The "Buckle-Up" Dashboard Sticker: An Effective Environmental Intervention for Safety Belt Promotion

Bruce A. Thyer
E. Scott Geller

A vehicle dashboard sticker that read "SAFETY BELT USE REQUIRED IN THIS VEHICLE" was found to double the use of safety belts by front-seat passengers. During an initial two-week baseline phase, 24 graduate students (who always buckled up when driving) recorded safety belt use by front-seat passengers in their automobiles. The mean baseline belt use of 476 passengers was 34%. Subsequently, buckle-up stickers were placed in the 24 vehicles, and passenger belt use increased to 70% (N = 448). Two weeks later the stickers were withdrawn and passenger belt use dropped to 41% (N = 406). Replacement of the 24 stickers for two final weeks resulted in 78% belt use by 392 front seat passengers.

(1)   During recent years, behavior change interventions have extended beyond the realm of clinical practice in mental health into the domain of public health programs. Examples of such research programs include the prevention of cigarette smoking (Schinke et al., 1985) and pregnancy among teenagers (Schinke et al., 1981), the widespread dissemination of behavioral methods to promote and maintain weight loss (Stuart, 1978), contingency management programs to motivate aerobic exercise (Thyer et al., 1984), and programs to encourage high-risk children to use dental services (Olson et al., 1981).

(2)   A major public health problem that is readily preventable is automobile accident-induced injury. In 1979 alone, traffic crashes were responsible for the death of 51,900 Americans and the disabling injuries of an additional two million (Sleet, 1984), and informed estimates indicate that at least half of these deaths and trauma could be prevented if vehicle occupants had

Reprinted with permission from *Environment and Behavior, 19*(4): 484-494. Copyright © 1987 by Sage Publications, Inc.

Bruce A. Thyer is Associate Professor of Social Work at Florida State University. He is interested in promoting behavior analysis with social work and within the fields of mental health and community practice.

E. Scott Geller is Professor of Psychology at Virginia Polytechnic Institute and State University. He is a Fellow of the American Psychological Association and has been an Associate Editor of *Environment and Behavior* since 1983. From 1983 to 1986, he was Associate Editor for the *Journal of Applied Behavior Analysis.* In 1982 he co-authored *Preserving the Environment: New Strategies for Behavior Change* (Pergamon Press) with Richard A. Winett and Peter B. Everett.

AUTHORS' NOTE: We acknowledge the conscientious efforts of the 24 Pensacola graduate social work students, the statistical advice of J. Timothy Stocks, and the helpful suggestions of Galen Lehman on an earlier draft of this article. Copies of the dashboard stickers and reprints are available from either author: Bruce A. Thyer, School of Social Work, Florida State University, Tallahassee, FL 32306 or E. Scott Geller, Department of Psychology, Virginia Tech, Blacksburg, VA 24061.

performed the simple behavior of buckling up their safety belts (Highway Safety Research Center, 1976). Despite the unambiguous evidence associating consistent safety belt use with injury reduction and prevention, fewer than 15% of American drivers regularly wear their safety belts (Tarrants, 1983). In recent years, various behavior change interventions have been employed in an attempt to increase safety belt use in the United States (see reviews by Geller, 1984b; Streff and Geller, 1986).

(3)　　Governmental application of contingency management principles has been limited to the establishment and enforcement of mandatory safety belt-use laws, typically involving punitive fines as penalties for not buckling up. Such belt use mandates are usually only moderately effective, unless they are rigorously enforced (see Jonah et al., 1982), and they have the disadvantage of imposing additional elements of aversive control on citizens already burdened with a surfeit of punitive legal sanctions.

(4)　　More acceptable programs to promote safety belt use involve the establishment of contrived contingencies of positive reinforcement. For example, Geller and his students have conducted a programmatic series of corporate and community safety belt programs incorporating elements of safety education, reminder flyers, and incentive/reward strategies. A driver could be eligible to participate in the safety belt lotteries by either signing a pledge card promising regular safety belt use or by being observed buckled up when driving (e.g., Geller et al., 1982). These contrived incentive programs have produced significant increases in safety belt use, and possess the advantage of avoiding the negative side

effects associated with aversive control. To date, however, the long-term gains in safety belt use from incentive programs have been modest, with increases on the order of from 26% belt use during baseline to 46% during incentives (Geller et al., 1982), from 20% to 56% and 17% to 31% (Geller, 1983), and from 6% to 23% (Geller, 1984a).

(5)　　Simple environmental (or stimulus control) strategies to promote safety belt use have been evaluated by Rogers (1984) and Geller, Bruff, and Nimmer (1985). Using a multiple baseline design, Rogers (1984) found that a small dashboard sticker that read "SAFETY BELT USE REQUIRED IN THIS VEHICLE" increased belt use by about 400% (i.e., from 10% to 38%) among the drivers of state-owned vehicles. Having drivers sign a signature sheet indicating that they had read the relevant state regulations mandating safety belt use when on state business had significant additional impact.

(6)　　Geller, Bruff, and Nimmer (1985) prepared 11" X 14" "Flash-for-Life" signs reading "PLEASE BUCKLE UP — I CARE" on one side, and "THANK YOU FOR BUCKLING UP" on the other. In their community-based study, Geller et al. (1985) had seven different automobile passengers "flash" the buckle-up side of the sign at unbuckled passengers and drivers of other automobiles. Over a seven-week period, 1087 unbuckled drivers were thus "flashed," of whom 185 complied with the buckle-up prompt. When this was observed, the "flasher" reversed the sign, displaying the "thank you" message. A further study of the "Flash-for-Life" strategy involved pedestrian "flashers" displaying the sign to drivers exiting parking lots

Figure 1. The "buckle-up" dashboard sticker (actual size) used as the experimental intervention. The letters were blue on a white background.

(Thyer et al., 1986). An A-B-A-B design with two-week phases showed that this environmental change intervention doubled safety belt use by drivers, from about 20% use during baseline conditions to approximately 40% use when the "Flash-for-Life" cards were displayed.

(7)   These simple environmental interventions possess several advantages over alternative behavior change interventions for increasing safety belt use. The absence of aversive contingencies is one desirable feature, and the second is their relative ease of implementation. Given the success of these strategies and their low cost, the present study examined the effectiveness of dashboard stickers in promoting safety belt use in privately owned and operated automobiles.

Method

Participants and Setting

(8)   The study was conducted in the city of Pensacola, Florida, and its environs. At the time of this study, Florida did not have a mandatory safety belt law pertaining to adults. A total of 24 graduate students (mean age = 38) with personal automobiles containing func-

tional shoulder and lap belts in the front seat served as data recorders.

(9)   While wearing a combination shoulder and lap belt, each observer/driver independently and unobtrusively recorded whether or not front-seat passengers of their automobiles buckled up their safety belts at the beginning of each trip. Only data from passengers who did not know about the study were included. These data were turned in on a weekly basis to the senior author who aggregated the individual records on a day-by-day basis, calculating the total number of passengers driven by 24 graduate students each day, and the percentage of passengers each day who buckled up.

Intervention and Experimental Design

(10)   After a two-week baseline period, the 1.5" X 2.5" adhesive sticker depicted in Figure 1 was applied to the passenger-side dashboard of the 24 automobiles. If questioned by their passengers, the drivers casually stated "I always prefer that my passengers wear their seat belts." They did not otherwise argue with or cajole their passengers or employ other tactics designed to encourage safety belt use (e.g., refuse to proceed until the

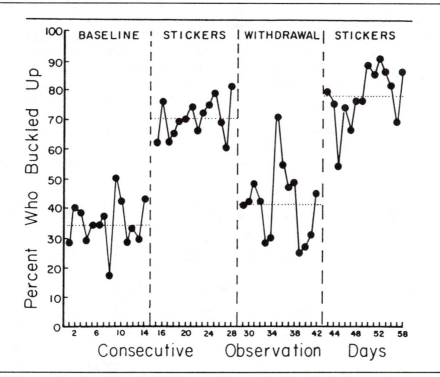

Figure 2. The percentage of passengers who buckled up over 58 consecutive observation days, two-weeks per consecutive baseline, intervention, withdrawal, and intervention phase.

passenger was properly buckled). Data were unobtrusively recorded on a standard form[1] for a two-week intervention phase, and then at the end of the two weeks of intervention, the dashboard stickers were removed, initiating a two-week withdrawal phase. Finally, the stickers were replaced and data collected for a second and final two-week intervention period. This data collection and intervention/withdrawal program thus conformed to an A-B-A-B time-series experimental design (Barlow and Hersen, 1984).

Results

(11)   The daily mean percentages of those passengers who wore their safety belts are displayed in Figure 2. During initial baseline, the daily number of passengers ranged from 19 to 50, with a mean (and standard deviation) of 34 (9.3). Safety belt use ranged from 17% to 50%, with a mean of 34(7.8)% of the passengers buckled up.

(12)   During the first intervention phase, the daily number of passengers ranged from 21 to 46, with a mean (and standard deviation) of 32(6.7). The percentage of buckled passengers ranged from 60 to 81, with a mean of 70(6.3)%.

(13)   During the withdrawal phase, when the stickers had been removed, the aggregated daily number of passengers ranged from 19 to 36, with a mean (and standard deviation) of 29(5.7). Safety belt use ranged from 25% to 71%, with a mean (and standard deviation) of 41(12)%.

(14)   During the second intervention phase, the daily number of passengers ranged from 20 to 43, with a mean (and standard deviation) of 28(5.9). Daily safety belt use was reported to range from 54% to 90% of the passengers, with a mean (and standard deviation) of 78(9.5)%.

(15)   A one-way analysis of variance (ANOVA) demonstrated a statistically significant difference across phases in the percentage of passengers who buckled up [$F(3, 52) = 69.5; p < .01$]. This difference was isolated using post hoc Scheffé comparisons (reported in Table 1), which indicated that the two baseline conditions were not significantly different from each other, nor were the two experimental phases different with respect to safety belt use (Scheffé, 1953). Both of the two baseline phases, however, were significantly lower in mean safety belt use than either of the two experimental phases. The proportion of the variance in safety belt use that may be attributed to the intervention was 79%.

(16)   An overwhelming number of passengers buckled their safety belts without questioning the driver or protesting. Indeed, driver prompts (described above) were used on only 19% of the occasions when the passengers buckled up during the intervention phases.

Discussion

(17)   In the present study, a "buckle up" sticker placed on vehicle dashboards increased safety belt use by over 100%, resulting in approximately 70% belt wearing by front-seat passengers. In some cases, the "buckle-up" sticker elicited a remark from the passenger that in turn gave the drivers an opportunity to offer the simple verbal prompt, "I always prefer that my passengers wear their seat belts." The A-B-A-B design showed reliable functional control over safety belt use in this simple and convenient environmental intervention. Indeed, the demonstrated efficacy of the

Table 1. Scheffé Comparisons (F ratios) of the Differences in Daily Aggregated Percentage of Passengers Who Employed Safety Belts Between Phases of the Experiment

	First Baseline (A1)	—		
Phase of	First Intervention (B1)	93.79*	—	
Experiment	Second Baseline (A2)	3.12**	65.64*	—
	Second Intervention (B2)	142.78*	4.33**	103.67*	—
		A1	B1	A2

*$p < .05$; **n.s.

[1]Copies of this data sheet and the detailed research protocol that the graduate students followed are available upon request to either author.

242

"buckle-up" sticker was among the most significant ever reported by experimental studies of safety belt promotion, rivaling or exceeding compliance induced by mandatory safety belt use legislation, educational campaigns, stimulus control procedures, or incentive/reward programs (e.g., see reviews by Geller, 1984b; Streff and Geller, 1986; Nichols, 1982).

(18)   The success of this environmental intervention may possibly be attributed to the fact that most individuals have a learning history that has vigorously reinforced rule-governed behavior, a special case of operant control responsible for much of what is referred to as civilized comportment (Zettle and Hayes, 1983). In an earlier study, Geller et al. (1985) showed that 25% of 787 drivers in a university town followed the request of a "buckle up" sign that was "flashed" from another vehicle, whereas significantly less compliance (i.e., 14%) was found in a nearby rural community. In that study, it was presumed that the modeling of safety belt use by the sign "flasher" was a contributing factor in intervention impact. Likewise, in the present study, safety belt use by the vehicle drivers was probably necessary for the prominent behavior-change success of the dashboard stickers.

(19)   A drawback of the present study was the sole reliance upon data obtained by graduate students in the absence of reliability checks. This criticism is mitigated by the use of 24 mature individuals (mean age = 38) who were taught to appreciate objective, behavioral observations, and by the emphasis placed on reporting accurate data. During the training of the data collectors, experimental hypotheses were not entertained; and intervention effects much less pronounced than those observed were expected by the authors and by those students who discussed their findings with us. In addition, the small number of passengers per day riding with each student typically rendered data collection an extremely simple and straightforward task.

(20)   The long-term effects of the dashboard sticker remain to be determined. The fact that there was no trend in the data indicating a lessening impact of the stickers at the end of the two intervention periods supports the continuing efficacy of this simple program. Actually, mean belt use was slightly higher during the second than first baseline and intervention phases. This shows some promise for residual effects of the short-term intervention, as has also been observed in university incentive programs (Rudd and Geller, 1985) and community-based sign displays (Thyer et al., 1987) for safety belt promotion.

(21)   The traffic accident is currently the number one public health problem in the United States, given that it is the leading cause of death from age 5 to 34 and results in more than two million disabling injuries per year (Sleet, 1984). Because one-half or more of the injuries and fatalities to vehicle occupants could be prevented if safety belts were consistently worn, the large-scale promotion of safety belt use is an urgent and critical target for primary prevention in public health. The present study demonstrated the remarkable effectiveness of a simple environmental intervention that could be readily integrated with other behavior change approaches to safety belt promotion (e.g., mandatory use laws, incentives, and public awareness programs). In other words, a comprehensive effort to increase the nationwide use of vehicle safety belts should include the dissemination and application of "buckle up" dashboard stickers.

References

BARLOW, D. H. and M. HERSEN (1984) Single-Case Experimental Designs. New York: Pergamon.

GELLER, E. S. (1983) "Rewarding safety belt usage at an industrial setting: tests of treatment generality and response maintenance." J. of Applied Behavior Analysis 16: 189-202.

GELLER, E. S. (1984a) "A delayed reward strategy for large-scale motivation of safety belt use: a test of long-term impact." Accident Analysis and Prevention 16: 457-463.

GELLER, E. S. (1984b) Motivating Safety Belt Use with Incentives: A Critical Review of the Past and a Look to the Future. SAE Technical Paper Series, No. 840326. Warrendale, PA: Society of Automotive Engineers.

GELLER, E. S., C. D. BRUFF, and J. G. NIMMER (1985) "'Flash for Life': community-based prompting for safety belt promotion" J. of Applied Behavior Analysis 18: 145-159.

GELLER, E. S., L. DAVIS, and K. SPICER (1983) "Industry-based rewards to promote seat belt usage: differential impact on white-collar versus blue-collar employees." J. of Organizational Behavior Management 5:17-29.

GELLER, E. S. and H. A. HAHN (1984) "Promoting safety belt use at industrial sites: an effective program for blue collar employees." Professional Psychology: Research and Practice 15: 553-564.

GELLER, E. S., L. PATERSON, and E. TALBOT (1982) "A behavioral analysis of incentive prompts for motivating seat belt use." J. of Applied Behavior Analysis 18: 403-415.

Highway Safety Research Center (1976) "Belts: questions and answers." Highway Safety Highlights 10:1.

JONAH, B. A., N. E. DAWSON, and G. A. SMITH (1982) "Effects of a selective traffic enforcement program on seat belt use." J. of Applied Psychology 67: 84-96.

NICHOLS, J. (1982) Effectiveness and Efficiency of Safety Belt and Child Restraining Usage Programs. (Report No. DOT-HS-806-142.) Washington, DC: U.S. Department of Transportation, National Highway Traffic Safety Administration.

OLSON, D. G., R. L. LEVY, C. A. EVANS, and S. K. OLSON (1981) "Enhancement of high risk children's utilization of dental services." Amer. J. of Public Health 71:631-634.

ROGERS, R. W. (1984) "Promoting safety belt use among state employees: the effects of prompting, stimulus control and a response-cost intervention." Unpublished doctoral dissertation. Florida State University, Tallahassee.

RUDD, J. R. and E. S. GELLER (1985) "A university-based incentive program to increase safety belt use: toward cost-effective institutionalization." J. of Applied Behavior Analysis 18: 215-226.

SCHEFFÉ, H. (1953) "A method for judging all contrasts in the analysis of variance." Biometrika 40: 87-104.

SCHINKE, S. P., B. J. BLYTHE, L. D. GILCHRIST, and G. A. BURT (1981) "Primary prevention of adolescent pregnancy." Social Work with Groups 4: 121-135.

SCHINKE, S. P., L. D. GILCHRIST, and W. H. SNOW (1985) "Skills intervention to prevent cigarette smoking among adolescents." Amer. J. of Public Health 75: 665-667.

SLEET, D. A. (1984) A Preventative Health Orientation in Safety Belt and Child Safety Seat Use. SAE Technical Paper Series, No. 840325. Warrendale, PA: Society of Automotive Engineers.

STUART, R. B. (1978) Act Thin, Stay Thin. New York: Norton.

STREFF, F. M. and E. S. GELLER (1986) "Strategies for motivating safety belt use: the application of applied behavior analysis." Health Education Research: Theory and Practice 1: 47-59.

TARRANTS, W. (1983) "Evaluation news and notes." Traffic Safety Evaluation Research Rev. 2:1-4.

THYER, B. A., E. S. GELLER, M. WILLIAMS, and E. PURCELL (1987) "Community based 'flashing' to increase safety belt use." Journal of Experimental Education 55: 155-159.

THYER, B. A., S. IRVINE, and C. A. SANTA (1984) "Contingency management of exercise by chronic schizophrenics." Perceptual and Motor Skills 58: 419-425.

ZETTLE, R. D. and S. C. HAYES (1983) "Rule-governed behavior: a potential theoretical framework for cognitive behavior therapy," pp. 73-118 in P. C. Kendall (ed.) Advances in Cognitive Behavioral Research and Therapy, Vol 1. New York: Academic Press.

Factual Questions

1. What percentage of American drivers regularly wear their safety belts?

2. Which researcher first evaluated the effect of a dashboard sticker encouraging the use of safety belts?

3. How does the present study differ from that done by Rogers (1984)?

4. Who recorded the data for this study?

5. How were the drivers to respond if the passengers questioned the driver about the dashboard sticker or refused to buckle-up?

6. What was the mean daily percentage of passengers wearing safety belts during the initial baseline period? during the first intervention phase? During the withdrawal phase? During the second intervention phase?

7. To what does the 7.8 which appears in parentheses in paragraph 11 refer?

8. How does the effectiveness of the dashboard sticker compare to other methods used to promote safety belt use?

9. According to the authors, what factors lessen the problem that arises from the absence of reliability checks in this study?

10. What is the basis for the authors' suspicion that the effect of dashboard stickers in promoting safety belt use is not solely short-term?

Questions for Discussion

11. Does the introduction provide a clear notion of the research problem, the purpose of the research, and its significance?

12. Does the literature review seem relevant to the research problem?

13. Do the 1,722 passengers observed in this study represent 1,722 different persons or a smaller number of persons who repeatedly rode in these cars?

14. Is the number of passengers observed sufficient? To what population would you generalize the results of this study?

15. What are the advantages of the A-B-A-B designed used by the authors compared to a simple A-B design?

16. Is there enough information on the research instruments and procedures to allow you to replicate this study?

17. Do the research instruments and procedures have adequate reliability and validity?

18. Does the analysis include sufficient statistical information? Are the statistics that are used appropriate?

19. Are the conclusions supported by and do they logically follow from the data that have been presented?

20. Are the findings discussed in terms of their implications and/or practical significance?

Article 32

New Methods for Measuring Homelessness and the Population at Risk: Exploratory Research in Colorado

Franklin J. James

This article applies a new methodology for estimating the scale and characteristics of the homeless population in an analysis of homelessness in Colorado. Also presented is a preliminary, crude attempt to estimate the size and characteristics of the population at risk of homelessness in the state. To implement the methods, more than 900 people were interviewed in April 1988 at soup lines, shelters, health clinics, and places on the streets known to be sleeping sites for homeless people. People were defined as homeless if they reported that they lacked a permanent residence. It is estimated that the point prevalence of homelessness in the state was 2,605 in April 1988 and that about 8,000 different people were homeless at some time during that year. Strikingly, it is estimated that half of these homeless people were drawn from a relatively small group of 21,000 Colorado residents at high (that is, more than 10 percent) chance of being homeless in any given year.

(1)   Inconsistent and unreliable documentation of the nature and extent of homelessness has forestalled needed empirical research on its causes and on strategies for its amelioration. Several social or "structural" factors are likely contributors to the current scale of homelessness, including the following:

♦ tight urban housing markets, especially markets for low-cost rental housing; such markets are the result of cutbacks in federal housing assistance and of private market forces (Apgar, 1990)

♦ changes in federal and state mental health care policies, especially the deinstitutionalization or "noninstitutionalization" programs of the 1970s and 1980s (Dear & Wolch, 1987)

♦ rising national poverty associated with changes in family structure and with the shift to a postindustrial economy; these trends have had an especially deleterious impact on the economic status of women, children, and minorities (Wilson, 1987)

♦ the fraying of social "safety net" programs for the needy (Danziger & Weinberg, 1986).

(2)   All of these factors are plausible, but their importance has yet to be measured or established, in part because of the paucity of statistical or quantitative information on homelessness. At a minimum, empirical assessment of potential social and economic causes of homelessness would require reliable measures of trends and levels of homelessness in several states or

Reprinted with permission from *Social Work Research and Abstracts,* 28 (2): 9-14. Copyright © 1992 by National Association of Social Workers, Inc.

Franklin J. James, PhD, is Professor of Public Policy, Graduate School of Public Affairs, University of Colorado at Denver, 1445 Market Street, Denver, CO 80202.

metropolitan areas. Unfortunately, such data do not exist, even for the nation as a whole. Two high-quality studies have estimated the national scale of homelessness (Burt & Cohen, 1989; U.S. Department of Housing and Urban Development, 1984). They suggest that the number of homeless people may have doubled during the 1980s. However, the methods used in these studies were quite different, effectively precluding such an inference.

(3)   This article presents a new, efficient methodology for estimating the scale and characteristics of the homeless population in a metropolitan area or state. This methodology is applied in an exploratory analysis of homelessness in Colorado and was developed as part of a collaborative effort with the Colorado Coalition for the Homeless and the Denver Department of Social Services (Parvensky, 1988). It is hoped that the Colorado experience may stimulate interest in using the methodology elsewhere. The successful application of the methodology in other states and areas could serve as a basis for generating some of the basic data needed for systematic hypothesis testing.

(4)   This article also makes a preliminary, crude attempt to estimate the size and characteristics of the population at risk for homelessness in Colorado; better documentation of the characteristics of the population at risk could facilitate preventive policies. This article also identifies types of people within the high-risk population who make an especially large contribution to the overall prevalence of homelessness, either because they tend to experience long or chronic spells of it or because they experience repeated or serial episodes of homelessness.

(5)   Evidence from poverty policy illustrates the potential usefulness of such research. Poverty research has documented that approximately half of the overall person-years of poverty suffered in the United States are suffered by the so-called persistently poor, people who are poor for at least eight out of 10 years (Duncan, 1984). However, these persistently poor people account for only about one-tenth of the people who are poor sometime in a decade. These findings suggest that a targeting of antipoverty efforts on the persistently poor could, if successful, have a disproportionate impact on reducing the nation's poverty problem. Targeting the chronically or episodically homeless could have the same benefits for policy regarding homelessness.

(6)   It cannot be assumed that patterns of homelessness in Colorado are representative of patterns

in other states or communities. The research reported here should thus be considered exploratory.

Methodology

(7)   Previous efforts to measure homelessness have frequently focused on the numbers and characteristics of people in emergency shelters. However, shelters are used by only a portion of homeless people. For instance, only 71 percent of Colorado's adult homeless people reported having used a shelter within 30 days of the homeless survey (Governor's Task Force on the Homeless, 1988). When attempted, past efforts to count homeless people on the streets have generally underestimated the size of this population. Studies in Boston, Nashville, and other places have toured urban streets, relying on peoples' appearances to identify them as homeless. However, many homeless people are indistinguishable from people with housing (Roth, Bean, Lust, & Saveanu, 1985). Street surveys have also overlooked possibly substantial numbers of out-of-sight homeless people in covert sleeping places (James, 1988). Very little solid empirical research has attempted to count or estimate numbers of homeless people staying on an emergency basis with friends or family.

(8)   The new research methodology used in this study is designed to provide as comprehensive an estimate of homelessness as possible. The data come from an April 1988 survey of 920 people in Colorado at soup lines (community kitchens), emergency shelters, day shelters, a health clinic for homeless people, the streets, and hidden sleeping places. The methods designed to analyze these data ascertained the numbers and characteristics of homeless soup line users and patterns of soup line use by subgroups of the homeless population. These two sets of information were then combined to generate an estimate of overall homelessness in the state. Research suggests that soup lines and day shelters serve a broader spectrum of homeless people than do emergency shelters (Piliavin & Sosin, 1987; Rossi, Fisher, & Willis, 1986; Roth et al., 1985).

(9)   In the Denver metropolitan area, estimates of numbers and characteristics of soup line users were based on 418 interviews with a probability sample of soup line users. Estimates of soup line use by street people were based on 73 interviews. Sixty-eight people were interviewed after 9:30 p.m. at a sample of locations known by search-and-rescue personnel of the Salvation Army to be sleeping sites for homeless people. An additional five people spending the night on the streets were surveyed at day shelters and clinics for the homeless. Soup line use by shelter residents was

estimated on the basis of a probability sample of 136 interviews (92 in residential shelters and 44 at the day shelters or health clinic mentioned above). (Details of the field research are presented in Appendix A in James, 1988.)

(10)   Based on these interviews, it was estimated that 64 percent of metropolitan area street people and 40 percent of metropolitan area shelter residents used soup lines in an average 24-hour period in April 1988. Numbers of homeless soup line users on the streets and in shelters were factored into estimates of the overall homeless population in these groups by multiplying numbers of homeless soup line users from the two groups by the following ratio:

$$\frac{\text{homeless soup line users} + \text{homeless nonusers}}{\text{homeless soup line users}}$$

This is the inverse of the proportion of homeless people who use soup lines.

(11)   Outside the metropolitan area, no attempt was made to interview homeless people on the streets because of insufficient knowledge about where to find them. Research outside the metropolitan area focused on homeless people in emergency shelters and other homeless people who used soup lines.

(12)   Only adults were interviewed in these surveys. Estimates of numbers of homeless children were based on the reports of homeless parents. An important homeless group that was not adequately counted comprised runaway or "thrownaway" youths (young people rejected by parents or guardians). Such young people frequently avoid soup lines and emergency shelters for homeless people because of the fear of sexual or physical abuse by older homeless males (Don Krasniewski, Colorado Coalition for the Homeless, personal communication, April 1990; Price, 1987) and because shelters are frequently required by law to report youths living without parents to the police (Committee on Health Care for Homeless People, 1988).

Defining Homelessness

(13)   The definition of homelessness differs — sometimes significantly — among studies. The Stewart B. McKinney Act (1987) provides the following definition of homeless person for purposes of federal policy:

(1) An individual who lacks a fixed, regular, and adequate nighttime residence; and (2) an individual who

has a primary nighttime residence that is (a) a supervised publicly or privately operated shelter designed to provide temporary living accommodations (including welfare hotels, congregate shelters, and transitional housing for the mentally ill), (b) an institution that provides a temporary residence for individuals intended to be institutionalized, or (c) a public or private place not designated for, or ordinarily used as, a regular sleeping accommodation for human beings.

(14)   In line with this basic definition, the Colorado research counted people and families as homeless if they reported that they did not have a permanent residence — a simplified version of criterion 1 of the McKinney definition — at the time of the survey. Survey procedures provided comprehensive estimates of numbers of people living in emergency shelters for homeless people [criterion 2(a)] or on the streets, in cars, or in abandoned buildings [criterion 2(c)]. Other people lacking a permanent address were also counted as homeless if they were using soup lines. These included people staying with friends or family and in hotels, detoxification facilities, hospitals, or jails.

Prevalence of Homelessness in Colorado

(15)   Table 1 presents the best available quantitative estimates of numbers of homeless people in Colorado on an average day in April 1988. The figures indicate that there were an average of 1,815 homeless people each day in the Denver metropolitan area, including 1,550 adults and 265 children under 18. Another 790 homeless people — 710 adults and 80 children — were estimated for the rest of the state. As was pointed out above, these estimates for the rest of the state include only residents of emergency shelters and homeless soup line users and are thus conservative. Overall, the survey resulted in estimates that there were 2,605 homeless people — 2,260 adults and 345 children — in the state on an average day in April 1988.

(16)   To assess the accuracy of the estimation procedures in Denver, a census was taken of emergency shelters and transitional housing in the metropolitan area. Shelter operators were asked the number of people sheltered on April 6 and on April 27, 1988. This count averaged 1,316 people on the two dates (James, 1988). The estimate in Table 1 is 1,225, clearly very close.

(17)   The two estimates are closer than they appear; a small number of shelter users have permanent residences elsewhere and are not included in the counts of homeless people reported here. In 1984, the U.S. Department of Housing and Urban Development estimated

Table 1. Number of Homeless People in Colorado

Area	Where Spent the Night			Total
	Shelters	Streets	Other[a]	
Denver metropolitan area[b]				
Adults 18 or older	1,000	390	160	1,550
Children	225	20	20	265
Total	1,225	410	180	1,815
Rest of State[c]				
Adults 18 or older	500	210		710
Children	30	50		80
Total	530	260		790
Colorado, total				
Adults 18 or older	1,500	760		2,260
Children	255	90		345
Total	1,755	850		2,605

Source: Graduate School of Public Affairs Analysis of Colorado Homeless Survey, April 1988.

[a]People without a permanent residence are included who use soup lines, who are staying with friends or family and in hotels and detoxification programs, or who have just been released from jail.

[b]The Denver metropolitan area comprises Denver, Adams, Arapahoe, and Jefferson counties.

[c]Outside the metropolitan area, no attempt was made to estimate numbers of homeless people on the streets who were not soup line users. As a result, figures outside the metropolitan area understate the overall number of homeless people.

the point prevalence of homelessness in the metropolitan area to be 2,500 as of 1983, close to the new estimate.

(18)   More recent research indicates that the rate of homelessness in Colorado is considerably lower than in the United States as a whole. The most recent high-quality estimates of national homelessness indicate a 1987 national rate of 21 homeless people per 10,000 population (Burt & Cohen, 1989). Applying the national rate implies an expected homeless population in Colorado of 6,930 more than twice the actual rate. The estimated size of Colorado's homeless population is plausible; contrary to patterns elsewhere in the nation, housing markets in most areas of the state are very soft because of pervasive weakness in the state economy. Rental vacancy rates in the Denver metropolitan area are estimated to have exceeded 10 percent at the time of the survey. Rents and housing values have been stable or declining in many parts of the state for several years (Governor's Task Force on the Homeless, 1988).

(19)   Far more than 2,605 people are homeless in Colorado at some time in a year. The annual prevalence

of homelessness is the number of separate individuals homeless at any time during a year. Some types of service needs are linked more strongly to annual prevalence than to point prevalence, including preventive or curative policies such as employment and training or education services and transitional or permanent housing for homeless people. In contrast, the need for emergency services is more closely linked to point prevalence.

(20)   The annual prevalence of homelessness can be estimated as the sum of the numbers of people homeless at the start of the year plus new cases that emerge during the year. At the time of the survey, 18 percent of respondents had become homeless in the previous month. On the assumption that this rate of monthly incidence is constant over the year and that the April count of homeless people also remains fairly constant over the year, then the annual prevalence of homelessness would be around 8,000, or about 3.2 times the point prevalence of homelessness. Analysis in Chicago has estimated lower multipliers — between 1.8 and 2.7 — apparently because of the great prevalence of long-term homelessness in that city (Rossi et al., 1986).

People at Risk for Homelessness

(21) People who are homeless during a particular day or year are the tip of an iceberg of the larger problem of people with unstable and inadequate housing or living arrangements. For each person who actually experiences homelessness, there are several people who are at high risk for homelessness.

(22) The most appropriate research strategy for identifying the population at risk (and the extent and causes of their risk) is through surveys of incidence of homelessness within the overall population, including the housed as well as the homeless population. The author proposed that the U.S. Department of Housing and Urban Development incorporate such information into the American Housing Survey or some other major national data sources. Questions to accomplish this purpose were field tested in the 1991 metropolitan area survey of approximately 5,000 households, with the intent of adding effective questions to the 1992 national survey of approximately 38,000 households.

(23) Crude evidence from the Colorado survey implies that a small pool of people at high risk accounts for a substantial portion of the overall homelessness problem in the state. The pool of people at risk for homelessness may be roughly estimated from numbers of currently homeless people.

(24) In mathematical terms, the population of homeless people was weighted by the numeric value

$$[(Age-16)/Spells] \times [12/(Length \times 2)],$$

where *spells* is the overall number of spells of homelessness reported by the respondent; *age* is the reported age of respondent; and *length* is the number of months the person reported having been homeless in the current spell. This weighting procedure involves a number of assumptions:

♦ all reported spells occurred during adult years

♦ on average, respondents were contacted halfway through their current spell

♦ the length of the current spells indicates the likely future lengths of spells

♦ the overall risk of homelessness will remain constant at 1988 levels.

(25) For example, if a homeless respondent reported two spells of homelessness per decade of adult life and if the expected overall length of his or her spells of homelessness was estimated to be six months, it seems reasonable to assume the person was representative of a pool of 10 people facing similar risk. Because the probability the person would experience homelessness in a given year was 20 percent (two spells per decade), it would require a pool of five such people to produce an average of one such homeless person a year. Because the expected length of the person's spell of homelessness is six months, it would take an average of two such homeless people each year to yield one person-year of homelessness. The overall pool of such people at risk would thus be five times two, or 10.

(26) Table 2 uses this methodology to estimate the overall pool of people in Colorado who face a high — more than 10 percent per year — risk of homelessness. A person or family with a 10 percent chance of homelessness in any given year would have a 65 percent chance of homelessness in a 10-year period. This assumes that the probability of homelessness in any given period can be modeled as a simple binomial process. However, homelessness may have a malignant effect on a person in that each experience with homelessness may magnify a person's future probability of homelessness (Jahiel, 1987).

(27) As can be seen, this pool is estimated to be 21,000, or about 0.6 percent of the overall state population. Table 2 also provides an estimate of the pool of people who face lower but still significant risks of

Table 2. People at Risk for Homelessness in Colorado in 1988, by Level of Risk

People at Risk	Lower Risk[a]	High Risk[b]	Total State Population[c]
Adults	60,000	18,000	2,401,000
Children under 18	4,800	3,200	866,000
Total	64,800	21,200	3,267,000

Source: Graduate School of Public Affairs Anaysis of Colorado Homeless Survey, April 1988.
[a] People with more than 3 percent and less than 10 percent chance of homelessness per year; a 10 percent annual chance of homelessness implies a 65 percent chance of homelessness during a decade.
[b] People with greater than a 10 percent chance of homelessness each year.
[c] Source: U.S. Bureau of the Census. (1987). *Statistical abstract of the United States: 1988.* Washington, DC: U.S. Government Printing Office.

homelessness — between a 3 percent and a 10 percent chance of homelessness in any given year. About 65,000 people, or 2 percent of Colorado's population, are estimated to be in the lower-risk pool.

(28)   Strikingly, the evidence indicates that half (50.3 percent) of the point prevalence of homelessness in Colorado is attributable to the high-risk pool of 21,000 people, and another 42.5 percent is attributable to the lower-risk pool. Thus, over 90 percent of people homeless in Colorado at the time of the survey were drawn from a tiny slice — 2.6 percent — of the state's population. To put this figure in perspective, the 1979 poverty rate in the state was 10.1 percent; at that time, 285,000 people were classified as impoverished (U.S. Bureau of the Census, 1987). The figure today would be higher. Thus, no more than one in three of the state's impoverished population is at significant — more than 3 percent per year — risk of homelessness.

(29)   Until more research is done, the characteristics of homeless people provide the best available evidence on the characteristics of people at risk. Presumably, groups of people who are overrepresented among homeless people will also be overrepresented among people at risk. Adult homeless people are predominantly male (80 percent in Colorado), and most (in Colorado, 68 percent) are in the relatively young age group of 18 to 40. Though most homeless people are non-Hispanic white, black and Hispanic people are substantially overrepresented among homeless people. Living alone without children is also far more common among homeless people than among other adults (James, in press).

(30)   It is also well documented that monthly incomes are extremely low among homeless people. In Colorado, almost one-fourth (23 percent) report no income. The median overall monthly income during the month prior to the survey was under $100. Clearly, homeless people are predominantly low-skilled or unskilled workers at the bottom of the occupational ladder or out of the labor force altogether.

(31)   Finally, evidence from previous studies has shown that the prevalence of mental illness or substance abuse is high among homeless people (Committee on Health Care for Homeless People, 1988). Estimates of the current mental health status of homeless people imply that 25 to 50 percent of homeless adults have a major mental illness such as schizophrenia or affective disorder. Available data suggest that from one-half to three-fourths of homeless people suffer from either major mental illness or substance abuse problems (Committee on Health Care for Homeless People, 1988).

(32)   The overall profile of the population at high risk for homelessness is thus reasonably clear. It disproportionately comprises young men without families, black and Hispanic people, people with poor education and earning potential, and people with substance abuse problems or mental illness. One important qualifier should be raised regarding substance abuse and mental illness: These problems are simultaneously causes and consequences of homelessness. Substance abuse can be a form of self-medication for the pain of homelessness, and affective disorders and certain other mental illnesses can be caused or exacerbated by homelessness.

Chronic and Serial Homelessness

(33)   Within this high-risk population, two groups of homeless people contribute disproportionately to person-days of homelessness and impose disproportionate demands on emergency services such as shelters or soup lines. These are chronically homeless people, who are homeless for long spells, and serially homeless people, who experience repeated spells. Chronic and serial homelessness are related; serial homelessness is especially frequent among chronically homeless people. This may be the result of a number of episodes caused by the same factors. Alternatively, long-term homelessness may have maleficent effects on a person's ability to achieve a stable work or residential situation (Jahiel, 1987). Research has shown that long-term homelessness alters a person's expectations and self-image in ways that are likely to make the homeless situation more tolerable or acceptable (Snow & Anderson, 1987).

(34)   Two studies have systematically assessed the characteristics of homeless people that place them at risk for chronic or serial homelessness. One study examined patterns of homelessness among 331 homeless people in Minneapolis (Piliavin & Sosin, 1987). In this study, the main measure of the period of time a person had been homeless was the cumulative number of years a person reported being homeless during his or her life, aggregated over all spells of homelessness. Compared to other homeless people, the likelihood of chronic homelessness (cumulative homelessness of two years or more) was found to be lower among black people, people with more continuous employment experience, people not living alone, and people without a criminal record.

(35)   Strikingly, this study found that people with alcohol abuse problems or those who had received treatment for the problem were no more likely to be chronically homeless than were other homeless people. People

with a history of hospitalization for mental health problems were more likely to be chronically homeless than were people without a record of institutionalization. Surprisingly, however, people whose first experiences in mental institutions preceded their first spell of homelessness were no more likely to be chronically homeless than were people with no record of institutionalization. Institutionalization boosted the likelihood of chronic homelessness only when it coincided with or followed homelessness. The explanation of this finding is unclear. The study also found that people who had experienced an out-of-home childhood placement were more likely to be chronically homeless (Piliavin & Sosin, 1987).

(36)   The second study examined the factors associated with chronic homelessness and serial homelessness in Colorado (James, in press). In this study, the indicator of chronic homelessness was the number of months since a person last had a permanent residence. The indicator of serial homelessness was the overall lifetime number of spells of homelessness reported by the person.

(37)   The Colorado study found that the characteristics of respondents with the strongest statistical association with the nature of homelessness are substance abuse and mental health problems. On average, people identified as having drug or alcohol problems reported having been homeless for over 10 months longer than were otherwise similar people without such problems. People with mental health problems were estimated to have an average of 0.5 more spells of homelessness than did people not reporting mental illness. There is no significant tendency for people identified as having mental health problems to have longer spells of homelessness. However, people reporting both substance abuse and mental health problems tended to suffer from both high probabilities of serial homelessness and long spells of homelessness (James, in press).

(38)   With respect to race and ethnicity, black people stand out as likely to have both fewer spells of homelessness (compared to other homeless people) and as likely to have shorter spells of homelessness. These findings are similar to those of Piliavin and Sosin (1987). Family status does not appear to be related to length or frequency of spells of homelessness in Colorado. In contrast, the Minneapolis research found families with children to be overrepresented among the short-term homeless (Piliavin & Sosin, 1987).

(39)   Two indicators of the characteristics of a person's support network — community ties and the receipt of public program benefits — showed some significant relationships to homelessness in Colorado. First, people who had lived in their community for a year or more (an indicator of community ties) had expected spells of homelessness that were longer by three months than those of more transient homeless people. This finding is difficult to explain. Second, homeless people receiving social program benefits reported shorter but more frequent spells of homelessness than did homeless people not receiving benefits (James, in press). This finding is not surprising; Colorado offers meager benefits to its needy citizens compared to other states (Shapiro & Greenstein, 1988). As a result, people dependent on public assistance live lives of great insecurity.

(40)   Two additional relationships are of note. First, homeless people who are employed were found to be less likely to be chronically homeless. Their expected spell of homelessness was shorter by six months, other things being equal, compared to homeless people who were not employed. In addition, residence in the Denver metropolitan area (compared to residence elsewhere in the state) was associated with briefer spells of homelessness and fewer repeat spells. Other things being equal, spells of homelessness are shorter by five months for homeless people in the Denver metropolitan area than for people in the rest of the state. The chronic nature of homelessness in Colorado's smaller cities and rural areas suggests that a major homelessness problem may be concealed in such areas elsewhere in the nation (James, in press).

Conclusion

(41)   The new methods applied to estimate the numbers and characteristics of the homeless population show promise. Hopefully, the methods will be applied and prove equally useful in other places.

(42)   It appears that the bulk of Colorado's homeless population is drawn from a very small subset of the state's population that is at significant risk for homelessness. The evidence also shows that a disproportionate amount of the state's homelessness problem is the result of chronic or serial homelessness among an even smaller group of homeless people. The small size of the at-risk group implies considerable promise for efforts to target preventive services, if such services are targeted accurately.

References

Apgar, W C., Jr. (1990). Rental housing in the United States: A focus on metropolitan and urban areas. In M. Kaplan & F. James (Eds.), *The future of national urban policy* (pp. 101-130). Durham, NC: Duke University Press.

Burt, M.R., & Cohen, B.F. (1989). *America's homeless: Numbers, characteristics, and programs that serve them.* Washington, DC: Urban Institute Press.

Committee on Health Care for Homeless People. (1988). *People, homelessness, health and human needs.* Washington, DC: National Academy Press.

Danziger, S.H., & Weinberg, D.H. (1986). *Fighting poverty: What works and what doesn't.* Cambridge, MA: Harvard University Press.

Dear, M., & Wolch, J. (1987). *Landscapes of despair: From deinstitutionalization to homelessness.* Princeton, NJ: Princeton University Press.

Duncan, G.J. (1984). *Years of poverty/years of plenty.* Ann Arbor: University of Michigan Survey Research Center.

Governor's Task Force on the Homeless. (1988). *Report of the governor's task force on the homeless.* Denver: State of Colorado.

Jahiel, R. (1987). Homeless women and children. In R. Bingham, R. Green, & S. White (Eds.), *The homeless in contemporary society* (pp. 99-118). Boston: Boston Foundation.

James, F.J. (1988). *Numbers and characteristics of the homeless: A preliminary application in Colorado of a new methodology.* Denver: University of Colorado Graduate School of Public Affairs.

James, F.J. (in press). *Factors which shape the risks of homelessness: Preliminary observations from Colorado.* Denver: University of Colorado Graduate School of Public Affairs.

Parvensky, J. (1988). *In search of a place to call home: A profile of homelessness in Colorado.* Denver: Colorado Coalition for the Homeless.

Piliavin, I., & Sosin, M. (1987). Tracking the homeless. *Focus, 10*(4), 20-24.

Price, V. (1987). Runaways and homeless street youth. In *Homelessness: Critical issues for policy and practice* (pp. 24-28). Boston: Boston Foundation.

Rossi, P., Fisher, G., & Willis, G. (1986). *The condition of the homeless in Chicago.* Amherst: University of Massachusetts at Amherst, Social and Demographic Research Institute.

Roth, D., Bean, J., Lust, N., & Saveanu, T. (1985). *Homelessness in Ohio: A study of people in need.* Columbus: Office of Program Evaluation and Research, Ohio Department of Mental Health.

Shapiro, I., & Greenstein, R. (1988). *Holes in the safety net: Colorado.* Washington, DC: Center on Budget and Policy Priorities.

Snow, D., & Anderson, L. (1987). Identity work among the homeless: The verbal construction and avowal of personal identities. *American Journal of Sociology, 92*, 1336-1371.

Stewart B. McKinney Homeless Assistance Act. (1987). 101 Stat. 482.

U.S. Bureau of the Census. (1987). *Statistical Abstract of the United States: 1988.* Washington, DC: U.S. Government Printing Office.

U.S. Department of Housing and Urban Development. (1984). *A report to the secretary on the homeless and emergency shelters.* Washington, DC: U.S. Government Printing Office.

Wilson, W.J. (1987). *The truly disadvantaged: The inner city, the underclass, and public policy.* Chicago: University of Chicago Press.

Accepted January 11, 1991

Factual Questions

1. The 1989 study by Burt and Cohen reported more people homeless in the U.S. than the 1984 study of homelessness by the U.S. Department of Housing and Urban Development. Why does the author hesitate to conclude that homelessness in the U.S. increased during the late 1980s?

2. What reason does the author give for treating this research as exploratory in nature?

3. How many soup line users were interviewed? Estimates of soup line use by street people were based

on how many interviews? Estimates of soup line use by shelter residents were based on how many interviews?

4. The author mentions two different groups of homeless that were not well counted in this study. Which groups were they and why were they not adequately counted?

5. How many homeless individuals were estimated to be in the state of Colorado on an average day in April 1988?

6. What is the difference between point prevalence and annual prevalence?

7. Using the formula in paragraph 24, one currently homeless person who is 36 years old, experiencing her second spell of homelessness, and has now been homeless for three months represents how large a pool of persons at-risk of being homeless?

8. Describe the overall profile of the population at high risk for homelessness.

9. What is the difference between chronic homelessness and serial homelessness?

10. In the author's study of chronic and serial homelessness in Colorado, how were chronic and serial homelessness measured?

Questions for Discussion

11. Does the introduction provide a clear notion of the research problem, the purpose of the research, and its significance?

12. Does the literature review seem relevant to the research problem?

13. Is the number of research subjects sufficient? To what population would you generalize the results of this study?

14. Is there enough information on the research instruments and procedures to allow you to replicate this study?

study (in press) found alcohol abuse strongly related to chronic homelessness. How is it possible for two studies to arrive at such different conclusions?

15. Do the research instruments and procedures have adequate reliability and validity?

20. Are the findings discussed in terms of their implications and/or practical significance?

16. Does the analysis include sufficient statistical information? Are the statistics that are used appropriate?

17. For this study, 627 homeless persons were interviewed in the Denver metropolitan area. Yet Table 1 reports an estimate of 1,815 homeless persons in the Denver metropolitan area. How was that estimate made?

18. Why can we not say with certainty that drug abuse and mental illness are causes of homelessness?

19. Two studies of chronic and serial homelessness are compared toward the end of this article. The study by Piliavin and Sosin (1987) found alcohol abuse unrelated to chronic homelessness while the James

Article 33

Emptying the Nest and Parental Well-Being: An Analysis of National Panel Data

Lynn White
University of Nebraska–Lincoln

John N. Edwards
Virginia Polytechnic University

Panel data from a national random sample are used to investigate the effects of children leaving home on parental well-being. The "empty nest" is associated with significant improvements in marital happiness for all parents, regardless of parent's or children's characteristics. Overall life satisfaction improves significantly only under two conditions: when there is frequent contact with nonresident children or when there were young teens in the 1983 household. For both measures of parental well-being, the positive effects of the empty nest appear to be strongest immediately after the children leave. These findings, coupled with the high levels of post-launching contact, suggest that while parents experience a modest post-launch honeymoon, the parental role remains important to parental well-being.

(1)   The effect of the child-leaving phase of the family life cycle on parental well-being has been the topic of much discussion and several influential studies, but empirical findings are sketchy. Most studies rely on cross-sectional data, and only two studies examine the change in parental well-being associated with launching. We follow a national sample of 402 parents of older children over a four-year period and compare changes in marital happiness and life satisfaction between those who did and did not empty their nest. We

Reprinted with permission from *American Sociological Review*, 55(2): 235-242. Copyright © 1990 by American Sociological Association.

This study was supported in part by Grant No. 5 RO1 AG4146 from the National Institute on Aging. The contributions of co-investigators Alan Booth and David R. Johnson are gratefully acknowledged. The paper also benefitted from the helpful comments of anonymous ASR reviewers.

Lynn White is Professor of Sociology at the University of Nebraska–Lincoln. Her research focuses on the family over the life course.

John N. Edwards is Professor of Sociology at Virginia Polytechnic Institute and State University. The present report represents one in a series of papers dealing with marriage over the life course derived from a national longitudinal survey of married women and men. He is also currently involved in a study in Bangkok, Thailand, of the effects of household crowding on family relations.

also examine whether the effects of the empty nest depend upon the stressfulness of the parental role or amount of post-launch contact.

Previous Work

Theoretical Perspectives

(2)   Three theoretical perspectives offer hypotheses about the effects of the empty nest: role identity theories, role change theories, and role conflict theories.

(3)   Role identity theories derive from the structural school of symbolic interaction. Thoits (1983, p. 183) argues, for example, that "Social identities provide actors with existential meaning and behavioral guidance, and that these qualities are essential to psychological well-being and organized, functional behavior." According to this perspective, the more roles one has, the better off one is. This perspective predicts that role loss will have negative effects on psychological functioning, suggesting that child-leaving will be associated with decreases in parental well-being. This prediction rests on the questionable premise that launching one's children means exiting the parental role. Generally, scholars working in this tradition reject this premise: respondents are counted as occupying a parental role if they have ever had children (cf. Thoits 1983).

(4)   The role change perspective is associated with the work of Holmes and Rahe (1967). Their work, which is the basis of a long research tradition, suggests that any role change (whether addition or deletion) will have negative effects on psychological and physical well-being. This perspective also predicts a negative effect of emptying the nest. Because the negative effect of role change may be short-lived, it may not be observed in a four-year panel.

(5)   Finally, a general perspective that we call role stress argues that the effect of change depends on the degree of conflict and stress associated with the role (Barnett and Baruch 1985). If there is role strain or role conflict, loss of the role may be beneficial. Because several studies find that parenthood is a stressful role (McLanahan and Adams 1987), this perspective suggests that the empty nest should lead to improvements in parental well-being.

(6)   The sociological literature on launching has generally used some form of role identity or role stress theory. The "empty nest syndrome" of early work is clearly a form of role identity theory: loss of a major role brings alienation, dissatisfaction, and loneliness (Phillips 1957). On the other hand, more recent commentators seem to assume that parenthood is a stressful role, and that its loss should bring relief (Glenn 1975; Miller and Myers-Walls 1983).

Empirical Findings

(7)   Although two early clinical studies (Curlee 1969; Bart 1972) report depression following the empty-nest period, most cross-sectional studies of the general population reveal modest positive outcomes (Rollins and Feldman 1970; Deutscher 1973; Glenn 1975; Harkins 1978; Campbell 1981).

(8)   Several studies use the family life cycle approach of grouping a cross-sectional sample into four or five categories that correspond roughly to stages of family development. Most of these studies report a U-shaped pattern in which marital happiness is highest during the honeymoon stage, lowest when the children are schoolage or teens, and higher when the children are older or gone (Rollins and Feldman 1970; Rollins and Cannon 1974; Anderson, Russell, and Schumm 1983). The effect is rather small, however, and sometimes absent (Spanier, Lewis, Cole 1975).

(9)   Studies by Glenn (1975) and Glenn and McLanahan (1982), using national cross-sectional data, show that families with children in the home are generally worse off in terms of global and marital satisfaction than families without children. In support of the argument that parenthood is a generally stressful role, Glenn and McLanahan found no group for whom presence of children was positively correlated with marital satisfaction.

(10)   These cross-sectional studies have several drawbacks. In addition to the possibility that the observed relationships are cohort effects (empty-nest parents come from earlier cohorts than parents currently with children in the home), selection biases are possible (Spanier et al. 1975; Schram 1979). A selection effect for presence of children and lower happiness could occur in two ways. First, children slow the divorce process suggesting an overrepresentation of unsatisfactory marriages among families with children in the home (White, Booth, and Edwards 1986). Second, the evidence that children are an important source of satisfaction to people in poor marriages (Luckey and Bain 1970: Lauer and Lauer 1986) suggests that people in poor marriages may hang on to their children longer. In addition to these general problems of cross-sectional research, the Glenn (1975) and Glenn and McLanahan (1982) studies are hampered by inexact comparisons:

Because their data sets only measured presence of children under 18, they were forced to include childless families and families with resident adult children in the post-launch category.

(11)   Two studies examine *change* in parental well-being associated with emptying the nest. Both report generally positive effects of completing the launching process. Menaghan (1983), in a sample of 639 Chicagoans interviewed in 1972 and 1976, reports the effects of the empty nest on two measures — an index of marital affection-fulfillment and an index of perceived equity. Comparing 34 respondents whose youngest (last?) child had left home with respondents who were already empty nesters or who still had children in the home, Menaghan concludes that launching the youngest child results in significant improvement in perceived equity but not in affection-fulfillment. Using a larger sample from the Panel Study of Income Dynamics, McLanahan and Sorensen (1985) investigate whether child-leaving changes self-satisfaction (Are you satisfied or dissatisfied with yourself?) between 1968 and 1972. They find that on-time departures (i.e.,when parents were over 40) are associated with significant increases in women's self-satisfaction but not men's. Off-time departures (i.e.. before the parent reached 40) are associated with decreased self-satisfaction for fathers. Because they used the departure of any child rather than the completion of the launching process as their independent variable, McLanahan and Sorensen may have underestimated the effect of emptying the nest on parental well-being.

(12)   These two panel studies are milestones in the assessment of the launching process. They provide the first evidence that change in parental status is associated with positive change in parental well-being. Because neither study was designed to tap changes in parental well-being, however, both use dependent variables that relate only indirectly to previous research.

The Issues

(13)   We examine the effects of entering and completing the launching process on two indicators of parental well-being: marital happiness and life satisfaction. We test the hypothesis that launching will have a positive effect on parental well-being and that this effect will be stronger for parents who experience the most stress from parenting.

(14)   Previous studies suggest that mothers find parenting more stressful than fathers (McLanahan and Adams 1987), that parents argue more with sons than daughters (Suitor and Pillemer 1988), and that stepchildren cause more family tension than biological children (White and Booth 1985). In addition, we hypothesize that parenting will be more stressful when parents hold nontraditional gender roles or are highly educated. The latter variables have been shown by Goldscheider and Goldscheider (1988) to predict early departure of children from the parental home. Mother's employment and number of children in the household are also included as indicators of parental stress. We test to see whether the effects of launching on parental well-being are modified by these indicators of parental stress. We also include age of youngest child, which acts as a proxy for recency of emptying the nest as well as tapping amount of active parenting required by resident children.

(15)   Finally, we test whether the effect of launching depends upon contact with nonresident children. If contact and obligations continue to be high, launching may have little effect on parental well-being.

Study Design

Sample

(16)   This research is based on a national sample interviewed in 1980 and again in 1983 and 1988. In 1980, telephone interviews were conducted with a random sample of 2,033 married individuals under the age of 55. In 1983, reinterviews were completed with 1,592 individuals of whom 1,331 were interviewed a third time in 1988. Careful analysis shows that the 1983 and 1988 panels are largely representative of the nation's married couples.[1] Because information on relationships with nonresident children is available only for the 1988 wave, this study is based on a comparison of the 1983-1988 panel. Analysis is restricted to the 402 respondents who met the following criteria: 1) interviewed in 1983 and 1988; 2) marriage intact between

---

[1] In 1980, sample households were chosen using random digit dialing procedures. A second random procedure was used to select the respondent. Only married individuals under 55 were included in the sample. Interviews were completed with 65 percent of those estimated to be eligible; among households where an eligible respondent was contacted, the completion rate was 76 percent. The 1980 sample was comparable to national distributions of married individuals under 55 on age, race, household size, tenure, and region. Analysis of panel attrition over the following two waves demonstrates that the sample remains representative of our target population, although men, renters, and those with low education were more likely to drop out of the sample. Probit analysis demonstrates that the probability of dropping out of the sample is unrelated to marital happiness scores on the prior interview. We feel confident that, with appropriate controls for background factors, the panel remains an effective tool for evaluating factors associated with change in marital quality.

1983 and 1988; and 3) had at least one child 14 or older in the home in 1983.

Dependent Variables

(17)   To maximize comparability with previous literature, we use marital happiness and life satisfaction as dependent variables. Marital happiness is measured by an 11-item summed scale with an alpha reliability of .87.[2] The mean for this scale, which has a possible range of 11 to 33, was 29.2 in 1983 with a standard deviation of 4.0. Life satisfaction is measured by the standard single-item indicator: "Taking everything together, how would you say you are these days? Would you say you are very happy (=3), pretty happy (=2). or not too happy? (=1)." In 1983, the mean on this variable was 2.3 and the standard deviation was .56. This item has been used in previous research (e.g., Glenn 1975).

Independent Variables

(18)   To distinguish between entering and completing the launching process, we use two measures. EMPTY NEST is coded 1 if the respondent reports no children in the household in 1988 and 0 if there are children in the household in 1988. (All of the respondents had at least one child 14 or older in the household in 1983.) Using this definition, 123 of the 402 respondents (31 percent) launched all of their children by 1988. Nearly three-fourths (194) of those coded 0 on the empty nest variable entered the launching process and have at least one nonresident child in addition to the children still in the household. The dummy variable PARTIAL LAUNCH identifies these parents who have started but not completed the launching process. A comparison of the effects of these two variables tells us more precisely what stage of the launching process affects parental well-being.

Background Variables

(19)   Gender-role traditionalism is measured by a 7-item Likert-type scale asking about normative behavior for men and women. The scale has an alpha reliability of .71. Mother's employment is a dummy variable (1 = employed more than 35 hours per week). Presence of stepchildren is coded 1 if there are children of the respondent or his/her spouse in the household who are more than one year older than the current marriage. Boys is a dummy variable scored 1 if any of the children in the household in 1983 were boys.

Findings

(20)   Because the dependent variables are continuous, OLS regression is used. To assess whether changes in well-being are associated with childleaving, we regress the 1988 score for the dependent variable on the 1983 score of the dependent variable and the launching variables. The effective dependent variable is change in well-being, i.e., that part of the 1988 score that is not predicted from the 1983 score. Control variables include respondent's sex, age, education, and gender-role traditionalism, the number of children in the household, whether any of the children were boys, presence of stepchildren, age of youngest child, and mother's employment status.

The Effect of Launching, 1983-1988

(21)   We first ask whether the launching process is associated with significant changes in life satisfaction or marital happiness between 1983 and 1988. The results are presented in columns 1 and 5 of Table 1.

(22)   EMPTY NEST has a significant positive effect on marital happiness, but not on life satisfaction.[3] Column 1 shows that having launched all of one's children is associated with a 1.10-point increase on the marital happiness scale. The positive effect of the empty nest on marital happiness but not on life satisfaction coincides with Glenn's (1975) finding that the correlation of empty nest with marital happiness is stronger than with life satisfaction.

(23)   PARTIAL LAUNCH has no effect on either life satisfaction or marital happiness. A comparison of the results for the two independent variables suggests that total absence of children rather than simply older children or fewer children is necessary before the launching process improves marital happiness.

---

[2] The scale includes seven items asking about happiness with specific aspects of marriage (understanding, love, agreement, sexual relationship, taking care of things around the house, companionship, and faithfulness) and four global satisfaction items (overall happiness of marriage, rating of own marriage compared to others, strength of love for spouse, and whether the marriage is getting better or worse).

[3] Because of inconsistencies in data availability across the three waves, the full analysis cannot be replicated for the other panel components. A replication of the analysis in columns 1 and 5 of Table 1 for the 1980-1988 panel, however, produces very similar results. Using 517 individuals with children 10 or older in 1980, the effect of EMPTY NEST on change in marital happiness was significant and positive (b = 1.03, p = .009) and on life satisfaction was insignificant (b = .01, p = .84).

Table 1. OLS Regression Equations Showing the Effect of Child-Leaving on Change in Marital Happiness and Life Satisfaction Between 1983 and 1988 (Unstandardized coefficients; standard errors in parentheses)

| Variable | Marital Happiness, 1988 | | | | Life Satisfaction, 1988 | | | |
| | Total | | Launchers[a] | | Total | | Launchers[a] | |
	(1)	(2)	(3)	(4)	(5)	(6)	(7)	(8)
PARTIAL LAUNCH	.06	-.06	----	----	-.03	-.05	----	----
	(.45)	(.45)	----	----	(.07)	(.07)	----	----
EMPTY NEST	1.10*	3.83*	1.21*	2.83	.04	.40	.05	.06
	(.53)	(1.48)	(.42)	(1.99)	(.09)	(.24)	(.07)	(.32)
EMPTY NEST × age youngest		-.16*		-.15		-.02		-.03*
		(.08)		(.09)		(.01)		(.01)
EMPTY NEST × CONTACT[a]		----		1.02		----		.52*
		----		(1.48)		----		(.24)
Control Variables, 1983								
Marital happiness	.77**	.77**	.74**	.74**	----	----	----	----
	(.04)	(.04)	(.05)	(.05)	----	----	----	----
Life satisfaction	----	----	----	----	.39**	.39**	.41**	.42**
	----	----	----	----	(.05)	(.05)	(.06)	(.05)
Sex	.40	.40	.19	.22	-.12*	-.12*	-.13*	-.12
	(.35)	(.34)	(.39)	(.39)	(.06)	(.06)	(.06)	(.06)
Education	-.03	-.02	-.05	-.04	.02*	.03*	.02	.02*
	(.07)	(.07)	(.07)	(.07)	(.01)	(.01)	(.01)	(.01)
Age	.01	.02	.01	.02	-.01	-.01	-.01	-.01
	(.03)	(.03)	(.04)	(.04)	(.01)	(.01)	(.01)	(.01)
Gender role traditionalism	-.09	-.10	-.07	-.08	-.00	-.00	-.00	-.00
	(.07)	(.07)	(.08)	(.08)	(.01)	(.01)	(.01)	(.01)
Boys	.12	.04	-.24	-.34	.07	.06	.05	.03
	(.38)	(.39)	(.42)	(.42)	(.06)	(.06)	(.07)	(.07)
Age of youngest child	.00	.05	-.02	.03	.01	.02*	.02	.03**
	(.05)	(.05)	(.05)	(.06)	(.01)	(.01)	(.04)	(.01)
Number of children in household	.30	.39	.27	.34	.03	.04	.02	.04
	(.21)	(.21)	(.23)	(.23)	(.03)	(.03)	(.04)	(.04)
Mother's employment	.36	.34	.10	.09	-.02	-.02	-.08	-.08
	(.35)	(.35)	(.38)	(.38)	(.06)	(.06)	(.06)	(.06)
Presence of stepchildren	-.51	-.36	.05	.24	-.04	-.02	-.04	-.02
	(.54)	(.55)	(.58)	(.59)	(.09)	(.09)	(.09)	(.09)
CONTACT with nonresident children, 1988[b]	----	----	-.57	-.81	----	----	.08	-.02
	----	----	(.56)	(.62)	----	----	(.09)	(.10)
Intercept	6.01	5.26	8.02	7.34	1.32	1.22	1.39	1.28
R²	.50	.50	.48	.50	.17	.17	.21	.21
N	402		317		402		317	

*p < .05   **p < .01

[a] Includes empty nest parents and partial launch parents. PARTIAL LAUNCH variable is not defined for this group.

[b] CONTACT is defined only for respondents with nonresident children.

Interaction Effects: Parental Stress Indicators

(24)   Next we examine whether the effects of the empty nest are general across all parents or whether they depend on extent of parental strain. In the case of life satisfaction, we ask whether more highly stressed parents experience improvement following launch. We hypothesized that stress would be greater under the following conditions: respondent was female, more highly educated, or reported nontraditional gender roles, the number of children was larger, any of the children were boys or stepchildren, mother was employed, or age of youngest child was low. All stress indicators were drawn from the 1983 data. The tests involved adding a multiplicative term (e.g., EMPTY NEST x gender-role traditionalism) to the equations in columns 1 and 5. Because EMPTY NEST rather than PARTIAL LAUNCH appears to be the relevant variable, the interactions were restricted to the EMPTY NEST variable.

(25)   Only one of the 16 tests of interaction was significant: the lower the age of youngest child, the greater the improvement in marital happiness following the empty nest (columns 2 and 6). For life satisfaction, the term was also negative, but not significant (p =.09). The equation predicts an improvement on the marital happiness scale of 1.59 points for an empty nest respondent whose youngest child in 1983 was 14, compared to a decrease in marital satisfaction for respondents whose youngest resident child in 1983 was 24 or older. (The contingent intercepts are 6.0 and 6.4 respectively.)

(26)   Although one of 16 tests would be significant by chance alone, we are inclined to interpret this result substantively. The greater relief from the exit of younger children may stem from the greater demands that teenage children place on parents compared to young adults. Age of youngest child also stands as a rough proxy for recency of the empty nest stage: everything else equal, the younger the youngest child, the more recently the empty nest is likely to have occurred. Viewed in this light, the positive impact of recency effectively repudiates role change theory, which predicts a strong deleterious effect when the change is recent. Instead, these results suggest the possibility of a modest post-launch honeymoon stage.

(27)   Overall, this examination of possible interaction effects suggests that the empty nest is associated with significant improvements in marital happiness for nearly all parents, but is not associated with significant changes in life satisfaction. This finding supports the most general form of the stressful role hypothesis. The general absence of interaction effects for the marital happiness finding suggests that even the best of children of the most conventional parents tend to be a source of strain in the marital relationship. The one interaction effect, between EMPTY NEST and age of youngest child on marital happiness, however, suggests that this barrier is stronger when the children are teenagers rather than young adults.

Post-Launch Relationships

(28)   One plausible reason for the relatively small effect of emptying the nest found in this and previous studies is that children continue to be very much a part of their parents' lives after they leave home. Among respondents with nonresident children, 88 percent reported that they had seen or talked to one of their nonresident children in the three days prior to the interview and 80 percent had seen or talked to a child the previous day. Out of the house is rarely out of sight, much less out of mind.

(29)   The 1988 data set includes two measures of post-launch relationships. One is a Likert-type measure that asks, "Do obligations to (child/children) not living with you take a lot of your time and energy, quite a bit, a little, or hardly any?" The second is a summary of questions asking, for each child living away from home, "How many days has it been since you have seen or talked to (child)?" CONTACT is a dummy variable indicating whether the respondent has seen or talked to a nonresident child in the last three days. The measures of post-launch contact are available only for the 317 respondents who have some or all of their children living away from home.

(30)   Only a few parents (4 percent) reported that their nonresident children required a lot of time and energy. This variable had no main or joint effects on either measure of parental well-being, nor did it reduce the coefficients for EMPTY NEST (results not shown). Regardless of how much or how little trouble nonresident children are, the empty nest is associated with an increase in marital happiness and unrelated to change in life satisfaction.

(31)   Contact with children had no main or joint effects on marital happiness (columns 3 and 4), indicating that no matter how often the children dropped by or called, their nonresidence status improved marital happiness. There was, however, a significant joint effect of CONTACT and EMPTY NEST on life satisfaction (column 8). Among parents with nonresident children, the multiplicative term for age of youngest child and EMPTY NEST was also significant for life satisfaction.

(32)   The empty nest has a positive effect on life satisfaction (b = .52) when there is contact with nonresident children, but a negative effect (b = -.40) when there has not been recent contact.[4] Among parents with nonresident children (before as well as after the addition of the interaction term for CONTACT), there is a significant interaction for age of youngest child similar to that for marital happiness: the lower the age of the youngest child, the greater the improvement in life satisfaction following the empty nest. When the youngest child in 1983 was 14, the empty nest entailed a .10-point increase in life satisfaction; when the youngest child in 1983 was older than 18, the effect of empty nest was actually negative. Again, a plausible explanation is that the positive impact of the empty nest is strongest in the period immediately after the children leave.

(33)   Although the positive conditional effect of contact contradicts our initial expectations, the strength of parental attachment and identification with children makes it understandable that the positive effects of emptying the nest depend on not being estranged from one's children. The finding of a positive, conditional effect of contact with children supports the view that parenthood is an important, identity-affirming role. Although actually living with one's teen-age children may pose obstacles to the marital relationship, it appears that life satisfaction depends on continued affirmation of the parental role.

Discussion and Conclusion

(34)   This study adds to the literature on the family life cycle by using a relatively large national panel to assess changes in marital happiness and life satisfaction associated with children leaving home.

(35)   Emptying the nest is associated with significant improvements in *marital happiness,* regardless of parent's or children's characteristics. The effect however, is significantly stronger when there had been young teens in the household. Having entered the launching stage (having launched some children, but not all) does not affect marital happiness.

(36)   Emptying the nest has no main effect on changes in *life satisfaction*. Analysis of parents who have launched some or all of their children shows that the empty nest is associated with improvements in life

satisfaction under two conditions: when there is frequent contact with the nonresident children or there were young teens in the household in 1983.

(37)   These findings directly contradict predictions from role change theory. Assuming that age of youngest child in the household in 1983 stands as a rough proxy for recency of launch, these findings suggest that the empty nest produces greater improvement in marital happiness and life satisfaction immediately after the children leave.

(38)   The generally positive effects of the empty nest on parental well-being support the hypothesis that parenting is a stressful role and that parents are relieved to see an end to co-residence. The general absence of interaction effects suggests that the mere presence of children — regardless of number, sex, provenance, parent's gender roles, and other indicators of parental stress — creates a modest obstacle for their parents' marriage. These findings echo and extend the work of Glenn and McLanahan (1982): all parents experience a modest increase in marital happiness following the empty nest.

(39)   Launching teens produces greater improvements in both marital happiness and life satisfaction than the launching of older children. Because none of the other indicators of parental stress modified the effect of the empty nest, we are inclined to interpret this finding as a reflection of timing rather than stress. It suggests that the positive effect of the empty nest is strongest in the period immediately after the children leave home.

(40)   These data also provide support for role identity theory: The empty nest is associated with significantly greater improvement in life satisfaction when the empty nest includes frequent contact between parents and children. Although parents respond positively to the end of co-residence, continuation of the parental role appears to be important to parental well-being. Our data suggest that when the empty nest results in the end of the parental role, indicated by infrequent contact between parent and children, life satisfaction is reduced. For most parents, however, the end of co-residence does not end the parental role. Instead, most of these respondents see or talk to a nonresident child daily.

(41)   The end of co-residence has a generally positive effect on parental well-being, resulting in a modest

---

[4]The coefficient for EMPTY NEST reported in column 8 is the effect of EMPTY NEST when both CONTACT and age of youngest child are zero. In order to evaluate the effect of each interaction term separately, this term was recalculated at the mean for the other variable. For example, when age of youngest child is at its mean value (15.3), then the effect of empty nest without CONTACT is -.40. Similarly, when CONTACT is at its mean (.88), then the effect of the empty nest when age of youngest child is zero is .52.

post-launch honeymoon. A thoughtful examination of parenthood in our society suggests that any more substantial outcome is unlikely. First, 20-25 years of active parenthood leave a mark on dyadic relationships and individual personalities that cannot be eliminated simply because the children are gone. As Lee (1988) notes, the distinct gender roles associated with parenthood have a permanent effect on parents' lives and relationships. Second, the impact of the empty nest is reduced by the close ties and frequent contact between parents and children that suggests that separate residence is a relatively minor act of disengagement. As long as the normative, economic, and psychological links between parents and children continue, it is unrealistic to expect that a simple change of residence will raise the burdens from parental shoulders and enable them to gambol off into a carefree sunset.

References

Anderson, S. A., C. S. Russell, and W. R. Schumm. 1983. "Perceived Marital Quality and Life-Cycle Categories: A Further Analysis." *Journal of Marriage and the Family* 45:127-39.

Barnett, R. C. and G. K. Baruch. 1985. "Women's Involvement in Multiple Roles and Psychological Distress." *Journal of Personality and Social Psychology* 49: 135-45.

Bart, P. B. 1972. "Depression in Middle-Age Women." Pp. 163-68 in *Women in Sexist Society*, edited by V. Gornick and B. K. Moran. New York: The New American Library.

Campbell, A. 1981. *The Sense of Well-Being in America.* New York: McGraw-Hill.

Curlee, J. 1969. "Alcoholism and the Empty-Nest." *Bulletin of the Menninger Clinic* 33:165-71.

Deutscher, I. 1973. "Socialization for Postparental Life." Pp. 510-17 in *Love, Marriage, Family: A Developmental Approach*, edited by M. Lasswell and T. Lasswell. Glenview: Scott, Foresman.

Glenn. N. D. 1975. "Psychological Well-Being in the Post-Parental State: Some Evidence from National Surveys." *Journal of Marriage and the Family* 37:105-10.

Glenn, Norval and Sara McLanahan. 1982. "Children and Marital Happiness: A Further Specification of the Relationship." *Journal of Marriage and the Family"* 44:63-72.

Goldscheider, Frances and Calvin Goldscheider. 1988. "Family Structure and Conflict: Nest-Leaving Expectations of Young Adults and Their Parents." *Journal of Marriage and the Family* 51:87-97.

Harkins, E. 1978. "Effects of Empty Nest Transition on Self-Report of Psychological and Physical Well-Being." *Journal of Marriage and the Family* 40:549-56.

Holmes, J. D. and R. H. Rahe. 1967. "The Social Readjustment Rating Scale." *Journal of the Psychosomatic Research* 11:213-18.

Lauer, Robert and Jeanette Lauer. 1986. "Factors in Long-Term Marriages." *Journal of Marriage and the Family* 7:382-90.

Lee, Gary. 1988. "Marital Satisfaction in Later Life: The Effect of Nonmarital Roles" *Journal of Marriage and the Family* 50:775-83.

Luckey, Eleanore and Joyce Bain. 1970. "Children: A Factor in Marital Satisfaction." *Journal of Marriage and the Family* 32:43-44.

McLanahan, Sara and Julia Adams. 1987. "Parenthood and Psychological Well-Being." *Annual Review of Sociology* 13:237-57.

McLanahan, S. S. and A. B. Sorensen. 1985. "Life Events and Psychological Well-Being Over the Life Course." Pp. 217-38 in *Life Course Dynamics*, edited by G. H. Elder. Ithaca: Cornell University Press.

Menaghan, Elizabeth. 1983. "Marital Stress and Family Transitions: A Panel Analysis." *Journal of Marriage and the Family* 45:371-86.

Miller, Brent and Judith Myers-Walls. 1983. "Parenthood: Stresses and Coping Strategies." Pp. 54-73 in *Stress in the Family, Vol. 1: Coping with Normative Transitions*, edited by H. McCubbin and C. Figley. New York: Brunner/Mazel.

Phillips. B. S. 1957. "A Role Theory Approach to Adjustment in Old Age." *American Sociological Review* 22:212-17.

Rollins, Boyd and Kenneth Cannon. 1974. "Marital Satisfaction Over the Family Life Cycle: A Reevaluation." *Journal of Marriage and the Family* 36:271-83.

Rollins, Boyd and H. Feldman. 1970. "Marital Satisfaction Over the Family Life Cycle." *Journal of Marriage and the Family* 32:20-28.

Schram, R. W. 1979. "Marital Satisfaction Over the Family Life Cycle: A Critique and Proposal." *Journal of Marriage and the Family* 41:7-12.

Spanier, G., R. A. Lewis, and C. L. Cole. 1975. "Marital Adjustment Over the Life Cycle: The Issue of Curvilinearity." *Journal of Marriage and the Family* 37:263-275.

Suitor, Jill and Karl Pillemer. 1988. "Explaining Intergenerational Conflict when Adult Children and Elderly Parents Live Together." *Journal of Marriage and the Family* 50:1037-47.

Thoits, Peggy. 1983. "Multiple Identities and Psychological Well-Being: A Reformulation and Test of the Social Isolation Hypothesis." *American Sociological Review* 48:174-87.

White, Lynn and Alan Booth. 1985. "The Quality and Stability of Remarriages: The Role of Stepchildren." *American Sociological Review* 50:689-98.

White, Lynn, Alan Booth, and John Edwards. 1986. "Children and Marital Happiness: Why the Negative Correlation?" *Journal of Family Issues* 7:131-49.

Factual Questions

1. What three theoretical perspectives offer hypotheses relevant to this study?

2. In what way are the Glenn (1975) and Glenn and McLanahan (1982) studies hampered by inexact comparisons?

3. What types of individuals were more likely to drop out of the sample when individuals were reinterviewed in 1983 and 1988?

4. What criteria did subjects have to meet to be included in the study?

5. What are the dependent variables for the study?

6. The 11 items that compose the marital happiness scale ask about what things?

7. What effect does EMPTY NEST have on the two dependent variables?

8. What effect does PARTIAL LAUNCH have on the two dependent variables?

9. What percentage of respondents with non-resident children reported that they had seen or talked with one of their non-resident children the previous day?

10. How does the extent of parental contact with non-resident children determine the effect of emptying the nest on parental life satisfaction?

Questions for Discussion

11. Does the introduction provide a clear notion of the research problem, the purpose of the research, and its significance?

12. Does the literature review seem relevant to the research problem?

13. Is the number of research subjects sufficient? To what population would you generalize the results of this study?

14. Is there enough information on the research instruments and procedures to allow you to replicate this study?

15. Do the research instruments and procedures have adequate reliability and validity?

16. Does the analysis include sufficient statistical information? Are the statistics that are used appropriate?

17. Why did the authors examine possible interaction effects?

18. Are the conclusions supported by and do they logically follow from the data that have been presented?

19. Why do the authors conclude that the results do not support the role change perspective?

20. Are the findings discussed in terms of their implications and/or practical significance?

Article 34

A Snowball's Chance in Hell: Doing Fieldwork with Active Residential Burglars

Richard Wright
Scott H. Decker
Allison K. Redfern
Dietrich L. Smith

Criminologists long have recognized the importance of field studies of active offenders. Nevertheless, the vast majority of them have shied away from researching criminals "in the wild" in the belief that doing so is impractical. This article, based on the authors' fieldwork with 105 currently active residential burglars, challenges that assumption. Specifically, it describes how the authors went about finding these offenders and obtaining their cooperation. Further, it considers the difficulties involved in maintaining an on-going field relationship with those who lead chaotic lives. And lastly, the article outlines the characteristics of the sample, noting important ways in which it differs from one collected through criminal justice channels.

(1)   Criminologists long have recognized the importance of field studies of active offenders. More than 2 decades ago, for example, Polsky (1969, p. 116) observed that "we can no longer afford the convenient fiction that in studying criminals in their natural habitat, we would discover nothing really important that could not be discovered from criminals behind bars." Similarly, Sutherland and Cressey (1970) noted that:

Those who have had intimate contacts with criminals "in the open" know that criminals are not "natural" in police stations, courts, and prisons, and that they must be studied in their everyday life outside of institutions if they are to be understood. By this is meant that the investigator must associate with them as one of them, seeing their lives and conditions as the criminals themselves see them. In this way, he can make observations which can hardly be made in any other way. Also, his observations are of unapprehended criminals, not the criminals selected by the processes of arrest and imprisonment. (p. 68)

Reprinted with permission from *Journal of Research in Crime and Delinquency, 29*(2): 148-161. Copyright © 1992 by Sage Publications, Inc.

The research on which this article is based was funded by Grant No. 89-IJ-CX-0046 from the National Institute of Justice, Office of Justice Programs, U.S. Department of Justice. Points of view or opinions expressed in this document are those of the authors and do not necessarily represent the official position or policies of the U.S. Department of Justice. Correspondence should be sent to: Richard Wright, Department of Criminology and Criminal Justice, University of Missouri–St. Louis, St. Louis, MO 63121.

And McCall (1978, p. 27) also cautioned that studies of incarcerated offenders are vulnerable to the charge that they are based on "unsuccessful criminals, on the supposition that successful criminals are not apprehended or at least are able to avoid incarceration." This charge, he asserts, is "the most central bogeyman in the criminologist's demonology" (also see Cromwell, Olson, and Avary 1991; Hagedorn 1990; Watters and Biernacki 1989).

(2)   Although generally granting the validity of such critiques, most criminologists have shied away from studying criminals, so to speak, in the wild. Although their reluctance to do so undoubtedly is attributable to a variety of factors (e.g., Wright and Bennett 1990), probably the most important of these is a belief that this type of research is impractical. In particular, how is one to locate active criminals and obtain their cooperation?

(3)   The entrenched notion that field-based studies of active offenders are unworkable has been challenged by Chambliss (1975) who asserts that:

> The data on organized crime and professional theft as well as other presumably difficult-to-study events are much more available than we usually think. All we really have to do is to get out of our offices and onto the street. The data are there; the problem is that too often [researchers] are not. (p. 39)

Those who have carried out field research with active criminals would no doubt regard this assertion as overly simplistic, but they probably would concur with Chambliss that it is easier to find and gain the confidence of such offenders than commonly is imagined. As Hagedorn (1990, p. 251) has stated: "Any good field researcher . . . willing to spend the long hours necessary to develop good informants can solve the problem of access."

(4)   We recently completed the fieldwork for a study of residential burglars, exploring, specifically, the factors they take into account when contemplating the commission of an offense. The study is being done on the streets of St. Louis, Missouri, a declining "rust belt" city. As part of this study, we located and interviewed 105 active offenders. We also took 70 of these offenders to the site of a recent burglary and asked them to reconstruct the crime in considerable detail. In the following pages, we will discuss how we found these offenders and obtained their cooperation. Further, we will consider the difficulties involved in maintaining an ongoing field relationship with these offenders, many of whom lead chaotic lives. Lastly, we will outline the characteristics of our sample, suggesting ways in which it differs from one collected through criminal justice channels.

Locating the Subjects

(5)   In order to locate the active offenders for our study, we employed a "snowball" or "chain referral" sampling strategy. As described in the literature (e.g., Sudman 1976; Watters and Biernacki 1989), such a strategy begins with the recruitment of an initial subject who then is asked to recommend further participants. This process continues until a suitable sample has been "built."

(6)   The most difficult aspect of using a snowball sampling technique is locating an initial contact or two. Various ways of doing so have been suggested. McCall (1978), for instance, recommends using a "chain of referrals":

> If a researcher wants to make contact with, say, a bootlegger, he thinks of the person he knows who is closest in the social structure to bootlegging. Perhaps this person will be a police officer, a judge, a liquor store owner, a crime reporter, or a recently arrived Southern migrant. If he doesn't personally know a judge or a crime reporter, he surely knows someone (his own lawyer or a circulation clerk) who does and who would be willing to introduce him. By means of a very short chain of such referrals, the researcher can obtain an introduction to virtually any type of criminal. (p. 31)

(7)   This strategy can be effective and efficient, but can also have pitfalls. In attempting to find active offenders for our study, we avoided seeking referrals from criminal justice officials for both practical and methodological reasons. From a practical standpoint, we elected not to use contacts provided by police or probation officers, feeling that this would arouse the suspicions of offenders that the research was the cover for a "sting" operation. One of the offenders we interviewed, for example, explained that he had not agreed to participate earlier because he was worried about being set up for an arrest: "I thought about it at first because I've seen on T.V. telling how [the police] have sent letters out to people telling 'em they've won new sneakers and then arrested 'em." We also did not use referrals from law enforcement or corrections personnel to locate our subjects owing to a methodological concern that a sample obtained in this way may be highly unrepresentative of the total population of active offenders. It is likely, for instance, that such a sample would include a disproportionate number of unsuccessful criminals, that is,

those who have been caught in the past (e.g., Hagedorn 1990). Further, this sample might exclude a number of successful offenders who avoid associating with colleagues known to the police. Rengert and Wasilchick (1989, p. 6) used a probationer to contact active burglars, observing that the offenders so located "were often very much like the individual who led us to them."

(8)   A commonly suggested means of making initial contact with active offenders other than through criminal justice sources involves frequenting locales favored by criminals (see Chambliss 1975; Polsky 1969; West 1980). This strategy, however, requires an extraordinary investment of time as the researcher establishes a street reputation as an "all right square" (Irwin 1972, p. 123) who can be trusted. Fortunately, we were able to short-cut that process by hiring an ex-offender (who, despite committing hundreds of serious crimes, had few arrests and no felony convictions) with high status among several groups of Black street criminals in St. Louis. This person retired from crime after being shot and paralyzed in a gangland-style execution attempt. He then attended a university and earned a bachelor's degree, but continued to live in his old neighborhood, remaining friendly, albeit superficially, with local criminals. We initially met him when he attended a colloquium in our department and disputed the speaker's characterization of street criminals.

(9)   Working through an ex-offender with continuing ties to the underworld as a means of locating active criminals has been used successfully by other criminologists (see e.g., Taylor 1985). This approach offers the advantage that such a person already has contacts and trust in the criminal subculture and can vouch for the legitimacy of the research. In order to exploit this advantage fully, however, the ex-offender selected must be someone with a solid street reputation for integrity and must have a strong commitment to accomplishing the goals of the study.

(10)   The ex-offender hired to locate subjects for our project began by approaching former criminal associates. Some of these contacts were still "hustling," that is, actively involved in various types of crimes, whereas others either had retired or remained involved only peripherally through, for example, occasional buying and selling of stolen goods. Shortly thereafter, the ex-offender contacted several street-wise law-abiding friends, including a youth worker. He explained the research to the contacts, stressing that it was confidential and that the police were not involved. He also informed them that those who took part would be paid a small

sum (typically $25.00). He then asked the contacts to put him in touch with active residential burglars.

(11)   Figure 1 outlines the chain of referrals through which the offenders were located. Perhaps the best way to clarify this process involves selecting a subject, say 064, and identifying the referrals that led us to this person. In this case, the ex-offender working on our project contacted a street-wise, noncriminal acquaintance who put him in touch with the first active burglar in the chain, offender 015. Offender 015 referred 7 colleagues, one of whom — 033 — put us in touch with 3 more subjects, including 035, who in turn introduced us to 038, who referred 8 more participants. Among these participants was offender 043, a well-connected burglar who provided 12 further contacts, 2 of whom — 060 and 061 —convinced 064 to participate in the research. This procedure is similar to that described by Watters and Biernacki (1989, p. 426) in that "the majority of respondents were not referred directly by research staff." As a consequence, our sample was strengthened considerably. After all, we almost certainly would not have been able to find many of these individuals on our own, let alone convince them to cooperate.

(12)   Throughout the process of locating subjects, we encountered numerous difficulties and challenges. Contacts that initially appeared to be promising, for example, sometimes proved to be unproductive and had to be dropped. And, of course, even productive contact chains had a tendency to "dry up" eventually. One of the most challenging tasks we confronted involved what Biernacki and Waldorf (1981, p. 150) have termed the "verification of eligibility," that is, determining whether potential subjects actually met the criteria for inclusion in our research. In order to take part, offenders had to be both "residential burglars" and "currently active." In practice, this meant that they had to have committed a residential burglary within the past 2 weeks. This seems straightforward, but it often was difficult to apply the criteria in the field because offenders were evasive about their activities. In such cases, we frequently had to rely on other members of the sample to verify the eligibility of potential subjects.

(13)   We did not pay the contacts for helping us to find subjects and, initially, motivating them to do so proved difficult. Small favors, things like giving them a ride or buying them a pack of cigarettes, produced some cooperation, but yielded only a few introductions. Moreover, the active burglars that we did manage to find often were lackadaisical about referring associates because no financial incentive was offered. Eventually, one of the informants hit on the idea of "pimping"

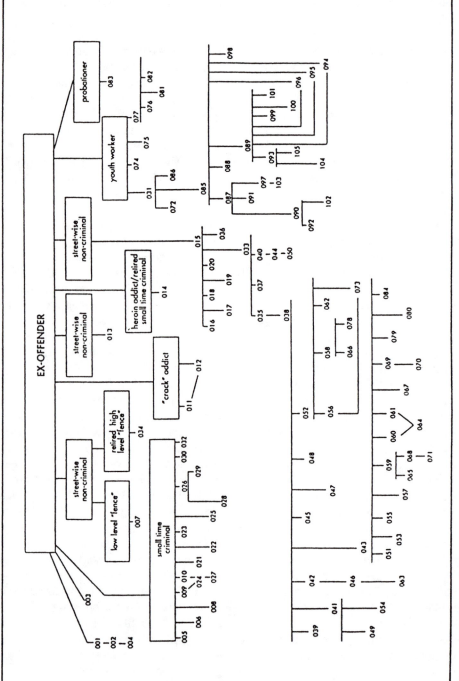

Figure 1: "Snowball" Referral Chart

colleagues, that is, arranging an introduction on their behalf in exchange for a cut of the participation fee (also see Cromwell et al. 1991). This idea was adopted rapidly by other informants and the number of referrals rose accordingly. In effect, these informants became "locators" (Biernacki and Waldorf 1981), helping us to expand referral chains as well as vouching for the legitimacy of the research, and validating potential participants as active residential burglars.

(14)　　The practice of pimping is consistent with the low level, underworld economy of street culture, where people are always looking for a way to get in on someone else's deal. One of our contacts put it this way: "If there's money to make out of something, I gotta figure out a way to get me some of it." Over the course of the research, numerous disputes arose between offenders and informants over the payment of referral fees. We resisted becoming involved in these disputes, reckoning that such involvement could only result in the alienation of one or both parties (e.g., Miller 1952). Instead, we made it clear that our funds were intended as interview payments and thus would be given only to interviewees.

Field Relations

(15)　　The success of our research, of course, hinged on an ability to convince potential subjects to participate. Given that many of the active burglars, especially those located early in the project, were deeply suspicious of our motives, it is reasonable to ask why the offenders were willing to take part in the research. Certainly the fact that we paid them a small sum for their time was an enticement for many, but this is not an adequate explanation. After all, criminal opportunities abound and even the inept "nickel and dime" offenders in the sample could have earned more had they spent the time engaged in illegal activity. Moreover, some of the subjects clearly were not short of cash when they agreed to participate; at the close of one interview, an offender pulled out his wallet to show us that it was stuffed with thousand dollar bills, saying:

> I just wanted to prove that I didn't do this for the money. I don't need the money. I did it to help out [the ex-offender employed on our project]. We know some of the same people and he said you were cool.

(16)　　Without doubt, many in our sample agreed to participate only because the ex-offender assured them that we were trustworthy. But other factors were at work as well. Letkemann (1973, p. 44), among others, has observed that the secrecy inherent in criminal work

means that offenders have few opportunities to discuss their activities with anyone besides associates — which many of them find frustrating. As one of his informants put it: "What's the point of scoring if nobody knows about it." Under the right conditions, therefore, some offenders may enjoy talking about their work with researchers.

(17)　　We adopted several additional strategies to maximize the cooperation of the offenders. First, following the recommendations of experienced field researchers (e.g., Irwin 1972; McCall 1978; Walker and Lidz 1977; Wright and Bennett 1990), we made an effort to "fit in" by learning the distinctive terminology and phrasing used by the offenders. Here again, the assistance of the ex-offender proved invaluable. Prior to entering the field, he suggested ways in which questions might be asked so that the subjects would better understand them, and provided us with a working knowledge of popular street terms (e.g., "boy" for heroin, "girl" for cocaine) and pronunciations (e.g., "hair ron" for heroin). What is more, he sat in on the early interviews and critiqued them afterwards, noting areas of difficulty or contention and offering possible solutions.

(18)　　A second strategy to gain the cooperation of the offenders required us to give as well as take. We expected the subjects to answer our questions frankly and, therefore, often had to reciprocate. Almost all of them had questions about how the information would be used, who would have access to it, and so on. We answered these questions honestly, lest the offenders conclude that we were being evasive. Further, we honored requests from a number of subjects for various forms of assistance. Provided that the help requested was legal and fell within the general set "of norms governing the exchange of money and other kinds of favors" (Berk and Adams 1970, p. 112) on the street, we offered it. For example, we took subjects to job interviews or work, helped some to enroll in school, and gave others advice on legal matters. We even assisted a juvenile offender who was injured while running away from the police, to arrange for emergency surgery when his parents, fearing that they would be charged for the operation, refused to give their consent.

(19)　　One other way we sought to obtain and keep the offenders' confidence involved demonstrating our trustworthiness by "remaining close-mouthed in regard to potentially harmful information" (Irwin 1972, p. 125). A number of the offenders tested us by asking what a criminal associate said about a particular matter. We declined to discuss such issues, explaining that the promise of confidentiality extended to all those participating in our research.

(20)   Much has been written about the necessity for researchers to be able to withstand official coercion (see Irwin 1972; McCall 1978; Polsky 1969) and we recognized from the start the threat that intrusions from criminal justice officials could pose to our research. The threat of being confronted by police patrols seemed especially great given that we planned to visit the sites of recent successful burglaries with offenders. Therefore, prior to beginning our fieldwork, we negotiated an agreement with police authorities not to interfere in the conduct of the research, and we were not subjected to official coercion.

(21)   Although the strategies described above helped to mitigate the dangers inherent in working with active criminals (see e.g., Dunlap et al. 1990), we encountered many potentially dangerous situations over the course of the research. For example, offenders turned up for interviews carrying firearms including, on one occasion, a machine gun; we were challenged on the street by subjects who feared that they were being set up for arrest; we were caught in the middle of a fight over the payment of a $1 debt. Probably the most dangerous situation, however, arose while driving with an offender to the site of his most recent burglary. As we passed a pedestrian, the offender became agitated and demanded that we stop the car: "You want to see me kill someone? Stop the car! I'm gonna kill that motherfucker. Stop the fuckin' car!" We refused to stop and actually sped up to prevent him jumping out of the vehicle; this clearly displeased him, although he eventually calmed down. The development of such situations was largely unpredictable and thus avoiding them was difficult. Often we deferred to the ex-offender's judgment about the safety of a given set of circumstances. The most notable precaution that we took involved money; we made sure that the offenders knew that we carried little more than was necessary to pay them.

Characteristics of the Sample

(22)   Unless a sample of active offenders differs significantly from one obtained through criminal justice channels, the difficulties and risks associated with the street-based recruitment of research subjects could not easily be justified. Accordingly, it seems important that we establish whether such a difference exists. In doing so, we will begin by outlining the demographic characteristics of our sample. In terms of race, it nearly parallels the distribution of burglary arrests for the City of St. Louis in 1988, the most recent year for which data are available. The St. Louis Metropolitan Police Department's Annual Report (1989) reveals that 64% of burglary arrestees in that year were Black, and 36% were White. Our sample was 69% Black and 31% White. There is divergence for the gender variable, however; only 7% of all arrestees in the city were female, while 17% of our sample fell into this category. This is not surprising. The characteristics of a sample of active criminals, after all, would not be expected to mirror those of one obtained in a criminal justice setting.

Table 1. Contact with Criminal Justice System

	Frequency	Percent
Subject ever arrested (for any offense)?		
No	28	28
Yes	72	72
	100	
Subject ever arrested, convicted, incarcerated (for burglary)?		
No arrests	44	42
Arrest, no conviction	35	33
Arrest, conviction, no jail/prison	4	4
Arrest, conviction, jail/prison	22	21
	105	

(23) Given that our research involved only currently active offenders, it is interesting to note that 21 of the subjects were on probation, parole, or serving a suspended sentence, and that a substantial number of juveniles — 27 or 26% of the total — were located for the study. The inclusion of such offenders strengthens the research considerably because approximately one third of arrested burglars are under 18 years of age (Sessions 1989). Juveniles, therefore, need to be taken into account in any comprehensive study of burglars. These offenders, however, seldom are included in studies of burglars located through criminal justice channels because access to them is legally restricted and they often are processed differently than adult criminals and detained in separate facilities.

(24) Prior contact with the criminal justice system is a crucial variable for this research. Table 1 sets out whether, and to what degree, those in our sample have come into official contact with that system. Of primary interest in this table is the extent to which our snowball sampling technique uncovered a sample of residential burglars unlikely to be encountered in a criminal justice setting, the site of most research on offenders.

(25) More than one-quarter of the offenders (28%) claimed never to have been arrested. (We excluded arrests for traffic offenses, "failure to appear" and similar minor transgressions, because such offenses do not adequately distinguish serious criminals from others.) Obviously, these offenders would have been excluded had we based our study on a jail or prison population. Perhaps a more relevant measure in the context of our study, however, is the experience of the offenders with the criminal justice system for the offense of burglary, because most previous studies of burglars not only have been based on incarcerated offenders, but also have used the charge of burglary as a screen to select subjects (e.g., Bennett and Wright 1984; Rengert and Wasilchick 1985). Of the 105 individuals in our sample, 44 (42%) had no arrests for burglary, and another 35 (33%) had one or more arrests, but no convictions for the offense. Thus 75% of our sample would not be included in a study of incarcerated burglars.

(26) We turn now to an examination of the patterns of offending among our sample. In order to determine how many lifetime burglaries the offenders had committed, we asked them to estimate the number of completed burglaries in which they had taken part. We "bounded" this response by asking them (a) how old they were when they did their first burglary, (b) about significant gaps in offending (e.g., periods of incarceration), and (c) about fluctuations in offending levels. The subjects typically estimated how many lifetime burglaries they had committed in terms of a range (e.g., 50-60), then were prompted with questions about the variation in their rate of offending over the course of their burglary career. We recorded what offenders agreed was a conservative estimate of the number of lifetime burglaries. More than half of the sample (52%) admitted to 50 or more lifetime burglaries. Included in this group are 41 offenders (40% of the total) who have committed at least 100 such crimes.

(27) The measure of lifetime burglaries, of course, does not provide an estimate of the *rate* of offending. For that, we calculated "lambda" (Blumstein and Cohen 1979) — that is, the annual number of lifetime burglaries — for each subject by using our interview data. We arrived at this figure by subtracting age at first burglary from age at time of initial interview; from this, we subtracted the number of years each offender spent "off the street" in a secure residential facility (prison, jail, secure detention, or treatment center). This gave us the denominator for the lambda measure, the number of years at risk. The number of lifetime burglaries was divided by years at risk to get lambda. Approximately two thirds of the sample (68%) averaged 10 or fewer burglaries a year over the course of their offending careers — a finding not out of line with lambda estimates for burglary derived from arrest data (Blumstein and Cohen 1979). It should be noted, however, that there was great variability in the rate of offending among our sample; 34% committed, on average, less than five burglaries a year while, at the other extreme, 7% committed more than 50 such crimes yearly. This subgroup of exceptionally high rate offenders accounted for 4,204 of the 13,179 residential burglaries (32%) reported by our subjects. This result compliments previous research based on self-reports by prison inmates that has shown great variability in individual crime rates, with a small group of very active criminals being responsible for a disproportionate number of offenses (e.g., Greenwood 1982; Petersilia, Greenwood, and Lavin 1977).

(28) The final portion of the analysis compares offenders who have and have not ever been arrested *for anything* in terms of (a) their total lifetime burglaries, and (b) their lambda (see Table 2).

(29) The differences for these measures are pronounced. The mean lifetime burglaries for those who have never been arrested for anything is nearly double that for those who have been arrested. The variability in the group that has not been arrested is evident in the standard deviation (s = 324). A small subsample of this group has committed very few lifetime burglaries.

Table 2. Comparisons of Sample Members by Any Previous Arrest Status

	Number	Mean	s	t*
		Total lifetime burglaries by any previous arrest		
Yes	67	120	166	
				0.04
No	20 N=87	232	324	
		Lifetime burglary lambdas		
Yes	67	13	21	
				0.03
No	20 N=87	28	38	

*Because sample selection was not random, the *t*-test results must be interpreted cautiously.

Those in this subsample are mostly juvenile females who have offended infrequently over a very short period of time. But for this, there would be even larger differences between the groups. The mean lambda for those who have not been arrested is twice that for their arrested counterparts. This measure also displays considerable variation, as evidenced by the high standard deviation. Nevertheless, among those who have not been arrested, there are a number of offenders whose existence often has been doubted, namely high-rate criminals who successfully have avoided apprehension altogether.

Conclusion

(30)   By its nature, research involving active criminals is always demanding, often difficult, and occasionally dangerous. However, it is possible and, as the quantitative information reported above suggests, some of the offenders included in such research may differ substantially from those found through criminal justice channels. It is interesting, for example, that those in our sample who had never been arrested for anything, on average, offended *more* frequently and had committed *more* lifetime burglaries than their arrested counterparts. These "successful" offenders, obviously, would not have shown up in a study of arrestees, prisoners, or probationers — a fact that calls into question the extent to which a sample obtained through official sources is representative of the total population of criminals.

(31)   Beyond this, researching active offenders is important because it provides an opportunity to observe and talk with them outside the institutional context. As Cromwell et al. (1991) have noted, it is difficult to assess the validity of accounts offered by institutionalized criminals. Simply put, a full understanding of criminal behavior requires that criminologists incorporate field studies of active offenders into their research agendas. Without such studies, both the representativeness and the validity of research based on offenders located through criminal justice channels will remain problematic.

References

Bennett, Trevor and Richard Wright. 1984. *Burglars on Burglary: Prevention and the Offender.* Aldershot, England: Gower.

Berk, Richard and Joseph Adams. 1970. "Establishing Rapport with Deviant Groups." *Social Problems* 18:102-17.

Biernacki, Patrick and Dan Waldorf. 1981. "Snowball Sampling: Problems and Techniques of Chain Referral Sampling." *Sociological Methods & Research* 10:141-63.

Blumstein, Alfred and Jacqueline Cohen. 1979. "Estimation of Individual Crime Rates from Arrest Records." *Journal of Criminal Law and Criminology* 70:561-85.

Chambliss, William. 1975. "On the Paucity of Research on Organized Crime: A Reply to Galliher and Cain." *American Sociologist* 10:36-39.

Cromwell, Paul, James Olson, and D'Aunn Avary. 1991. *Breaking and Entering: An Ethnographic Analysis of Burglary.* Newbury Park, CA: Sage.

Dunlap, Eloise, Bruce Johnson, Harry Sanabria, Elbert Holliday, Vicki Lipsey, Maurice Barnett, William Hopkins, Ira Sobel, Doris Randolph, and Ko-Lin Chin. 1990. "Studying Crack Users and Their

Criminal Careers: The Scientific and Artistic Aspects of Locating Hard-to-Reach Subjects and Interviewing Them about Sensitive Topics." *Contemporary Drug Problems* 17: 121-44.

Greenwood, Peter. 1982. *Selective Incapacitation.* Santa Monica, CA: RAND.

Hagedorn, John. 1990. "Back in the Field Again: Gang Research in the Nineties." Pp. 240-59 in *Gangs in America,* edited by C. Ronald Huff. Newbury Park, CA: Sage.

Irwin, John. 1972. "Participant Observation of Criminals." Pp. 117-37 in *Research on Deviance,* edited by Jack Douglas. New York: Random House.

Letkemann, Peter. 1973. *Crime as Work.* Englewood Cliffs, NJ: Prentice-Hall.

McCall, George. 1978. *Observing the Law.* New York: Free Press.

Miller, S. M. 1952. "The Participant Observer and Over-Rapport." *American Sociological Review* 17:97-99.

Petersilia, Joan, Peter Greenwood, and Marvin Lavin. 1977. *Criminal Careers of Habitual Felons.* Santa Monica, CA: RAND.

Polsky, Ned. 1969. *Hustlers, Beats, and Others.* Garden City, NJ: Anchor.

Rengert, George and John Wasilchick. 1985. *Suburban Burglary: A Time and a Place for Everything.* Springfield, IL: Thomas.

_____. 1989. *Space, Time, and Crime: Ethnographic Insights into Residential Burglary.* Final report submitted to the National Institute of Justice, Office of Justice Programs, U.S. Department of Justice.

Sessions, William. 1989. *Crime in the United States — 1988.* Washington, DC: U.S. Government Printing Office.

St. Louis Metropolitan Police Department. 1989. *Annual Report — 1988/89.* St. Louis, MO: St. Louis Metropolitan Police Department.

Sudman, Seymour. 1976. *Applied Sampling.* New York: Academic Press.

Sutherland, Edwin and Donald Cressey. 1970. *Criminology — 8th Edition.* Philadelphia, PA: Lippincott.

Taylor, Laurie. 1985. *In the Underworld.* London: Unwin.

Walker, Andrew and Charles Lidz. 1977. "Methodological Notes on the Employment of Indigenous Observers." Pp. 103-23 in *Street Ethnography,* edited by Robert Weppner. Beverly Hills, CA: Sage.

Watters, John and Patrick Biernacki. 1989. "Targeted Sampling: Options for the Study of Hidden Populations." *Social Problems* 36: 416-30.

West, W. Gordon. 1980. "Access to Adolescent Deviants and Deviance." Pp. 31-41 in *Fieldwork Experience, Qualitative Approaches to Social Research,* edited by William Shaffir, Robert Stebbins, and Allan Turowitz. New York: St. Martin's.

Wright, Richard and Trevor Bennett. 1990. "Exploring the Offender's Perspective: Observing and Interviewing Criminals." Pp. 138-51 in *Measurement Issues in Criminology,* edited by Kimberly Kempf. New York: Springer-Verlag.

Factual Questions

1. To what convenient methodological fiction did Polsky refer over two decades ago?

2. What is probably the most important belief among criminologists that prevents them from doing field-based research?

3. How many research subjects were interviewed?

4. What type of sample is used by the researchers and how is it conducted?

5. What is a "chain of referrals" technique?

6. Why did the researchers not use initial referrals from criminal justice officials?

7. Who made the initial contacts that resulted in research subjects for the researchers?

8. To what does the phrase 'verification of eligibility' refer?

9. Are the differences between the sample and the police records of persons arrested for burglary greater for race or for gender?

10. What percentage of the sample had never been convicted of burglary?

11. What is lambda?

12. What was the mean number of lifetime burglaries for persons in the sample who have been arrested at least once for any reason? What was the mean number of lifetime burglaries for persons in the sample who have never been arrested even once for any reason?

Questions for Discussion

13. Does the introduction provide a clear notion of the research problem, the purpose of the research, and its significance?

14. Does the literature review seem relevant to the research problem?

15. Is the number of research subjects sufficient? To what population would you generalize the results of this study?

16. What were some of the reasons why subjects were willing to talk to the researchers?

17. What were some of the things the researchers did to gain the confidence of the subjects?

18. Is there enough information on the research instruments and procedures to allow you to replicate this study?

19. Should there be information about the reliability and validity of the research instruments and procedures?

20. Does the analysis include sufficient statistical information? Are the statistics that are used appropriate?

21. Are the conclusions supported by and do they logically follow from the data that have been presented?

22. Are the findings discussed in terms of their implications and/or practical significance?

Notes:

Appendix A

Reading Research Reports:
A Brief Introduction

David A. Schroeder
David E. Johnson
Thomas D. Jensen

(1)   To many students, the prospect of reading a research report in a professional journal elicits so much fear that no information is, in fact, transmitted. Such apprehension on the part of the reader is not necessary, and we hope that this article will help students understand more clearly what such reports are all about and will teach them how to use these resources more effectively. Let us assure you that there is nothing mystical or magical about research reports, although they may be somewhat more technical and precise in style, more intimidating in vocabulary, and more likely to refer to specific sources of information than are everyday mass media sources. However, once you get beyond these intimidating features, you will find that the vast majority of research reports do a good job of guiding you through a project and of informing you of important points of which you should be aware.

(2)   A scientific research report has but one purpose: to communicate to others the results of one's scientific investigations. To ensure that readers will be able to appreciate fully the import and implications of the research, the author of the report will make every effort to describe the project so comprehensively that even a naive reader will be able to follow the logic as he or she traces the author's thinking through the project.

(3)   A standardized format has been developed by editors and authors to facilitate effective communication. The format is subject to some modification, according to the specific needs and goals of a particular author for a particular article, but, in general, most articles possess a number of features in common. We will briefly discuss the six major sections of research articles and the purpose of each. We hope that this selection will help you take full advantage of the subsequent articles and to appreciate their content as informed "consumers" of social psychological research.

Heading

(4)   The heading of an article consists of the title, the name of the author or authors, and their institutional affiliations. Typically the title provides a brief description of the primary independent and dependent variables that have been investigated in the study. This information should help you begin to categorize the study into some implicit organizational framework that will help you keep track of the social psychological material. For example, if the title includes the word *persuasion*, you should immediately recognize that the article will be related to the attitude-change literature, and you should prepare yourself to identify the similarities and differences between the present study and the previous literature.

(5)   The names of the authors may also be important to you for at least two reasons. First, it is quite common for social psychologists to use the names of authors as a shorthand notation in referring among

themselves to critical articles. Rather than asking, "Have your read 'Videotape and the attribution process: Reversing actors' and observers' points of view'?", it is much easier to say, "Have you read the Storms (1973) article?" In addition, this strategy gives the author(s) credit for the material contained in the article. Second, you will find that most researchers actively pursue programs of research that are specific to a particular area of interest. For example, you will eventually be able to recognize that an article written by Albert Bandura is likely to be about social learning processes, while an article by Leonard Berkowitz is probably going to discuss aggression and violence. Once you begin to identify the major researchers in each area, you will find that you will be able to go beyond the information presented within an article and understand not only how a piece of research fits into a well-defined body of literature but also how it may be related to other less obvious topics.

Abstract

(6)   The Abstract is a short (often less than 150 words) preview of the contents of the article. The Abstract should be totally self-contained and intelligible without any reference to the article proper. It should briefly convey a statement of the problem explored, the methods used, the major results of the study, and the conclusions reached. The Abstract helps to set the stage and to prepare you for the article itself. Just as the title helps you place the article in a particular area of investigation, the Abstract helps pinpoint the exact question or questions to be addressed in the study.

Introduction

(7)   The Introduction provides the foundation for the study itself and therefore for the remainder of the article. Thus it serves several critical functions for the reader. First, it provides a context for the article and the study by discussing past literature that is relevant to and has implications for the present research. Second, it permits a thorough discussion of the rationale for the research that was conducted and a full description of the independent and dependent variables that were employed. Third, it allows the hypotheses that were tested to be stated explicitly, and the arguments on which these predictions were based to be elucidated. Each of these functions will be considered in detail.

(8)   The literature review that is typically the initial portion of the Introduction is not intended to provide a comprehensive restatement of all the published articles that are tangentially relevant to the present research. Normally, a selective review is presented — one that

carefully sets up the rationale of the study and identifies deficiencies in our understanding of the phenomena being investigated. In taking this approach, the author is attempting to provide insights into the thought processes that preceded the actual conducting of the study. Usually the literature review will begin by discussing rather broad conceptual issues (e.g., major theories, recognized areas of investigation) and will then gradually narrow its focus to more specific concerns (e.g., specific findings from previous research, methods that have been employed). It may be helpful to think of the introduction as a funnel, gradually drawing one's attention to a central point that represents the critical feature of the article.

(9)   Following the review of the past literature, the author typically presents the rationale for his or her own research. A research study may have one of several goals as its primary aim: (1) it may be designed to answer a question specifically raised by the previous literature but left unanswered. (2) It may attempt to correct methodological flaws that have plagued previous research and threaten the validity of the conclusions reached. (3) It may seek to reconcile conflicting findings that have been reported in the literature, typically by identifying and/or eliminating confounding variables by exerting greater experimental control. (4) It may be designed to assess the validity of a scientific theory by testing one or more hypotheses that have been deduced or derived from that theory. (5) It may begin a novel line of research that has not been previously pursued or discussed in the literature. Research pursuing any of these five goals may yield significant contributions to a particular field of inquiry.

(10)   After providing the rationale for the study, the author properly continues to narrow the focus of the article from broad conceptual issues to the particular variables that are to be employed in the study. Ideally, in experimental studies, the author clearly identifies the independent and dependent variables to be used; in correlational studies, the predictor and criterion variables are specified. For those readers who do not have an extensive background in research methodology, a brief explanation of experimental and correlational studies may be in order.

(11)   *Experimental studies.* An experimental study is designed to identify cause-effect relationships between independent variables that the experimenter systematically manipulates and the dependent variable that is used to measure the behavior of interest. In such a study, the researcher controls the situation to eliminate or neutralize the effects of all extraneous factors that

may affect the behavior of interest in order to assess more precisely the impact of the independent variables alone. In most instances, only the tightly controlled experimental method permits valid inferences of cause-effect relationships to be made.

(12) *Correlational studies.* In some circumstances the researcher cannot exert the degree of control over the situation that is necessary for a true experimental study. Rather than giving up the project, the researcher may explore alternative methods that may still permit an assessment of his or her hypotheses and predictions. One such alternative is the correlational approach. In a correlational study, the researcher specifies a set of measures that should be related conceptually to the display of a target behavior. The measure that is used to assess the target behavior is called the criterion variable; the measure from which the researcher expects to be able to make predictions about the criterion variable is called the predictor variable. Correlational studies permit the researcher to assess the degree of relationship between the predictor variable(s) and the criterion variable(s), but inferences of cause and effect cannot be validly made because the effects of extraneous variables have not been adequately controlled. Correlational studies are most frequently used in naturalistic or applied situations in which researchers must either tolerate the lack of control and do the best they can under the circumstances or give up any hope of testing their hypotheses.

(13) After the discussion of these critical components of the study, the author explicitly states the exact predictions that the study is designed to test. The previous material should have set the stage sufficiently well for you as a reader to anticipate what these hypotheses will be, but it is incumbent on the author to present them nonetheless. The wording of the hypotheses may vary, some authors preferring to state the predictions in conceptual terms (e.g., "The arousal of cognitive dissonance due to counterattitudinal advocacy is expected to lead to greater attitude change than the presentation of an attitude-consistent argument.") and others preferring to state their predictions in terms of the actual operationalizations that they employed (e.g., "Subjects who received a $1 incentive to say that an objectively boring task was fun are expected to subsequently evaluate the task as being more enjoyable than subjects who were offered a $20 incentive to say that the task was interesting.")

(14) In reading a research report, it is imperative that you pay attention to the relationship between the initial literature review, the rationale for the study and the statement of the hypotheses. In a well-conceived and well-designed investigation, each section will flow logically from the preceding one; the internal consistency of the author's arguments will make for smooth transitions as the presentation advances. If there appear to be discontinuities or inconsistencies throughout the author's presentation, it would be wise to take a more critical view of the study — particularly if the predictions do not seem to follow logically from the earlier material. In such cases, the author may be trying to present as a prediction a description of the findings that were unexpectedly uncovered when the study was being conducted. Although there is nothing wrong with reporting unexpected findings in a journal article, the author should be honest enough to identify them as what they really are. As a reader, you should have much more confidence in the reliability of predictions that obtain than you do in data that can be described by postdictions only.

Method

(15) To this point, the author has dealt with the study in relatively abstract terms, and has given little attention to the actual procedures used in conducting it. In the Method section, the author at last describes the operationalizations and procedures that were employed in the investigation. There are at least two reasons for the detailed presentation of this information. First, such a presentation allows interested readers to reconstruct the methodology used, so that a replication of the study can be undertaken. By conducting a replication using different subject populations and slightly different operationalizations of the same conceptual variables, more information can be gained about the validity of the conclusions that the original investigator reached. Second, even if a replication is not conducted, the careful description of the method used will permit you to evaluate the adequacy of the procedures employed.

(16) The Method section typically comprises two or more subsections, each of which has a specific function to fulfill. Almost without exception, the Method section begins with a subject subsection, consisting of a complete description of the subjects who participated in the study. The number of subjects should be indicated, and there should be a summary of important demographic information (e.g., numbers of male and female subjects, age) so that you can know to what populations the findings can be reasonably generalized. Sampling techniques that were used to recruit subjects and incentives used to induce volunteering should also be clearly specified. To the extent that subject characteristics are of primary importance to the goals of the research,

greater detail is presented in this subsection, and more attention should be directed to it.

(17)   A procedures subsection is also almost always included in the Method section. This subsection presents a detailed account of the subjects' experiences in the experiment. Although other formats may also be effective, the most common presentation style is to describe the subjects' activities in chronological order. A thorough description of all questionnaires administered or tasks completed is given, as well as any other features that might be reasonably expected to affect the behavior of the subjects in the study.

(18)   After the procedures have been discussed, a full description of the independent variables in an experimental study, or predictor variables in a correlational study, is typically provided. Verbatim description of each of the different levels of each independent variable is presented, and similar detail is used to describe each predictor variable. This information may be included either in the procedures subsection or, if the description of these variables is quite lengthy, in a separate subsection.

(19)   After thoroughly describing these variables, the author usually describes the dependent variables in an experimental study, and the criterion variables in a correlational study. The description of the dependent and/or criterion variables also requires a verbatim specification of the exact operationalizations that were employed. When appropriate and available, information about the reliability and validity of these measures is also presented. In addition, if the investigator has included any questions that were intended to allow the effectiveness of the independent variable manipulation to be assessed, these manipulation checks are described at this point. All of this information may be incorporated in the procedures subsection or in a separate subsection.

(20)   After you have read the Method section, there should be no question about what has been done to the subjects who participated in the study. You should try to evaluate how representative the methods that were used were of the conceptual variables discussed in the Introduction. Manipulation checks may help to allay one's concerns, but poorly conceived manipulation checks are of little or no value. Therefore, it is important for you as a reader to remember that you are ultimately responsible for the critical evaluation of any research report.

Results

(21)   Once the full methodology of the study has been described for the reader, the author proceeds to report the results of the statistical analyses that were conducted on the data. The Results section is probably the most intimidating section for students to read, and often the most difficult section for researchers to write. You are typically confronted with terminology and analytical techniques with which you are at best unfamiliar, or at worst totally ignorant. There is no reason for you to feel badly about this state of affairs; as a neophyte in the world of research, you cannot expect mastery of all phases of research from the start. Even experienced researchers are often exposed to statistical techniques with which they are unfamiliar, requiring them either to learn the techniques or to rely on others to assess the appropriateness of the procedure. For the student researcher, a little experience and a conscientious effort to learn the basics will lead to mastery of the statistical skills necessary.

(22)   The author's task is similarly difficult. He or she is attempting to present the findings of the study in a straightforward and easily understood manner, but the presentation of statistical findings does not always lend itself readily to this task. The author must decide whether to present the results strictly within the text of the article or to use tables, graphs, and figures to help to convey the information effectively. Although the implications of the data may be clear to the researcher, trying to present the data clearly and concisely so that the reader will also be able to discern the implications is not necessarily assured. In addition, the author is obligated to present all the significant results obtained in the statistical analyses, not just the results that support the hypotheses being tested. Although this may clutter the presentation and detract from the simplicity of the interpretation, it must be remembered that the researcher's primary goal is to seek the truth, not to espouse a particular point of view that may not be supported by the data.

Discussion

(23)   The Discussion section is the part of the manuscript in which the author offers an evaluation and interpretation of the findings of the study, particularly as they relate to the hypotheses that were proposed in the Introduction. Typically the author will begin this section with a brief review of the major findings of the study and a clear statement of whether the data were consistent or inconsistent with the hypotheses. The discussion will then address any discrepancies between the

predictions and the data, trying to resolve these inconsistencies and offering plausible reasons for their occurrence. In general, the first portion of the Discussion is devoted to an evaluation of the hypotheses that were originally set forward in the Introduction, given the data that were obtained in the research.

(24) The Discussion may be seen as the inverse of the introduction, paralleling the issues raised in that section in the opposite order of presentation. Therefore, after discussing the relationship of the data with the hypotheses, the author often attempts to integrate the new findings into the body of research that provided the background for the study. Just as this literature initially provided the context within which you can understand the rationale for the study, it subsequently provides the context within which the data can be understood and interpreted. The author's responsibility at this point is to help you recognize the potential import of the research, without relying on hype or gimmicks to make the point.

(25) The Discussion continues to expand in terms of the breadth of ideas discussed until it reaches the broad, conceptual issues that are addressed by the superordinate theoretical work that originally stimulated the past research literature. If a particular piece of research is to make a significant contribution to the field, its findings must either clarify some past discrepancy in the literature, identify boundary conditions for the applicability of the critical theoretical work, reconcile differences of opinion among the researchers in the field, or otherwise contribute to a more complete understanding of the mechanisms and mediators of important social phenomena.

(26) Once the author has reached the goals that are common to most journal articles, attention may be turned to less rigorous ideas. Depending on a particular journal's editorial policy and the availability of additional space, the author may finish the article with a brief section about possible applications of the present work, implications for future work in the area, and with some restraint, speculations about what lies ahead for the line of research. Scientists tend to have relatively little tolerance for conclusions without foundation and off-the-cuff comments made without full consideration. Therefore authors must be careful not to overstep the bounds of propriety in making speculations about the future. But such exercises can be useful and can serve a heuristic function for other researchers if the notions stated are well conceived.

(27) Finally, particularly if the article has been relatively long or complex, the author may decide to end it with a short Conclusion. The Conclusion usually simply restates the major arguments that have been made throughout the article, reminding the reader one last time of the value of the work.

(28) As we suggested earlier, not all articles will follow the format exactly. Some latitude is allowed to accommodate the particular needs of the author and the quirks of the research being described. Given that the goal is effective communication of information, it would not be reasonable for the format to dictate what could and could not be included in a manuscript. We hope that this introduction will help to demystify research articles and provide you with some insights into what an author is trying to accomplish at various points in the report. Let us end with a word of encouragement: Your enjoyment of social psychology will be enhanced by your fuller appreciation of the sources of the information to which you are being exposed, and, to the extent that you are able to read and understand these original sources for yourself, your appreciation of this work will be maximized.

Reference

Storms, M. D. Videotape and the attribution process: Reversing actors' and observers' points of view. *Journal of Personality and Social Psychology*, 1973, **27**, 165-175.

Factual Questions

1. What four elements should the abstract contain?

2. If there is a research hypothesis, should it be explicitly stated in the introduction?

3. Normally, should the literature review be selective or comprehensive in research reports?

4. Should the introduction to a research report start with a narrow discussion of variables or with a discussion of broad conceptual issues?

5. What is a *criterion variable* in a correlational study?

6. The method section usually begins with a description of what?

7. According to the authors, what is probably the most intimidating section of a research report for students?

8. How should the discussion section of a research report typically begin?

9. Name an area in which you are interested in identifying cause-and-effect relationships but in which a correlational study would probably be more appropriate than an experimental study.

10. Do you believe that *post hoc* explanations are ever acceptable in a research article?

11. Name some demographic information that might be of interest to you in a typical social science research article in addition to the examples given in paragraph 16.

12. Do you agree that possible applications and implications of the research should be discussed only if the editorial policy and space permit?

Appendix B

Reading and Critiquing Research Manuscripts

David Royse

(1)   Students have a tendency to believe that any research that manages to appear in print is "good" research. I wish that this were so. Unfortunately, some pretty shoddy research can be found in journals without too much difficulty. As I stated in the beginning of this book, one reason you are required to enroll in a research methods course is to help you recognize poor or inadequate research. Flawed research (if unrecognized) could lead you to conclusions that are not warranted and could be dangerous to your clients.

(2)   Using the major content areas of research reports, we can construct a set of criteria to use in evaluating research reports, journal articles, or manuscripts. (These criteria can also be used to double-check your manuscripts.) I'm indebted to Garfield (1984) for his observations and guidelines on this topic.

Criteria for Evaluating Research Reports

1. Does the Introduction provide a clear notion of (a) the problem, (b) the purpose of the research, and (c) its significance?
2. Are the stated hypotheses reasonable? Do they appear to logically follow from the review of the literature?
3. Is the literature review (a) relevant to the study, (b) thorough, and (c) current?
4. Is a research design stated? Do the subjects appear to have been selected without overt bias? If there is a control group, does it seem to be an appropriate group for comparison? Is the number of subjects sufficient?

5. Is there a discussion of the reliability and validity of the instruments that are used?
6. Is there enough information on (a) the procedures, and (b) the instruments and the operational definitions of the variables to allow you to replicate this study?
7. Are statistical tests present when needed? If statistical tests are used, are they the appropriate tests?
8. Are the findings discussed in terms of their implications and practical significance? Are the conclusions supported by and do they logically follow from the data that have been presented? Is the author guilty of overgeneralizing? Has actual or potential bias been recognized?

(3)   When evaluating a research report, you should find yourself answering "yes" to most of the criteria questions. Strong research articles will elicit a greater number of affirmative responses. Weak articles will receive a larger number of negative responses. You can use these criteria not only to evaluate the research reports prepared by others, but also to check your own report or manuscript to insure that you have included all of the crucial elements.

Reference

Garfield, S. L. (1984). The evaluation of research: An editorial perspective. In A. S. Bellack and M. Hersen (eds.), *Research Methods in Clinical Psychology*. New York: Pergamon Press.
